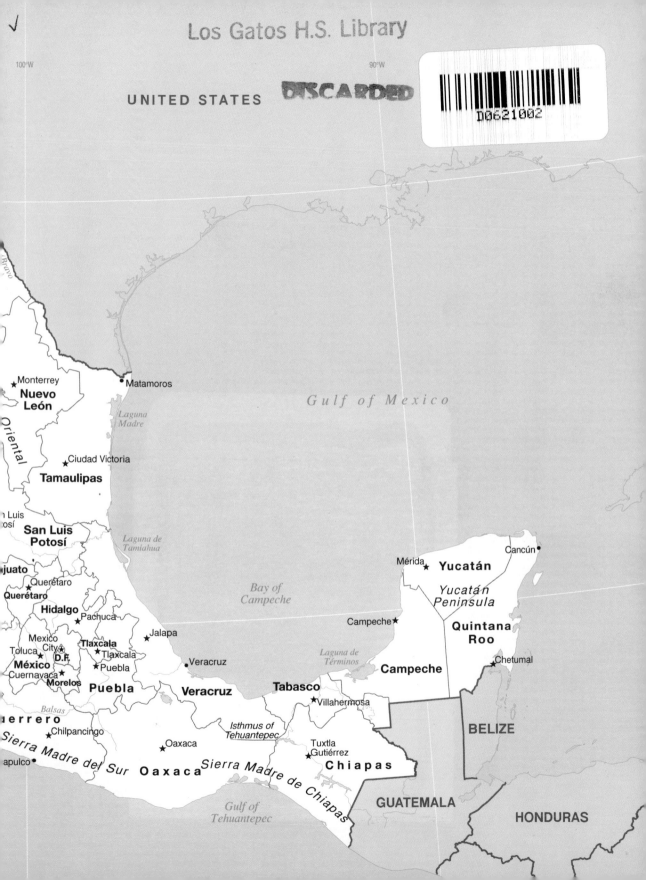

100°W

90°W

UNITED STATES

Bravo

★ Monterrey
**Nuevo
León**

● Matamoros

*Laguna
Madre*

Gulf of Mexico

Oriental

★ Ciudad Victoria

Tamaulipas

n Luis
osí

**San Luis
Potosí**

*Laguna de
Tamiahua*

juato

● Querétaro

Querétaro

Hidalgo

★ Pachuca

Bay of
Campeche

Mérida ●
★ **Yucatán**

Cancún ●

*Yucatán
Peninsula*

Jalapa ★

Campeche ★

**Quintana
Roo**

Mexico
City ★
Toluca ●

Tlaxcala
★ Tlaxcala

D.F.
México

★ Puebla

Cuernavaca ●
Morelos

Puebla

● Veracruz

Veracruz

*Laguna de
Términos*

● Chetumal ★

Campeche

Tabasco

★ Villahermosa

BELIZE

Balsas

uerrero

● Chilpancingo

*Isthmus of
Tehuantepec*

Oaxaca ★

Sierra Madre del Sur **O a x a c a** *Sierra Madre de Chiapas*

Tuxtla
Gutiérrez ★

Chiapas

apulco ●

GUATEMALA

HONDURAS

*Gulf of
Tehuantepec*

Junior Worldmark Encyclopedia of the Mexican States

Junior Worldmark Encyclopedia of the Mexican States

U·X·L

An imprint of Thomson Gale,
a part of The Thomson Corporation

THOMSON
‐✷‐ ™
GALE

Detroit • New York • San Francisco • San Diego • New Haven, Conn. • Waterville, Maine • London • Munich

THOMSON
™
GALE

Junior Worldmark Encyclopedia of the Mexican States

Project Editor
Mary Rose Bonk

Editorial
Allison McNeill

Imaging and Multimedia
Christine O'Bryan

Research
Denise Buckley

Manufacturing
Rita Wimberley

Rights Acquisitions
Mari Masalin-Cooper

Product Design
Pamela A. E. Galbreath

```
          Library of Congress Cataloging-in-Publication Data
Junior Worldmark encyclopedia of the Mexican states / [Timothy L. Gall and
Susan Bevan  Gall, editors].-- 1st ed.
      p. cm.
  Includes bibliographical references and index.
  ISBN 0-7876-9161-5 (hardcover : alk. paper)
 1.  Mexican states--Encyclopedias, Juvenile. 2.  Mexico--Encyclopedias,
Juvenile. I. Title: Encyclopedia of the Mexican states. II. Gall, Timothy
L. III. Gall, Susan B.
  F1204.J86 2004
  972'.003--dc22
                                                        2004008307
```

This title is also available as an e-book
ISBN 0-7876-9361-8
Contact your Thomson Gale sales representative for ordering information.

Printed in the United States of America
10 9 8 7 6 5 4 3 2 1

Table of Contents

Reader's Guide. vi

Guide to Articles. ix

Words to Know. x

Aguascalientes 1

Baja California. 9

Baja California Sur. 21

Campeche. 31

Chiapas. 41

Chihuahua 51

Coahuila 61

Colima 71

Distrito Federal 81

Durango 91

Guanajuato 101

Guerrero. 111

Hidalgo. 121

Jalisco 129

México 139

Michoacán 149

Morelos. 161

Nayarit 171

Nuevo León 179

Oaxaca 189

Puebla. 201

Querétaro 209

Quintana Roo. 217

San Luis Potosí. 227

Sinaloa 235

Sonora. 245

Tabasco. 255

Tamaulipas 263

Tlaxcala 273

Veracruz 281

Yucatán 291

Zacatecas 301

Mexico 309

Index. 327

Reader's Guide

Junior Worldmark Encyclopedia of the Mexican States, presents profiles of the 31 states and the Distrito Federal (federal district) of Mexico. Entries are arranged alphabetically in one volume. Following the state entries is an article on the country of Mexico itself. The *Worldmark* design organizes facts and data about every state in a common structure. Every profile contains a map showing the state and its location in the nation.

Sources

Due to the broad scope of this encyclopedia many sources were consulted in compiling the information and statistics presented in this volume. However, special recognition is due to the many agencies of the Mexican states, from Aguascalientes to Zacatecas, that contributed data, answered questions, and provided information. Statistical information was gathered with the help of Instituto Nacional de Estadística Geografia e Informatica (INEGI), the agency that oversees publication of statistics on many aspects of Mexico and its citizens. Among the sources consulted during the compilation of this first edition of *Junior Worldmark*

Encyclopedia of the Mexican States were XII Censo General de Población y Vivienda 2000 (12th General Census of Population 2000).

The sections on history and government were prepared by Patricio Navia, Ph.D., who is on the faculty of both the Center for Latin American and Caribbean Studies, New York University and the Escuela de Ciencia Politica, Universidad Diego Portales, Santiago, Chile. The editors also acknowledge the assistance provided by staff members of the History and Geography Department, Cleveland Public Library, and Barbara Appel Tenenbaum, Ph.D., Specialist in Mexican Culture, Hispanic Division, Library of Congress.

Profile Features

This first edition of *Junior Worldmark Encyclopedia of the Mexican States* follows the numbered heading structure, which allows students to compare two or more states in a variety of ways, that is the hallmark of the *Junior Worldmark* series. *Junior Worldmark Encyclopedia of the Mexican States* features 27 numbered headings. Each state entry is accompanied by a map specially prepared for this first edition.

Each province profile begins by presenting basic information about the state, including the pronunciation and origin of the state name, the capital, the date it entered the country, a description of the official coat of arms, and the holidays observed. (The entries also inform the student researcher that the states of Mexico have no official state flags.) The introductory information ends with the standard time given by time zone in relation to Greenwich mean time (GMT). The world is divided into 24 time zones, each one hour apart. The Greenwich meridian, which is 0 degrees, passes through Greenwich, England, a suburb of London. Greenwich is at the center of the initial time zone, known as Greenwich mean time. All times given are converted from noon in this zone. The time reported for each state is the official time zone.

Because many terms used in this encyclopedia will be new to students, a Words to Know section appears at the beginning of the volume.

Organization

The body of each profile is arranged in 27 numbered headings as follows:

1   Location and Size. Statistics are given on area, with a comparison to a US state. The names of the geographic features that surround the state (other states, bodies of water, or countries) are provided. The number of municipalities identified in each state is included, along with the name of the capital. Latitude and longitude are given, along with a general geographic location of the state within the country of Mexico. An overview of the topography, with principal mountains (and elevations), valley, plains, and islands are listed. The state's major lakes and rivers, along with

any other notable geographic features, are described briefly.

2   Climate. Temperature and rainfall are given for the various regions of the state in both English and metric units.

3   Plants and Animals. Described here are the plants and animals native to the state.

4   Environmental Protection. Information on efforts to preserve the environment are described here. Information on unique or protected animal and plant species are also included.

5   Population, Ethnic Groups, Languages. Statistics from the 2000 census for total population and population by gender are provided. Population density for the state overall, and the population of the capital are given, along with information on languages spoken by the citizens.

6   Religions. Statistics from the 2000 census describe the breakdown of the population according to religion and/or denominations.

7   Transportation. Information on the state's network of roads, railways, and waterways is provided. In addition, the principal airports and seaports serving the state are provided.

8   History. Includes a concise summary of the state's history from ancient times (where appropriate) through the arrival of European explorers, missionaries, and conquerors, to the present.

9   State and Local Government. The election cycle for governor is provided, along with information on the state's legislature. The state's constitution, along with the name of the seat of government, are briefly described. Finally, details of the form of municipal government found in the state are given.

10 **Political Parties.** Describes the significant political parties through history, where appropriate, and the influential parties as of 2004. The current governor is named, and the year of the next scheduled gubernatorial election is provided.

11 **Judicial System.** Structure of the court system and the jurisdiction of courts in each category is provided.

12 **Economy.** This section presents the key elements of the economy. Major industries are summarized.

13 **Industry.** Key industries are listed, and important aspects of industrial development, including the effects of the North American Free Trade Agreement (NAFTA) are described where applicable.

14 **Labor.** An overview of employment, unemployment, and labor relations is provided.

15 **Agriculture.** Information on agricultural activity, principal crops, and livestock of the state are given.

16 **Natural Resources.** Information on principal natural resources, such as minerals mined, is provided.

17 **Energy and Power.** Description of the state's power resources, including electricity produced and oil reserves and production, are provided.

18 **Health.** Information on the primary public health facilities (hospitals and medical facilities) appear here.

19 **Housing.** General information on the condition of housing in the state is given here.

20 **Education.** Statistical data from the 2000 census on numbers of school-age children in the state is provided. Major universities are listed.

21 **Arts.** A summary of the major cultural institutions is provided.

22 **Libraries and Museums.** Statistics on the number of branches of the national library in the state are provided. Major museums are listed.

23 **Media.** Major newspapers are listed. Information on telephone and Internet service is also provided where appropriate.

24 **Tourism, Travel, and Recreation.** Under this heading, the student will find a summary of the important sites of interest to tourists in the state. Major festivals and fairs hosted in the state are also mentioned.

25 **Sports.** The major sports teams and principal stadiums in the state are summarized.

26 **Famous People.** In this section, some of the best-known citizens of the state through history are listed.

27 **Bibliography.** The bibliographic and web site listings at the end of each profile are provided as a guide for further research.

A keyword index completes the volume.

Comments and Suggestions

We welcome your comments on the *Junior Worldmark Encyclopedia of the Mexican States,* as well as your suggestions for features to be included in future editions. Please write: Editors, *Junior Worldmark Encyclopedia of the Mexican States,* U•X•L, 27500 Drake Road, Farmington Hills, MI 48331-3535; or call toll-free: 1-800-877-4253.

Guide to Articles

All information contained within an article is uniformly keyed by means of a number to the left of the subject headings. A heading such as "History," for example, carries the same key numeral (8) in every article. Therefore, to find information about the history of Aguascalientes, consult the table of contents for the page number where the Aguascalientes article begins and look for section 8.

Introductory matter for each province includes:
Pronunciation
Origin of state name
Capital
Entered country
Coat of arms
Holidays
Flag
Time zone

Sections listed numerically

1 Location and Size
2 Climate
3 Plants and Animals
4 Environmental
     Protection
5 Population, Ethnic
     Groups, Languages
6 Religions
7 Transportation
8 History
9 State and Local
     Government
10 Political Parties
11 Judicial System
12 Economy
13 Industry

14 Labor
15 Agriculture
16 Natural Resources
17 Energy and Power
18 Health
19 Housing
20 Education
21 Arts
22 Libraries and Museums
23 Media
24 Tourism, Travel, and
     Recreation
25 Sports
26 Famous People
27 Bibliography

Alphabetical listing of sections

Agriculture	15	Libraries and Museums	22
Arts	21	Location and Size	1
Bibliography	27	Media	23
Climate	2	Natural Resources	16
Economy	12	Plants and Animals	3
Education	20	Political Parties	10
Energy and Power	17	Population, Ethnic	
Environmental Protection	4	Groups, Languages	5
Famous People	26	Religions	6
Health	18	Sports	25
History	8	State and Local	
Housing	19	Government	9
Industry	13	Tourism, Travel, and	
Judicial System	11	Recreation	24
Labor	14	Transportation	7

Explanation of symbols

A fiscal split year is indicated by a stroke (e.g. 1999/00).
The use of a small dash (e.g., 1990–94) normally signifies the
    full period of calendar years covered (including the end year indicated).

Words to Know

A

abdicate: To formally give up a claim to a throne; to give up the right to be king or queen.

aboriginal: The first known inhabitants of a country. A species of animals or plants which originated within a given area.

acid rain: Rain (or snow) that has become slightly acid by mixing with industrial air pollution.

adobe: A brick made from sun-dried heavy clay mixed with straw, used in building houses. A house made of adobe bricks.

adult literacy: The ability of adults to read and write.

agrarian economy: An economy where agriculture is the dominant form of economic activity. A society where agriculture dominates the day-to-day activities of the population is called an agrarian society.

air link: Refers to scheduled air service that allows people and goods to travel between two places on a regular basis.

airborne industrial pollutant: Pollution caused by industry that is supported or carried by the air.

althing: A legislative assembly.

amendment: A change or addition to a document.

Amerindian: A contraction of the two words, American Indian. It describes native peoples of North, South, or Central America.

amnesty: An act of forgiveness or pardon, usually taken by a government, toward persons for crimes they may have committed.

animal husbandry: The branch of agriculture that involves raising animals.

animism: The belief that natural objects and phenomena have souls or innate spiritual powers.

annex: To incorporate land from one country into another country.

annual growth rate: The rate at which something grows over a period of 12 months.

appeasement: To bring to a state of peace.

appellate: Refers to an appeal of a court decision to a high authority.

aquaculture: The culture or "farming" of aquatic plants or other natural produce, as in the raising of catfish in "farms."

aquatic resources: Resources that come from, grow in, or live in water, including fish and plants.

aquifer: An underground layer of porous rock, sand, or gravel that holds water.

arable land: Land that can be cultivated by plowing and used for growing crops.

archipelago: Any body of water abounding with islands, or the islands themselves collectively.

archives: A place where records or a collection of important documents are kept.

aristocracy: A small minority that controls the government of a nation, typically on the basis of inherited wealth.

asylum: To give protection, security, or shelter to someone who is threatened by political or religious persecution.

atoll: A coral island, consisting of a strip or ring of coral surrounding a central lagoon.

austerity measures: Steps taken by a government to conserve money or resources during an economically difficult time, such as cutting back on federally funded programs.

authoritarianism: A form of government in which a person or group attempts to rule with absolute authority without the representation of the citizens.

autonomous state: A country which is completely self-governing, as opposed to being a dependency or part of another country.

autonomy: The state of existing as a self-governing entity. For instance, when a country gains its independence from another country, it gains autonomy.

average inflation rate: The average rate at which the general prices of goods and services increase over the period of a year.

average life expectancy: In any given society, the average age attained by persons at the time of death.

B

Baptist: A member of a Protestant denomination that practices adult baptism by complete immersion in water.

barren land: Unproductive land, partly or entirely treeless.

barter: Trade practice where merchandise is exchanged directly for other merchandise or services without use of money.

bedrock: Solid rock lying under loose earth.

bicameral legislature: A legislative body consisting of two chambers, such as the U.S. House of Representatives and the U.S. Senate.

bill of rights: A written statement containing the list of privileges and powers to be granted to a body of people, usually introduced when a government or other organization is forming.

Biosphere: The part of the earth and its atmosphere that is capable of supporting life.

bituminous coal: Soft coal; coal which burns with a bright-yellow flame.

black market: A system of trade where goods are sold illegally, often for excessively inflated prices. This type of trade usually develops to avoid paying taxes or tariffs levied by the government, or to get around import or export restrictions on products.

bloodless coup: The sudden takeover of a country's government by hostile means but without killing anyone in the process.

bog: Wet, soft, and spongy ground where the soil is composed mainly of decayed or decaying vegetable matter.

bonded labor: Workers bound to service without pay; slaves.

border dispute: A disagreement between two countries as to the exact location or length of the dividing line between them.

broadleaf forest: A forest composed mainly of broadleaf (deciduous) trees.

buffer state: A small country that lies between two larger, possibly hostile countries, considered to be a neutralizing force between them.

bullfighting: Sport popular in Spain and Mexico where a man fights against a bull, eventually killing it, in front of large crowds of spectators.

bureaucracy: A system of government that is characterized by division into bureaus of administration with their own divisional heads. Also refers to the inflexible procedures of such a system that often result in delay.

C

CACM see Central American Common Market.

cactus: Type of plant that thrives in a hot, dry climate.

canton: A territory or small division or state within a country.

capital punishment: The ultimate act of punishment for a crime, the death penalty.

capitalism: An economic system in which goods and services and the means to produce and sell them are privately owned, and prices and wages are determined by market forces.

carnivore: Flesh-eating animal or plant.

carob: The common English name for a plant that is similar to and sometimes used as a substitute for chocolate.

cash crop: A crop that is grown to be sold rather than kept for private use.

cassation: The reversal or annulling of a final judgment by the supreme authority.

cassava: The name of several species of stout herbs, extensively cultivated for food.

Caucasian or Caucasoid: The white race of human beings, as determined by genealogy and physical features.

cease-fire: An official declaration of the end to the use of military force or active hostilities, even if only temporary.

cenote: A deep hollow in limestone rock where water collects. A cenote often connects to a cavern or underground cave.

censorship: The practice of withholding certain items of news that may cast a country in an unfavorable light or give away secrets to the enemy.

census: An official counting of the inhabitants of a state or country with details of sex and age, family, occupation, possessions, etc.

cession: Withdrawal from or yielding to physical force.

cholera: An acute infectious disease characterized by severe diarrhea, vomiting, and, often, death.

Christianity: The religion founded by Jesus Christ, based on the Bible as holy scripture.

circuit court: A court that convenes in two or more locations within its appointed district.

city-state: An independent state consisting of a city and its surrounding territory.

civil court: A court whose proceedings include determinations of rights of individual citizens, in contrast to criminal proceedings regarding individuals or the public.

civil jurisdiction: The authority to enforce the laws in civil matters brought before the court.

civil law: The law developed by a nation or state for the conduct of daily life of its own people.

civil rights: The privileges of all individuals to be treated as equals under the laws of their country; specifically, the rights given by certain amendments to the U.S. Constitution.

civil unrest: The feeling of uneasiness due to an unstable political climate, or actions taken as a result of it.

civil war: A war between groups of citizens of the same country who have different opinions or agendas. The Civil War of the United States was the conflict between the states of the North and South from 1861 to 1865.

climatic belt: A region or zone where a particular type of climate prevails.

coastal belt: A coastal plain area of lowlands and somewhat higher ridges that run parallel to the coast.

coastal plain: A fairly level area of land along the coast of a land mass.

coca: A shrub native to South America, the leaves of which produce organic compounds that are used in the production of cocaine.

coke: The solid product of the carbonization of coal, bearing the same relation to coal that charcoal does to wood.

collective bargaining: The negotiations between workers who are members of a union and their employer for the purpose of deciding work rules and policies regarding wages, hours, etc.

collective farming: The system of farming on a collective where all workers share in the income of the farm.

colloquial: Belonging to ordinary, everyday speech: often especially applied to common words and phrases which are not used in formal speech.

colonial period: The period of time when a country forms colonies in and extends control over a foreign area.

colonist: Any member of a colony or one who helps settle a new colony.

colony: A group of people who settle in a new area far from their original country, but still under the jurisdiction of that country. Also refers to the newly settled area itself.

commerce: The trading of goods (buying and selling), especially on a large scale, between cities, states, and countries.

commercial catch: The amount of marketable fish, usually measured in tons, caught in a particular period of time.

commercial crop: Any marketable agricultural crop.

commission: A group of people designated to collectively do a job, including a government agency with certain law-making powers. Also, the power given to an individual or group to perform certain duties.

commodity: Any items, such as goods or services, that are bought or sold, or agricultural products that are traded or marketed.

common law: A legal system based on custom and decisions and opinions of the law courts. The basic system of law of England and the United States.

common market: An economic union among countries that is formed to remove trade barriers (tariffs) among those countries, increasing economic cooperation. The European Community is a notable example of a common market.

commonwealth: A commonwealth is a free association of sovereign independent states that has no charter, treaty, or consti-

tution. The association promotes cooperation, consultation, and mutual assistance among members.

commune: An organization of people living together in a community who share the ownership and use of property. Also refers to a small governmental district of a country, especially in Europe.

communism: A form of government whose system requires common ownership of property for the use of all citizens. All profits are to be equally distributed and prices on goods and services are usually set by the state. Also, communism refers directly to the official doctrine of the former U.S.S.R.

compulsory: Required by law or other regulation.

compulsory education: The mandatory requirement for children to attend school until they have reached a certain age or grade level.

conciliation: A process of bringing together opposing sides of a disagreement for the purpose of compromise. Or, a way of settling an international dispute in which the disagreement is submitted to an independent committee that will examine the facts and advise the participants of a possible solution.

concordat: An agreement, compact, or convention, especially between church and state.

confederation: An alliance or league formed for the purpose of promoting the common interests of its members.

coniferous forest: A forest consisting mainly of pine, fir, and cypress trees.

conifers: Cone-bearing plants. Mostly evergreen trees and shrubs which produce cones.

conquest: Forcibly taking over control of territory.

conquistador: Someone involved in the Spanish conquest of America, especially Mexico and Peru.

conscription: To be required to join the military by law. Also known as the draft. Service personnel who join the military because of the legal requirement are called conscripts or draftees.

conservative party: A political group whose philosophy tends to be based on established traditions and not supportive of rapid change.

constituency: The registered voters in a governmental district, or a group of people that supports a position or a candidate.

constituent assembly: A group of people that has the power to determine the election of a political representative or create a constitution.

constitution: The written laws and basic rights of citizens of a country or members of an organized group.

constitutional monarchy: A system of government in which the hereditary sovereign (king or queen, usually) rules according to a written constitution.

constitutional republic: A system of government with an elected chief of state and elected representation, with a written constitution containing its governing principles. The United States is a constitutional republic.

consumer goods: Items that are bought to satisfy personal needs or wants of individuals.

continental climate: The climate of a part of the continent; the characteristics and peculiarities of the climate are a result of the land itself and its location.

continental shelf: A plain extending from the continental coast and varying in width that typically ends in a steep slope to the ocean floor.

copra: The dried meat of the coconut; it is frequently used as an ingredient of curry, and to produce coconut oil. Also written cobra, coprah, and copperah.

cordillera: A continuous ridge, range, or chain of mountains.

corvette: A small warship that is often used as an escort ship because it is easier to maneuver than larger ships like destroyers.

counterinsurgency operations: Organized military activity designed to stop rebellion against an established government.

county: A territorial division or administrative unit within a state or country.

coup d'ètat or coup: A sudden, violent overthrow of a government or its leader.

court of appeal: An appellate court, having the power of review after a case has been decided in a lower court.

court of first appeal: The next highest court to the court which has decided a case, to which that case may be presented for review.

court of last appeal: The highest court, in which a decision is not subject to review by any higher court. In the United States, it could be the Supreme Court of an individual state or the U.S. Supreme Court.

criminal law: The branch of law that deals primarily with crimes and their punishments.

cultivable land: Land that can be prepared for the production of crops.

cyclone: Any atmospheric movement, general or local, in which the wind blows spirally around and in towards a center. In the northern hemisphere, the cyclonic movement is usually counter-clockwise, and in the southern hemisphere, it is clockwise.

D

decentralization: The redistribution of power in a government from one large central authority to a wider range of smaller local authorities.

deciduous species: Any species that sheds or casts off a part of itself after a definite period of time. More commonly used in reference to plants that shed their leaves on a yearly basis as opposed to those (evergreens) that retain them.

declaration of independence: A formal written document stating the intent of a group of persons to become fully self-governing.

deforestation: The removal or clearing of a forest.

deity: A being with the attributes, nature, and essence of a god; a divinity.

delta: Triangular-shaped deposits of soil formed at the mouths of large rivers.

demarcate: To mark off from adjoining land or territory; set the limits or boundaries of.

democracy: A form of government in which the power lies in the hands of the people, who can govern directly, or can be governed indirectly by representatives elected by its citizens.

denationalize: To remove from government ownership or control.

deportation: To carry away or remove from one country to another, or to a distant place.

depression: A hollow; a surface that has sunken or fallen in.

deregulation: The act of reversing controls and restrictions on prices of goods, bank interest, and the like.

desalinization plant: A facility that produces freshwater by removing the salt from saltwater.

desegregation: The act of removing restrictions on people of a particular race that keep them socially, economically, and, sometimes, physically, separate from other groups.

desertification: The process of becoming a desert as a result of climatic changes, land mismanagement, or both.

devaluation: The official lowering of the value of a country's currency in relation to the value of gold or the currencies of other countries.

developed countries: Countries which have a high standard of living and a well-developed industrial base.

development assistance: Government programs intended to finance and promote the growth of new industries.

dialect: One of a number of regional or related modes of speech regarded as descending from a common origin.

dictatorship: A form of government in which all the power is retained by an absolute leader or tyrant. There are no rights granted to the people to elect their own representatives.

diplomatic relations: The relationship between countries as conducted by representatives of each government.

direct election: The process of selecting a representative to the government by balloting of the voting public, in contrast to selection by an elected representative of the people.

dissident: A person whose political opinions differ from the majority to the point of rejection.

dogma: A principle, maxim, or tenet held as being firmly established.

domain: The area of land governed by a particular ruler or government, sometimes referring to the ultimate control of that territory.

dormant volcano: A volcano that has not exhibited any signs of activity for an extended period of time.

dowry: The sum of the property or money that a bride brings to her groom at their marriage.

draft constitution: The preliminary written plans for the new constitution of a country forming a new government.

dry forest: A type of tropical forest where the climate features a long dry season and a short rainy season. Most trees in the dry forest lose their leaves during the dry season. Also called tropical dry forest or tropical deciduous forest.

due process: In law, the application of the legal process to which every citizen has a right, which cannot be denied.

durable goods: Goods or products which are expected to last and perform for several years, such as cars and washing machines.

dynasty: A family line of sovereigns who rule in succession, and the time during which they reign.

E

earned income: The money paid to an individual in wages or salary.

ecclesiastical: Pertaining or relating to the church.

ecological balance: The condition of a healthy, well-functioning ecosystem, which includes all the plants and animals in a natural community together with their environment.

ecology: The branch of science that studies organisms in relationship to other organisms and to their environment.

economic depression: A prolonged period in which there is high unemployment, low production, falling prices, and general business failure.

economically active population: That portion of the people who are employed for wages and are consumers of goods and services.

ecotourism: Broad term used to describe travel that focuses on nature, adventure, and learning about different cultures. The term is also used to describe travel that is sensitive to protecting the environment. Scientific, educational, or academic purposes (such as biotourism, archetourism, and geotourism) are also forms of ecotourism.

elected assembly: The persons that comprise a legislative body of a government who received their positions by direct election.

electoral system: A system of choosing government officials by votes cast by qualified citizens.

electoral vote: The votes of the members of the electoral college.

electorate: The people who are qualified to vote in an election.

emancipation: The freeing of persons from any kind of bondage or slavery.

embargo: A legal restriction on commercial ships to enter a country's ports, or any legal restriction of trade.

emigration: Moving from one country or region to another for the purpose of residence.

empire: A group of territories ruled by one sovereign or supreme ruler. Also, the period of time under that rule.

enclave: A territory belonging to one nation that is surrounded by that of another nation.

encroachment: The act of intruding, trespassing, or entering on the rights or possessions of another.

endangered species: A plant or animal species whose existence as a whole is threatened with extinction.

endemic: Anything that is peculiar to and characteristic of a locality or region.

epidemic: As applied to disease, any disease that is temporarily prevalent among people in one place at the same time.

Episcopal: Belonging to or vested in bishops or prelates; characteristic of or pertaining to a bishop or bishops.

excommunicated: Officially banned from the church, especially the Roman Catholic Church.

exports: Goods sold to foreign buyers.

F

faction: People with a specific set of interests or goals who form a subgroup within a larger organization.

federal: Pertaining to a union of states whose governments are subordinate to a central government.

federation: A union of states or other groups under the authority of a central government.

final jurisdiction: The final authority in the decision of a legal matter. In the United States, the Supreme Court would have final jurisdiction.

fiscal year: The twelve months between the settling of financial accounts, not necessarily corresponding to a calendar year beginning on January 1.

fodder: Food for cattle, horses, and sheep, such as hay, straw, and other kinds of vegetables.

folk religion: A religion with origins and traditions among the common people of a nation or region that is relevant to their particular life-style.

foreign exchange: Foreign currency that allows foreign countries to conduct financial transactions or settle debts with one another.

foreign policy: The course of action that one government chooses to adopt in relation to a foreign country.

fossil fuels: Any mineral or mineral substance formed by the decomposition of organic matter buried beneath the earth's surface and used as a fuel.

free enterprise: The system of economics in which private business may be conducted with minimum interference by the government.

free-market economy: An economic system that relies on the market, as opposed to government planners, to set the prices for wages and products.

fundamentalist: A person who holds religious beliefs based on the complete acceptance of the words of the Bible or other holy scripture as the truth. For instance, a fundamentalist would believe the story of creation exactly as it is told in the Bible and would reject the idea of evolution.

G

GDP *see* gross domestic product.

global warming: Also called the greenhouse effect. The theorized gradual warming of the earth's climate as a result of the burning of fossil fuels, the use of man-made chemicals, deforestation, etc.

GMT *see* Greenwich Mean Time.

GNP *see* gross national product.

Greenwich (Mean) Time: Mean solar time of the meridian at Greenwich, England, used as the basis for standard time throughout most of the world. The world is divided into 24 time zones, and all are related to the prime, or Greenwich mean, zone.

gross domestic product: A measure of the market value of all goods and services produced within the boundaries of a nation, regardless of asset ownership. Unlike gross national product, GDP excludes receipts from that nation's business operations in foreign countries.

gross national product: A measure of the market value of goods and services produced by the labor and property of a nation. Includes receipts from that nation's business operation in foreign countries

groundwater: Water located below the earth's surface, the source from which wells and springs draw their water.

guano: The excrement of seabirds and bats found in various areas around the world. Gathered commercially and sold as a fertilizer.

gubernatorial election: An election to choose a governor.

guerrilla: A member of a small radical military organization that uses unconventional tactics to take their enemies by surprise.

H

hardwoods: The name given to deciduous trees, such as cherry, oak, maple, and mahogany.

heavy industry: Industries that use heavy or large machinery to produce goods, such as automobile manufacturing.

hoist: The part of a flag nearest the flagpole.

homogeneous: Of the same kind or nature, often used in reference to a whole.

human rights activist: A person who vigorously pursues the attainment of basic rights for all people.

human rights issues: Any matters involving people's basic rights which are in question or thought to be abused.

humanist: A person who centers on human needs and values, and stresses dignity of the individual.

humanitarian aid: Money or supplies given to a persecuted group or people of a country at war, or those devastated by a natural disaster, to provide for basic human needs.

hydrocarbon: A compound of hydrogen and carbon, often occurring in organic substances or derivatives of organic substances such as coal, petroleum, natural gas, etc.

hydrocarbon emissions: Organic compounds containing only carbon and hydrogen, often occurring in petroleum, natural gas, coal, and bitumens, and which contribute to the greenhouse effect.

hydroelectric potential: The potential amount of electricity that can be produced hydroelectrically. Usually used in reference to a given area and how many hydroelectric power plants that area can sustain.

hydroelectric power plant: A factory that produces electrical power through the application of waterpower.

I

immigration: The act or process of passing or entering into another country for the purpose of permanent residence.

imports: Goods purchased from foreign suppliers.

indigenous: Born or originating in a particular place or country; native to a particular region or area.

industrialized nation: A nation whose economy is based on industry.

infanticide: The act of murdering a baby.

inflation: The general rise of prices, as measured by a consumer price index. Results in a fall in value of currency.

installed capacity: The maximum possible output of electric power at any given time.

insurgency: The state or condition in which one rises against lawful authority or established government; rebellion.

insurgent. A person who rebels against the established authority of government.

insurrectionist: One who participates in an unorganized revolt against an authority.

interim government: A temporary or provisional government.

interim president: One who is appointed to perform temporarily the duties of president during a transitional period in a government.

internal migration: Term used to describe the relocation of individuals from one region to another without leaving the confines of the country or of a specified area.

isthmus: A narrow strip of land bordered by water and connecting two larger bodies of land, such as two continents, a continent and a peninsula, or two parts of an island.

J

Jesuit order: A religious group that is part of the Roman Catholic Church.

Judaism: The religious system of the Jews, based on the Old Testament as revealed to Moses and characterized by a belief in one God and adherence to the laws of scripture and rabbinic traditions.

Judeo-Christian: The dominant traditional religious makeup of the United States and other countries based on the worship of the Old and New Testaments of the Bible.

junta: A small military group in power of a country, especially after a coup.

K

kwh: The abbreviation for kilowatt-hour.

L

labor force: The number of people in a population available for work, whether actually employed or not.

labor movement: A movement in the early to mid-1800s to organize workers in groups according to profession to give them certain rights as a group, including bargaining power for better wages, working conditions, and benefits.

land reforms: Steps taken to create a fair distribution of farmland, especially by governmental action.

landlocked: An area that does not have direct access to the sea; it is completely surrounded by other states or countries.

least developed countries: A subgroup of the United Nations designation of "less developed countries;" these countries generally have no significant economic growth, low literacy rates, and per person gross national product of less than $500. Also known as undeveloped countries.

leeward: The direction identical to that of the wind. For example, a leeward tide is a tide that runs in the same direction that the wind blows.

leftist: A person with a liberal or radical political affiliation.

legislative branch: The branch of government which makes or enacts the laws.

less developed countries (LDC): Designated by the United Nations to include countries with low levels of output, living standards, and per person gross national product generally below $5,000.

literacy: The ability to read and write.

M

maize: Another name (Spanish or British) for corn or the color of ripe corn.

majority party: The party with the largest number of votes and the controlling political party in a government.

mangrove: A tree which abounds on tropical shores in both hemispheres. Characterized by its numerous roots which arch out from its trunk and descend from its branches, mangroves form thick, dense growths along the tidal muds, reaching lengths hundreds of miles long.

manioc: The cassava plant or its product. Manioc is a very important food-staple in tropical America.

maquiladora: An assembly plant located in Mexico but owned by a company based in another country. There, lower-paid Mexican workers assemble products using parts that have been imported. Finished products are then exported.

marine life: The life that exists in, or is formed by the sea.

maritime climate: The climate and weather conditions typical of areas bordering the sea.

maritime rights: The rights that protect navigation and shipping.

market access: Market access refers to the openness of a national market to foreign products. Market access reflects a government's willingness to permit imports to compete relatively unimpeded with similar domestically produced goods.

market economy: A form of society which runs by the law of supply and demand. Goods are produced by firms to be sold to consumers, who determine the demand for them. Price levels vary according to the demand for certain goods and how much of them is produced.

market price: The price a commodity will bring when sold on the open market. The price is determined by the amount of demand for the commodity by buyers.

massif: A central mountain-mass or the dominant part of a range of mountains.

mean temperature: The air temperature unit measured by the National Weather Service by adding the maximum and minimum daily temperatures together and diving the sum by 2.

mestizo: A person of mixed European (usually Spanish) and American Indian (Amerindian) parentage.

migratory birds: Those birds whose instincts prompt them to move from one place to another at the regularly recurring changes of season.

migratory workers: Usually agricultural workers who move from place to place for employment depending on the growing and harvesting seasons of various crops.

military coup: A sudden, violent overthrow of a government by military forces.

military junta: The small military group in power in a country, especially after a coup.

military regime: Government conducted by a military force.

military takeover: The seizure of control of a government by the military forces.

militia: The group of citizens of a country who are either serving in the reserve military forces or are eligible to be called up in time of emergency.

millet: A cereal grass whose small grain is used for food in Europe and Asia.

minority party: The political group that comprises the smaller part of the large overall group it belongs to; the party that is not in control.

missionary: A person sent by authority of a church or religious organization to spread his religious faith in a community where his church has no self-supporting organization.

monarchy: Government by a sovereign, such as a king or queen.

money economy: A system or stage of economic development in which money replaces barter in the exchange of goods and services.

Moors: One of the Arab tribes that conquered Spain in the eighth century.

mouflon: A type of wild sheep characterized by curling horns.

mulatto: One who is the offspring of parents one of whom is white and the other is black.

municipality: A district such as a city or town having its own incorporated government.

N

NAFTA *see* North American Free Trade Agreement

nationalism: National spirit or aspirations; desire for national unity, independence, or prosperity.

nationalization: To transfer the control or ownership of land or industries to the nation from private owners.

native tongue: One's natural language. The language that is indigenous to an area.

natural gas: A combustible gas formed naturally in the earth and generally obtained by boring a well. The chemical makeup of natural gas is principally methane, hydrogen, ethylene compounds, and nitrogen.

natural harbor: A protected portion of a sea or lake along the shore resulting from the natural formations of the land.

naturalize: To confer the rights and privileges of a native-born subject or citizen upon someone who lives in the country by choice.

nature preserve: An area where one or more species of plant and/or animal are protected from harm, injury, or destruction.

neutrality: The policy of not taking sides with any countries during a war or dispute among them.

news censorship *see* censorship

North American Free Trade Agreement: NAFTA, which entered into force in January 1994, is a free trade agreement between Canada, the United States, and Mexico. The agreement progressively eliminates almost all U.S.-Mexico tariffs over a 10–15 year period.

nuclear power plant: A factory that produces electrical power through the application of the nuclear reaction known as nuclear fission.

nuclear reactor: A device used to control the rate of nuclear fission in uranium. Used in commercial applications, nuclear reactors can maintain temperatures high enough to generate sufficient quantities of steam which can then be used to produce electricity.

O

OAS (Organization of American States): The OAS (Spanish: Organizaciûn de los Estados Americanos, OEA), or the Pan American Union, is a regional organization which promotes Latin American economic and social development. Members include the United States, Mexico, and most Central American, South American, and Caribbean nations.

occupied territory: A territory that has an enemy's military forces present.

official language: The language in which the business of a country and its government is conducted.

oligarchy: A form of government in which a few people possess the power to rule as opposed to a monarchy which is ruled by one.

open economy: An economy that imports and exports goods.

open market: Open market operations are the actions of the central bank to influence or control the money supply by buying or selling government bonds.

opposition party: A minority political party that is opposed to the party in power.

organized labor: The body of workers who belong to labor unions.

overfishing: To deplete the quantity of fish in an area by removing more fish than can be naturally replaced.

overgrazing: Allowing animals to graze in an area to the point that the ground vegetation is damaged or destroyed.

overseas dependencies: A distant and physically separate territory that belongs to another country and is subject to its laws and government.

P

pact: An international agreement.

Paleolithic: The early period of the Stone Age, when rough, chipped stone implements were used.

panhandle: A long narrow strip of land projecting like the handle of a frying pan.

paramilitary group: A supplementary organization to the military.

parasitic diseases: A group of diseases caused by parasitic organisms which feed off the host organism.

parochial: Refers to matters of a church parish or something within narrow limits.

partisan politics: Rigid, unquestioning following of a specific party's or leader's goals.

patriarchal system: A social system in which the head of the family or tribe is the father or oldest male. Kinship is determined and traced through the male members of the tribe.

per capita: Literally, per person; for each person counted.

periodical: A publication whose issues appear at regular intervals, such as weekly, monthly, or yearly.

petrochemical: A chemical derived from petroleum or from natural gas.

pharmaceutical plants: Any plant that is used in the preparation of medicinal drugs.

plantain: The name of a common weed that has often been used for medicinal purposes, as a folk remedy and in modern medicine. Plaintain is also the name of a tropical plant producing a type of banana.

political climate: The prevailing political attitude of a particular time or place.

political refugee: A person forced to flee his or her native country for political reasons.

potable water: Water that is safe for drinking.

private sector: The division of an economy in which production of goods and services is privately owned.

privatization: To change from public to private control or ownership.

proportional representation: A form of election where representatives to a legislature are designated according to the proportion of the total votes won by the specific political parties.

protectorate: A state or territory controlled by a stronger state, or the relationship of the stronger country toward the lesser one it protects.

Protestant: A member or an adherent of one of those Christian bodies which descended from the Reformation of the sixteenth century. Originally applied to those who opposed or protested the Roman Catholic Church.

Protestant Reformation: In 1529, a Christian religious movement begun in Germany to deny the universal authority of the pope, and to establish the Bible as the only source of truth. (*Also see* Protestant)

proved reserves: The quantity of a recoverable mineral resource (such as oil or natural gas) that is still in the ground.

provisional government: A temporary government set up during time of unrest or transition in a country.

pulses: Beans, peas, or lentils.

purge: The act of ridding a society of "undesirable" or unloyal persons by banishment or murder.

R

rate of literacy: The percentage of people in a society who can read and write.

recession. A period of reduced economic activity in a country or region.

referendum: The practice of submitting legislation directly to the people for a popular vote.

reforestation: Systematically replacing forest trees lost due to fire or logging.

Reformation *see* Protestant Reformation.

refugee: One who flees to a refuge or shelter or place of safety. One who in times of persecution or political commotion flees to a foreign country for safety.

revolution: A complete change in a government or society, such as in an overthrow of the government by the people.

right-wing party: The more conservative political party.

Roman Catholic Church: The designation of the church of which the pope or Bishop of Rome is the head, and that holds him as the successor of St. Peter and heir of his spiritual authority, privileges, and gifts.

roundwood: Timber used as poles or in similar ways without being sawn or shaped.

runoff election: A deciding election put to the voters in case of a tie between candidates.

S

sack: To strip of valuables, especially after capture.

salinization: An accumulation of soluble salts in soil. This condition is common in desert climates, where water evaporates quickly in poorly drained soil due to high temperatures.

savanna: A treeless or near treeless plain of a tropical or subtropical region dominated by drought-resistant grasses.

secession: The act of withdrawal, such as a state withdrawing from the Union in the Civil War in the United States.

sect: A religious denomination or group, often a dissenting one with extreme views.

segregation: The enforced separation of a racial or religious group from other groups, compelling them to live and go to school separately from the rest of society.

seismic activity: Relating to or connected with an earthquake or earthquakes in general.

self-sufficient: Able to function alone without help.

separation of power: The division of power in the government among the executive, legislative, and judicial branches and the checks and balances employed to keep them separate and independent of each other.

separatism: The policy of dissenters withdrawing from a larger political or religious group.

Seventh-day Adventist: One who believes in the second coming of Christ to establish a personal reign upon the earth.

shamanism: A religion of some Asians and Amerindians in which shamans, who are priests or medicine men, are believed to influence good and evil spirits.

shantytown: An urban settlement of people in flimsy, inadequate houses.

shoal: A place where the water of a stream, lake, or sea is of little depth. Especially, a sand-bank which shows at low water.

sierra: A chain of hills or mountains.

slash-and-burn agriculture: A hasty and sometimes temporary way of clearing land to make it available for agriculture by cutting down trees and burning them.

slave trade: The transportation of black Africans beginning in the 1700s to other countries to be sold as slaves—people owned as property and compelled to work for their owners at no pay.

social insurance: A government plan to protect low-income people, such as health and accident insurance, pension plans, etc.

social security: A form of social insurance, including life, disability, and old-age pension for workers. It is paid for by employers, employees, and the government.

socialism: An economic system in which ownership of land and other property is distributed among the community as a whole, and every member of the community shares in the work and products of the work.

socialist: A person who advocates socialism.

softwoods: The coniferous trees, whose wood density as a whole is relatively softer than the wood of those trees referred to as hardwoods.

sorghum: Plant grown in various parts of the world for its valuable uses, such as for grain, syrup, or fodder.

staple crop: A crop that is the chief commodity or product of a place, and which has widespread and constant use or value.

state: The politically organized body of people living under one government or one of the territorial units that make up a federal government, such as in the United States.

student demonstration: A public gathering of students to express strong feelings about a certain situation, usually taking place near the location of the people in power to change the situation.

subcontinent: A land mass of great size, but smaller than any of the continents; a large subdivision of a continent.

subsistence economy: The part of a national economy in which money plays little or no role, trade is by barter, and living standards are minimal.

subsistence farming: Farming that provides the minimum food goods necessary for the continuation of the farm family.

subtropical climate: A middle latitude climate dominated by humid, warm temperatures and heavy rainfall in summer, with cool winters and frequent cyclonic storms.

suffrage: The right to vote.

T

tariff: A tax assessed by a government on goods as they enter (or leave) a country. May be imposed to protect domestic industries from imported goods and/or to generate revenue.

temperate zone: The parts of the earth lying between the tropics and the polar circles. The northern temperate zone is the area between the tropic of Cancer and the Arctic Circle. The southern temperate zone is the area between the tropic of Capricorn and the Antarctic Circle.

terrorism: Systematic acts of violence designed to frighten or intimidate.

thermal power plant: A facility that produces electric energy from heat energy released by combustion of fuel or nuclear reactions.

Third World: A term used to describe less developed countries; as of the mid-1990s, it is being replaced by the United Nations designation Less Developed Countries, or LDC.

topography: The physical or natural features of the land.

torrid zone: The part of the earth's surface that lies between the tropics, so named for the character of its climate.

totalitarian party: The single political party in complete authoritarian control of a government or state.

trade unionism: Labor union activity for workers who practice a specific trade, such as carpentry.

treaty: A negotiated agreement between two governments.

tribal system: A social community in which people are organized into groups or clans descended from common ancestors and sharing customs and languages.

U

unemployment rate: The overall unemployment rate is the percentage of the work force (both employed and unemployed) who claim to be unemployed.

unicameral legislature: A legislative body consisting of one chamber.

UNICEF: An international fund set-up for children's emergency relief: United Nations Children's Fund (formerly United Nations International Children's Emergency Fund).

urban guerrilla: A rebel fighter operating in an urban area.

urbanization: The process of changing from country to city.

W

wildlife sanctuary: An area of land set aside for the protection and preservation of animals and plants.

workers' compensation: A series of regular payments by an employer to a person injured on the job.

World Bank: The World Bank is a group of international institutions which provides financial and technical assistance to developing countries.

Y

yellow fever: A tropical viral disease caused by the bite of an infected mosquito, characterized by jaundice.

Z

Zapatistas: A rebel group centered mainly in the Mexican state of Chiapas.

zócalo: Central square in a city or town.

Aguascalientes

Pronunciation: ah-gwas-kah-lee-EHN-tehs.

Origin of state name: Spaniards settling in the area in the 1500s discovered the hot springs, or aguas calientes ("hot waters" in Spanish). They named their settlement Villa de Nuestra Señora de la Asunción de las Aguas Calientes (Home of Our Lady of the Assumption of the Hot Springs). This name was eventually shortened to Aguascalientes (which means hot waters).

Capital: Aguascalientes.

Entered country: 1835.

Coat of Arms: The coat of arms of Aguascalientes has a fountain, a caldron, and coals. These represent the hot springs that are a main feature of the state. The image of Our Lady of the Assumption, accompanied by two cherubs, represents the foundation of the city. The gold chain, which is incomplete and surrounded by lips, depicts freedom and the emergence of the independent state. The grapes and dam signify agriculture supported by state irrigation systems. The bee imprisoned within a wheel represents the ordered, constant, and progressive labor of the inhabitants of Aguascalientes.

Holidays: Año Nuevo (New Year's Day—January 1); Día de la Constitución (Constitution Day—February 5); Benito Juárez's birthday (March 21); Primero de Mayo (Labor Day—May 1); Revolution Day, 1910 (November 20); and Navidad (Christmas—December 25).

Flag: There is no official state flag.

Time: 6 AM = noon Greenwich Mean Time (GMT).

1 ▪ Location and Size

Aguascalientes, located in the center of the country, has an area of 5,197 square kilometers (2,007 square miles). It is about the same size as the US state of Delaware. It is bordered on the north by the Mexican state of Zacatecas and on the south by the Mexican state of Jalisco. Aguascalientes has 11 municipalities. The capital is also named Aguascalientes.

The state of Aguascalientes lies on the western side of the Mexican highlands between 21°23′ and 22°28′ north latitude and 101°53′ and 102°50′ west longitude.

The state has mountains (sierra), valleys, and plains. Its elevation averages 1,800 meters (5,940 feet) above sea level. The mountains lie in the western part of the state and form part of the Zacatecas Sierra. These mountains belong to the great mountain range known as the Sierra Madre Occidental. The best-known mountains are the Sierra Fria, El Pinal, Guadalupe, Laurel, Comanja and Tepezalá. There are 2 main valleys, the Aguascalientes and the Huajúcar (or Calvillo). The plains are located in the southeastern part of the state.

The most important rivers are the Aguascalientes (or San Pedro) and Calvillo; these form part of the larger Lerma-Santiago River system, which runs into the Pacific Ocean. Tributaries of the Aguascalientes River include the Morcinique, Chicalote, and Santiago Rivers.

2 ▧ Climate
The climate is dry and warm, with summer rains. Temperatures are fairly constant year round, averaging 19°C (66°F), while its average yearly rain level is 480 millimeters (20 inches).

3 ▧ Plants and Animals
Native plants include scrubby pine trees and oak trees.

4 ▧ Environmental Protection
Sierra Fría is an ecological preserve where dwarf pine trees, oak forests, and a variety of animals can be found, including pumas, lynxes, boar, white-tailed deer, wild turkey, and raccoons.

5 ▧ Population, Ethnic Groups, Languages
Aguascalientes had a total population of 944,285 in 2000; of the total, 456,533 were men and 487,752 were women. The population density was 168 people per square kilometer (435 people per square mile). In 2000, the capital, Aguascalientes,

had a population of 643,360. The majority of the population speak Spanish. A small percentage (0.2%) speak one of the many indigenous Amerindian languages.

6 ▧ Religions
According to the 2000 census, 83% of the population, or 785,614 people, were Roman Catholic; less than 2%, or 15,857 people, were Evangelical Protestant. That year there were also 1,316 Mormons, 4,467 Jehovah's Witnesses, and nearly 12,700 people who reported no religion.

7 ▧ Transportation
Aguasclientes has a well-developed system of highways and roads. Until the 1980s, when travel by railroad declined, Aguascalientes was home to the country's largest railroad repair facility. The Aguascalientes Airport serves the state.

8 ▧ History
The area of Aguascalientes was originally inhabited by different Chichimec (Amerindian) groups. Aguascalientes was first conquered by Spanish soldiers under the command of Cristobal de Oñate around 1530. The conquest was very bloody. The Spaniards indiscriminately killed natives and forcefully took their lands. The native resistance was strong and lasted for centuries.

Spanish settlers founded the city of Nuestra Señora de la Asunción de Aguascalientes in 1575. Twelve colonizers were given land rights. Vineyard agriculture and other fruit products were produced by the new settlers. Soon the area became an exporter of grapes and other fruits. Some wool production and iron- and wood-crafted products

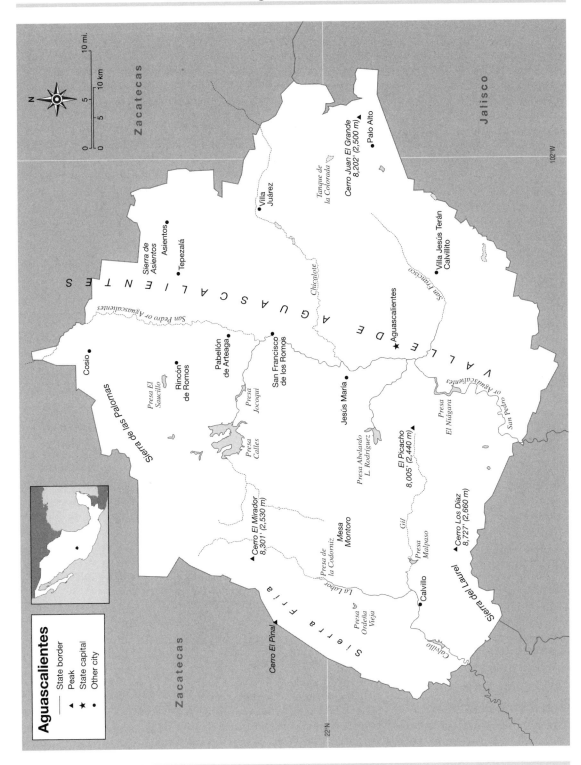

Aguascalientes

— State border
◄ Peak
★ State capital
● Other city

Zacatecas

Jalisco

Villa Juárez

Tanque de la Colorada

Cerro Juan El Grande 8,202' (2,500 m) ◄
● Palo Alto

Sierra de Asientos
● Asientos
● Tepezalá

Villa Jesús Terán ●
Calvillito

Chicalote

San Pedro or Aguascalientes

SIERRA DE AGUASCALIENTES

VALLE DE AGUASCALIENTES

★ Aguascalientes

San Francisco

Cosio ●

Presa El Saucillo

Rincón de Romos ●

Pabellón de Arteaga ●

San Francisco de los Romos ●

Presa Jocoqui

Presa El Niágara

San Pedro or Aguascalientes

Sierra de las Palomas

Presa Calles

Jesús María ●

Presa Abelardo L. Rodríguez

El Picacho 8,005' (2,440 m) ◄

Gil

Cerro El Mirador 8,301' (2,530 m) ◄

Presa de la Codorniz

Mesa Montoro

La Labor

Presa Malpaso

Cerro Los Díaz 8,727' (2,660 m) ◄

Sierra del Laurel

Calvillo ●

Sierra Fría

Cerro El Pinal ◄

Presa Ordeña Vieja

Calvillo

Zacatecas

22°N

102°W

The costumes worn by these members of Ballet Folklorico de Mexico are typical of traditional Aguascalientes. Women's dresses combine traditional embroidery and European influences.

converted Aguascalientes into a small but significant economic regional center.

Mining evolved in the municipality of Asientos de Ibarra, helping boost the local economy. Because of its central geographic location, the city of Aguascalientes became a commercial and transportation center between the Zacatecas and Jalisco regions.

In 1767, the members of the Roman Catholic Jesuit order were expelled from Mexico. This began a period of economic decline. The Jesuits owned a vast amount of land in Aguascalientes, so their departure severely hindered the local economy. In 1785, Aguascalientes was made a section of the Zacatecas Intendancy, a territory with connections to Europe. This caused discontent among the local leaders. They wanted more freedom to conduct their business and make their own decisions. A widespread famine in the late 1780s further hurt the local economy and reduced the population.

A series of public works initiatives and Roman Catholic Church constructions help boost the economy in the years before independence. Several local leaders helped promote independence ideas. Among them, Pedro Parga, Rafael Iriarte, Francisco Primo de Verdad y Ramos, and Valentín Gómez Farías championed the independence cause.

On October 9, 1821, a month after the national declaration of independence, Aguascalientes patriots arrested Spanish authorities and joined the movement headed by priest Miguel Hidalgo y Castilla in central Mexico. Rafael Iriarte formed a 1,500-man battalion that joined the independence army.

After independence was formally declared in 1821, Aguascalientes was made a part of the state of Zacatecas. Independence leader Gómez Farías went on to serve as vice president and president in the 1830s. The political instability that characterized Mexico from the 1830s to the 1860s affected Aguascalientes. It was declared an autonomous state of Mexico several times, only to be periodically incorporated into Zacatecas, depending on the political alliances that controlled the military and political elites in Mexico.

Aguascalientes was occupied by French invaders in the civil war of 1863. The state joined forces with the reform army of Mexican revolutionary and statesman Benito Juárez (1806–1872) to resist the French. During the long government of Porfirio Díaz—who was president from 1877 to 1880, and again from 1884 to 1911—Aguascalientes progressed economically. Railroads were built and electricity was brought to the state in 1890. Telephone lines were installed in 1901.

During the Mexican Revolution (1910–1920), different factions fiercely fought for control of Aguascalientes because of its strategic location. Local elites were divided among the different factions. When Álvaro Obregón became president (1920–24) and his faction emerged as winner of the revolution, control of Aguascalientes was easily achieved.

The Institutional Revolutionary Party (PRI) went on to control Aguascalientes from 1934 to 1998, when the conservative National Action Party (PAN) candidate became the first non-PRI governor of the state. As of 2004, Aguascalientes ranked 27 among the 31 states in population. Aguascalientes has had a role in Mexican history much greater than what its size and population might first imply.

9 ▌ State and Local Government

Aguascalientes holds gubernatorial elections every 6 years. The unicameral (one chamber) legislature is comprised of the Chamber of Deputies. Eighteen of the 27 Chamber members are elected from single member districts and 9 are elected at large, for proportional representation.

The state's constitution dates from 1950. It establishes formal separation of powers, an independent judiciary, and different mechanisms and provisions for government accountability and responsiveness. The state government is located in the municipality of Aguascalientes.

The state is comprised of 11 municipalities, each with its own government. Each elects a municipal president for nonrenewable 3-year terms. Former municipal presidents can run again for office after 1 term out of office. In addition, each municipality has a city council whose members are elected for nonrenewable 3-year terms.

10 ▌ Political Parties

The three main political parties in all of Mexico are the Institutional Revolutionary Party (PRI), the National Action Party (PAN), and the Party of the Democratic Revolution (PRD). The PRI overwhelmingly controlled politics in Aguascalientes after the end of the Mexican Revolution. Otto Granados Roldán, governor from 1992 to 1998, was a close ally of Carlos Salinas de Gortari, Mexican president (1988–94). Otto Granados Roldán was the last PRI politician to win a gubernatorial election in the state. In 1998, Felipe González González from the PAN won the gubernatorial elections for a nonrenewable 6-year term. Statewide elections were scheduled for 2004.

11 ▧ Judicial System

The Supreme Tribunal of Justice of Aguascalientes is comprised of 7 members elected for nonrenewable 15-year terms. Candidates are elected from a list presented to the state governor by the state court. The president of the Supreme Tribunal is elected by its members for a nonrenewable 4-year term.

The state judicial system is independent and autonomous. Its rulings must not challenge the jurisprudence of the Mexican Supreme Court. Other courts in charge of administrative matters are also part of the state judicial system.

12 ▧ Economy

In 2004, the economy of Aguascalientes was one of the fastest growing of any Mexican state. From 1997 to 2002, the state economy grew at almost 7%. Roughly one-third of the state's economy was based in manufacturing industries (principally machinery and equipment), textiles, and nourishing products.

13 ▧ Industry

There are at least 6 industrial parks in Aguascalientes. Nissan, Xerox, and Texas Instruments are among the companies that have manufacturing facilities in the state. Automobile manufacturing accounts for 20% of industry. Textiles (15%) and dairy products (about 10%) are other large industries.

14 ▧ Labor

There is almost no unemployment in the state. Employer-worker relations are generally good. There has never been a labor strike in Aguascalientes.

The US Bureau of Labor Statistics reported that Mexican workers saw their wages increase 17%, from $2.09 per hour in 1999 to $2.46 per hour in 2000. (The average US worker earned $19.86 per hour in 2000.) The maximum work week is set at 48 hours by law. The average worker spends 40 to 45 hours per week on the job. Workers earn twice their regular hourly rate for up to 9 hours a week of overtime. When a worker works more than 9 hours overtime in a week, he or she earns 3 times the regular hourly rate.

15 ▧ Agriculture

About 35% of the land is devoted to agriculture. The wide plains are well suited to raising cattle and therefore good for the related production of dairy products. Aguascalientes is one of Mexico's leading producers of dairy products. Various crops thrive in the moderate climate. Crops include alfalfa, corn, wheat, and chilies. Peaches and grapes for wine are also grown.

16 ■ Natural Resources

The most notable natural resources are the hot springs that flow under about one-third of the state's land area.

17 ■ Energy and Power

Electricity is provided by the Federal Electricity Commission and Central Light and Power. Both utilities are run by the Mexican government. As of 2004, the government was considering allowing the development of private utilities.

18 ■ Health

The state of Aguascalientes has 9 general hospitals, 107 outpatient centers, and 28 surgical centers.

19 ■ Housing

Housing in Aguascalientes is some of the best available anywhere in Mexico. Most (85%) is in good repair. The majority of residents own their own homes. A large percentage of those renting their homes are citizens of other countries living and working in the state temporarily.

20 ■ Education

President Benito Juárez launched the system of public education in 1867. Public education in Mexico is free for students ages 6 to 16, but most who can afford to go to private schools. This has created a gap in education between the social classes. The number of school-age children in Aguascalientes (3–19) was 452,173 in 2000.

For post-secondary education, students may enroll in Universidad Autónoma de Aguascalientes (Autonomous University of Aguascalientes) or the Instituto Tecnológico de Aguascalientes (Technical Institute of Aguascalientes).

21 ■ Arts

Aguascalientes sponsors the Ballet Folklórico Ehécatl. There are many art galleries and 6 performing arts auditoriums in the state. There is also a cultural institute (Casa de Artesenias). There are 3 theaters: Teatro de Aguascalientes, an example of modern architecture, seats 1,650; the Teatro Morelos, originally a parish house; and the Teatro del Parque Victor Sandoval, used for theatrical, musical, and film presentations.

22 ■ Libraries and Museums

The national library system has 57 branches in the state of Aguascalientes.

Aguascalientes has 15 museums dedicated to art, science, religion, bullfighting, and railroading. The Aguascalientes Museum (Museo de Aguascalientes), the main museum of fine arts, was built in 1903. Other museums in the state include the Museum of Contemporary Art (Museo del Arte Contemporáneo); the Interactive Museum of Science and Technology, which houses an IMAX theater; a museum dedicated to the works of José Guadalupe Posada, a revolutionary artist; and the Museum of Regional History. Specialized museums include La Cristiada, which commemorates the Roman Catholic Church's struggle against the government; the Museo Taurino, which showcases bullfighting; and the Museo Ferrocarril, a museum of the railroad.

23 ▨ Media

The capital city, Aguascalientes, has 2 newspapers: *El Sol del Centro* and *Hidrocalido.*

In 1991, the government-owned phone company, Teléfonos de Mexico, was sold to private investors. Since then service has improved but rates have risen. Teléfonos de Mexico provides 95% of telephone service in Mexico.

24 ▨ Tourism, Travel, and Recreation

Aguascalientes is famous for its therapeutic hot springs. There are many parks and recreation centers for camping, mountain biking, rock climbing, and fishing. El Tunel de Poterillo offers a beautiful canyon with waterfalls and native flora and fauna. The park at El Ocote has prehistoric wall paintings of humans and animals. The Sierra de Laurel has a wildlife park and places to go mountain biking. The Cerro de Muerte offers rock climbing and rappelling. The San Marcos National Fair, held in late April or early May each year, features art exhibits, rodeos, bullfights, a gambling casino, pageants, and music.

25 ▨ Sports

The city of Aguascalientes has a professional basketball team, the Panteras. The baseball team, Los Rayos de Nexaca, also plays in Aguascalientes at the 20,000-seat Estadio Victoria (Victoria Stadium). Another baseball team, Los Gallos de Aguascalientes, plays in the 10,000-seat Estadio Municipal (Municipal Stadium). There are two bullfighting rings; the 16,000-seat Plaza Monumental and the smaller 5,000-seat Plaza San Marcos.

26 ▨ Famous People

Early leaders in the movement for independence were Pedro Parga (1792–1873), Rafael Iriarte, Francisco Primo de Verdad y Ramos (b. Jalisco, 1760–1808), and Valentín Gómez Farías (b. Jalisco, 1781–1858). Sculptor Jesús Contreras (1866–1902) created 18 statues of famous Mexicans that line the Paseo de la Reforma (Avenida Reforma) in Mexico City. Other notable citizens include composers Alfonso Esparza Oteo (1894–1950) and Manuel M. Ponce (1882–1948), and poet Ramón López Velarde (1888–1921).

27 ▨ Bibliography

Books

Carew-Miller, Anna. *Famous People of Mexico.* Philadelphia: Mason Crest Publishers, 2003.

DeAngelis, Gina. *Mexico.* Mankato, MN: Blue Earth Books, 2003.

Supples, Kevin. *Mexico.* Washington, DC: National Geographic Society, 2002.

Web Sites

Gobierno de del Estado Aguascalientes (Government of the State of Aguascalientes), English version. http://www.aguascalientes.gob.mx/english/ (accessed on June 11, 2004).

Mexico for Kids. http://www.elbalero.gob.mx/index_kids.html (accessed on June 11, 2004).

Baja California

Pronunciation: BAH-hah kah-lee-FOHR-nee-ah.

Origin of state name: The name "California" comes from a 16th-century Spanish novel. California was an island close to paradise. Baja comes from the Spanish word for lower. (The US state of California was once known as Alta California, with Alta meaning higher.)

Capital: Mexicali.

Entered country: 1952.

Coat of Arms: The emblem represents the past, the present, and the future of the state. The upper part depicts the Sun, symbol of light, the main element of nature and an inexhaustible source of energy, heat, and life. On each side, two human figures, with hands joined in the middle, project a beam of light, symbol of energy. The man is holding a book, representing culture. The woman is holding items representing intellectual activities and science. The central silhouette represents the missionaries who came to the region during the conquest and evangelized the indigenous population. The planted field in the upper left corner represents the agriculture of the present. On the horizon, a mountain range suggests the possibilities of mining. The silhouette of a factory and a cog (gear tooth) represent industry and the future. In the middle is the desert, and on the bottom is the Colorado River, which flows to the sea. Two waves on either side symbolize the western and eastern coasts.

Holidays: Año Nuevo (New Year's Day—January 1); Día de la Constitución (Constitution Day—February 5); Benito Juárez's birthday (March 21); Primero de Mayo (Labor Day—May 1); Revolution Day, 1910 (November 20); and Navidad (Christmas—December 25).

Flag: There is no official state flag.

Time: 4 AM = Greenwich Mean Time (GMT).

1 ■ Location and Size

Baja California lies on the Baja California peninsula, a long finger of land in western Mexico extending south from the US state of California. The state of Baja California covers the northern part of the peninsula and has an area of 71,576 square kilometers (27,635 square miles). It is slightly larger in area than the US state of West Virginia. Its north-south length is similar to the state of Florida. Baja California is bordered on the north by California, on the west by the Pacific Ocean, on the east by the Golfo de California and the Colorado River, and on the south by Baja California Sur. Baja California is divided into 5 municipalities. The capital, Mexicali, is

© Robert Frerck/Woodfin Camp

South of Loreto, the Sierra de la Giganta.

located in the north on the border with California.

The peninsula is covered with mountains (sierras), with broad valleys lying between the mountain peaks. The larger cities and towns, including Mexicali, Las Palmas, Tijuana, Guadalupe, and Real de Castillo, lie in valleys.

Water runs down the slopes of the mountain ranges into the Pacific Ocean and the Sea of Cortés, which is part of the Golfo de California. Due to its geological formation and to long-lasting droughts, the state of Baja California has no large rivers. Springs are scarce and offer little water.

There are 35 islands, most of them lying in the Golfo de California. A few islands lie close to the west coast. Guadalupe Island lies 94 kilometers (150 miles) west of Baja California in the Pacific Ocean.

2 ■ Climate

The climate is dry, with annual rainfall averaging 30 to 60 centimeters (12 to 24 inches). Fog and winter rains are typical in the coastal area around Tijuana near the border with the United States. In the northeast and the south, the climate has wide temperature differences between the hot days and the very cold nights. The center of the state is cooler, with cold

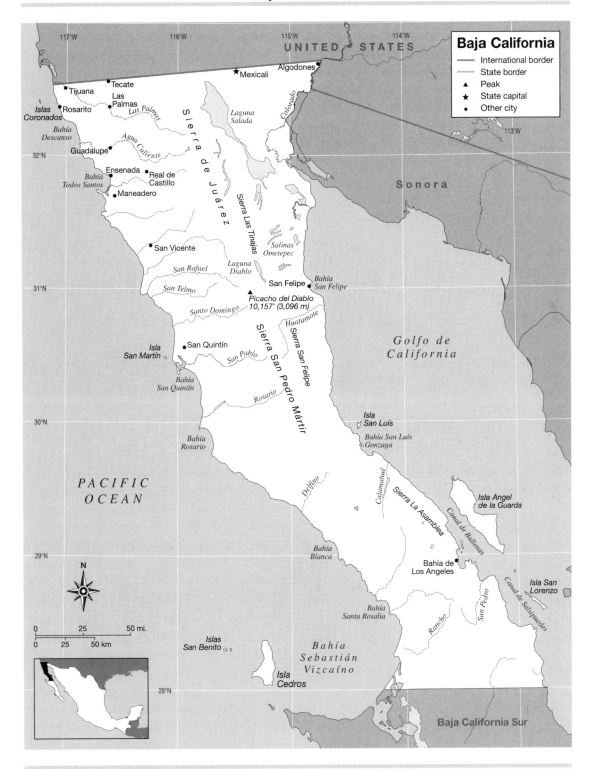

Baja California

- International border
- State border
- ▲ Peak
- ★ State capital
- • Other city

UNITED STATES

★ Mexicali

• Algodones

• Tijuana
• Tecate
Las Palmas
Islas Coronados • Rosarito
Las Palmas
Agua Caliente
• Guadalupe
Bahía Descanso
Laguna Salada
Colorado

Sonora

S i e r r a   d e   J u á r e z

Laguna Salada

32°N

Bahía Todos Santos
• Ensenada
• Real de Castillo
• Maneadero

Sierra Las Tinajas

• San Vicente

Salinas Ometepec

San Rafael
Laguna Diablo
San Telmo
• San Felipe
Bahía San Felipe

31°N

Santo Domingo
▲ Picacho del Diablo
10,157' (3,096 m)

Isla San Martín •
• San Quintín
San Pablo
Huatamote

Sierra San Felipe

Sierra San Pedro Mártir

Bahía San Quintín
Rosario

Golfo de California

Isla San Luís

30°N

Bahía Rosario
Bahía San Luís Gonzaga

PACIFIC OCEAN

Delfino
Calamahué

Sierra La Asamblea

Isla Angel de la Guarda

N

Bahía Blanca

29°N

Bahía de Los Angeles

Isla San Lorenzo

Canal de Ballenas
Canal de Salsipuedes

San Pedro
Rancho

0   25   50 mi.
0   25   50 km

Bahía Santa Rosalia

Islas San Benito

Bahía Sebastián Vizcaíno

Isla Cedros

28°N

Baja California Sur

117°W   116°W   115°W   114°W   113°W

Cabo San Lucas harbor and marina.

winters (when most of the rain falls) and cool summers.

3 ■ Plants and Animals

Tourists enjoy watching gray whales give birth in the protected waters along the coast. Many species of ducks and other marine birds find habitat in the coastal areas.

In the mountains, there are coyotes, white-tailed deer, puma, lynx, wild sheep, and many species of snakes. Species of eagles and red-tailed hawk soar above the mountain peaks.

Plants of the state may be categorized by their environments: salt marshes; coastal dunes; chaparral scrub; and forest, which is found in the mountains. Of a total of 450 important plant species in Mexico, 211 (47%) are found in Baja California. Jojoba and palmilla (also called soaptree yucca) are both widespread because they tolerate dry growing conditions. Jojoba seeds have many commercial uses, such as in lubricants, cosmetics, and medicines. The mountainous regions have alpine plants and pine forests. Coastal areas have various low-growing shrubs and cactus.

4 ■ Environmental Protection

The government is concerned about improving air and water quality. Management of hazardous waste is also a concern. Water quality is a particular concern in the Colorado River basin, where untreated sewage and power plant waste are a problem.

5 ▨ Population, Ethnic Groups, Languages

Baja California had a total population of 2,487,367 in 2000; of the total, 1,252,581 (just over 50%) were men and 1,234,786 (just under 50%) were women. The population density was 35 people per square kilometer (91 people per square mile). In 2000, the capital of Mexicali had 764,902 residents. As of 2000, almost all residents speak Spanish as their first language; about 2% of the citizens of Baja California speak one of the Amerindian languages.

Since the 1980s, hundreds of thousand of people have migrated from the states of southern Mexico to find work in Baja California. Many hope to eventually cross the border into the United States.

6 ▨ Religions

According to the 2000 census, 66% of the population, or 1.6 million people, were Roman Catholic; 6%, or 158,874 people, were Protestant. That year there were also 6,653 Seventh-Day Adventists, 6,334 Mormons, 41,472 Jehovah's Witnesses, and nearly 155,000 people who reported no religion.

7 ▨ Transportation

Baja California has about 11,000 kilometers (7,000 miles) of roadways. Four-lane highways connecting the 4 main cities make up just over 500 kilometers (200 miles).

Four international airports—Tijuana, Mexicali, San Felipe, and Ensenada—provide commercial air service.

8 ▨ History

Before the first Spaniards reached the region in 1533, different groups of hunters and gatherers occupied Baja California. The Yumano and Cucapás civilizations reached a considerable level of religious and artistic development prior to 1533.

Spaniard Hernán Cortés (1485–1547) led two expeditions to Baja California in 1535 and 1536. He wanted to conquer what he believed was an island. In 1602, Sebastián Vizcaíno (c. 1550–1616) led an expedition that renamed the old Santa Cruz port with its modern name, La Paz. Although there were some efforts to establish a Spanish colony in the 1600s, the first permanent non-indigenous settlement was a Jesuit (an order of the Roman Catholic Church) mission created in 1697.

Jesuit priests introduced new crops and helped the natives with agricultural techniques. The Spaniards enslaved the native people and brought diseases from home. These two factors combined to decimate (greatly reduce) the native population throughout the 1700s.

The Jesuits were expelled from Mexico in 1767 by a decree issued by the Spanish crown. This allowed Franciscan monks (from another order of the Roman Catholic Church) the freedom to move in to populate Baja California. Together with Alta California (now the US state of California), Baja California was made a Spanish province in the mid-1700s. It then officially merged with Alta California to create a territory of the Spanish viceroyalty (territory ruled by Spain) of Mexico.

Carnival the week before the Christian holiday, Ash Wednesday, in Ensenada.

In 1804, Baja and Alta California were divided again into two separate provinces. Because of their physical isolation, the people living in Baja California did not join in the drive for independence in 1810. Governor Fernando de la Toba declared Baja California's independence in 1822. A constitution was created in 1824. Baja California and Alta California were once again merged into a Mexican province, with San Diego as its capital and José María de Echandía as governor.

In 1829, the provincial capital was moved to La Paz, which is the modern-day capital of the state of Baja California Sur.

During the Mexican-American War (1846–48), Baja California was disputed territory. Mexican patriots fought against US soldiers. In the Treaty of Guadalupe Hidalgo in 1848, Mexico ceded Alta California to the United States, and it became the state of California. Mexico kept Baja California. Conflicts over control of Baja California persisted. American pirate William Walker attacked Baja California in 1853 and occupied La Paz and Cabo San Lucas. He declared independence and claimed to be president of the new republic. He was later expelled and deported to the United States.

From 1876 to 1910, Baja California witnessed widespread persecution of native indigenous groups. Lands of the native people were taken by the government for agricultural use in the name of Mexican progress and development. The International Company of Mexico, a Connecticut-based corporation, was granted almost half of the territory for different economic initiatives starting in 1886.

The Mexican Revolution took place from 1910 to 1920. Revolution sympathizers attacked Mexicali in 1911. Political instability in the rest of Mexico led many on both sides of the California border to push for the annexation of Baja California to the United States. Some activists in the United States promoted a movement for Baja California to secede (break away) from Mexico. Opposition from Mexican patriots who wanted to keep Baja California as part of Mexico prevented this from happening.

After the Mexican Revolution, a new constitution established the country of Mexico, but the government was not stable. The new Mexican government took control of Baja California and discouraged the idea that Baja California join the United States. Baja California was a territory of Mexico for the next 35 years.

Baja California was restructured into the Baja California Norte (North) and Baja California Sur (South) territories in 1952. The central Mexican government appointed governors in Baja California Norte and Baja California Sur, solidifying the division of the peninsula into two different provinces.

In 1952, Baja California became Mexico's 29th state, while Baja California Sur remained a territory. Braulio Maldonado Sandez, a member of the Institutional Revolutionary Party (PRI), became the first state governor under the new constitution.

9 ▪ State and Local Government

Baja California became Mexico's 29th state officially on December 31, 1952. Its constitution was accepted in 1953. Braulio Maldonado Sandez, a member of the Institutional Revolutionary Party (PRI), became the first state governor under the new constitution. In 2001, Eugenio Elorduy Walther of the National Action Party (PAN) won the election to become the 12th governor. His 6-year nonrenewable term will expire in 2008. A unicameral (single chamber) legislature is comprised of a 25-member Chamber of Deputies. The deputies are elected for a nonrenewable 3-year term. Sixteen of the deputies are elected from single-member districts and 9 are elected at large.

The governments of Baja California's 5 municipalities enjoy limited autonomy (self-government). The municipal president is elected to a nonrenewable 3-year term. The president governs with a local municipal council. The state legislature has the power to intervene in municipal government under certain circumstances. By controlling budget allocation, the state government exerts immense influence over local authorities.

10 ▪ Political Parties

The 3 main political parties in all of Mexico are the Institutional Revolutionary Party (PRI), the National Action Party (PAN), and the Party of the Democratic Revolution (PRD). As in the rest of Mexico, the PRI was the most powerful and influential party in Baja California until the late 1980s, controlling the state and most municipal governments. In 1989, PAN leader Ernesto Ruffo became the first non-PRI state governor. In 1995, Hector

Terán won the state for the PAN again. Eugenio Elorduy Walther obtained a third consecutive PAN victory in 2001.

11 ▌ Judicial System

The Supreme Tribunal of Justice is comprised of 13 justices elected for nonrenewable 6-year terms. The Supreme Tribunal president is elected by the 13 justices for a nonrenewable 2-year term. Justices are appointed by a two-thirds majority in the legislature from among a list of nominees presented by the Supreme Tribunal. Only qualified lawyers can be appointed to the Supreme Tribunal. In addition, there is a tribunal of electoral justice comprised of 3 members elected for 3-year terms. Local tribunals complete the state judicial system.

12 ▌ Economy

Agriculture, maquiladora (manufacturing assembly plants), tourism, and mining are important parts of the economy. Baja California has 6 highway border crossing points into the US state of California. In 2000, approximately 180,000 cars crossed the border each day. The busiest border crossing is between Tijuana, Baja California, and San Ysidro, California. About 50,000 cars cross the border there each day, with 25,000 people crossing on foot. The Port of Ensenada is located on the Pacific Ocean and provides services for international trade.

13 ▌ Industry

Baja California has many industrial parks. In Tijuana and Mexicali, there are dozens of industrial parks devoted to auto parts and electronics manufacturing.

14 ▌ Labor

The United States Bureau of Labor Statistics reported that Mexican workers saw their wages increase 17%, from $2.09 per hour in 1999 to $2.46 per hour in 2000. (By comparison, the average American worker earned $19.86 per hour in 2000.) After one year, workers are entitled by law to six days paid vacation.

Amerindian migrant agricultural workers, primarily of Mixtec and Zapotec descent, have been discriminated against throughout the state's history. As of 2004, migrant workers were attempting to organize, through the Independent Confederation of Farm Workers and Peasants (CIOAC), to demand better treatment by their employers and the government.

15 ▌ Agriculture

Agriculture is important to the state economy. Most agriculture is done in the region around Mexicali. The main products are wheat, tomato, broccoli, alfalfa, cotton, sorghum, and garlic. Other crops include grapes, dates, carob, lemons, and oranges. Agricultural crops grown for export to the United States, Canada, Europe, and Asia are chives, radishes, asparagus, melons, celery, lettuce, onions, and watermelon.

16 ▌ Natural Resources

Fishing in the coastal waters off Baja California is an important economic activity. Principal fish caught include sole, tuna, sardines, mackerel, and lobster. The extraction of salt from ocean saltwater is

© Mireille Vautier/Woodfin Camp

Tijuana lies on the border with the US state of California.

another important activity. Sport fishing is enjoyed by tourists year round.

17 ▪ Energy and Power

Electricity is generated by 10 power plants, with a total capacity of 2,285 megawatts. Four of these are geothermal (using heat from the earth's interior), representing 720 megawatts. Baja California generates enough electricity to satisfy the state's needs and to export energy to neighboring Sonora and to the United States.

Mexicali has natural gas resources; as of 2004 a pipeline between Mexicali and Tijuana with the capacity to carry 14 million cubic meters (500 million cubic feet) of natural gas per day was under construction.

18 ▪ Health

The state of Baja California has 20 general hospitals, 220 outpatient centers, and 67 surgical centers.

Most of the Mexican population is covered under a government health plan. The IMSS (Instituto Mexicano de Seguro Social) covers the general population. The ISSSTE (Instituto de Seguridad y Servicios Sociales de Trabajadores del Estado) covers state workers.

© Mireille Vautier/Woodfin Camp

The Tijuana Cultural Center.

19 ▪ Housing

In 2000, there are an average of 4.2 people per household. About 95% of the houses in the state have electricity, 77% have sewer connections, and 87% have running water. Some 73% of the houses are owner-occupied, and 27% are occupied by renters.

The influx of hundreds of thousands of people who have moved from the southern states of Mexico north toward the US border has produced a severe shortage of land and housing.

20 ▪ Education

President Benito Juárez (1806–1872) launched the system of public education in 1867. Public education in Mexico is free for students ages 6 to 16, but most who can afford it go to private schools. This has created a gap in education between the social classes. The population of school-age children (3–19) was 452,173 in 2000.

Students may enroll in Universidad Autónoma de Aguascalientes (Autonomous University of Aguascalientes) or the Instituto Tecnológico de Aguascalientes (Technical Institute of Aguascalientes).

21 ▪ Arts

The state of Baja California sponsors many dance groups including the Balleto Folklórico de Ticuan, a jazz ensemble (Dat'Z Jazz), Groupo Almalafa, and Groupo Mal Paso. Baja California also has a professional orchestra. The city of Ensenada is home to the Galería de Perez Meillon, which showcases native crafts such as the traditional willow baskets of the Pai-Pai Indians.

22 ▮ Libraries and Museums

There are 44 branches of the national library in the state of Baja California.

Among the 20 museums of Baja California are several history museums in Ensenada and a wax museum and a pre-Columbian museum in Tijuana.

23 ▮ Media

The capital city, Mexicali, has two papers: *La Crónica de Baja California* and *La Voz de la Frontera*. Tijuana has three papers: *El Sol de Tijuana*, *La Frontera*, and *Zeta*.

24 ▮ Tourism, Travel, and Recreation

Outdoor water sports such as deep sea fishing, scuba diving, and snorkeling provide vacationers with reasons to visit Baja California. Rosarito Beach, Ensenada, and Mexicali are easy access points from San Diego, California. There is tourist shopping in the border town of Tijuana.

The state capital of Mexicali offers many tourist attractions. The Plaza Calafia offers tourists a look at real bullfighting. The city park has a zoo and local marketplace. In October, Mexicali hosts its annual fair, the Fiesta del Sol. There are beautiful beaches at San Felipe on the Sea of Cortés.

© Mireille Vautier/Woodfin Camp

Modern building in Tijuana.

25 ▮ Sports

Mexicali's baseball team, the Aguilas, plays in the Nido Aguilas (Eagle's Nest) Mexicali stadium, seating 12,000 people. Los Mochis's baseball team, the Cañeros, plays in the Emilio Ibarra Almada stadium holding 15,000 people.

Major bullfighting venues include the Plaza de Toros in Tijuana, with seating for 21,621. It is part of the large complex, Playas Tijuana, which also has a racetrack. Mexicali's bullfighting ring, Plaza Calafia, seats 10,000.

Tijuana's soccer team plays in the National de Tijuana stadium, where there is seating for 12,000. Tijuana's basketball team, the Tazmania Diablos, plays in the Fausto Gutierrez Moreno stadium, where there is seating for 4,500.

26 ▨ Famous People

Fernando de la Toba declared independence in Baja California. Braulio Maldonado Sandez (1903–1990), a member of the PRI (Institutional Revolutionary Party), became the first state governor. Missionary Eusebio Kino (1645–1711) attempted to establish a mission program in Baja California in the 1670s.

27 ▨ Bibliography

Books

Supples, Kevin. *Mexico.* Washington, DC: National Geographic Society, 2002.

Williams, Jack, *The Magnificent Peninsula: The Comprehensive Guidebook to Mexico's Baja California.* Redding, CA: H. J. Williams, 2001.

Web Sites

Government of Baja California, English-language version. http://www.bajacalifornia.gob.mx/english/home.htm (accessed on June 11, 2004).

Mexico for Kids. http://www.elbalero.gob.mx/index_kids.html (accessed on June 11, 2004).

Baja California Sur

Pronunciation: bah-hah kah-lee-FOHR-nee-ah SOOR.

Origin of state name: The name "California" comes from a 16th-century Spanish novel. California was an island close to paradise. Baja comes from the Spanish word for lower. Sur is Spanish for south.

Capital: La Paz.

Entered country: 1974.

Coat of Arms: The navy blue represents justice, truth, and loyalty. The fish represents the resources of the ocean. The center section is divided in half: the red and gold represent unity, wealth, and courage. The shell symbolizes the battle that citizens have fought to defend their borders.

Holidays: Año Nuevo (New Year's Day—January 1); Día de la Constitución (Constitution Day—February 5); Benito Juárez's birthday (March 21); Primero de Mayo (Labor Day—May 1); Revolution Day, 1910 (November 20); and Navidad (Christmas—December 25).

Flag: There is no official flag.

Time: 4 AM = Greenwich Mean Time (GMT).

1 ■ Location and Size

Baja California Sur, a very narrow state in western Mexico, covers the southern half of the Baja California peninsula. (The peninsula is a long finger of land extending south from the border with the US state of California.) Baja California Sur's total area is 71,428 square kilometers (27,578 square miles), slightly smaller than the state of South Carolina. Baja California Sur has 5 municipalities. The capital, La Paz, is located in the southeast.

Making up part of Baja California Sur are the islands of Natividad, Magdalena, and Santa Margarita in the Pacific Ocean; and the islands of San Marcos, Coronados, Carmen, Monserrat, Santa Catalina, Santa Cruz, San Diego, San José, San Francisco, Partida, Espíritu Santo and Cerralvo in the Sea of Cortés (Golfo de California).

Baja California Sur, with a coastline of more than 2,000 kilometers (1,250 miles), has the longest coastline of any Mexican state. It is bordered to the east and south by the Golfo de California. This gulf separates the peninsula from the mainland Mexican

Many species of cactii, including the cardón cactus, thrive in Baja California Sur. The cardón cactus may reach 21 meters (70 feet) in height.

states of Sinaloa and Sonora. To the west is the Pacific Ocean. Baja California Sur's largest rivers are the San Ignacio and the Raymundo.

Mountains (sierras) form a chain that follows the eastern coastline, ending at the southern tip of the peninsula near Cabo San Lucas (Cape San Lucas).

2 ■ Climate

The climate is mild, with temperatures averaging 24°C (75°F) during the day and 13°C (55°F) at night in January. In July, temperatures average 32°C (90°F) during the day and 27°C (80°F) at night. The cli-mate is dry, with annual rainfall averaging 30 to 60 centimeters (12 to 24 inches) per year.

3 ■ Plants and Animals

Baja California Sur is host to many sea animals along its two coasts. These include iguanas, snakes, turtles, several species of sea birds, swallows, and pelicans. There are many migrating whales and sport fish in the waters along the coast. The desert has mesquite trees; cactus; and small, shrubby pines. The higher elevations are home to deer and mountain lions, rabbits, squirrels, and big-horned sheep.

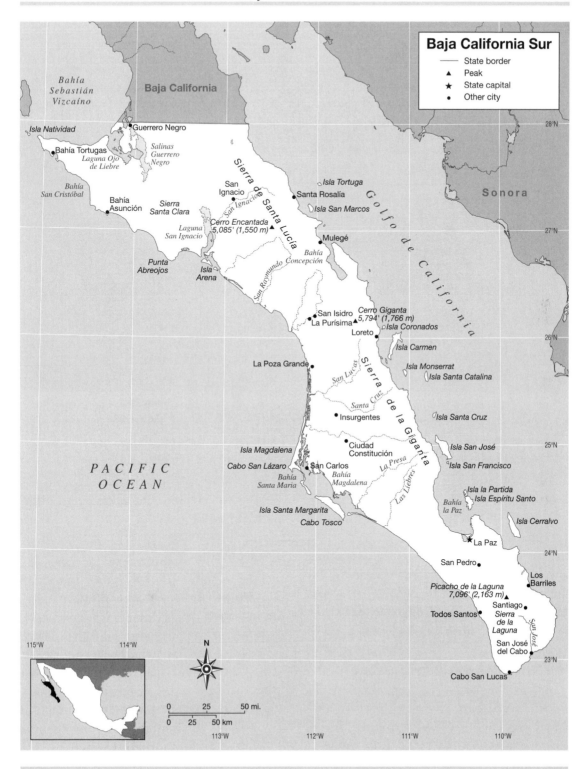

Baja California Sur
— State border
▲ Peak
★ State capital
• Other city

Bahía Sebastián Vizcaíno

Baja California

Isla Natividad

Guerrero Negro

Bahía Tortugas

Salinas Guerrero Negro

Laguna Ojo de Liebre

Bahía San Cristóbal

Sierra Santa Clara

Bahía Asunción

San Ignacio

Laguna San Ignacio

Cerro Encantada 5,085' (1,550 m) ▲

Isla Tortuga

Santa Rosalía

Isla San Marcos

Mulegé

Golfo de California

Sonora

Punta Abreojos

Isla Arena

Bahía Concepción

San Isidro
La Purísima ▲

Cerro Giganta 5,794' (1,766 m) ▲

Isla Coronados

Loreto

Isla Carmen

La Poza Grande

San Lucas

Sierra de la Giganta

Isla Monserrat

Isla Santa Catalina

Santa Cruz

Insurgentes

Isla Santa Cruz

PACIFIC OCEAN

Isla Magdalena

Cabo San Lázaro

Bahía Santa Maria

San Carlos

Ciudad Constitución

Bahía Magdalena

La Presa

Las Liebres

Isla San José

Isla San Francisco

Isla la Partida
Isla Espíritu Santo

Isla Santa Margarita

Cabo Tosco

Bahía la Paz

Isla Cerralvo

★ La Paz

San Pedro •

Los Barriles

Picacho de la Laguna 7,096' (2,163 m) ▲

Santiago
Sierra de la Laguna

Todos Santos •

San José

San José del Cabo

Cabo San Lucas

115°W 114°W 113°W 112°W 111°W 110°W

28°N 27°N 26°N 25°N 24°N 23°N

N

0   25   50 mi.
0   25   50 km

Henk Sierdsema/Saxifraga/EPD Photos

The inland area north of the resort, San José del Cabo, is sparcely populated.

The cardón cactus, the world's largest cactus, thrives on the Baja California peninsula. It grows slowly and may reach heights of 21 meters (70 feet).

The landscape in the mountainous areas of Baja California Sur is tropical dry forest. The dry forest has a long dry season and a short rainy season, opposite the climate where the rain forest thrives.

4 ■ Environmental Protection

The fish populations in the Golfo de California to the east of Baja California have been depleted by overfishing. Fishing also endangers turtles and other marine animals that get caught accidentally by fishing equipment (hooks or nets). International environmental groups are pressuring the Mexican government to control fishing there.

5 ■ Population, Ethnic Groups, Languages

Baja California Sur had a total population of 424,041 in 2000; of the total, 216,250 (51%) were men and 207,791 (49%) were women. The population density was 6 people per square kilometer (15 people per square mile). In 2000, the capital, La Paz, had a population of 213,045.

Almost all residents speak Spanish. There is a small percentage (1.4%) who speak one of the Amerindian languages.

6 ■ Religions

According to the 2000 census, 79% of the population, or 333,156 people, were Roman Catholic; 3.5%, or 15,083 people, were Protestant. That year there were also 665 Seventh-Day Adventists, 995 Mormons, 5,611 Jehovah's Witnesses, and nearly 18,000 people who reported no religion.

7 ■ Transportation

There are highways stretching the length of the Baja California peninsula, but there are relatively few gas stations. Drivers must plan carefully to avoid running out of fuel. La Paz-Manuel de Leon Airport provides international flights to and from Baja California Sur. Los Cabos International Airport at San Jose del Cabo is an international airport serving Cabo San Lucas. There is shipping across the Golfo de California to the mainland states of Sonora and Sinaloa.

8 ■ History

In addition to different groups of hunters and gatherers, there were Yumano and Cucapás civilizations in the area before the arrival of the Spaniards in Baja California. The first Spaniards reached the region in 1533. Spaniard Hernán Cortés (1485–1547) led two expeditions in 1535 and 1536 to conquer what he believed was an island. In 1602, Sebastián Vizcaíno (c. 1550–1616) led an expedition that renamed the old Santa Cruz port with its modern name, La Paz. Although there were some colonization efforts in the 1600s, the first permanent nonindigenous settlement was a Jesuit (an order of the Roman Catholic Church) mission created in 1697. Jesuit priests introduced new crops and helped the natives with new agricultural techniques. Diseases brought by the Spaniards and the enslavement of the indigenous population helped decimate the native population throughout the 1700s.

The expulsion of the Jesuits in 1767 by decree of the Spanish crown gave way to a centralized effort to populate Baja California with Franciscan monks (from the Franciscan order of the Roman Catholic Church) and military garrisons. Together with Alta California (now the US state of California), Baja California was made a Spanish province in the mid-1700s. It then officially merged with Alta California to create a territory of the Spanish viceroyalty (territory ruled by Spain) of Mexico. In 1804, Baja and Alta California were divided again into two separate provinces.

The drive for independence in 1810 took hold in many Mexican states, but not in Baja California because of its physical isolation. Governor Fernando de la Toba finally declared Baja California's independence from Spain in 1822. A constitution was ratified (approved) in 1824 and Baja and Alta California were once again merged into a Mexican province with San Diego as its capital and José María de Echandía as governor. In 1829, the provincial capital was moved to La Paz.

During the Mexican-American War (1846–48), Baja California was disputed territory. Mexican patriots fought against US soldiers. In the Treaty of Guadalupe Hidalgo of 1848, Mexico ceded (gave up) Alta California but kept Baja California. Conflicts over control of Baja California persisted. American pirate William Walker attacked Baja California in 1853 and occupied La Paz and Cabo San Lucas, declaring independence and claiming to be president of the new republic. He was later expelled and deported to the United States.

From 1876 to 1910, Baja California witnessed widespread persecution of native indigenous groups. Native lands were forcibly taken for agricultural use in the name of Mexican progress and development. The International Company of Mexico, a Connecticut-based corporation, was granted almost half of the territory for different economic initiatives starting in 1886. When the Mexican Revolution (1910–1920) toppled the regime of Porfirio Díaz (1830–1915), Baja California was comprised of the Norte (North) and Sur (South) provinces.

After the revolution, the new Mexican government took control of Baja California and suppressed the move towards annexation by the United States. The central government appointed governors in Baja California Norte and Baja California Sur, consolidating the division of the peninsula into two different provinces. From 1916 to 1974, 10 governors were appointed for Baja California Sur. During this period, much progress was made, including the construction of roads, a water system, a system for electricity, and a education system. A shipping route was established with the mainland states. Baja California Sur became a federal state in 1974 under the presidency of Luis Echeverría, with 3 municipalities: La Paz, Comondú, and Mulegé. Félix Agramont Cota, the appointed governor, convened a constitutional assembly. The new constitution was ratified (approved) on January 9, 1975. The first constitutional governor was

Ángel César Mendoza Aramburu. As the population grew, the state further divided its territory, adding the municipality of Los Cabos in 1981 and Loreto in 1992.

9 ▪ State and Local Government

The state governor is elected for a nonrenewable 6-year term. Leonel Cota Montaño was elected in 1999 and his term will expire in 2005. The legislature is comprised of a unicameral (single chamber) state assembly. Fifteen of its 21 members are elected in single member districts, and 6 by proportional representation, all for nonrenewable 3-year terms. Legislators can seek election again after sitting out 1 term of the assembly. Power is highly centralized in the office of the governor, but re-election restrictions and the small size of the state have made the Baja California Sur governor relatively weak when compared to other Mexican states.

Comprised of 5 municipalities, Baja California has a highly centralized government. Municipal presidents are elected for nonrenewable 3-year terms. Each municipality also elects a local council, whose size varies according to the municipal population. Municipal council members are also elected for nonrenewable 3-year terms.

10 ▪ Political Parties

The 3 main political parties in all of Mexico are the Institutional Revolutionary Party (PRI), the National Action Party (PAN), and the Party of the Democratic Revolution (PRD). As in the rest of Mexico, candidates of these 3 parties compete for most elected offices. The PRI has exercised dominance over the political system since the state was officially separated from Baja California. All state governors have belonged to the PRI. The PAN is the second strongest party in the state, but the leftist PRD also has some electoral presence.

11 ■ Judicial System

A Superior Tribunal of Justice is the highest judicial authority in the state. Its 7 members are appointed by the legislature from a 3-person list presented by the state governor. Justices must be qualified lawyers and they cannot be immediately reappointed after their 6-year terms expire. In addition there is a state electoral tribunal and local courts in each municipality. The state electoral tribunal is comprised of 3 members elected by a two-thirds majority in the legislature for nonrenewable 6-year terms.

12 ■ Economy

Tourism and sport fishing are the most important segments of the economy. Agriculture and salt mining (in the northern part of the state) are also important economic activities. A small commercial cotton growing operation exists in the state.

13 ■ Industry

There is little industry, except for tourism-related activities, in the state. Salt is mined in the northern desert.

14 ■ Labor

The United States Bureau of Labor Statistics reported that Mexican workers saw their wages increase 17%, from $2.09 per hour in 1999 to $2.46 per hour in 2000. (By comparison, the average American worker earned $19.86 per hour in 2000.)

After 1 year, workers are entitled by law to 6 days paid vacation.

15 ■ Agriculture

Agriculture is an important economic activity. Principal crops are wheat, corn, green chiles, tomatoes, alfalfa, sorghum, and chickpeas (garbanzo beans). Other crops include oranges, avocados, mangoes, and dates. Honey is also produced.

Ranchers in Baja California Sur raise cattle, goats, pigs, and chickens for both meat and egg production.

16 ■ Natural Resources

Fishing in the coastal waters yields abalone, tuna, clams, lobster, and shrimp, among other species. Fishing is an important economic activity, with fish processing facilities located at Santa Rosalía on the east coast.

The state produces salt, plaster, and phosphorite, mostly to be exported. The salt is extracted from ocean saltwater. One of the largest extraction facilities is located on the west coast at Guerrero Negro near the border with Baja California. There are hundreds of shallow tanks there, all filled with ocean water, which is allowed to evaporate. When the water has completely evaporated, the bottoms of the tanks are filled with salt. The salt is purified and sold as table salt, or as a food preservative.

17 ■ Energy and Power

Geothermal power (from the heat of the earth's interior) has potential in the state. A geothermal plant was built near Las Tres Vírgenes (Three Virgins), a volcano near the Golfo de California that last erupted in the 1700s. In rural areas, residents formerly paid a flat fee for electricity, with no meter to measure how much electricity was being used. By the late 1990s, most homes had metered electricity.

18 ▨ Health

There are 18 general hospitals, 130 outpatient centers, and 28 surgical centers in Baja California Sur. AmeriMed (American hospitals) also has a medical center in Cabo San Lucas.

Most of the Mexican population is covered under a government health plan. The IMSS (Instituto Mexicano de Seguro Social) covers the general population. The ISSSTE (Instituto de Seguridad y Servicios Sociales de Trabajadores del Estado) covers state workers.

19 ▨ Housing

There is a slight housing shortage in Baja California Sur. Most of the housing is in good condition, with less that 10% requiring significant upgrading.

20 ▨ Education

The system of public education was started by President Benito Juárez (1806–1872) in 1867. Public education in Mexico is funded by the state and is free for students ages 6 to 16. There were 88,376 school-age children in the state in 2000. Many students elect to go to private schools.

The thirty-one states of Mexico all have at least one state university. The Universidad Internacional de la Paz (International University of La Paz) is located in the capital.

21 ▨ Arts

There are over 8 theaters, including the Teatro Juárez in La Paz. The city of La Paz also has an open-air theater. The city of Todos Santos is an artists' community that often hosts various art fairs. The Galería de Todos Santos is a fine arts gallery showcasing the works of many famous Mexican artists. There is also El Boleo Centro Cultural in the city of Mulegé, and the French cultural society Alianza Francesa has a chapter.

22 ▨ Libraries and Museums

There are 40 branches of the national library system in Baja California Sur.

There is a museum of archeology and a museum of natural history in the city of La Paz and a Jesuit museum in the city of Loreto.

23 ▨ Media

The capital city, La Paz, has *El Sudcaliforniano*.

24 ▨ Tourism, Travel, and Recreation

The two main cities of Cabo San Lucas and San Juan del Cabo offer many hotels and recreational facilities. Whale watching (from January through March), deep sea fishing, golf and tennis, motorcycling, scuba diving, and snorkeling are all area attractions. The "Corridor," is a main highway between the two towns. Medano Beach has windsurfing and at the tip of Baja California Sur is a rock formation known as Los Arcos, famous to all photographers. The town of Mulegé offers sport fishing and diving along with tours of prehistoric caves and their paintings.

25 ▪ Sports

People in Baja California Sur enjoy the sporting venues of Baja California to the north. There are no major sports venues in Baja California Sur.

26 ▪ Famous People

Ángel César Mendoza Aramburu was the first governor; Juan Antonio Flores Ojeda was the governor as of 2004.

27 ▪ Bibliography

Books

Sobol, Richard. *Adelina's Whales.* New York: Dutton, 2003.

Williams, Jack. *The Magnificent Peninsula: The Comprehensive Guidebook to Mexico's Baja California.* Redding, CA: H. J. Williams, 2001.

Web Sites

Mexico for Kids. http://www.elbalero.gob.mx/index_kids.html (accessed on June 11, 2004).

Campeche

Pronunciation: kahm-PEH-cheh.

Origin of state name: The name Campeche is of Mayan origin and has three possible meanings: It may be derived from the words *can* (snake) and *pech* (tick)—the place of snakes and ticks. Some speculate that Can Pech means "the place where the snake is worshipped," because snakes appear on many ancient structures.

Capital: Campeche.

Entered country: 1862.

Coat of Arms: The red background of the upper left and lower right quarters represents the bravery of Campecheans and contrasts with the silver towers. This silver color is the reflection of solidness and honor of its inhabitants, and the towers signify the strength of Campecheans in the defense of their land. The other two quarters bear a sailing ship with a raised anchor, which reminds viewers of the importance of Campeche as a maritime port. The four quarters rest upon a blue background that represents the loyalty and noble sentiments of Campecheans. Finally, above the coat of arms there is a crown decorated with precious stones symbolizing the nobility and grandeur of the state.

Holidays: Año Nuevo (New Year's Day—January 1); Día de la Constitución (Constitution Day—February 5); Benito Juárez's birthday (March 21); Primero de Mayo (Labor Day—May 1); Revolution Day, 1910 (November 20); and Navidad (Christmas—December 25).

Flag: There is no official flag.

Time: 6 AM = noon Greenwich Mean Time (GMT).

1 ■ Location and Size

Campeche, in eastern Mexico on the Yucatán Peninsula, covers an area of 56,789 square kilometers (21,926 square miles). Campeche is about the same size as the US state of Iowa. Campeche is bordered by the Mexican state of Quintana Roo on the east; by the Mexican state of Tabasco and the Gulf of Mexico on the west; by the Mexican state of Yucatán on the north; and by the Central American nation of Guatemala on the south. It is divided into eleven municipalities. The capital city is also called Campeche.

Campeche has 404 kilometers (252 miles) of coastline and includes the Isla del Carmen, Jaina, Triángulo, and Cayo Arcas.

The mountains (*sierras*) are situated in the northern and eastern parts of the state. A great flat plain stretches to the south. The region also includes *cenotes,* natural pools that formed when water seeped through the limestone of underground caves.

There are small lakes throughout Campeche, and the coastline is dotted with lagoons. The main rivers are the Candelaría and the Champotón. The Usumacinta forms the border with Tabasco. The Laguna de Términos (Términos Lagoon) lies on the southern part of the coastline with the Gulf of Mexico and is fed by several rivers, including the Candelaría.

2 ▨ Climate

The warm waters of the Gulf of Mexico contribute to the climate, which is generally warm and humid. The average temperatures is 24°C to 28°C (76°F to 82°F). Annual rainfall averages 38 inches (96.5 centimeters). The highest monthly average rainfall occurs in August and September.

3 ▨ Plants and Animals

The state has rich rain forests. The jaguar population, most of which may be found in the Calakmul Biosphere Reserve, is estimated at four hundred. It is one the largest jaguar populations anywhere in the world. Orchids and other plants of the rain forest are native to the state.

4 ▨ Environmental Protection

The Calakmul Biosphere Reserve, on the southern border with Guatemala, is the second largest protected area in Mexico. The reserve, located 320 kilometers (200 miles) from the capital, Campeche, was created in 1993. There also are extensive ruins of ancient civilizations in Campeche.

Much of the forest areas in Campeche have been cut down and the wood used for housing materials and for cooking and heating. Forests were also cleared to make way for livestock. The government has instituted preservation programs to stop further environmental destruction.

5 ▨ Population, Ethnic Groups, Languages

Campeche had a total population of 690,689 in 2000; of the total, 344,334 were men and 346,355 were women. The population density was 12 people per square kilometer (31 people per square mile). In 2000, the capital, Campeche, had a population of 216,735.

About 85% of all citizens speak Spanish as their first language. Campeche has a fairly large population of indigenous (native) people, primarily Mayan. About 15% of citizens speak one of the Mayan languages as their first language.

6 ▨ Religions

According to the 2000 census, 63% of the population, or 432,457 people, were Roman Catholic; 12%, or 79,994 people, were Protestant. That year there were also 11,558 Seventh-Day Adventists, 2,264 Mormons, 14,585 Jehovah's Witnesses, and nearly 65,000 people who reported no religion.

7 ▨ Transportation

Campeche International Airport and Ciudad del Carmen Airport provide international flights to and from Campeche.

There are approximately 2,942 kilometers (1,839 miles) of paved roads and about 400 kilometers (250 miles) of railroad

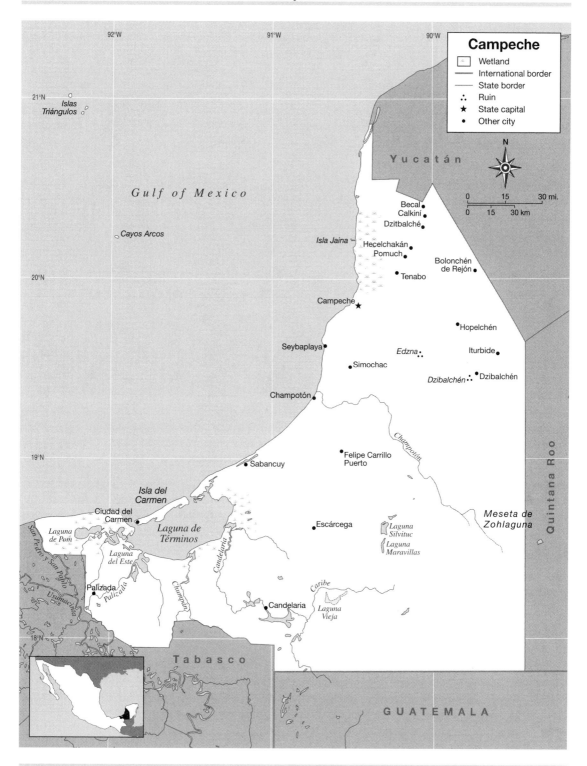

Campeche
- Wetland
- International border
- State border
- ∴ Ruin
- ★ State capital
- • Other city

Islas Triángulos

Yucatán

Gulf of Mexico

Cayos Arcos

Becal
Calkiní
Dzitbalché
Isla Jaina
Hecelchakán
Pomuch
Bolonchén
de Rejón
Tenabo

Campeche

Hopelchén

Seybaplaya
Edzna
Iturbide
Simochac
Dzibalchén
Dzibalchén

Champotón

Champotón

Felipe Carrillo
Puerto

Sabancuy

Isla del
Carmen

Ciudad del
Carmen

Laguna
de Pom
Laguna de
Términos

Candelaria

Laguna
del Este

Laguna
Silvituc

Laguna
Maravillas

Meseta de
Zohlaguna

Escárcega

Quintana Roo

San Pedro y San Pablo

Usumacinta

Palizada
Palizada

Candelaria

Caribe

Laguna
Vieja

Tabasco

GUATEMALA

Small cargo sailboat on the waters of the Bahía de Campeche (Bay of Campeche).

track, mostly serving tourists wishing to visit Mayan ruins. A highway, known historically as the royal highway, connects the two important cities on the Yucatán Peninsula— Campeche and Merida. Other highways link the capital, Campeche, with Villahermosa, the capital of Tabasco.

Cayo Arcas is one of Mexico's principal ports for exports. Laguna Azul is the port at Ciudad del Carmen.

8 ■ History

The history of Campeche, which lies on the Yucatán Peninsula, begins in the era from 300 to 900 A.D. The Maya built sev-

eral cities in the Yucatán. The Toltec culture arrived in 987 A.D., led by its leader Quetzalcóatl. Toltec became the dominate culture in the region before the arrival of the Spanish.

The first Spaniards to visit the region were the survivors of a shipwreck. Two survivors, Jerónimo de Aguilar and Gonzalo Guerrero, became incorporated into Mayan civilization. Guerrero married the daughter of the Chetumal tribal chief, and their son was the first officially recorded Mestizo (mixed Indian and Spanish) in Mexico. Jerónimo de Aguilar was later rescued by Spanish explorer Hernán Cortés's (1485– 1547) expedition.

Spanish explorer Francisco de Montejo initiated the conquest of Yucatán in 1527. The Amerindian resistance was so strong that he fled. He returned three years later with his son Francisco de Montejo y León but was again unsuccessful in his effort to overpower the native Indians. A third attempt in 1537 proved successful. De Montejo founded the cities of Campeche in 1540 and Mérida in 1542. Franciscan priests (from an order of the Roman Catholic Church) built more than thirty convents in an effort to convert the indigenous people to the Catholic faith. Indigenous revolts during the colonial period consolidated Yucatán's reputation as a region whose fierce Indians would not easily surrender to Spanish rule. The Spanish built a wall around the city of Campeche to protect it from other European invaders and from indigenous warriors.

Yucatán did not participate in the independence movement of 1810. The Spanish authorities controlled the region and prevented any insurgencies. In 1821, with the Plan of Iguala, Yucatán was made a part of independent Mexico. After the Independence of Mexico, Campeche became one of the five important seats of government that formed Yucatán. Yucatán was formally made a state in 1823 and a new constitution became law in 1825. On August 7, 1857, civil war divided Campeche from Yucatán. A new region was created that was given the name Campeche, with the city of Campeche as the capital.

The constitution was written in 1861, and the Mexican Congress voted in favor of accepting Campeche as a state in 1862, during the presidency of Benito Juárez (1806–1872).

Under the long presidency of Porfirio Díaz (1830–1915), Campeche lost the Quintana Roo territory. Díaz made Quintana Roo

a separate province in 1902. Quintana Roo was returned to Campeche during the short Ortiz Rubio presidency (1930–1932). Finally, President Lázaro Cárdenas, who held office from 1934 to 1940, separated Campeche and Quintana Roo permanently by creating a new Quintana Roo state in 1974.

Also in the mid-19th century, Campeche segregationists sought to force the central government to create a new province independent of Yucatán. Tomás Aznar, Pedro and Perfecto de Baranda, Francisco and Rafael Carvajal, Leando and Miguel Domínguez, and Irineo Lavalle were among the leaders of Campechean separation. Segregationist Campeche leaders occupied Mérida, the Yucatán capital, in the early 1860s.

The invasion of French troops into Mexico in the mid-1860s forced Campeche leaders to decide whether to join the occupying forces, as Yucatán had done, or to resist the foreign invaders. The city of Campeche was attacked and eventually overpowered by the French invading forces. Carlota, the French emperor's wife, visited Campeche during their short tenure as Mexican monarchs. Pro-republican forces occupied Campeche to fight against French emperor Maximilian (1832–1867) and the French invaders. The end of the war and the consolidation of power under Díaz did not bring peace to Campeche, however. From 1876 to 1910, twenty-five different governors ruled Campeche.

The discovery of oil fields off the coast turned Campeche into an extremely important area for the rest of Mexico. Military and political control of the state became central to any government that sought to exercise control over the rest of Mexico. Despite the local instability, the central government has continuously exercised direct control over the area where the oil fields are located.

During the Mexican Revolution (1910–1920) Campeche witnessed confrontations by different factions. A new government assumed control of the state shortly before the Mexican Constitution was approved in 1917. Since then, the party that eventually became the Institutional Revolutionary Party (PRI) has exercised political control over Campeche.

When President Cárdenas created the state of Quintana Roo in 1974, dividing the old state of Campeche, opposition from some Campechean leaders was quickly suppressed with promises of industrial and economic incentives. The presence of the most important oil fields off the coast of Campeche has made the state into one of the most strategically important units of the Mexican federation.

Some efforts at forming guerrilla movements in the region were undertaken in the mid-1960s. The strategic economic importance of the state led the central government to heavily intervene in state politics and to exercise an unusual level of centralized control over the Campechean state affairs.

Following the passage of the North American Free Trade Agreement (NAFTA) in 1992, a trade agreement between Mexico, the United States, and Canada, Campeche became home to many new manufacturing enterprises.

9 ■ State and Local Government

The state government is highly centralized and most powers reside with the governor, who is elected by popular vote for a six-year nonrenewable term. The state congress is comprised of thirty-five legislators elected in twenty-one single member districts and fourteen multimember districts to promote the representation of minority parties. Legislators are elected for nonrenewable three-year terms. Although there is a formal, well-established separation of power with provisions for checks and balances, state governors have historically exercised strong influence over the legislative branch of government.

Comprised of eleven municipalities, local governments are restricted in their powers and attributions. In spite of this, the wave of democratization that swept Mexican politics since the early 1990s has also brought increased democratization to local governments in Campeche. Municipal presidents are elected for nonrenewable three-year terms as are municipal council members. The size of municipal councils varies according to the population of each municipality.

10 ■ Political Parties

The three main political parties in all of Mexico are the Institutional Revolutionary Party (PRI), the National Action Party (PAN), and the Party of the Democratic Revolution (PRD).

As in the rest of Mexico, the PRI heavily controlled politics in Campeche during most of the 20th century. Campeche's strategic importance as an oil producing region made the PRI political control of the state more evident than in most other states. The last two governors, Antonio González (1997–2003) and Jorge Carlos Hurtado Valdez (2003–2009), both belonged to the PRI.

11 ■ Judicial System

Comprised of a Superior Tribunal of Justice, an electoral tribunal, and local courts, the judicial system is autonomous and independent. Superior Tribunal justices are appointed by the governor with the legislature's approval. Appointees must be qualified lawyers with previous judicial experience. Appointments are made for six-year terms. After a term expires, if the justice is confirmed, he or she will continue in office for life or until a mandatory retirement age of sixty-five.

12 ■ Economy

About 45% of the state's economy relates to the oil fields just off the shores of Campeche. Tourism (15%) is the next most important sector of the economy. Financial and real estate services (15%) are also important economic activities.

13 ■ Industry

Over half of Mexico's oil and over one-fourth of the country's natural gas are produced by the wells off the coast of Campeche. PEMEX, Mexico's oil company, has significant operations in the state. Tourism is also an important industry, with Mayan ruins being a significant draw for visitors.

14 ■ Labor

The United States Bureau of Labor Statistics reported that Mexican workers saw their wages increase 17%, from $2.09 per hour in 1999 to $2.46 per hour in 2000. (By comparison, the average American worker earned $19.86 per hour in 2000.) After one year, workers are entitled by law to six days paid vacation.

15 ■ Agriculture

Agriculture and livestock are an important part of the economy in the northeast, where there is less rainfall. Fruit orchards produce mangoes, citrus fruits, watermelon, cantaloupe, and papaya. Other crops grown in the state include corn, rice, beans, sorghum, soy, jalapeño peppers, peanuts, and several varieties of squash. Cattle, pig, and goat production are other sources of income to the state, as well as beekeeping.

16 ■ Natural Resources

The oil fields off the Campeche coast are the state's most important mineral resource.

Fishing is an important and growing activity, with facilities for shipping already in existence. There are refrigerated warehouses in the port areas, as well as training centers for fishermen.

17 ■ Energy and Power

Over 90% of people living in cities and 85% of those living in rural areas have electricity.

18 ■ Health

Campeche has 20 general hospitals, 256 outpatient centers, and 28 surgical centers.

Most of the Mexican population is covered under a government health plan. The IMSS (Instituto Mexicano de Seguro Social) covers the general population. The ISSSTE (Instituto de Seguridad y Servicios Sociales de Trabajadores del Estado) covers state workers.

© Peter Langer/EPD Photos

Xpuhil Tower on Structure I, part of the ancient ruins preserved in the Calakmul Biosphere Reserve.

19 ■ Housing

The population of Campeche is growing at about 5% per year. More than one-fourth of the housing available in Campeche is of poor quality and requires major upgrading or replacement. Less than half of Campeche's housing is considered satisfactory or in need of just minor improvements.

20 ■ Education

The system of public education was first started by President Benito Juárez in 1867. Public education in Mexico is funded by the state and is free for all students from ages six to sixteen. There are over 180,000 school-age children living in the state. Many students elect to go to private schools.

The thirty-one states of Mexico all have at least one state university. A university was established under Governor Alberto Trueba Urbina's administration (1955–1961). It became known as the Universidad Autonoma de Campeche (Independent University of Campeche) in 1989.

21 ■ Arts

Campeche has nine theaters and seven auditoriums, all located in the city of Campeche. There are six cultural centers, two of which are located in the city of

Carmen. The *jarana,* the traditional dance of Campeche, is performed at many of the cultural centers. Many local markets sell crafts made by local artisans.

22 ▪ Libraries and Museums

The state of Campeche has forty-eight branches of the national library. There are five museums in Campeche. There is an archaeology museum in the city of Campeche and a local history museum in Hecelchakán.

23 ▪ Media

The capital city, Campeche, has two news-papers: *El Sur de Campeche* and *La Tribuna de Campeche.* There are thirteen AM and five FM radio stations broadcasting in the state. About half of the state's territory has broad-cast television service; 20% of the state's residents have access to cable television. Internet service is not widely available, but several companies had begun offering access as of 2003.

There are 35,000 to 40,000 telephone lines in service in the state. Two mobile phone companies provide cellular phone service.

24 ▪ Tourism, Travel, and Recreation

The city of Campeche is an old fortified colonial city with walls meant to protect it from pirate attacks. Tourists can visit the many citadels (fortresses) and thick-walled fortifications (called *baluartes*). There are also many Mayan ruins as a result of Spain's attempt to convert the natives to Christianity. The museum at San Miguel Fort has a collection of pre-Columbian artifacts. There are also Mayan ruins in the town of Edzna, where visitors can see the Temple of Five Stories. The towns of Rio Bec and Calakmul also have ruins.

25 ▪ Sports

Mexico's oldest baseball league, Liga Mexicana (Minor League Baseball), was organized in 1925. The Piratas (Pirates) of Campeche are members of this league. The baseball season in Mexico is from April to August.

26 ▪ Famous People

Notable citizens born in Campeche in-clude lawyer and politician Pablo García Montilla (1824–1895), who was involved in the establishment of the state's gov-ernment and judicial system; lawyer and journalist Justo Sierra (1848–1912), one of the founders of the University of Mexico; Impressionist painter Joaquin Clausell (1866–1935); writer and folk historian Juan de la Cabada Vera (1899–1986); and musician and historian Francisco Alvares Suarez (1838–1916).

27 ▪ Bibliography

Books

Supples, Kevin. *Mexico.* Washington, DC: National Geographic Society, 2002.

Web Sites

Mayan World. http://www.mayan-world.com/ (accessed on June 11, 2004).

Mexico for Kids. http://www.elbalero.gob.mx/index_kids.html (accessed on June 11, 2004).

Chiapas

Pronunciation: chee-AH-pahs.

Origin of state name: The name of Chiapas is taken from the ancient city of Chiapan, which in Náhuatl means the place where the chia (a kind of sage) grows.

Capital: Tuxtla Gutiérrez.

Entered country: 1841.

Coat of Arms: The coat of arms was initially the emblem of Ciudad Real, now known as San Cristóbal de las Casas, a colonial city located one and one-half hours away from the capital of Tuxlta Gutiérrez. It was founded in 1535 by the Spaniards. The lions, castle, and crown represent the power and authority held by King Carlos V (1500–1558) of Spain.

Holidays: Año Nuevo (New Year's Day—January 1); Día de la Constitución (Constitution Day—February 5); Benito Juárez's birthday (March 21); Primero de Mayo (Labor Day—May 1); Revolution Day, 1910 (November 20); and Navidad (Christmas—December 25).

Flag: There is no official flag.

Time: 6 AM = noon Greenwich Mean Time (GMT).

1 ■ Location and Size

Chiapas is situated in southern Mexico. It has an area of 73,724 square kilometers (28,465 square miles). It is slightly smaller than the US state of South Carolina. Chiapas is bordered on the north by the Mexican state of Tabasco, on the south by the Pacific Ocean, on the east by the Central American nation of Guatemala, and on the west by the Mexican states of Oaxaca and Veracruz. Chiapas has 111 municipalities. Its capital, Tuxtla Gutiérrez, lies near the center of the state.

Chiapas has a coastal plain along the Pacific Ocean to the south. In the north, the coastal plain that begins in Tabasco extends into Chiapas. The Sierra Madre is a chain of high mountains that run from the northwest to the southeast. The highest peak is the Tacaná volcano (4,093 meters/13,428 feet in elevation), which lies on the border with Guatemala. The Grijalva River flows northwest through the center of the state until it empties into the Bahía de Campeche. There are three major dams along the Grijalva. The spectacular Cañon del Sumidero (Sumidero Canyon) was formed by the Grijalva River. A high plateau, the highest region in the state, lies in the center of Chiapas.

2 ▦ Climate

Temperatures are fairly constant year round, with variation depending on elevation. The north is dry with little rainfall, but the southern part of the state is more humid. The average temperature is 20°C (68°F), but temperatures may reach as high as 40°C (104°F) and as low as 0°C (32°F).

3 ▦ Plants and Animals

Orchids and bromeliads (plants of the pineapple family) are native to the tropical areas of the state. Mangrove trees are also native. The forest area has jaguars, flying squirrels, monkeys, white-tailed deer, tapirs, toucans, and parrots. At higher elevations there are hardwood trees such as mahogany and cedar. Crocodiles and hundreds of species of birds live along the Pacific coast.

4 ▦ Environmental Protection

In the 1990s, Chiapas began to protect and preserve its cloud forests (forest at high elevations) and coastal areas. The El Triunfo Biosphere Reserve is located in the south in the Sierra Madres. It ranks as one of the most biologically diverse places on the planet and encompasses approximately 300,000 acres.

La Encrucijada Biosphere Reserve is located in the Pacific coastal area of Chiapas and covers 357,824 acres. This reserve offers the tallest mangroves on the Pacific coast and healthy numbers of crocodiles, jaguars, raccoons, and iguanas.

5 ▦ Population, Ethnic Groups, Languages

Chiapas had a total population of 3,920,892 in 2000; of the total, 1,941,880 were men and 1,979,012 were women. The population density was 53 people per square kilometer (137 people per square mile). In 2000, the capital, Tuxtla Gutiérrez, had a population of 433,544. About 25% of the population speaks one of the Mayan languages. Chiapas has the third largest population of indigenous language speakers (after the Mexican states of Yucatán and Oaxaca).

6 ▦ Religions

According to the 2000 census, 53% of the population, or 2.1 million people, were Roman Catholic; 12%, or 457,736 people, were Protestant. That year there were also 173,772 Seventh-Day Adventists, 82,646 Jehovah's Witnesses, and nearly 470,000 people who reported no religion.

7 ▦ Transportation

Most of the state's 7,000 kilometers (4,375 miles) of highways are paved. Many rural areas are accessible only by rough dirt roads.

Tuxtla Gutiérrez-Llano San Juan Airport provides international flights to and from Chiapas.

8 ▦ History

Human presence in Chiapas dates as far back as 600 A.D. Located in the heart of the region of Mayan influence, Chiapas was home to some of the most important Mayan ceremonial centers, like Palenque, Bonampak, Yaxchilán, and Lacanjá. Chiapa Indians eventually conquered

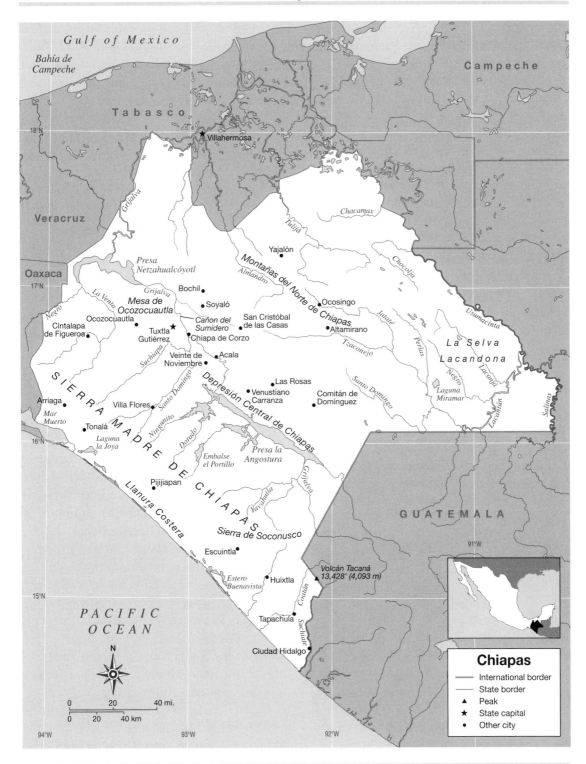

Gulf of Mexico

Bahía de
Campeche

Campeche

Tabasco

Veracruz

★ Villahermosa

18°N

Chacamax

Oaxaca

17°N

Presa
Netzahualcóyotl

Tulijá

Yajalón

Almandro

Montañas del Norte de Chiapas

Chocolja

Usumacinta

La Venta

Grijalva

Bochil

Mesa de
Ocozocuautla

Soyaló

Ocosingo

Jataté

La Selva
Lacandona

Negro

Ocozocuautla

Cañon del
Sumidero

San Cristóbal
de las Casas

Cintalapa
de Figueroa

Tuxtla
Gutiérrez ★

Chiapa de Corzo

Altamirano

Tzaconejo

Negro

Perlas

Lacantún

Veinte de
Noviembre

Acala

Laguna
Miramar

Salinas

Suchiapa

Santo Domingo

Las Rosas

S I E R R A

Arriaga

Villa Flores

Venustiano
Carranza

Comitán de
Domínguez

Santo Domingo

Lacantún

Mar
Muerto

Ningunito

Tonalá

Dorado

M A D R E

D E

Depresión Central de Chiapas

Grijalva

16°N

Laguna
la Joya

Embalse
el Portillo

Presa la
Angostura

C H I A P A S

Pijijiapan

Yatahuala

GUATEMALA

Llanura Costera

91°W

Sierra de Soconusco

Escuintla

Volcán Tacaná
13,428' (4,093 m) ▲

15°N

Estero
Buenavista

Huixtla

Coatán

PACIFIC
OCEAN

Tapachula

Suchiate

N

Ciudad Hidalgo

Chiapas

- ~~~~~ International border
- ——— State border
- ▲ Peak
- ★ State capital
- • Other city

0   20   40 mi.
0   20   40 km

94°W   93°W   92°W

the territory. By the 15th century, Aztecs dominated the area, but they were not able to rule over the Chiapa.

When the Spaniards arrived, the Chiapa and a number of other indigenous groups inhabited different parts of the Chiapas region. After five years of fierce fighting between the Spanish and the indigenous peoples (1522–1528), the Spanish conquistadores (conquerors) dominated enough land to found a city, Villa Real, known today as San Cristóbal. As part of Guatemala in the 17th century, the indigenous people in Chiapas continued to stage revolts against Spanish occupation. In 1712, several groups waged a bloody war on the Spanish colonizers, fighting against slavery and other forms of oppression.

Chiapas was highly identified with Spanish colonial rule and connected to its southern neighbor, Guatemala. So Chiapas did not immediately join the drive for Mexico's independence. Catholic priest Matías Antonio de Córdoba declared independence from Spanish rule in 1821. A plebiscite (vote) in 1824 ratified Chiapas's union with Mexico. A new state constitution was created in 1826. Despite Guatemala's protest, Chiapas was fully incorporated into Mexico in 1841.

Conflicts between the colonial landowners and the indigenous people continued throughout the 19th century. The Mexican Revolution, which started in 1910, barely extended to Chiapas. Nevertheless, large landowners in Chiapas actively participated in the debates that surrounded the conflicts. Many revolutionary leaders demanded reform of the way farm land was distributed and used. Indigenous groups did not join the revolution in favor of land reform demands.

When the revolution came to an end, the Institutional Revolutionary Party (PRI) emerged as the only important political party. An alliance between PRI leaders and large Chiapas landowners prevented the land reforms from reaching Chiapas and benefiting the indigenous communities. Chiapas remained one of the poorest states, with one of the largest indigenous populations. In Chiapas, unlike other states, the indigenous population remained autonomous and experienced little interaction with the local government, controlled primarily by the landed state elite.

An indigenous revolt triggered by the enactment of the North American Free Trade Agreement (NAFTA), a trade agreement between Mexico, the United States, and Canada, caused worldwide controversy in 1994. The indigenous armed revolt, initiated on January 1, 1994, combined opposition to globalization, rejection of free trade, and indigenous demands for land, respect, and political and cultural autonomy. The Zapatista Army of National Liberation (EZLN) was led by a popular revolutionary leader known as Marcos and by several indigenous leaders. Although the movement successfully brought indigenous demands and concerns over their values and cultural traditions to the forefront of the international debate, the movements' ambitious goals of evolving into a new national revolutionary force that could topple the PRI government eventually failed when the rest of Mexico experienced a process of democratic consolidation starting in the mid 1990s and ending with the PRI defeat in the 2000 presidential elections.

In January 2003, about 20,000 masked militants from the EZLN moved into San Cristóbal. They carried machetes and sticks and lit bonfires in the center of the city to protest government actions. The

Chiapas was home to important Mayan ceremonial centers, like this one at Palenque.

EZLN protests government treatment of indigenous people.

9 ■ State and Local Government

The state governor is the most influential and powerful political figure. Elected for a nonrenewable six-year term, the governor is the chief executive. A ministerial cabinet is appointed by and accountable to the governor. Formal separation of power and check-and-balance provisions also provide for a unicameral (one chamber) legislature. The state congress is comprised of forty deputies. Twenty-four are elected in single member districts and sixteen are elected at large for proportional representation. All deputies serve for nonrenewable three-year terms.

Comprised of 116 municipalities, Chiapas is one of the most ethnically diverse states in Mexico. Local governments have strong power to determine their own rules, especially in the independent indigenous communities. Political conflicts resulting from the opposition of federal authorities to increased power by indigenous communities regularly force courts to assess the limits of local authorities in exercising power.

The spectacular Cañon del Sumidero (Sumidero Canyon) was formed by the Grijalva River.

10 ▪ Political Parties

The three main political parties in all of Mexico are the Institutional Revolutionary Party (PRI), the National Action Party (PAN), and Party of the Democratic Revolution (PRD). The PRI, in association with large traditional land-owning families, exercised political control of the state throughout most of the 20th century. The 1994 indigenous revolt propelled the Zapatista Army of National Liberation (EZLN) to the forefront of national and state politics. The EZLN rejects electoral politics as a legitimate means of reaching power. This helped the two national opposition parties, the conservative PAN and the leftist PRD, to gain ground and capitalize on discontent against the PRI. Former PRI leader, Pablo Salazar, won the 2000 gubernatorial election with support from the PAN and PRD.

11 ▪ Judicial System

The Supreme Tribunal of Justice is the highest court in Chiapas. Its members are appointed by a two-thirds majority in the legislature from a three-person list presented by the governor. Supreme Tribunal justices serve nonrenewable seven-year terms. In addition, the Chiapas judicial system includes an electoral tribunal, a civil service tribunal, and local and indigenous courts. There are additional complexities resulting from Chiapas's strong indigenous presence. The indigenous communities use alternative courts and legal systems.

12 ▪ Economy

Crude oil production, manufacturing, and small-scale agriculture are important segments of the economy. Chiapas is a major producer of coffee for export.

13 ▪ Industry

In 2002, the state's first maquiladora (assembly plant) opened in San Cristóbal, to manufacture sweaters and T-shirts for sale in the United States. Overall there is little industry in Chiapas.

14 ▪ Labor

Many workers in Chiapas live in homes with no electricity or running water. They are among the lowest paid workers in Mexico. The US Bureau of Labor Statistics reported that Mexican workers saw their wages increase 17%, from $2.09 per hour in 1999 to $2.46 per hour in 2000. (The average US worker earned $19.86 per hour in 2000.) After one year, workers are entitled by law to six days paid vacation.

15 ▪ Agriculture

Coffee is the most valuable agricultural product; about 60% of Mexico's total coffee output comes from Chiapas. Chiapas ranks second among the Mexican states in the production of cacao, the product used to make chocolate.

Other crops grown in Chiapas include sugarcane, cotton, bananas, and other fruits. These are grown especially in the lowland regions near the Pacific coast. Some land is devoted to pasture for livestock. There are nearly a million chickens, turkey, and ducks raised by farmers each year; milk is another major product produced in the state.

16 ▪ Natural Resources

Chiapas has rich natural resources, including the watershed of the Grijalva River, tropical rainforests, oil, gas, uranium, iron, aluminum, copper, and amber. One-third of Mexico's crude oil is produced by Chiapas.

Lumber production more than doubled in the 1990s. About 80% of the lumber produced is pine. Fishing for shrimp, mullet, and sea bass is carried out in the coastal Pacific Ocean waters.

17 ▪ Energy and Power

Electricity in the state is produced by seven hydroelectric plants and four thermal plants. Nearly 25% of all of the country's electricity is generated in Chiapas. A 210-megawatt hydroelectric plant was due to begin operation at Copainalá in 2008. Mexico's existing natural gas reserves are located primarily in the southwestern states of Tabasco and Chiapas.

18 ▪ Health

There are 42 general hospitals, 1,510 outpatient centers, and 83 surgical centers in various cities.

Most of the Mexican population is covered under a government health plan. The IMSS (Instituto Mexicano de Seguro Social) covers the general population. The ISSSTE (Instituto de Seguridad y Servicios Sociales de Trabajadores del Estado) covers state workers.

Government health care services are not always available in zones where there is conflict between the government and rebels.

19 ▪ Housing

Housing in Chiapas is of generally poor quality, with almost half of the available housing in need of replacement or significant improvements. An estimated two-thirds of houses have dirt floors. About one-third of all homes, mostly in rural areas, do not have electricity.

20 ▪ Education

The system of public education was first started by President Benito Juárez (1806–1872) in 1867. Public education in Mexico is free for students from ages six to sixteen. Many students elect to go to private schools. The thirty-one states of Mexico all have at least one state university. The State University of Chiapas (UNACH) is in Tapachula.

Children in the small Mayan communities in rural areas may attend local schools specifically structured to preserve Mayan language and culture.

21 ▪ Arts

The state of Chiapas hosts at least six major theaters including El Teatro de Bellas Artes and Teatro de la Ciudad Emilio Rabasa. The Cultural Center of Chiapas Jaime Sabines, named for the well-known poet, hosts art exhibits and performances of all types. There is also a chapter of the French cultural society Alianza Francesa in the capital city of Tuxtla Gutiérrez. The Coro de Cámara Canto Nuevo (Choir of New Song) was founded in 2002.

22 ▪ Libraries and Museums

The state of Chiapas has 332 branches of the national library. There are about fifty museums. In the capital, Tuxla Gutiérrez, there is a botanical gardens and a museum of paleontology (the study of fossils).

23 ▪ Media

The capital, Tuxtla Gutiérrez, has three daily newspapers: *Cuarto Poder, Este Sur,* and *La República en Chiapas.* Tapachula has two daily newspapers: *El Orbe* and *Noticias de Chiapas.*

Television networks Televisa, TV Azteca, and Polytechnic broadcast in the state. There is limited cable service in the cities. There are over twenty radio stations broadcasting in Chiapas.

24 ▪ Tourism, Travel, and Recreation

Tuxtla Gutiérrez is the home of the 17th-century Cathedral of San Marcos. The church tower has marching statues of the twelve apostles, which move to mark every hour, accompanied by forty-eight church bells. One of the best zoos in the country, the Miguel Alvarez del Toro Zoo in Tuxtla Gutiérrez, has an interesting collection of native animals.

25 ▪ Sports

The soccer team, Jaguares, from the city of Tuxtla Gutiérrez plays in the Victor Manuel Reyna stadium, which holds 25,000 people.

26 ▪ Famous People

Emilio Rabasa (1856–1930), from Ocozocoautla, who became governor and ambassador to the United States, was a prominent legal scholar. Poet Jaime Sabines (1926–1999) was born in Tuxtla Gutiérrez. The rebels of the Zapatista Army of National Liberation (EZLN) take their name from Emiliano Zapata (1879–1919), born in Morelos, leader of a revolution in the early 20th century. Miguel Alvarez del Toro (1917–1996) was a prominent naturalist; the zoo in Tuxtla Gutiérrez is named in his honor.

27 ▪ Bibliography

Books

Carew-Miller, Anna. *Famous People of Mexico.* Philadelphia: Mason Crest Publishers, 2003.

DeAngelis, Gina. *Mexico.* Mankato, MN: Blue Earth Books, 2003.

Jacobson, Marcey. *The Burden of Time: Photographs from the Highlands of Chiapas.* Stanford, CA: Stanford University Press, 2001.

Ortiz, Teresa. *Never Again a World Without Us: Voices of Mayan Women in Chiapas, Mexico.* Washington, DC: EPICA, 2001.

Supples, Kevin. *Mexico.* Washington, DC: National Geographic Society, 2002.

Web Sites

Mexico for Kids. http://www.elbalero.gob.mx/index_kids.html (accessed on June 11, 2004).

Chihuahua

Pronunciation: chee-WAH-wah.

Origin of state name: Uncertain. May come from the Nahuatl word for "dry, sandy place."

Capital: Chihuahua.

Entered country: 1824.

Coat of Arms: The coat of arms is shield-shaped, with a red border. Across the top is a depiction of the old aqueduct of Chihuahua. In the center section a head of a Spaniard (left) and an Amerindian (right) represents the mestizo, or blending of two peoples; the lower third depicts Chihuahua Cathedral.

Holidays: Año Nuevo (New Year's Day—January 1); Día de la Constitución (Constitution Day—February 5); Benito Juárez's birthday (March 21); Primero de Mayo (Labor Day—May 1); Revolution Day, 1910 (November 20); and Navidad (Christmas—December 25).

Flag: There is no official flag.

Time: 5 AM = noon Greenwich Mean Time (GMT).

1 ▪ Location and Size

Chihuahua, the largest state, lies in northern Mexico. It has an area of 245,945 square kilometers (94,960 square miles), about one-third the size of the US state of Texas. Chihuahua is bordered on the north by the US states of New Mexico and Texas, on the south by the Mexican state of Durango, on the east by the Mexican state of Coahuila, on the west by the Mexican state of Sonora, and on the southwest by the Mexican state of Sinaloa. Chihuahua has sixty-seven municipalities. Its capital is also called Chihuahua.

The natural regions of Chihuahua are plateau and mountains (*sierras*). Chihuahua's sierras have steep peaks with narrow gorges. The rest of the state is made up of high plateau.

Rivers run generally west from the mountains and reach the Golfo de California. Rivers include the Papigochic, Urique, Batopilas, and Basasseachi. The Conchos River joins the Río Bravo (known as the Rio Grande in the United States) along the Texas border. The Río Bravo flows east to the Gulf of Mexico.

2 ▪ Climate

The climate is dry to semi-arid although there is regular rainfall. The average annual temperature is 20°C (68°F). Annual rainfall ranges from 221 millimeters (8.7 inches) to 1,023 millimeters (40.3 inches).

3 ▪ Plants and Animals

In the high plateau region and on the plains, native plants include lechuguilla (an evergreen succulent), mesquite (a common desert shrub), guayule (a rubber producing plant), and ocotillo (a succulent plant with red flowers). Native animal life includes lizards, rattlesnakes, and small birds and animals such as quail, shrews, rabbits, squirrels, skunks, wild boars, and porcupines.

In the mountains (*sierras*), native plants include pine and fir trees, poplars, and white cedar trees. Native animals include bats, moles, rats, bears, white-tailed deer, wolves, gray foxes, raccoons, and squirrels. There are nearly three hundred species of migratory and native birds, including spotted owls and blue-throated hummingbirds, along with over eighty species of reptiles.

4 ▪ Environmental Protection

Chihuahua has air quality problems in certain areas where there is heavy traffic. Many roads are not paved, and trucks create dusty conditions. In the border area around El Paso, Texas, and Ciudad Juárez, Chihuahua, safety of the water supply is sometimes threatened. The Conchos River, which eventually joins the Río Grande, is polluted by waste water. After the North American Free Trade Agreement (NAFTA) was passed in 1992, the Border Environmental Cooperation Com-

mission (BECC) was created to protect the environment in the border areas where development was rapid.

5 ▪ Population, Ethnic Groups, Languages

Chihuahua had a total population of 3,052,907 in 2000; of the total, 1,519,972 (49.8%) were men and 1,532,935 (50.2%) were women. The population density was 12 people per square kilometer (31 people per square mile). In 2000, the capital, Chihuahua, had a population of 670,208. Most people in Chihuahua speak Spanish, but a small percentage (3.2%) speak indigenous languages. About 85% of the indigenous language-speakers are Tarahumara.

6 ▪ Religions

According to the 2000 census, 72% of the population, or 2.2 million people, were Roman Catholic; 6%, or 185,665 people, were Protestant. That year there were also 5,817 Seventh-Day Adventists, 12,016 Mormons, 34,006 Jehovah's Witnesses, and over 160,000 people who reported no religion.

7 ▪ Transportation

The network of highways and roads is over 16,985 kilometers (10,615 miles) and connects all parts of the state. Over 2,200 kilometers (1,375 miles) of railroad serves the state, especially the tourists areas. By the end of 1910 there were three rail lines in operation. In 1961, the completion of the Chihuahua-Pacifico, known as ChP or Chepe, changed life in Chihuahua. Now remote areas could be reached and both mining and tourism expanded. In 1998, Ferromex, a private company, took over

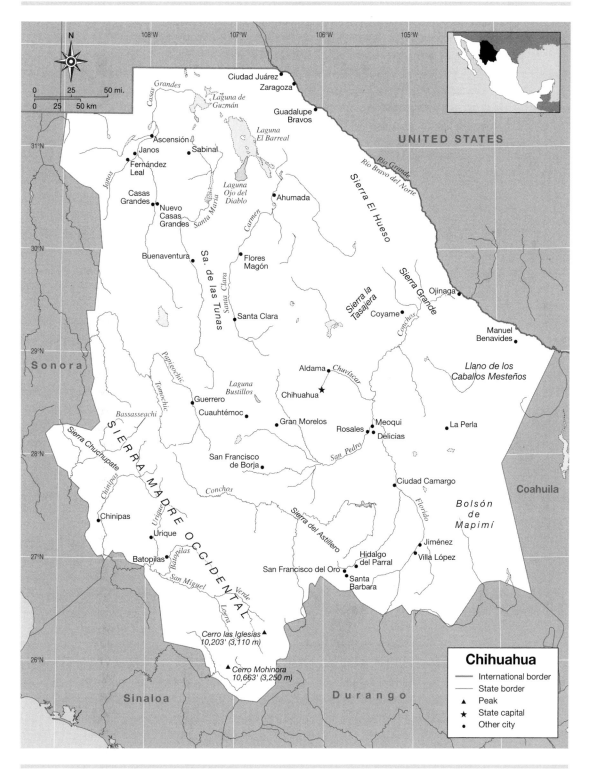

Chihuahua

International border
State border
▲ Peak
★ State capital
• Other city

control of the railroad from the government.

There is an international airport in the city of Chihuahua.

8 ▒ History

When the Spaniards first arrived, Chihuahua was inhabited by more than one hundred different indigenous groups. Among them were the Taraumara, Apache, Comanche, and Guarojío. The first Spaniard to visit was Alvar Nuñez Cabeza de Vaca, whose expedition covered territory from the US state of Florida to the Mexican state of Sinaloa.

The first Spanish settlements date back to the 16th century, when haciendas (country estates) and mining centers were first established. Some Franciscan (Roman Catholic) missions and the Carapoa villages (which are now a single town) were also founded in the mid 1500s. In 1598, the military garrisons known as El Paso and Ciudad Juárez were first built. Yet, the Spanish colonizers only loosely controlled the region during most of the 16th century.

The growth of the mining industry in the 17th century generated more economic activity but also provoked more indigenous uprisings. Tensions developed between the miners and the hacienda owners, who were interested in forcing indigenous groups to work as slaves. The interest Roman Catholic priests had in converting the indigenous people motivated several interventions by the Spanish crown to reduce tensions in the region.

The Independence War provoked Chihuahua hacienda owners and miners to side with the royalist forces against the independence movement. Yet, by 1821 the inevitable Mexican independence led leaders in Chihuahua to join the new country. The Plan of Iguala of 1821 established the framework that consolidated the new republic. Later, the region of Durango was separated from Chihuahua to create a new province. Chihuahua officially became a state of Mexico in 1824. The first state constitution was ratified in 1825.

An ethnic war that sought to exterminate Apache and Comanche indigenous people in 1830 caused much bloodshed. It almost entirely achieved its goal, nearly wiping out the indigenous population. After Texas achieved independence, Chihuahua resisted an effort to annex the state to the United States. Yet, the Treaty of Guadalupe Hidalgo in 1848 gave the United States a significant part of a territory previously considered part of Chihuahua. With the help of Chihuahua's governor Luis Terrazas, liberal national leader Benito Juárez (1806–1872) resisted the French occupation in Chihuahua in the mid-1860s.

Chihuahua was a central battleground during the Mexican Revolution (1910–1920). There was discontent against the Díaz regime, but the historic tensions with neighboring Coahuila, Madero's home state, were strong as well. This tension prevented the discontent against the central government from becoming a fueling force for the revolution in Chihuahua. Yet, even the United States sent troops to the state and occupied it for almost a year. Peasant revolutionary leader Francisco Villa (1878–1923), known as Pancho Villa, extensively fought in Chihuahua. He demanded land distribution and recognition of the peasants as legitimate actors in Mexican politics. Villa's famous military Northern Division was first assembled in Chihuahua.

© Peter Langer/EPD Photos

Copper Canyon.

After the revolution, Chihuahua remained a center of Institutional Revolutionary Party (PRI) influence. Its location close to the United States made it a strategic state for Mexico. It also allowed for the development and eventual consolidation of the oldest and most important opposition party during PRI rule, the National Action Party (PAN). Chihuahua leader Luis H. Álvarez became the PAN presidential candidate in 1958, after an unsuccessful run for the state governorship. This showed Chihuahua's emergence as a center of active political opposition against the ruling PRI. Economic development was strong in the cities and along the Texas border during the 1960s through the 1990s, but people in rural areas continued to live in poverty.

In 1992, Chihuahua was one of the first states to elect a governor who was not a member of the PRI. The North American Free Trade Treaty (NAFTA), a trade agreement between Mexico, the United States, and Canada, was signed in 1992 and took effect in 1994. Because Chihuahua shares a border with the United States, much economic development occurred in the state after NAFTA was signed. However, small farmers found it difficult to compete in the North American competitive market.

© Peter Langer/EPD Photos

The Chihuahua Pacifico Railway.

9 ■ State and Local Government

The governor's office is powerful. The governor is democratically elected every six years for a nonrenewable term. In addition, a thirty-three-member state congress is comprised of members elected for nonrenewable three-year terms. Twenty-two of the members are elected in single member districts and eleven in proportional representation. Separation of power provisions have strengthened and consolidated since the election of a non-PRI governor in 1992. Politics in Chihuahua are among the most democratic among the Mexican states, since there are two strong parties.

Chihuahua is comprised of sixty-seven municipalities that vary in range and population. Elections for municipal presidents and council members are held every three years and immediate re-election is not allowed. The competitive nature of politics at the state level has allowed the development of strong municipal governments.

10 ■ Political Parties

The three main political parties in all of Mexico are the Institutional Revolutionary Party (PRI), the National Action Party (PAN), and the Party of the Democratic Revolution (PRD). Chihuahua was the second state in Mexico to elect a non-PRI governor in the post-revolution period. After a contested election in 1986 where the PRI candidate emerged as winner, PAN's Francisco Barrio won the 1992 gubernatorial election. In 1998, Patricio Martínez García, a PRI militant, was elected governor, demonstrating the consolidation of a two party system in the state.

11 Judicial System

The Superior Tribunal of Justice is the highest court in the state. By law it must be made up of at least nine members. They are appointed by the legislature from a three-person list submitted by the executive in consultation with the legislature. Once ratified after their first three-year period, justices cannot be removed until a mandatory retirement age of 65. In addition, there is an electoral tribunal. Local courts complete the state judicial system.

12 Economy

Timber production and raising livestock were once the main components of the economy, but they represented less than 10% of economic activity as of 2003. Maquiladoras (assembly plants) that produce electronic components, automobile parts, and textile goods are now the primary economic activities. Manufacturing makes up about 23% of the economy. There are also a number of large breweries in the state. Tourism is an important and growing segment of the economy ever since railroad travel to the Copper Canyon area was upgraded following privatization of the railroad in 1998.

People living along the border often find barely enough water for drinking and cooking. There is much poverty in rural areas.

13 Industry

Over 350 maquiladoras (assembly plants) produce electronics, automobile parts, and wood products. Manufacturers such as Toshiba, JVC, and Honeywell have facilities in the many industrial parks that have been developed in the state. Chihuahua has one of the fastest growing economies in the country.

14 Labor

Labor-management relations in Chihuahua are generally good. Since the 1980s, the state's workforce has been known for producing high-quality products. The US Bureau of Labor Statistics reported that Mexican workers saw their wages increase 17%, from $2.09 per hour in 1999 to $2.46 per hour in 2000. (The average US worker earned $19.86 per hour in 2000.) After one year, workers are entitled by law to six days paid vacation.

After the North American Free Trade Agreement (NAFTA) was signed in 1992, relations between management and labor have been strained in the state. Union membership in Chihuahua is declining.

15 Agriculture

Despite its arid (dry) climate, agriculture is an important segment of the economy. Chihuahua farmers in the semi-arid coastal areas to the west produce sugar cane, oats, potatoes, wheat, cotton, corn, sorghum, peanuts, soy, alfalfa, and green chilies. In the valleys of eastern Chihuahua, farmers raise peaches, melons, nuts,

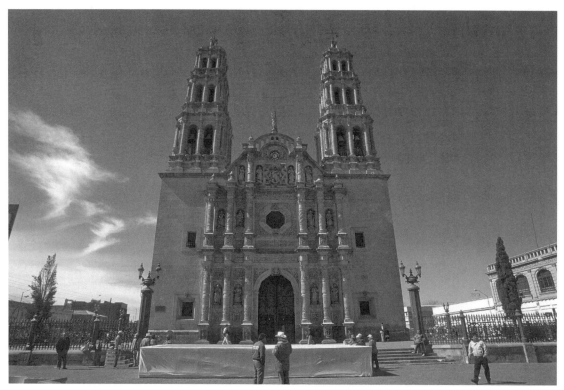

© Peter Langer/EPD Photos

The Roman Catholic cathedral in the capital, Chihuahua, is built of pink stone. It took almost 100 years to complete.

and apples. More than thirty species of apples are grown in the state.

Ranchers raise both beef and dairy cattle, as well as pigs, goats, and sheep on a smaller scale. Chihuahua is also an important producer of milk and cheese.

16 ■ Natural Resources

Forestry is an important economic activity in Chihuahua. Chihuahua has been known for its timber resources and livestock.

Chihuahua is known for its gold and silver mines. It is the country's second largest silver producer after Zacatecas. Silver, lead, and zinc are produced at the Naica mine.

Grupo Mexico operates two lead zinc mines, which both produce silver as a by-product.

Petroleos Mexicanos (Pemex), the state oil company, is the world's fifth largest oil company and the single most important entity in the Mexican economy. Pemex's natural gas pipeline connects to the US natural gas pipeline at nine locations, crossing the border into California, Arizona, and Texas (at the Chihuahua border at Ciudad Juárez, among other locations).

17 ■ Energy and Power

Mexico's first geothermal (using heat from the earth's interior) power plant began operation in 1973 at the Cierro Prieto in Chihuahua, near the US border. In the late 1990s, the government-owned Comision Federal de Electridad (Electric Commission or CFE) raised prices for electricity, triggering widespread protests.

18 ■ Health

The state of Chihuahua has 38 general hospitals, 530 outpatient centers, and 86 surgical centers.

Most of the Mexican population is covered under a government health plan. The IMSS (Instituto Mexicano de Seguro Social) covers the general population. The ISSSTE (Instituto de Seguridad y Servicios Sociales de Trabajadores del Estado) covers state workers.

19 ■ Housing

As of 2000, 66% of the housing in Chihuahua was considered in need of only minor repairs or of no repairs. About 24% needed moderate upgrading, while 11% needed to be replaced or completely remodeled.

20 ■ Education

The system of public education was first started by President Benito Juárez in 1867. Public education in Mexico is free for students ages six to sixteen. In 2000, there were about 638,067 school-age students in the state. Many students elect to attend private schools rather than the government-funded public schools. The thirty-one states of Mexico all have at least one state university. The Universidad Autónoma de Chihuahua celebrated its fiftieth anniversary in 2004.

21 ■ Arts

Chihuahua has many theaters including an open air theater, el Teatro de Camara del Instituto de Bellas Artes, and el Teatro de Héroes, an older theater of Victorian design that hosts operas, plays, music, and various types of theatrical presentations.

22 ■ Libraries and Museums

Chihuahua has 145 branches of the national library. There are many museums in Chihuahua including one dedicated to the history of the Mexican Revolution, a museum of modern art, a museum of sacred art, a museum of 19th century art, and a telephone museum.

23 ■ Media

The capital city, Chihuahua, has three papers: *El Diario, El Heraldo de Chihuahua,* and *Tiempo.* The city of Ciudad Juárez publishes *El Diario,* and the city of Parral has *El Sol de Parral.*

24 ■ Tourism, Travel, and Recreation

The city of Creel is the entryway to the western Sierra Madre mountain range known as Copper Canyon (Barranca del Cobre or Sierra Tarahumara). There are many tours of this region, which has six massive gorges that form a canyon system that is four times as large as the Grand Canyon of the United States. Four of the six canyons are deeper than the Grand Canyon. Copper Canyon takes its name from the copper-colored lichen (a type of mossy plant) that grows on the canyon walls. The culture of the indigenous Tarahumara people also attracts tourists to the area.

25 ▪ Sports

The city of Chihuahua has a basketball team, Los Dorados, which plays at the 1,500-seat Gimnasio R. M. Quevedo. There is also a 7,500-seat bullfighting ring. Ciudad Juárez has a baseball team (Los Gallos de Pelea) and a 15,000-seat bullfighting ring in the Plaza Monumental.

26 ▪ Famous People

Francisco "Pancho" Villa (1878–1923) was not born in Chihuahua but earned his reputation as a revolutionary leader in Chihuahua and Durango. Actor Anthony Rudolph Oaxaca Quinn (1915–2001) was born in Chihuahua but moved at age four to Los Angeles, California. His films included *Zorba the Greek* and *Lawrence of Arabia*. David Alfaro Siqueiros (1896–1974), a well-known muralist, has works at the National Preparatory School, Mexico City, and the Plaza Art Center in Los Angeles, California.

27 ▪ Bibliography

Books

DeAngelis, Gina. *Mexico.* Mankato, MN: Blue Earth Books, 2003.

Fisher, Richard D., et al. *The Copper Canyon, Chihuahua, Mexico.* Tucson, AZ: Sunracer, 2003.

Supples, Kevin. *Mexico.* Washington, DC: National Geographic Society, 2002.

Web Sites

Mexico for Kids. http://www.elbalero.gob.mx/index_kids.html (accessed on June 15, 2004).

Coahuila

Pronunciation: koh-ah-WEE-lah.

Origin of state name: The natives living in the territory were the Coahuilas. The Spaniards named them Coahuiltecos and called the territory New Extremadura. They later renamed it Coahuila.

Capital: Saltillo.

Entered country: 1917.

Coat of Arms: The lower section depicts walnut trees growing near the Monclova River, seen at sunrise to depict the state rising up after the Mexican Revolution. The Spanish town known as San Francisco de Coahuila (later renamed Monclova) was founded on the banks of the river; it was the capital of Coahuila for many years. In the left panel an oak tree and two wolves represent Biscay, the home province of many of the Spanish settlers. The right panel features a lion and a column, with a banner bearing the words Plus Ultra (Higher).

Holidays: Año Nuevo (New Year's Day—January 1); Día de la Constitución (Constitution Day—February 5); Benito Juárez's birthday (March 21); Primero de Mayo (Labor Day—May 1); Revolution Day, 1910 (November 20); and Navidad (Christmas—December 25).

Flag: There is no official flag.

Time: 6 AM = noon Greenwich Mean Time (GMT).

1 ▪ Location and Size

Coahuila, in northern Mexico, is one of the three largest states in Mexico. It has an area of 149,511 square kilometers (57,726 square miles), about the same size as the US state of Michigan. Coahuila is bordered on the north by the US state of Texas; on the east by the Mexican state of Nuevo León; on the south by the Mexican states of Zacatecas, Durango, and San Luis Potosí; and on the west by the Mexican state of Chihuahua. Coahuila has thirty-eight municipalities. Its capital is Saltillo.

The state is crossed from north to south by the Sierra Madre Oriental mountain range. (*Sierra* means mountains in Spanish.) Its mountains include the Sierra El Pino, Sierra Mojada, Melchor Ocampo, Los Novillos, Corazón del Toro, El Tunal, and El Jabalí.

Coahuila also has desert plains with sand dunes. The Bolsón de Mapimí desert is an enormous desert region. The fertile Comarca Lagunera lies in the southeast.

© Robert Frerck/Woodfin Camp

Bilbao dunes.

The most important rivers are the Bravo, Sabinas, San Rodrigo, San Diego, Santa Rosa, Castaños, Boquillas, and Canastas Rivers. The Nazas and Aguanaval Rivers have been dammed.

A large part of its territory is made up by the Bolsón de Mapimí, an enormous desert region characterized by little rain and scant vegetation.

2 ■ Climate

Temperatures average 12°C (53°F) in January and 23°C (73°F) in June and July. Annual rainfall averages 610 millimeters (24 inches), much of which falls during September and October.

3 ■ Plants and Animals

The native plants include species of pine trees and walnut trees. The fibers of the ixtle plant (a type of cactus) are used for handicrafts.

Tortoises nest in the coastal areas, and the waters are filled with all kinds of marine life. Animal life ranges from bears to prairie dogs, wild boars, wolves, raccoons, deer, and berrendos (which resemble deer). Bird species include dwarf parrots and eagles. The hot, dry desert supports rattlesnakes as well.

4 ■ Environmental Protection

As one of the states that borders the

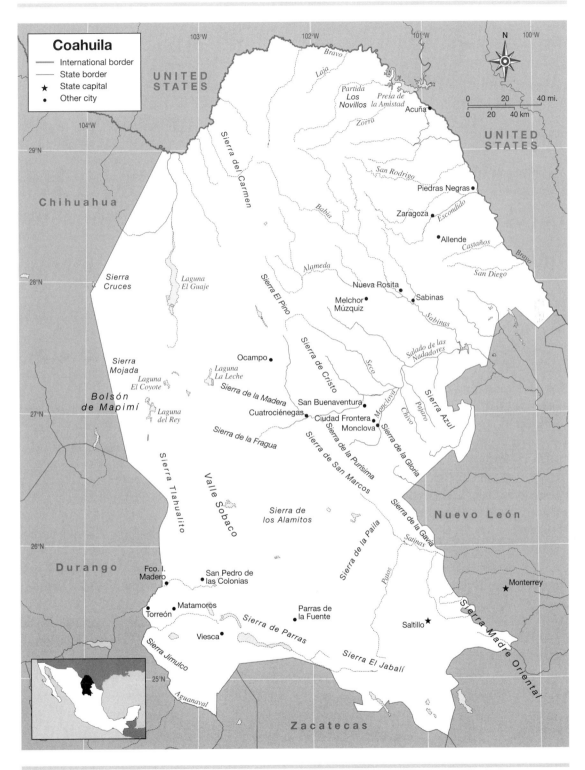

Coahuila

- International border
- State border
- ★ State capital
- • Other city

UNITED STATES

103°W   102°W   101°W   100°W

N

Bravo
Laja
Partida
Los
Novillos
Presa de
la Amistad
Zorra
Acuña

UNITED STATES

104°W

29°N

Chihuahua

Sierra del Carmen

Babía

San Rodrigo

Piedras Negras
Zaragoza *Escondido*
Allende
Castaños
San Diego
Bravo

0   20   40 mi.
0   20   40 km

Alameda

Nueva Rosita
Melchor
Múzquiz
Sabinas
Sabinas

28°N

Sierra
Cruces

Laguna
El Guaje

Sierra El Pino

Salado de las
Nadadores

Ocampo
Sierra de Cristo
Seco
Sierra Azul

Sierra
Mojada

Laguna
La Leche

Laguna
El Coyote

Sierra de la Madera

San Buenaventura
Monclova
Cuatrociénegas
Ciudad Frontera
Monclova
Sierra de la Gloria

27°N

Bolsón
de Mapimí

Laguna
del Rey

Sierra de la Fragua

Sierra de la Purísima

Chivo
Pajaro

Sierra de San Marcos

Nuevo León

Sierra Tlahualito

Valle
Sobaco

Sierra de
los Alamitos

Sierra de la Paila

Sierra de la Gavia
Salinas

26°N

Durango

Fco. I.
Madero

San Pedro de
las Colonias

Putos

Monterrey

Matamoros
Torreón

Parras de
la Fuente

Saltillo

Sierra de Parras

Sierra Madre Oriental

Viesca

Sierra Jimulco

25°N

Sierra El Jabalí

Aguanaval

Zacatecas

United States, Coahuila participates in the Border Environmental Cooperation Commission (BECC). Environmental issues include safety of the water supply and management of hazardous waste. Air pollution is generated by the burning of sugarcane fields.

5 Population, Ethnic Groups, Languages

Coahuila had a total population of 2,298,070 in 2000; of the total, 1,140,195 were men and 1,157,875 were women. The population density was 15 people per square kilometer (39 people per square mile). In 2000, the capital, Saltillo, had a population of 577,352. Almost all residents speak Spanish. A small percentage (0.2%) speak one of the Amerindian languages.

6 Religions

According to the 2000 census, 76% of the population, or 1.7 million people, were Roman Catholic; 6%, or 137,388 people, were Protestant. That year there were also 1,862 Seventh-Day Adventists, 8,108 Mormons, 25,370 Jehovah's Witnesses, and nearly 100,000 people who reported no religion.

7 Transportation

Three major highways connect the cities within Coahuila and connect Coahuila to its neighboring states. The capital, Saltillo, is linked by railroad to other major cities in the state, as well as to Monterrey in Nuevo León, Nuevo Laredo in Tamaulipas, and Mexico City.

There are two airports: Ramos Arizpe airport is 15 minutes away from Saltillo. Plan de Guadalupe International Airport, also near Saltillo, provides air service to Mexico City and to the Texas cities of Dallas, Forth Worth, and Houston.

8 History

When the Spaniards arrived in the mid-1500s, Coahuila was mostly inhabited by groups of hunters and gatherers. In the Lagunera Comarca region, indigenous people had constructed villages. They practiced rudimentary agriculture and fishing.

The Spaniards settled in the region in the late 16th century, when the city of Santiago del Saltillo del Ojo del Agua was founded. The Spaniards brought native people from neighboring Zacatecas to promote settlements, since the natives of Coahuila tended to migrate while hunting animals and gathering food. The conquest of territories by the Spaniards progressed slowly throughout the 17th century. In 1675, Saltillo mayor Antonio Balcárcel Rivadeneyra led an expedition that took control of the Río Grande River and ventured into what is now Texas.

When independence was declared in central Mexico in 1810, Coahuila mostly ignored the conflict between royalists (people loyal to Spain) and patriots (people interested in independence for Mexico). Landowners were more concerned with fighting indigenous revolts and transforming the precarious economy into a productive agricultural region. In 1811, Mariano Jiménez led troops in a movement to promote and consolidate independence in northern Mexico (including Texas). The failure of this effort caused Coahuila to remain under royalist control until 1821. That year the Plan of Iguala allowed for the consolidation of an independent Mexico.

When it declared independence in 1835, Texas was a territory under the jurisdiction of Coahuila. When the Mexican-American War (1846–48) broke out after Texas was annexed to the United States, leading the Mexicans was general and politician Antonio López de Santa Anna (1794–1876). Santa Anna abandoned the patriots of Saltillo, Coahuila, and they were left alone to resist US occupying forces. US troops occupied Saltillo until the war was over and the Guadalupe Hidalgo treaty was signed in 1848. In the treaty, Coahuila ceded all its territories north of the Río Grande. Although some leaders in Coahuila had expressed their intent to join Texas as part of the United States, most preferred to remain a part of Mexico.

Coahuila leader Francisco Madero (1873–1913) published *Presidential Succession,* a book that eventually launched his presidential candidacy in 1910. Some people believed that Porfirio Díaz (1830–1915), who had been leading the country as a dictator since 1876, should be replaced. Madero, angry about Díaz's rule, called for a revolution on November 20, 1910. Madero was elected president in 1911 but was assassinated two years later. His ally, Venustiano Carranza (1859–1920), successfully took control of Mexico and declared victory in the revolution. After a new constitution took effect in 1917, Carranza's national reputation grew. He became the first elected president of Mexico after the revolution.

Since it was the home state of two of the most important leaders of the Mexican Revolution (Madero and Carranza), Coahuila occupies an important role in Mexican history. It is also one of the key states where the dominant political party in Mexican politics, the Institutional Revolutionary Party (PRI), developed and grew.

9 ■ State and Local Government

The constitution dates from 1818, but reforms were adopted in 1951. Since then, the executive power has been vested in a governor, elected democratically every six years for a nonrenewable term. The legislature is comprised of a thirty-five-member Chamber of Deputies. Twenty of the deputies are elected in single member districts and the remaining fifteen by proportional representation. Deputies are elected for nonrenewable three-year terms. The formal separation of powers and check and balances provisions have been undermined by the excessive concentration of power on the hands of the PRI since the end of the revolution.

There are thirty-eight municipalities. Municipal governments are relatively weak, as the state government continues to exercise enormous influence over local authorities. Municipal presidents and councilors are elected for three-year terms and immediate reelection is not allowed.

10 ■ Political Parties

The three main political parties in all of Mexico are the Institutional Revolutionary Party (PRI), the National Action Party (PAN), and Party of the Democratic Revolution (PRD).

The PRI has exercised absolute control in Coahuila. The twenty-six governors who have occupied the office since revolutionary leader Venustiano Carranza abandoned the governorship to become president of Mexico have all belonged to the PRI. PRI candidate Enrique Martínez y Martínez was elected in 1999, reflecting the electoral strength of the party that ruled Mexico since 1917.

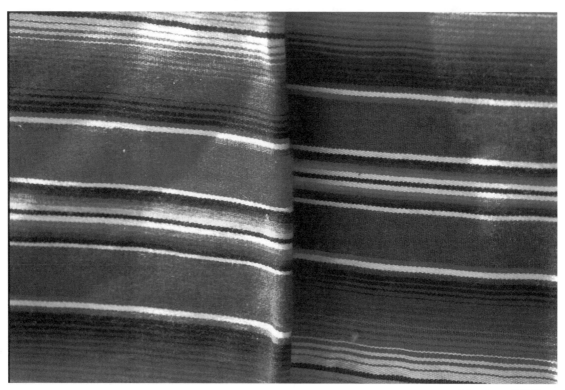

Traditional striped fabric of the serape.

11 ■ Judicial System

The judiciary is independent in theory. Historically the judicial system has been under the control of the state governor. The Superior Tribunal of Justice is comprised of seven members appointed for nonrenewable six-year terms by the governor, with legislature approval. Only qualified attorneys can be appointed. The Tribunal president is elected for a three-year term and can be reelected once. There is also an electoral tribunal. Local courts complete the state's judicial system.

12 ■ Economy

Mining, agriculture, and manufacturing are all important to the economy. The state produces over one-third of Mexico's steel, which supplies manufacturing facilities operated by US automakers General Motors and DaimlerChrylser. As one of the states that borders the United States, Coahuila has many processing plants, known as maquiladoras. The number and size of these plants grew rapidly after the North American Free Trade Agreement (NAFTA), a trade agreement between Mexico, the United States, and Canada, was enacted.

Among the agricultural products produced in Coahuila are cotton and various food crops, including dairy products.

13 ■ Industry

Much of the state's industry relates to the manufacture of automobiles, an industry that has developed since 1992 when the North American Free Trade Agreement (NAFTA) was signed. There are stamping plants, engine production plants, and vehicle assembly plants. There were about two hundred *maquiladoras* (assembly plants) employing about 100,000 workers in 2003.

14 ■ Labor

The US Bureau of Labor Statistics reported that Mexican workers saw their wages increase 17%, from $2.09 per hour in 1999 to $2.46 per hour in 2000. Wages for workers in Coahuila are slightly below (about 90%) the national average. (The average US worker earned $19.86 per hour in 2000.) After one year, workers are entitled by law to six days paid vacation.

15 ■ Agriculture

Agriculture is an important segment of the economy. Cotton, potatoes, grapes, watermelons, apples, alfalfa, wheat, oats, corn, sorghum, cotton, and nuts are among the state's agricultural crops. Several dams have been built to create reservoirs that can be used for irrigation.

Dairy cattle are raised to supply the state's milk-processing plants.

16 ■ Natural Resources

Mining is an important part of the economy. Although coal accounts for only 4% of Mexico's total energy requirements, the majority of the country's coal reserves are located in Coahuila.

Other minerals mined in Coahuila include iron, titanium, feldspar, lead, and dolomite.

17 ■ Energy and Power

Coal-fired plants supply a relatively small percentage of the country's electricity, but the Federal Electricity Commission (CFE) approves the use of coal to fuel power plants near the Coahuila mines. Coal is being replaced by natural gas in most power plants, since burning Mexican coal produces a high amount of ash and causes air pollution.

18 ■ Health

Coahuila has 38 general hospitals, 334 outpatient centers, and 93 surgical centers.

Most of the Mexican population is covered under a government health plan. The IMSS (Instituto Mexicano de Seguro Social) covers the general population. The ISSSTE (Instituto de Seguridad y Servicios Sociales de Trabajadores del Estado) covers state workers.

19 ■ Housing

Most of the state's housing is adequate. Only 5% of housing is in need of replacement or significant upgrading.

20 ■ Education

The system of public education was first started by President Benito Juárez (1806–1872) in 1867. Public education in Mexico is free for students from ages six to sixteen. Many students elect to go to private schools. There were nearly 500,000 school-age children in Coahuila in 2000.

The thirty-one states of Mexico all have at least one state university. The Universidad Autónoma de Coahuila (Independent University of Coahuila) is in Saltillo.

21 ▓ Arts
Coahuila has a dance group, DanzArte. The state is also famous for the serape (wool cape), and many artisans open their studios for people to watch the making of serapes and to purchase serapes. Coahuila is also noted for works made from wrought iron. There are many theaters and auditoriums featuring dance and music.

22 ▓ Libraries and Museums
Coahuila has 113 branches of the national library. There are twenty-nine museums. The capital, Saltillo, has a museum of science and technology and a bird museum. Torreón has a railroad museum and a museum of paleontology (fossils). Cepeda has a museum on the history of Mexican revolutionary and president Benito Juárez.

23 ▓ Media
The capital city, Saltillo, has two papers: *Palabra* and *Vanguardia.* The city of Piedras Negras has *Zócalo,* and the city of Torreón has four papers: *El Siglo de Torreón, La Opinión, Noticias de El Sol,* and *La Laguna.* There is both conventional and wireless telephone service available in the area around the capital, Saltillo.

24 ▓ Tourism, Travel, and Recreation
Saltillo is a popular tourist destination. The city is sometimes called "Athens of Mexico" because of its rich culture. It is also the "city of the serape" (the famous draping scarf worn by Mexican men and women).

Many buildings in Saltillo are constructed of pink quarry and limestone. Zaragoza Park is a large park in the city. The state fair is held in late July and early August each year in Saltillo. Monclova has the Devil's Cave, which has ancient cave paintings. Also in Monclava, an industrial city, the Feria de Acero (Steel Industry Fair) is held the second week of July each year.

25 ▓ Sports
Saltillo, the capital, hosts the basketball team Lobos. Saltillo's professional baseball team, Los Saraperos de Saltillo, plays in the Parque Francisco I. Madero, which seats 14,000.

Torreón's basketball team, Los Algodoneros de la Comarca, plays in the Municipal Stadium, which seats 2,500. Torreón's soccer team, the Santos Laguna, plays in the Corona stadium, which holds 25,500 people. Torreón also has a minor league baseball team, Los Algondoneros de la Unión Laguna, which plays in the Estdio de la Revolución holding 8, 500 people. Torreón also has a Plaza de Toros (bullfighting ring) that seats 10,000 people.

Monclova's baseball team, Los Acereros del Norte, plays in the Estadio Monclova, which holds 9,000 spectators.

26 ▓ Famous People
Francisco Indalécio Madero (1873–1913) was called the Father of the Revolution for working to overthrow the dictator Porfirio Díaz. Madero was born in Parras, Coahui-

la, on October 30, 1873, and was president from 1911 to 1913.

Revolutionary leader Venustiano Carranza (1859–1920) was born in Ciénegas on December 29, 1859. He was elected president of Mexico in 1917 but was assassinated in 1920 while still in office.

27 ▦ Bibliography

Books

Carew-Miller, Anna. *Famous People of Mexico.* Philadelphia: Mason Crest Publishers, 2003.

DeAngelis, Gina. *Mexico.* Mankato, MN: Blue Earth Books, 2003.

Pasztor, Suzanne B. *The Spirit of Hidalgo: The Mexican Revolution in Coahuila.* East Lansing, MI: Michigan State University Press, 2002.

Supples, Kevin. *Mexico.* Washington, DC: National Geographic Society, 2002.

Web Sites

Mexico for Kids. http://www.elbalero.gob.mx/index_kids.html (accessed on June 15, 2004).

Colima

Pronunciation: koh-LEE-mah.

Origin of state name: From the Náhuatl (Amerindian) word *collimaitl. Colli* means either ancestors or volcano, and *maitl* means domain of.

Capital: Colima.

Entered country: 1857.

Coat of Arms: The coat of arms bears a hieroglyph (a picture with special meaning) in the form of an arm. For the state's early inhabitants (Náhuatl), the arm represented the power of one person over all others. This authority essentially fell to the elders, who were greatly respected and obeyed. The coat of arms therefore symbolizes the strength of the people of Colima to improve their living conditions.

Holidays: Año Nuevo (New Year's Day—January 1); Día de la Constitución (Constitution Day—February 5); Benito Juárez's birthday (March 21); Primero de Mayo (Labor Day—May 1); Revolution Day, 1910 (November 20); and Navidad (Christmas—December 25).

Flag: There is no official flag.

Time: 6 AM = noon Greenwich Mean Time (GMT).

1 ▓ Location and Size

Colima lies in western Mexico. It is bordered on the north, east, and west by the Mexican state of Jalisco; on the southeast by the Mexican state of Michoacán; and on the south by the Pacific Ocean. Its capital city is Colima. The state has an area of 5,433 square kilometers (2,098 square miles), which is about the same size as the US state of Delaware. It is one of the smallest states in Mexico. (The only smaller states are Aguascalientes, Morelos, Tlaxcala, and the Distrito Federal—Federal District). Colima has ten municipalities.

Colima's landscape consists of mountains, hills, valleys, plains, and deep ravines. A branch of the Sierra Madre mountain range runs through the state. The highest peak in the state is the Colima Volcano at 4,240 meters (13,990 feet), the country's most active volcano. It lies on the border with Jalisco and has erupted over forty times since the 1500s. Damaging earthquakes, the most recent in 2003, are relatively frequent.

Colima's rivers flow from north to south into the Pacific Ocean. Major rivers include the Marabasco River and the Coahuayana (or the Naranjo) River. The Armería River, the largest of all, originates in Jalisco

The highest peak in the state is the Colima Volcano at 4,240 meters (13,990 feet), the country's most active volcano. It lies on the border with Jalisco and has erupted over forty times since the 1500s.

and crosses the central part of the state. The main fresh water lagoons are the Alcuzahue and the Amela in the municipality of Tecomán.

Colima has 160 kilometers (100 miles) of coastline. The Cuyutlán Lagoon is a large saltwater lagoon on the Pacific coast. It is used for salt production. The Manzanillo and Santiago Bays are both on the Pacific coastline.

The state includes the Revillagigedo Archipelago in the Pacific. It also includes Roca Partida, San Benedicto, Clarión, and Socorro islands.

2 ■ Climate

Temperatures are fairly constant year round, with variation depending on elevation. In the winter, temperatures range from 20°C to 28°C (68°F to 76°F). Summers are hotter, with temperatures ranging from 28°C to 34°C (82°F to 93°F). The rainy season falls from June through October, when much of the average annual rain falls. Rainfall during those months averages 1,010 millimeters (40 inches).

3 ■ Plants and Animals

Colima is one of the richest Mexican regions in species and one of the top

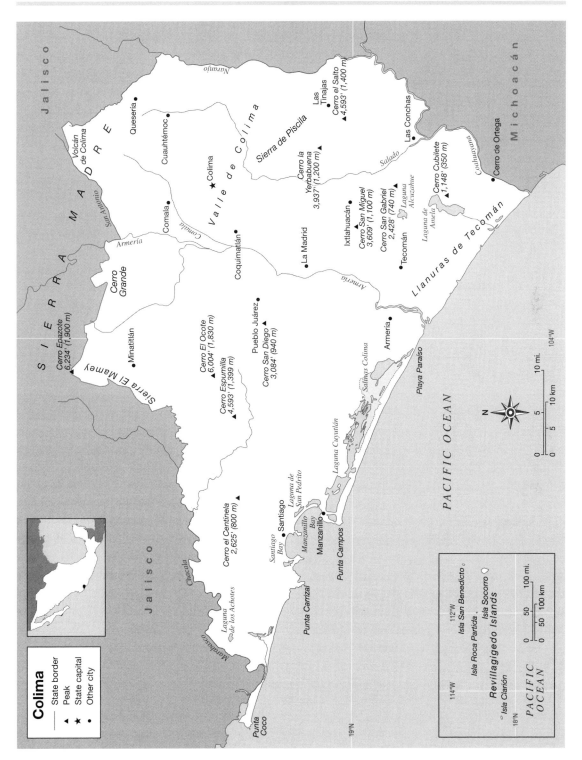

Colima

- State border
- ▲ Peak
- ★ State capital
- • Other city

Jalisco

Volcán de Colima

S I E R R A M A D R E

Cerro Epazote
6,234' (1,900 m)

Sierra El Mamey

Queseria

Cuauhtémoc

★Colima

Comala

Coquimatlán

Cerro Grande

Minatitlán

Cerro El Ocote
6,004' (1,830 m)

Cerro Espumilla
4,593' (1,399 m)

Pueblo Juárez

Cerro San Diego
3,084' (940 m)

Cerro el Centinela
2,625' (800 m)

Santiago

Santiago Bay

Manzanillo Bay

Manzanillo

Laguna de San Pedrito

Laguna Cuyutlán

Punta Campos

Punta Carrizal

Punta Coco

Laguna de los Achotes

Marabasco

Chacala

Jalisco

San Antonio

Armería

Comala

Naranjo

V a l l e d e C o l i m a

Sierra de Piscila

Cerro la Yerbabuena
3,937' (1,200 m)

Las Tinajas

Cerro el Salto
4,593' (1,400 m)

Las Conchas

Salado

Ixtlahuacán

Cerro San Miguel
3,609' (1,100 m)

Cerro San Gabriel
2,428' (740 m)

Laguna Alcuzáhue

Tecomán

La Madrid

Armería

Laguna de Amela

Cerro Cubilete
1,148' (350 m)

Coahuayana

Cerro de Ortega

M i c h o a c á n

Llanuras de Tecomán

Armería

Playa Paraíso

Salinas Colima

PACIFIC OCEAN

N

10 mi.
10 km
5
5
0
0

19°N

104°W

18°N

protected areas in North America for biodiversity.

4 ▪ Environmental Protection

In 2003, Colima received a federal grant to establish a system requiring industries to track pollutants. Sierra de Manantlan Biosphere Reserve straddles the border with Jalisco. Over 2,700 species of plants, 40% of which are native to Mexico, are protected there. About one-fourth of Mexico's species of mammals and one-third of its bird species find habitat in the reserve.

5 ▪ Population, Ethnic Groups, Languages

Colima had a total population of 542,627 in 2000; of the total, 268,192 (49%) were men and 274,435 (51%) were women. The population density was 96 people per square kilometer (249 people per square mile). In 2000, the capital, Colima, had a population of 129,454. Almost all the residents speak Spanish, with less than 1% speaking one of the Amerindian languages.

6 ▪ Religions

According to the 2000 census, 78% of the population, or 425,954 people, were Roman Catholic; just 2%, or 13,214 people, were Protestant. That year there were also 5,185 Jehovah's Witnesses, and nearly 12,000 people who reported no religion.

7 ▪ Transportation

There are 1,960 kilometers (1,225 miles) of highway connecting the state's ten cities. Eight of the ten municipalities have four-lane highways.

The Playa del Oro International Airport serves Manzanillo and the Miguel de la Madrid Airport is near the capital, Colima. Both provide domestic and international air service.

Manzanillo on the Pacific Ocean is Mexico's main deep-sea port. The port is equipped to unload large containers from ships and move them around on 13.5 kilometers (8.4 miles) of railway track. Agricultural grains and cement are among the many products shipped through Manzanillo's port. Manzanillo provides Mexico with shipping routes to the nations of Asia (Japan, South Korea, China, Indonesia, Australia, and New Zealand). It also provides shipping to other nations in the Americas, including Canada, the United States, Guatemala, Costa Rica, Colombia, and Peru.

There is no passenger train service in Colima, but 235 kilometers (147 miles) of railroad track transports cargo from the port and other Colima cities to other locations in Mexico.

8 ▪ History

The first human settlements date back to 300 A.D. Early civilizations, such as the Toltec (around 900) and the Chichimec (around 1100), were the first to build cities and introduce productive agriculture to the region. Colimán, an indigenous leader who ruled in the 15th century, converted Colima into a political, cultural, and military center of Mexico before the arrival on Europeans.

The Spanish tried three times in the early 1500s to colonize Colima but met with fierce resistance from the native population. Finally, Spaniard Gonzalo de Sandoval conquered the region and built a Spanish settlement, San Sebastián de Colina, in 1523. Later,

© Robert Frerck/Woodfin Camp

The Cuyutlán Lagoon is a large saltwater lagoon on the Pacific coast. It is used for salt production.

Viceroy Antonio de Mendoza (c. 1490–1552) visited the city and ordered the construction of a royal road between Mexico City and Colima. (A viceroy is a governor who rules as the representative of a king or queen, in this case of Spain.) By 1575, Colima was already a municipality. It evolved into an important economic, strategic, and cultural center during the colonial period.

When the independence movement broke out in 1810, Colima priest José Antonio Díaz led independence fighters who wanted to follow Miguel Hidalgo and his drive for Mexican independence from Spain. Hidalgo had previously lived and worked as a priest in Colima. Spanish royalists (follow- ers of the king) successfully prevented the independence fighters from gaining control of Colima. The independence struggle continued throughout the decade. Finally in 1821, the royalist forces accepted independence and signed the Plan of Iguala agreement that secured Mexico's independence from Spain.

In 1823, Colima was incorporated into the state of Jalisco. After a short period as a federal territory and as a territory of Michoacán, Colima was declared a state of the Mexican federation in 1857. For a brief period of three months, Colima was the federal capital, under the presidency of Benito Juárez (1806–1872). In November 1864, French troops occupied Colima and incorporated it into the lands effectively ruled by Mexican emperor Maximilian (1832–1867). After Maximilian's defeat, Juárez and, more importantly, Mexican general and politician Porfirio Díaz (1830–1915) received the support of the leaders in Colima. During Porfirio Díaz's presidency (from 1877 to 1880 and then again from 1884 to 1911), economic development favored Colima. A new railroad and important infrastructure investments helped expand agriculture and other economic activities.

In 1910 the Mexican Revolution began. It reached Colima in 1911, when the governor surrendered to the revolutionary forces. After the passage of the Mexican Constitution in 1917, Colima passed its own constitution later that year. The new governor, loyal to the revolutionary victors, assumed power shortly after. However, some political instability remained. Factions loyal to former revolutionary and antirevolutionary leaders continued to operate in Colima. Eventually, in 1943, stability was finally achieved and governors were able to complete their six-year terms without much opposition. The consolidation of Institutional Revolutionary Party (PRI, the most powerful political party in Mexico) rule also reached Colima. PRI candidates successfully won the gubernatorial races without much opposition from the conservative National Action Party (PAN) in the 1950s, 1960s, and 1970s, or the leftist Party of the Democratic Revolution (PRD) starting in the late 1980s.

The PRI candidate Gustavo Alberto Vázquez Montes was elected governor in 2003. He defeated the candidate of the joint PAN-PRD opposition.

9 ■ State and Local Government

With formal separation of powers and check-and-balances provisions, the state of Colima has a unicameral (one chamber) state congress and a strong executive power. The congress is elected every three years for nonrenewable terms. Sixteen of its twenty-five members are elected in single member districts; nine are elected by proportional representation. Because the PRI has exercised control of the powerful governor's office since the end of the revolution, the legislature has not been able to act independently. As politics become more competitive in Colima, the legislature should be more likely to act independently of the governor.

There are ten municipalities, each with a local government. These local governments have limited authority over administrative decisions. Tight control of budgets by the state government reduces the local authorities' leverage and influence. Municipal president and council members are elected for nonrenewable three-year terms.

10 ■ Political Parties

The three main political parties in all of Mexico are the Institutional Revolutionary Party (PRI), the National Action Party (PAN), and Party of the Democratic Revolution (PRD). The PRI has dominated Colima politics since the end of the Mexican Revolution (1910–1920). All Colima governors have belonged to that party. Despite more guarantees for opposition parties and free and fair elections since the early 1990s, the PRI continues to dominate politics in the state. A joint PAN-PRD effort to win the gubernatorial race in 2003 failed.

The PRI candidate successfully defeated the opposition consensus candidate.

11 ■ Judicial System

The highest court in Colima is the Superior Tribunal of Justice. Its members are appointed for nonrenewable six-year terms by the governor with congressional approval. Only qualified attorneys can be appointed to those posts. In addition, an electoral tribunal and several different local courts make up the judiciary in Colima. Yet, as is the case with the other state level powers, the dominance enjoyed by the PRI throughout most of the 20th century has made it difficult for any branch of government to function independently.

12 ■ Economy

The manufacture of iron, services, tourism, agriculture and agricultural product processing, mining, and fishing are the components of the economy in Colima. As of 2000, the economy was growing at about 5% annually. The per capita gross state product was P56,364 (P = pesos) per year, or just over US$5,000 per person.

13 ■ Industry

Colima ranks first among Mexico's states in the production of lemon oil and second in the production of iron. Iron ore is processed at Lázaro Cardenas. Other important industries include the manufacture of beverages (including dairy products), metal structures, food preservatives, and wooden furniture. There are also facilities where grains are processed into cereals. Colima also is home to a number of printers and publishing companies.

Tecomán, near the coast in the center of the state, is the main center where cement is produced. Also near Tecomán is one of the world's largest facilities where pectin is produced. Pectin is used to make jellies, among other things. The pectin is produced for export to the United States, Europe, and Asia.

14 ■ Labor

The US Bureau of Labor Statistics reported that Mexican workers saw their wages increase 17%, from $2.09 per hour in 1999 to $2.46 per hour in 2000. (The average US worker earned $19.86 per hour in 2000.) After one year, workers are entitled by law to six days paid vacation.

From 1999 to 2000, formal employment increased by 4,331 jobs. Unemployment stood at 1.9% in the cities of Colima and Villa de Alvarez, and less than 1% in the port city of Manzanillo.

15 ■ Agriculture

Colima is Mexico's largest producer of sour lemons, tamarind (long, brown pod with sweet/sour pulp), and guanabana (deep green fruit covered with small, soft spines). It is the country's second-largest producer of coconuts. Among the agricultural products are candies produced from coconuts.

Also produced in Colima are fruits including the Mexican lemon (limón), melons, mangoes, papaya, watermelon, yellow seedless watermelons, and bananas. Other crops include corn, sugar cane, jalapeño chiles, cherry tomatoes, and cucumbers.

Palms are also cultivated for use in landscaping, and palm fibers are used to weave hats, placemats, floor mats, and other items.

© Robert Frerck/Woodfin Camp

The city of Manzanillo lies on the Pacific coast.

16 ■ Natural Resources

The Pacific Ocean waters are rich with marine life. There is commercial fishing for tuna, giant squid, and shark, with processing plants located near the port of Manzanillo. Colima ranks second among all the states in tuna production. Sport fishing is also popular.

17 ■ Energy and Power

Electricity for the entire state is produced by two coal-burning power plants in Manzanillo. The plants also sell the surplus power (as much as 95% of the electricity produced) to other Mexican states and to other countries in the region.

18 ■ Health

The state of Colima has 10 general hospitals, 153 outpatient centers, and 16 surgical centers throughout the state.

Most of the Mexican population is covered under a government health plan. The IMSS (Instituto Mexicano de Seguro Social) covers the general population. The ISSSTE (Instituto de Seguridad y Servicios Sociales de Trabajadores del Estado) covers state workers.

19 ■ Housing

Housing styles vary widely. As of 2000, over 70% of Colima's housing stock was considered in good repair, with no problems requiring upgrading. A small percentage (8%) of the housing was categorized as needing "replacement or significant upgrading." In cities, many houses are stucco, often featuring large cracks, evidence of earthquake activity. In the small villages, housing may be constructed from cement blocks or twigs and corrugated iron.

20 ▦ Education

The system of public education was first started by President Benito Juárez in 1867. Public education is free for all students from ages six to sixteen. There were about 115,000 school-age children in the state in 2000. Many students elect to go to private schools. Families who can afford it send their children to private schools, while the poor often attend public schools with few materials.

The Universidad de Colima (University of Colima) and the Technological Institute of Colima are both located in the capital. The Monterrey Institute of Technology and Higher Education, the main campus of which is in Monterrey, Nuevo León, has a branch campus in Colima.

21 ▦ Arts

The state of Colima has over twenty theaters, many of them open-air style. One of the best known is the Teatro Hidalgo. Most major cities sponsor exhibitions and cultural fairs.

22 ▦ Libraries and Museums

Colima has 49 branches of the national library system. It also has 19 museums including the salt museum in the city of Armería. In the capital, Colima, are the Museo Regional de Historia (Museum of Regional History), the Museo de Artes Populares (Folk Art Museum), and the Museo de las Culturas de Occidente (Museum of Western Culture).

23 ▦ Media

In the capital of Colima, the newspaper *Diario de Colima* (Diary of Colima) is published. Internet service and cable television are available in Manzanillo and the city of Colima.

24 ▦ Tourism, Travel, and Recreation

The city of Colima is located at the base of an active volcano, the Volcan de Fuego. The Museo Regional de Historia (Museum of Regional History) houses displays of pre-Hispanic civilizations. The nearby village of Suchitlán is famous for its maskmakers. Manzanillo is known for its beautiful beaches. Sportfishing is popular: every February Manzanillo hosts the International Sailfish Tournament.

Beaches line the nearly 160 kilometer (100 mile) Pacific coast. Some beaches are covered with pebbles, while others have powdery white or black volcanic sand.

A favorite souvenir is the Colima dog, a replica of a ceramic dog figurine dating from the 1500s when Amerindian cultures flourished in the region.

25 ▦ Sports

Colima has a professional basketball team known as the Tuberos.

26 ▦ Famous People

José Antonio Díaz led the drive for independence starting in 1810. Vázquez Montes (b.1962) was elected governor in 2003.

27 ▪ Bibliography

Books

DeAngelis, Gina. *Mexico.* Mankato, MN: Blue Earth Books, 2003.

Supples, Kevin. *Mexico.* Washington, DC: National Geographic Society, 2002.

Web Sites

Mexico for Kids. http://www.elbalero.gob.mx/index_kids.html (accessed on June 15, 2004).

Distrito Federal

Pronunciation: dees-TREE-toh feh-deh-RAHL.

Origin of state name: Describes the location of the federal government of Mexico.

Capital: Ciudad de México (Mexico City).

Established: 1824.

Coat of Arms: The coat of arms contains a picture of a golden castle that is surrounded by three stone bridges. There are two lions supporting the castle tower. Around the border of the shield are ten thorny cactus leaves.

Holidays: Año Nuevo (New Year's Day—January 1); Día de la Constitución (Constitution Day—February 5); Benito Juárez's birthday (March 21); Primero de Mayo (Labor Day—May 1); Revolution Day, 1910 (November 20); and Navidad (Christmas—December 25).

Flag: There is no official flag.

Time: 6 AM = noon Greenwich Mean Time (GMT).

1 ■ Location and Size

The Distrito Federal (DF, Federal District) is the capital of Mexico. (Most of its territory is occupied by Mexico City.) It has an area of 1,547 square kilometers (597 square miles). It is about ten times the size of the District of Columbia, the US capital. Although there are no municipalities in Mexico's Distrito Federal, there are sixteen political districts.

The Distrito Federal is located in the center of the country. It is bordered on the north and west by the state of México and on the south by the Mexican state of Morelos.

The Distrito Federal lies on the high valley of Mexico, where the elevation is 2,280 meters (7,525 feet). (The high valley also encompasses parts of the Mexican states of Hidalgo, Puebla, Tlaxcala, and México.) The high valley is surrounded by mountains. Two volcanoes—Popocatépetl and Ixtaccíhuatl—are sometimes visible from the DF. One of the best-known canals in the Federal District is the Xochimilco canal.

2 ■ Climate

The climate is generally dry, with the greatest rainfall occurring during the

Henk Sierdsema/Saxifraga/EPD Photos

Aerial view of Mexico City.

summer months of June, July, and August. Average annual rainfall is 107 centimeters (42 inches). Average overall temperature is 14°C (58°F). In May, the warmest month, the average daily high temperature is 26°C (79°F). In January, the coldest month, the average daily high is 19°C (66°F).

In 1985, the DF region was struck by a devastating earthquake.

3 ■ Plants and Animals

The area was once home to dense forests. Deforestation and heavy development has reduced much of the habitat of the native animals. During the winter months, migrating butterfly species may be viewed around the DF.

The government has created special reserves for protection of native plants and animals. The Chichinautzin Ecological Reserve, established in the late 1980s, has volcanic craters that sprout unique vegetation. Ajusco National Park has pine and oak forests. Xochimilco floating gardens is a popular tourist spot. Native animals can be seen in the zoo in Chapultepec Park.

4 ■ Environmental Protection

Mexico City has some of the worst air pollution of any city in the world. In 1988, the government passed a law aimed at

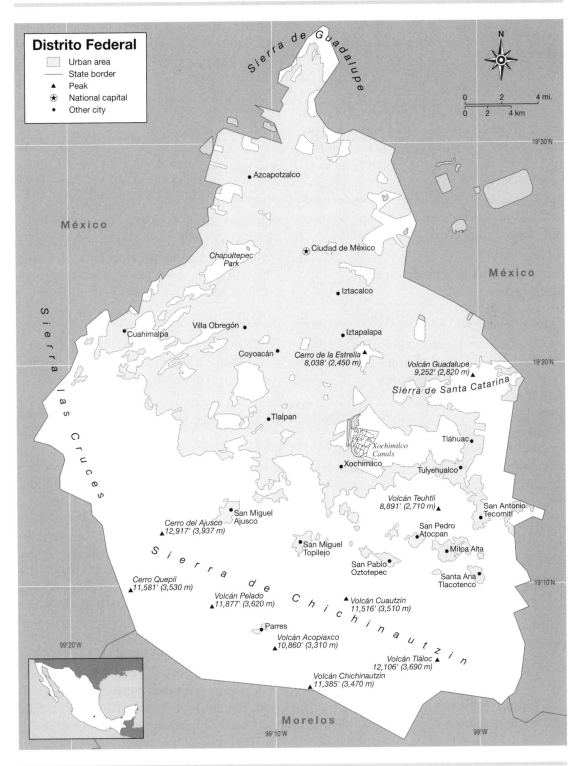

Distrito Federal

- Urban area
- State border
- ▲ Peak
- ⊛ National capital
- • Other city

N

| 0 | 2 | 4 mi. |
| 0 | 2 | 4 km |

Sierra de Guadalupe

19°30'N

• Azcapotzalco

México

Chapúltepec Park

⊛ Ciudad de México

México

• Iztacalco

Sierra las Cruces

Villa Obregón •
Cuahimalpa •

• Iztapalapa

Coyoacán •   Cerro de la Estrella ▲
              8,038' (2,450 m)

Volcán Guadalupe
9,252' (2,820 m) ▲

19°20'N

Sierra de Santa Catarina

• Tlalpan

Xochimilco Canals

Tláhuac •

• Xochimilco

Tulyehualco •

Volcán Teuhtli
8,891' (2,710 m) ▲

San Antonio
Tecomitl •

• San Miguel
Ajusco
Cerro del Ajusco
▲*12,917' (3,937 m)*

San Pedro
Atocpan •

• San Miguel
Topilejo

• Milpa Alta

Cerro Quepil
▲*11,581' (3,530 m)*

San Pablo
Oztotepec •

Santa Ana
Tlacotenco •

19°10'N

Volcán Pelado
▲*11,877' (3,620 m)*

▲ Volcán Cuautzin
11,516' (3,510 m)

• Parres

Volcán Acopiaxco
▲*10,860' (3,310 m)*

Volcán Tláloc ▲
12,106' (3,690 m)

Volcán Chichinautzin
▲*11,385' (3,470 m)*

Sierra de Chichinautzin

99°20'W

99°10'W

99°W

Morelos

improving air quality. Regulations aimed at reducing exhaust emissions from the four million cars registered in the DF have resulted in improved air quality as of 2004.

Mexico's first national park, Desierto de los Leones (Desert of the Lions), was established in the DF in 1917. It is a rich forest area (the name desert came from its remote location in 1917). In response, the government launched a program to try to restore the health of the forest. Trees are being replanted and woodpeckers are being reintroduced.

5 ▓ Population, Ethnic Groups, Languages

Distrito Federal had a total population of 8,605,239 in 2000; of the total, 4,110,485 (48%) were men and 4,494,754 (52%) were women. The population density was 5,799 people per square kilometer (15,019 people per square mile). The Distrito Federal is the most densely populated region of the country. Almost all residents speak Spanish, but about 1.8% of the population speaks one of the indigenous languages as their first language.

6 ▓ Religions

According to the 2000 census, 81% of the population, or 7 million people, were Roman Catholic; 3%, or 277,400 people, were Protestant. That year there were also 7,852 Seventh-Day Adventists, 21,893 Mormons, 74,140 Jehovah's Witnesses, and 18,380 Jews. Over 280,000 people reported no religion.

7 ▓ Transportation

Mexico-Benito Juárez Airport provides international flights to and from the Distrito Federal. Mexico City has been served by the Sistema de Transporte Colectivo Metro, an extensive metro system (over 200 kilometers/125 miles), since the 1960s. More than four million people travel on it each day. The fare is approximately US$0.20.

8 ▓ History

Mexico City is one of the oldest cities continuously inhabited in Latin America. Remains found at Tlatilco point to 1500 B.C. as the first time when a permanent settlement was built in Mexico City. Between 100 and 900 A.D. the center of human activity in the central valley of Mexico moved to Teotihuacán, an area north of modern day Mexico City. There, impressive pyramids were built as sites of worship for the Sun and the Moon. The valley where the city of Mexico is located was populated by Toltec Indians who began to grow and expand from southern Mexico and reached Teotihuacán after the Teotihuacán culture had begun its decline.

During the 13th century, Mexica Indians, also known as Aztecs, arrived in the region. According to the historical myth, they left a northern (probably mythical) city of Aztlán. They were led by their god, Huitzilopochtli, represented by a warrior-like figure. The myth says that when they arrived in the lake-filled region, the Aztecs witnessed the vision of an eagle devouring a snake while perched on a cactus. They believed that this was a message that their god wanted them to stay there. Tenochtitlán-Mexico was founded on June 8, 1325.

Under the leadership of monarchs Izcoatl, Montezuma I (Moctezuma I, d. 1469), Axayacatl (15th century), Tizoc, Ahuizotl (d. 1503), and Montezuma II (Moctezuma II,

1466–1520), the Aztecs emerged as the most important civilization in the central valley of Mexico. The highly disciplined warriors, who took the eagle and jaguar as their symbols, rapidly expanded the areas under Aztec domination. Yet, the Aztecs also absorbed and incorporated religious beliefs and cultural values of the groups they entered into contact with and dominated.

One of the most impressive constructions in Mexico City was the Templo Mayor, a double pyramid dedicated to the gods Tlaloc (god of water and rain) and Huitzilopochtli (god of war). They believed that Templo Mayor was the center of a universe, and human sacrifices were required to sustain it as such. In addition, there were other temples dedicated to Quetzalcóatl (father of civilization), Tezcatlipoca (god who creates and changes all things), and Ehecatl (god of wind). Together with the temples, the city rapidly grew as a commercial and military center of a vast Aztec empire. Located in the middle of a number of small lakes, the city gave way to the construction of a number of canals that surrounded plots of lands, called *chinampas*.

When the Spaniards arrived in the 1500s, Mexico-Tenochtitlán was probably one of the most populated cities in the world. Its structures and buildings must have deeply impressed the Spanish conquistadores (conquerors). Because of a religious myth, Aztecs expected the return of Quetalzcóatl. Believing Spanish explorer Hernán Cortés (1485–1547) was the returning god, Emperor Montezuma II met Cortés at the entrance of the city to welcome him. Cortés imprisoned Montezuma and moved on to kill many of the Aztec nobility. Despite the resistance of the Aztecs led by Cuahtémoc (c.

1495–1522), Cortés successfully conquered Mexico-Tenochtitlán on August 13, 1521.

Cortés quickly moved to control the rest of the central valley of Mexico but made Mexico-Tenochtitlán the capital city of the new Spanish territory. Roman Catholic churches were built on top of the ruins of Aztec temples, and the new government buildings replaced other sacred Aztec constructions. The Mexican presidential palace, the city's cathedral, and the main central square were located exactly in the same place where the Aztec's most important buildings were erected. That gives Mexico City a profound sense of the dramatic changes that occurred with the arrival of the Spanish conquistadores. It also reflects the deep history of a city that has been one of the world's greatest cities for centuries. Most of the people of Mexico are *mestizo* (mixed Amerindian and European descent). They are like Mexico City, where two rich and expanding civilizations came together.

After Cortés conquered it, Mexico-Tenochtitlan (now Mexico City) became the center of colonial rule—through the 16th, 17th, and 18th centuries, and through the heart of the independence movement between 1810 and 1821. It was at the center of the political instability that characterized Mexico between 1823 and 1867. It was the place where president Benito Juárez (1806–1872) began adopting his celebrated reforms. Mexico City was the main objective of the revolutionary leaders of 1910.

Plaza de la Constitución, the square in the center of the city (commonly referred to as the *Zócalo*), symbolizes the three cultures of Mexico City: the original Aztec, the invading Spanish, and the resulting Mexican culture that blends the two. The DF is one of the most populated cities in the world. It

Mosaics depicting Mexico's history and future cover the central library of the Universidad Nacional Autónoma de México (UNAM) in Mexico City. The mosaics, listed in the Guinness Book of World Records *as the largest in the world, measure over 40,000 square feet (4,000 square meters).*

was the site of the Olympic Games in 1968, when drug testing was first introduced. The city experienced rapid growth in the 1960s, 1970s, and 1980s.

By the 1970s, the city began to experience extreme problems with air pollution. Mountains surrounding the city exacerbated the problem, since they caused the air to be trapped over the city.

9 ■ State and Local Government

The chief of government (*jefe de gobierno*) is the chief executive (or mayor) in the Distrito Federal. Previously appointed by the president as a cabinet minister, since 1997 the chief executive has been democratically elected, by those residing in the Distrito Federal, for a six-year, nonrenewable term. The first elected chief of government was Cuauhtémoc Cárdenas Solórzano (b.1934). The legislative assembly of the DF is comprised of sixty-six members, forty elected in single member districts and twenty-six elected by proportional representation. The chief of government of the DF is elected concurrently with the president of Mexico on a separate ballot. As in other DFs, the federal government retains some authority to decide on matters that pertain to financial and administrative issues.

The local and state governments are the same, since the Federal District is the local government of the capital city of Mexico.

10 ▢ Political Parties

The three main political parties in all of Mexico are the Institutional Revolutionary Party (PRI), the National Action Party (PAN), and Party of the Democratic Revolution (PRD). These three parties have a strong presence in the DF. Voters first democratically elected their chief of government in 1997. Former PRD presidential candidate Cuauhtemoc Cárdenas Solórzano won the election. The PRD's Andrés Manuel López Obrador won the 2000 election and emerged as one of the most important contenders for the 2006 presidential election. The PRD is strongest in the DF, but the PAN has also made inroads. Since the PRI has mostly lost support in urban areas, its strength in the DF has also diminished significantly since the mid-1980s.

11 ▢ Judicial System

The Superior Tribunal of Justice is the highest court in the Distrito Federal. Its members are appointed by the chief of government, with congressional approval, for renewable six-year terms. Although there is also an electoral tribunal and lower courts, the presence of the national Supreme Court and the Federal Electoral Tribunal usually render the Federal District Superior Tribunal and Electoral Tribunal less important than its counterparts in the other thirty-one states. Yet, as the

Distrito Federal slowly changes from being a bureaucracy highly controlled by the federal government into a more state-like autonomous entity, the independence, the autonomy, and the importance of the federal district judicial system will become more important.

12 ▢ Economy

Over 10% of Mexico's gross domestic product (GDP) is produced in the DF. Many manufacturing concerns are headquartered in the DF; it is also a center for Mexico's tourism industry.

13 ▢ Industry

Major industries located in the DF include the manufacture of auto parts, food products, electrical equipment, electronics, machine tools, and heavy machinery.

14 ▢ Labor

The US Bureau of Labor Statistics reported that Mexican workers saw their wages increase 17%, from $2.09 per hour in 1999 to $2.46 per hour in 2000. (The average US worker earned $19.86 per hour in 2000.) After one year, workers are entitled by law to six days paid vacation.

15 ▢ Agriculture

A few small dairy farms lie on the outskirts of the city, with the milk and cheese sold locally. Some families also raise pigs and chickens in backyard pens. A typical family might keep three pigs and one or two dozen chickens. Some of the animals are consumed by the family, but most are raised to be sold by local butcher shops. Vegetables and fruits are also raised, but only in small family gardens.

16 ■ Natural Resources

There was once logging in the DF, but most of the forests are now protected.

17 ■ Energy and Power

The Federal Electricity Commission (CFE) manages the generation of electricity in Mexico; the smaller, but also government-owned, Luz y Fuerza del Centro (LFC) supplies electricity to much of the DF.

18 ■ Health

The Distrito Federal (Mexico City) has 109 general hospitals, 699 outpatient centers, and 589 surgical centers.

Most of the Mexican population is covered under a government health plan. The IMSS (Instituto Mexicano de Seguro Social) covers the general population. The ISSSTE (Instituto de Seguridad y Servicios Sociales de Trabajadores del Estado) covers state workers.

19 ■ Housing

Housing in the DF varies from luxury townhouses and apartments to housing built from poor quality materials. About 10% of the housing is in need of upgrading. The rapid growth in population in the DF means that there is an ongoing shortage of affordable housing.

20 ■ Education

The system of public education was first started by President Benito Juárez in 1867. Public education in Mexico is free for students from ages six to sixteen. There were about 1.5 million school-age children in the DF in 2000. Many students elect to go to private schools, especially those sponsored by the Roman Catholic Church. The thirty-one states of Mexico all have at least one state university. The National University of Mexico (UNAM) is located in the DF, as are El Colegio de Mexico (College of Mexico) and the Instituto Politécnico Nacional (National Polytechnic Institute).

21 ■ Arts

Mexico City is home to many dance and music performing arts groups. The Ballet Folklórico Nacional de Mexico (National Folk Ballet of Mexico) performs in the Palacio de Bellas Artes. Three other companies—Ballet Independiente, Ballet Neoclásico, and Ballet Contemporánea—perform in Mexico City. There are three major orchestras (including a children's symphony orchestra). ¡Que Payasos! (Clowns) is a popular rock-and-roll group that performs at festivals, especially for young people. There are over thirty-seven theaters and auditoriums sponsoring plays, concerts, and other types of performances.

22 ■ Libraries and Museums

There are 390 branches of the national library system in the Distrito Federal. There are also 127 museums. The most important museums are the art studio of famous painter Diego Rivera (1886–1957); an archeological museum; the home of artist Frida Kahlo (1907–1954); a national zoo; a science museum; a museum of paleontology (the study of fossils); a stamp museum; a mural museum dedicated to the art of Diego Rivera; a museum of the Mexican Revolution (1910–1920); a cultural institute of Mexico and Israel; the Palace of Fine Arts; the Basilica of the Virgin of Guadalupe (patron saint of

Mexico); a Bible museum; an Olympic museum; Chapultepec Castle (located in Chapultepec Park—a huge city park); the archeological museum of Xochimilco; and many others.

23 ▌ Media

Mexico City has numerous newspapers. Some of the most popular ones are *Cuestión, Diario de México, Diario Oficial de la Federación, El Economista, El Heraldo de México, El Sol de México, El Universal, Esto, Etcerera, Excelcior, Expanción, La Afición, La Crónica de Hoy, La Prensa, Novedades, Reforma,* and *Uno Mas Uno.*

24 ▌ Tourism, Travel, and Recreation

Mexico City's downtown area has a beautiful baroque cathedral called the Catedral Metropolitana. Alameda Central, dating from the 17th century, is the oldest park in the country. The Palacio de Bellas Artes has murals by Diego Rivera and David Alfaro Siqueiros (1896–1974) and crystal carvings of Mexico's famous volcanoes, Popocatépetl and Iztaccihuatl. The Zona Rosa (Pink Zone), a famous shopping area, also has two beautiful statues, La Diana Cazadora and the statue of Cristóbal Colón (Christopher Columbus). Chapultepec Park houses the castle of the former emperor Maximilian (1832–1867) and empress Carlotta (1840–1927), a zoo and botanical gardens, and the famous Museum of Anthropology, which has the old Aztec calendar and a huge statue of Tlaloc, the Aztec rain god. The main avenue of Mexico is La Avenida de la Independencia, featuring the statue of the Angel of Independence, a famous land-mark of the city. The shrine of Our Lady of Guadalupe, the patron saint of Mexico, is visited by thousands of pilgrims, some who climb the steps on their knees. The floating gardens of Xochimilco may be viewed by boat. University City houses the Universidad Autónoma de México (UNAM); its modern campus buildings feature murals and mosaics by Diego Rivera on their outer walls.

Bullfighting is popular in Mexico City. Spectators may choose to pay higher prices to guarantee seats in the shade, since the sun in Mexico City can be scorching.

25 ▌ Sports

Soccer is the most popular sport, and Mexico City has six soccer stadiums. Four teams—National Team, Atlante, América, and Necaxa—play their home games in the huge Estadio Azteca (Aztec Stadium); it seats 114,465 people and was the site of the World Cup finals in 1970 and 1986. The soccer team from the Universidad Autónoma de México plays in the 72,449-seat Olympic Stadium, built for the 1968 Olympics. Another soccer team, Cruz Azul, plays in a 39,000-seat stadium.

The professional baseball team, Diablos Rojos, plays in the 26,000-seat Foro Sol stadium. Mexico City also hosts bullfighting in the 40,000-seat Plaza Mexico and in the 10,000-seat Plaza de Toreo Cuatro Caminos. Toluca has minor league soccer teams that play in the 26,000-seat Nemesio Diez stadium. Nezahualcayotl has a professional soccer team, Neza, which plays in the 37,000-seat Neza 86 stadium.

26 ■ Famous People

Hernán Cortés (1485–1547) was a Spanish conquistador who conquered Aztec emperor Montezuma II to become the founder of Spanish Mexico. Though born in Spain, after his death his remains were placed in a vault at the Hospital de Jesus chapel, which he helped build. Octavio Paz (1914–1998), winner of the 1990 Nobel Prize for Literature, was born in Mexico City. Composer Carlos Chávez (1899–1978) produced works that combined Mexican, Indian, and Spanish-Mexican influences. Cantinflas (Mario Moreno Reyes 1911–1993) was a popular comedian, film producer, and writer who appeared in more than fifty-five films, including a role as Passepartoute in the 1956 version of *Around the World in Eighty Days.* Agustín Lara (1900–1970) was a popular composer who made his mark in the film industry from 1930 to 1950, a period known as the Golden Age of Mexican cinema. Carlos Fuentes (b. 1928) is a renowned writer, editor, and diplomat. He was head of the department of cultural relations in Mexico's ministry of foreign affairs from 1956 to 1959 and Mexican ambassador to France from 1975 to 1977. His fiction works deal with Mexican history and identity and include *A Change of Skin, Terra Nostra,* and *The Years with Laura Díaz* (all of which have been translated into English from Spanish). José Joaquín Fernández de Lizardi (1776–1827) was a journalist, satirical novelist, and dramatist, known by his pseudonym El Pensador Mexicano. His best known work is *El Periquillo Sarniento* (The Itching Parrot). Manuel Gutiérrez Nájera (1859–95) is considered to be one of the first Mexican modernist poets. The life of painter Frida Kahlo (1907–1954) was the subject of a 2002 feature film, *Frida,* starring Salma Hayek.

27 ■ Bibliography

Books

Caistor, Nick. *Mexico City: A Literary and Cultural Companion.* New York: Interlink Books, 2000.

Carew-Miller, Anna. *Famous People of Mexico.* Philadelphia: Mason Crest Publishers, 2003.

Laidlaw, Jill A. *Frida Kahlo.* Danbury, CT: Franklin Watts, 2003.

Supples, Kevin. *Mexico.* Washington, DC: National Geographic Society, 2002.

Web Sites

Mexico City. http://www.mexicocity.com (accessed on June 17, 2004).

Mexico for Kids. http://www.elbalero.gob.mx/index_kids.html (accessed on June 15, 2004).

Durango

Pronunciation: doo-RAHN-goh.

Origin of state name: The name is believed to have been given to the region by Spanish settlers from the Basque region of Spain. It means "fertile land, with rivers surrounded by mountains."

Capital: Durango.

Entered country: 1825.

Coat of Arms: The oak tree with two wolves represents Biscay, the home province of many of the Spanish settlers; the crown above the coat of arms represents the king of Spain.

Holidays: Año Nuevo (New Year's Day—January 1); Día de la Constitución (Constitution Day—February 5); Benito Juárez's birthday (March 21); Primero de Mayo (Labor Day—May 1); Revolution Day, 1910 (November 20); and Navidad (Christmas—December 25).

Flag: There is no official flag.

Time: 6 AM = noon Greenwich Mean Time (GMT).

1 ▌ Location and Size

Durango is located in northern Mexico. One of the largest states in Mexico, it covers an area of 121,776 square kilometers (47,018 square miles), about the same size as the US state of Mississippi. Durango is bordered by the Mexican state of Chihuahua on the north; by the Mexican states of Nayarit and Jalisco on the south; by the Mexican states of Zacatecas and Coahuila on the east; and by the Mexican state of Sinaloa on the west. Durango is divided into thirty-nine municipalities. The capital is also called Durango.

The Sierra Madre Occidental and other smaller mountain ranges (*sierras*) cross the state from northwest to southeast. Deep canyons and a flat plain are located between the valley and semi-desert regions. Valleys, including the Guadiana valley, are separated by the Oso, Guajalote, Magdalena, Coneto, and Gamón mountains (sierras).

The Florido River flows toward the Gulf of Mexico. Most of the state's rivers and streams run down from the mountains toward the Pacific Ocean. These include the Huyapan, Tamazula, Los Remedios, San Diego, and Mezquital rivers. The Nazas and Aguanaval rivers flow into the Bolsón de Mapimí, a barren river basin.

© Robert Frerck/Woodfin Camp

Rock outcroppings.

2 ■ Climate

Average temperature is 21°C (70°F). Average annual rainfall is 283 millimeters (11.2 inches). Monthly average rainfall in winter (November to April) is 8 millimeters (0.3 inch); monthly average rainfall in summer (May to October) is 36 millimeters (1.4 inches).

3 ■ Plants and Animals

Durango has huge evergreen forests and also a large section of the Chihuahuan Desert where many varieties of cactus thrive. The desert turtle was once fairly common but is now endangered in the state of Durango. Guayule, a source of rubber, is native to the state. Common plants of the desert include the fragrant gobernadora, ocotillo (with thorny branches growing toward the sky), yucca (with tall flower spikes in the spring), and candelilla (with a wax-like coating on its leaves to preserve water). Nopal cacti and mesquite (a common desert shrub) are plentiful.

Hundreds of species of butterflies are native to the state. Native animals include deer, badger, foxes, coyotes, squirrels, rabbits, kangaroo rats, and mice.

4 ■ Environmental Protection

Durango began a program in 2003 to require industry within the state to track

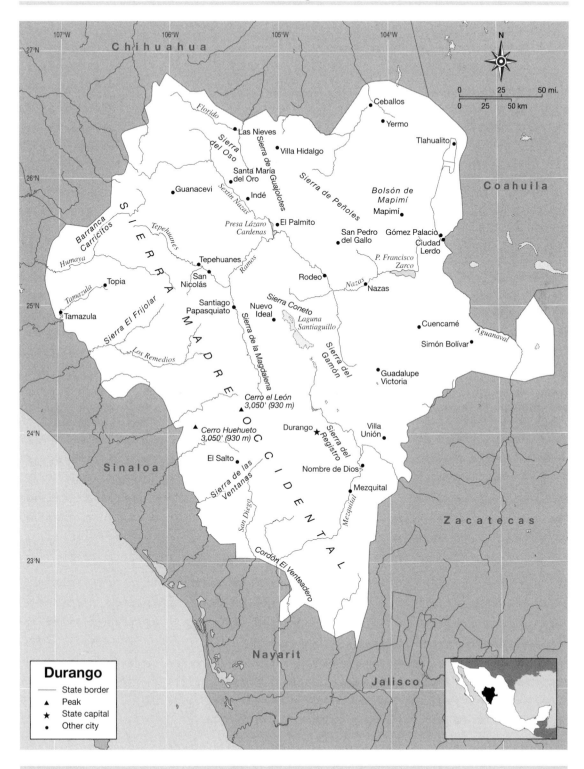

Durango

- State border
- ▲ Peak
- ★ State capital
- • Other city

Chihuahua

Coahuila

Sinaloa

Zacatecas

Nayarit

Jalisco

Ceballos
Yermo
Tlahualito
Las Nieves
Villa Hidalgo
Santa María del Oro
Guanacevi
Indé
El Palmito
Bolsón de Mapimí
Mapimí
San Pedro del Gallo
Gómez Palacio
Ciudad Lerdo
Presa Lázaro Cardenas
Tepehuanes
San Nicolás
Topia
Rodeo
Nazas
Tamazula
Santiago Papasquiato
Nuevo Ideal
Sierra Coneto
Laguna Santiaguillo
Cuencamé
Simón Bolívar
Guadalupe Victoria
Cerro el León 3,050' (930 m)
Cerro Huehueto 3,050' (930 m)
Durango
Villa Unión
El Salto
Nombre de Dios
Mezquital
Sierra del Registro

Florido
Sierra del Oso
Sierra de Guajolotes
Sierra de Peñoles
Sextin Nazas
Barranca Carricitos
Humaya
Tepehuanes
Tamazula
Sierra El Frijolar
Ramos
Nazas
P. Francisco Zarco
Aguanaval
Los Remedios
Sierra de la Magdalena
Sierra del Gamón
Sierra de las Ventanas
San Diego
Mezquital
Cordón El Venteadero

SIERRA MADRE OCCIDENTAL

N

0 25 50 mi.
0 25 50 km

107°W 106°W 105°W 104°W
27°N
26°N
25°N
24°N
23°N

pollutants they generate through manufacturing. There is a forest preserve, La Michilía Biosphere Reserve, on the eastern side of the Sierra Madre Occidental.

5 ▪ Population, Ethnic Groups, Languages
Durango had a total population of 1,448,661 in 2000; of the total, 709,521 were men and 739,140 were women. The population density was 12 people per square kilometer (31 people per square mile). In 2000, the capital, Durango, had a population of 490,245. Almost all citizens in Durango speak Spanish, but about 2% of the population speaks one of the indigenous languages as their first language.

6 ▪ Religions
According to the 2000 census, 79% of the population, or 1.1 million people, were Roman Catholic; 3%, or 48,794 people, were Protestant. That year there were also 19,515 Jehovah's Witnesses and nearly 50,000 people who reported no religion.

7 ▪ Transportation
Durango has 10,477 kilometers (6,548 miles) of roads providing links to the Pacific coast and to inland cities such as Monterrey, Nuevo Léon, and Saltillo, Coahuila. The two primary roads crossing the state are the Pan-American Road (running from México state to Ciudad Juárez, Chihuahua) and the Transoceanic Road (from the Mexican state of Tamaulipas through Matamoros, Coahuila, to Mazatlan, Sinaloa).

There is an international airport serving the capital, Durango, with flights to about a dozen cities in Mexico and to Los Angeles and Chicago in the United States. There are also rails links connecting the state to border cities with the United States to the north and with many other cities in Mexico.

8 ▪ History
Tepehuano indigenous groups inhabited Durango when the Spaniards first arrived in the 16th century. Captain Francisco de Ibarra was the first Spaniard to visit the region. The city of Durango was founded in 1563. Several indigenous revolts aimed at protesting the abuses and oppression by Spanish colonizers threw the region into turmoil for much of the 17th century.

Franciscan and Jesuit priests (from different orders of the Roman Catholic Church) built missions and sought to convert and work with the indigenous people of the area. Tensions with indigenous groups, including Apache and Comanche warriors, lasted well into the 19th century. This made it difficult for colonizers to promote economic development and introduce new agricultural technology to the region. Yet, the tensions also reflected the poor living conditions that the native inhabitants of the region experienced during the colonial period and throughout most of the 19th century.

Mexico witnessed the independence revolt led by Miguel Hidalgo (1753–1811) in 1810. Several local priests in Durango supported the revolt and attempted to rally the population. But local authorities, loyal to Spain, firmly opposed any uprising. Eventually, in the late 1810s, Pedro Celestino Negrete defeated the Spanish royalists in Durango and consolidated support for independence. Durango joined other states in signing the Plan of Iguala in 1821, which secured Mexico's independence.

Durango was officially recognized as a Mexican state in 1825 and the first state constitution was written in 1825. Santiago Baca Ortíz became the first constitutional governor of Durango. The conflicts between liberal and conservative factions reached Durango in the mid-1850s. The conservatives managed to control the state during most of the period, but eventually liberal forces won control. The leaders in Durango united behind Porfirio Díaz (1830–1915). As president, Díaz in turn promoted economic and infrastructure development in the state.

In 1909, wealthy and powerful citizens in Durango began to doubt that Díaz could continue to be effective as president. They supported Francisco Madero (1873–1913) in leading a revolution to oppose a new presidential term for the aging Díaz. Revolutionary leaders successfully gained control of Durango in 1911. It was not until 1917, however, that Domingo Arrieta successfully led the state to adopt a new constitution. Under his leadership, peace and order was restored to the state. Durango aligned with the winning faction of the Mexican Revolution (1910–1920) and signed the new 1917 constitution. But peace would not last long.

Francisco "Pancho" Villa (1878–1923), the legendary revolutionary leader, attempted a new uprising in 1923 in the Tepehuanes region in Durango but was quickly defeated. Yet, four years later, Durango was involved in the Cristero War (1926–1929). This war was launched by Roman Catholic militants who opposed the restrictions placed on the Catholic Church by the federal government. The "cristero" resistance was eventually defeated, but post-revolutionary peace arrived in Durango a couple of decades after it reached the rest of Mexico.

Following the passage of the North American Free Trade Agreement (NAFTA), a trade agreement between Mexico, the United States, and Canada, significant economic development took place in the state. The government invested significantly in new roads, upgrading of water systems, education and training, and improved health care systems.

Durango has been dominated by the Institutional Revolutionary Party (PRI) since the end of the revolution. In the 1980s, 1990s, and early 2000s, other parties were gaining strength in Mexico, and elections in Durango were becoming more competitive.

9 ■ State and Local Government

All of Durango governors have belonged to the Institutional Revolutionary Party (PRI) since the end of the revolution. Ángel Sergio Guerrero, elected governor for a six-year term (1998–2004), gave the PRI its most recent electoral victory. Durango has a unicameral (one chamber) state congress comprised of twenty-five deputies elected for nonrenewable three-year terms. Fifteen deputies are elected in single-member districts and ten by proportional representation. Although formal separation of powers and check-and-balance provisions exist in the constitution, the overwhelming power exercised by the PRI and the strong formal and informal attributions of the governor have limited the power and influence of the state legislature.

Comprised of thirty-eight municipalities, local governments in Durango are relatively weak and their attributions are mostly limited. Elections take place every three years for municipal presidents and council members. Immediate re-election is not allowed.

10 ▦ Political Parties

The three main political parties in all of Mexico are the Institutional Revolutionary Party (PRI), the National Action Party (PAN), and Party of the Democratic Revolution (PRD). Durango's politics have been dominated by the influential and powerful PRI. In the 1990s, Durango witnessed the emergence and consolidation of the PAN and PRD. Yet, as of 2004, those two parties had failed to transform their growing appeal into a statewide electoral victory.

11 ▦ Judicial System

The Superior Tribunal of Justice is Durango's highest court. Its eight members are elected for six-year, nonrenewable terms by the governor with legislative approval. Appointees must meet a number of stringent qualification requirements. In addition, an electoral tribunal and a number of local courts and tribunals comprise the judiciary system in Durango. Because of the dominance of one political party (PRI), the judiciary may not operate with total independence.

12 ▦ Economy

The economy of Durango was once limited to agriculture and mining. Since the passage of the North American Free Trade Agreement (NAFTA) in 1992, hundreds of maquiladoras (assembly plants) have developed. Among the companies that operate in Durango are Sam's Club, Honda, and Wal-Mart. Mining of silver and gold continue to be important economic activities as well.

13 ▦ Industry

Most industrial activity is centered around the capital, Durango, or in the east in a region known as La Laguna, around the cities of Gomez Palacio and Lerdo.

As of 2004, there were nearly 4,000 industrial enterprises employing more than 100,000 workers. The main industries represented in Durango are clothing, wood products, auto parts, mining, food processing, and electronics.

14 ▦ Labor

Durango collects a 2% payroll tax from all wage earners. The US Bureau of Labor Statistics reported that Mexican workers saw their wages increase 17%, from $2.09 per hour in 1999 to $2.46 per hour in 2000. (The average U.S. worker earned $19.86 per hour in 2000.) After one year, workers are entitled by law to six days paid vacation.

15 ▦ Agriculture

Durango ranks second among the Mexican states in production of goat's milk. It ranks fourth in production of poultry and sixth in production of cow's milk.

In rural areas, many families carry out small-scale agriculture on small plots, growing food for their own consumption or to sell locally. In the early 2000s, family farmers were concerned about the impact of genetically engineered maize (corn) on their crops.

Agriculture in Durango is based on crops like corn, beans, alfalfa, apples, zacate (a type of hay), sorghum, and oats for animal feed. The Guadiana valley is known for its aquaculture (cultivating products from the water) and the production of carp and

© Suzy Moore/Woodfin Camp

This Volkswagen dealership is in the city of Gomez Palacio. Most industrial activity is centered around three cities: the capital, Durango, Gomez Palacio, and Lerdo.

mojarra. Durango, San Dimas, and Otáez are known for their gold and silver mining activities, while lead is produced at Cuencamé and Guanaceví. Zinc, copper, and fluorite are also produced in various parts of the state.

16 Natural Resources

Mexico is the largest silver producer in the world; Durango is the third largest producer of silver (after the Mexican states of Zacatecas and Chihuahua). Lead, zinc, and copper are also mined in Durango.

The Guadiana valley is known for fish farms. Durango also is a leading producer of pine and oak lumber.

17 Energy and Power

Demand for electricity grew rapidly (from 1,321 gigawatt-hours in 1993 to nearly 2,000 gigawatt hours by 2000) after the North American Free Trade Agreement (NAFTA) went into effect in 1992. There is potential for development of hydroelectric power along the western slopes of the mountains.

18 Health

Durango has 18 general hospitals, 479 outpatient centers, and 38 surgical centers.

Most of the Mexican population is covered under a government health plan.

Durango movie set where many Hollywood Westerns were filmed.

The IMSS (Instituto Mexicano de Seguro Social) covers the general population. The ISSSTE (Instituto de Seguridad y Servicios Sociales de Trabajadores del Estado) covers state workers.

19 ■ Housing

The quality and quantity of available housing has not kept up with the rapid development of industry in the state since 1992. About half of all housing needs upgrading, with 20% requiring significant upgrading (including the installation of running water).

20 ■ Education

The system of public education was first started by President Benito Juárez (1806–

1872) in 1867. Public education in Mexico is free for students from ages six to sixteen. There were about 350,000 school-age students in the state in 2000. Many students elect to go to private schools.

21 ■ Arts

Durango has many theaters and galleries selling local handicrafts. In the capital, Durango, there is an art school where students may study painting and sculpture. The Durango Performing Arts area is on the north side of the capital. There, footprints of many famous Hollywood movie stars who came to Mexico to film have been preserved.

22 ▥ Libraries and Museums

There are 111 branches of the national library in Durango. There are thirty-six museums, including a museum of cinematography, a children's museum, a museum of contemporary art, a museum of the Mexican Revolution, and an archeology museum.

23 ▥ Media

The capital city of Durango has two daily newspapers, *El Siglo de Durango* and *El Sol de Durango*.

24 ▥ Tourism, Travel, and Recreation

The capital, Durango, has been the set for many cowboy movies. Some movie sets, Puebla del Oeste, Chupaderos, and Rancho La Joya, are still in operation. Guadiana Park has an artificial lake.

25 ▥ Sports

Durango has a basketball team, Leñadores, and a soccer team, the Alacranes. Soccer matches are played in the 18,000-seat Francisco Zarco stadium.

26 ▥ Famous People

Famous citizens born in Durango include composer Silvestre Revueltas (1899–1940), who drew on Mexican folk music themes in his works for orchestra. Francisco "Pancho" Villa (1878–1923), though not born in the state, was known as a revolutionary bandit in Chihuahua and Durango.

27 ▥ Bibliography

Books

Carew-Miller, Anna. *Famous People of Mexico.* Philadelphia: Mason Crest Publishers, 2003.

DeAngelis, Gina. *Mexico.* Mankato, MN: Blue Earth Books, 2003.

Supples, Kevin. *Mexico.* Washington, DC: National Geographic Society, 2002.

Web Sites

Mexico for Kids. http://www.elbalero.gob.mx/index_kids.html (accessed on June 15, 2004).

Guanajuato

Pronunciation: gwah-nah-WHAH-toh.

Origin of state name: From an Amerindian word that means "hill of frogs."

Capital: Guanajuato.

Entered country: 1824.

Coat of Arms: The coat of arms is supported by a base of colored marble with gold decoration. The base is a shell held by two laurel branches bound with a blue ribbon. The shell linking with the coat of arms symbolizes a stable home, opening to welcome guests. The gold background signifies nobility and represents the wealth of precious metals found in the state. The laurels stand for victory, and the acanthus flowers signify loyalty. This crest originally represented the city of Guanajuato but was later adopted by the state.

Holidays: Año Nuevo (New Year's Day—January 1); Día de la Constitución (Constitution Day—February 5); Benito Juárez's birthday (March 21); Primero de Mayo (Labor Day—May 1); Revolution Day, 1910 (November 20); and Navidad (Christmas—December 25).

Flag: There is no official state flag.

Time: 6 AM = noon Greenwich Mean Time (GMT).

1 ■ Location and Size

Guanajuato is in the center of Mexico. It covers an area of 30,768 square kilometers (11,880 square miles). Guanajuato is slightly larger than the US state of Maryland. It is bordered on the north by the Mexican states of San Luis Potosí and Zacatecas; on the east by the Mexican state of Querétaro; on the west by the Mexican state of Jalisco; and on the south by the Mexican state of Michoacán. Guanajuato is divided into forty-six municipalities. The capital, the city of Guanajuato, is located in approximately the center of the state.

Part of the Sierra Madre Oriental mountain range crosses the northeastern part of the state. Fertile valleys lie between the mountain ranges.

There are a number of rivers that flow into two river basins. The first of these river basins is the Pánuco, which flows northeast to the Gulf of Mexico. It is fed by the Santa María and Victoria Rivers. Other rivers run into the Río Lerma (Lerma River) basin, which, in turn, feeds the Río Santiago (Santiago River). Smaller rivers in the state

A plaza in the capital, Guanajuato.

include the Laja, Guanajuato, and Turbio Rivers.

2 ■ Climate

The climate is fairly dry. Average monthly rainfall from November to April is 1 centimeter (0.4 inches). Most of the rainfall occurs between May and September, when the average monthly rainfall is 9.5 centimeters (3.75 inches). The average temperature is 19°C (66°F).

3 ■ Plants and Animals

Trees in Guanajuato include oak, pine, birch, eucalyptus, guava, lemon, and many types of cactus and nopal (a type of cactus). Animals include rabbits, eagles, lizards, squirrels, deer, snakes, skunks, owls, heron, and quail.

4 ■ Environmental Protection

In 2003, Guanajuato was considering the establishment of a system requiring manufacturers to track their pollutants.

5 ■ Population, Ethnic Groups, Languages

Guanajuato had a total population of 4,663,032 in 2000; of the total, 2,233,315 were men and 2,429,717 were women. The

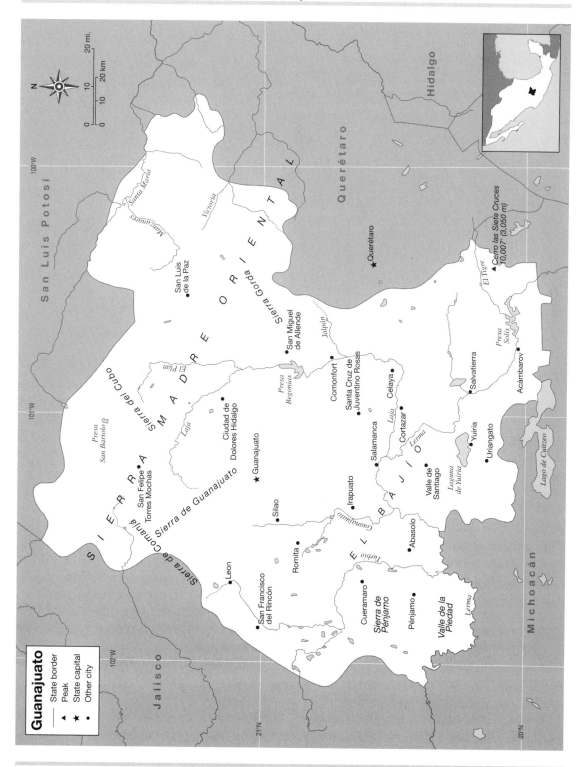

Guanajuato

— State border
▲ Peak
★ State capital
• Other city

20 mi.
20 km

San Luis Potosí

Jalisco

Hidalgo

Querétaro

Michoacán

Santa María
Manzanares
Victoria

San Luis
de la Paz

Sierra Gorda

San Miguel
de Allende

Querétaro ★

Cerro las Siete Cruces
10,007' (3,050 m)

El Tigre

S I E R R A   M A D R E   O R I E N T A L

Sierra del Cubo

El Plan

Jalpán

Comonfort

Santa Cruz de
Juventino Rosas

Celaya

Salvatierra

Presa
Solís

Acámbaro

Laja

Ciudad de
Dolores Hidalgo

Presa
Begoñas

★ Guanajuato

Cortazar

Lerma

Yuria

Uriangato

Presa
San Bartolo

Laja

Salamanca

Lago de Cuitzeo

San Felipe
Torres Mochas

S I E R R A

Sierra de Guanajuato

Silao

Irapuato

Valle de
Santiago

Laguna
de Yuria

Abasolo

Guanajuato

E L   B A J Í O

León

Romita

Turbio

Sierra de Comanja

San Francisco
del Rincón

Cueramaro

Sierra de
Pénjamo

Pénjamo

Valle de la
Piedad

Lerma

101°W

102°W

100°W

21°N

20°N

© Robert Frerck/Woodfin Camp

Monument to local hero in the battle for independence, Juan José de los Reyes Martínez (known as "Pipila").

population density was 152 people per square kilometer (394 people per square mile). In 2000, the capital, Guanajuato, had a population of 141,215. Almost everyone speaks Spanish, with a small percentage (0.3%) speaking one of the indigenous languages as their first language.

6 ■ Religions

According to the 2000 census, 84% of the population, or 3.9 million people, were Roman Catholic; just over 1%, or 53,390 people, were Protestant. That year there were also 24,020 Jehovah's Witnesses and

about 58,000 people who reported no religion.

7 ■ Transportation

Highways were constructed in the 1980s, helping the economy to grow by allowing goods to be transported. About 50% of all the people in Mexico live within 400 kilometers (250 miles) of Guanajuato, the capital of the state.

8 ■ History

The first human settlements in Guanajuato date back to 500 B.C. The Chupicuaro culture populated the region and left considerable cultural, religious, and traditional legacies. Before the arrival of the Spaniards, the region was inhabited by Guamare, Guaxabana, and Copuce indigenous groups. Prolonged human presence had left indelible traces of different cultures, often in tension with each other. Well-established settlements were also evident.

The first Spanish expedition arrived in 1522 led by Cristóbal de Olid (1488–1524). A year later, Spanish explorer Hernán Cortés (1485–1547) distributed some of the lands in the region to several of the lieutenants of his conquest expedition. In 1529, another Spanish explorer, Nuño de Guzmán (d. 1544), led an infamous expedition that killed many indigenous people and pillaged indigenous communities in the region. His pillaging included some communities that had already been conquered and assigned to colonizers under the encomienda (land tenure) system.

The discovery of silver mines in Zacatecas and Guanajuato helped promote Spanish settlements in the region in the late 16th and early 17th century. The city of Guanajuato was founded in 1557, two years after San Miguel (also in present-day Guanajuato) was founded and fourteen years before the foundation of Celaya. León, Guanajuato, was founded in 1574, reflecting the growing economic activity resulting from the exploitation of silver and other minerals. In 1762, the first inquisition official arrived in the region. The inquisition officials were priests appointed by the Catholic Church to combat followers of non-Catholic religions, particularly Protestants. The expulsion of the Jesuits (an order of the Roman Catholic Church) in 1767 provoked additional conflicts between local elites and the Catholic Church.

Guanajuato was one of the twelve regions that comprised Mexico in the 18th century, reflecting the economic and social importance of the agricultural and mineral producing region. The independence movement, which began in 1810, started in the city of Dolores, Guanajuato (known today as Dolores Hidalgo). Priest Miguel Hidalgo (1753–1811) called on peasants and patriots to revolt against the Spanish crown. A local hero, a miner named Juan José de los Reyes Martínez, is known by his nickname "Pipila." He was a hero in a battle in Guanajuato, and a statue commemorates his place in the state's history. Hidalgo organized an army that marched towards Mexico City. Although the rebellion was eventually defeated, the independence movement remained active in Guanajuato. In 1821 Guanajuato joined the rest of Mexico in signing the Plan of Iguala that secured the country's independence.

In the Mexican-American War (1846–48), a Guanajuato army fiercely fought the US occupation. During the political conflicts for power in the 1850s, Mexican revolutionary and later president Benito Juárez (1806–1872) made Guanajuato the provisional capital of his government. During the short French occupation (from 1863 to 1867) under the monarchy of Maximilian (1832–1867), Guanajuato was the most populated state of Mexico. Under Juárez, Guanajuato remained an economic and political power in Mexico. Benito Juárez and later President Porfirio Díaz (1830–1915) promoted economic development and improvements in infrastructure.

The Mexican Revolution, which started in 1910, was fiercely fought in Guanajuato. There revolutionary leaders organized militias and different factions faced each other in bloody battles. Francisco "Pan-

© Robert Frerck/Woodfin Camp

The Valenciana silver mine operated for over 250 years.

cho" Villa (1878–1923) and other revolutionary leaders occupied different cities during the revolt. However, no group dominated the entire state. After the end of the revolution, the Cristero War (1926–1929) brought new confrontations to the state. The Catholic Church's militant opposition to some of the policies of the new government and the uprising of Catholic loyalists generated much tension in Guanajuato. Eventually, the government made peace with the Catholic Church, but religious tensions remained present in the state.

Since the mid 1950s, the consolidation of anti-clerical (anti-Catholic) Institutional Revolutionary Party (PRI) rule in Mexico promoted the growth of the pro-Catholic National Action Party (PAN) party in Guanajuato. The election of PAN gubernatorial candidate Vicente Fox in 1995 represented the first state-wide electoral defeat for the PRI. Fox's gubernatorial victory in 1995 made Guanajuato the first state to elect a non-PRI governor since the end of the Mexican Revolution. Fox went on to become president of Mexico in 2000.

9 ■ State and Local Government

The governor is the most important and powerful figure in the state. With strong powers and attributions, the governor can assume an influential leadership role. The state congress is comprised of thirty-six deputies, twenty-two elected in single member districts and fourteen by proportional representation, for nonrenewable three-year terms. Balance of power provisions existing in the constitution were first implemented when a PAN candidate won the governorship in 1995. Democratic consolidation in Guanajuato has resulted in lively debates between two strong political parties. However, executive powers are now checked by the legislature.

The forty-six municipalities of the state elect municipal presidents and council members every three years for nonrenewable terms. The powers and attributions of the municipal governments are strong because of historical tradition and the importance of local governments during the colonial period. The process of democratic consolidation that Guanajuato experienced since the mid 1980s also supports the municipal government.

10 ▪ Political Parties

The three main political parties in all of Mexico are the Institutional Revolutionary Party (PRI), the National Action Party (PAN), and Party of the Democratic Revolution (PRD). Although the PRI was the sole political party during much of the post revolution 20th century, the PAN became a strong contender for political power and representation in the mid 1980s. PAN's Vicente Fox was the first non-PRI governor of the state. He went on to become the first non-PRI president of Mexico in 2000.

11 ▪ Judicial System

The Supreme Tribunal of Justice is the highest court of the state. Members are appointed by the governor with congressional approval. The president of the Supreme Tribunal is elected from among its members for a renewable two-year period. The state legal system is also comprised of an electoral tribunal and local courts with different powers and attributions. The process of democratization experienced in the mid 1980s and 1990s has helped strengthen the independence and autonomy of the Guanajuato judiciary.

12 ▪ Economy

The segments of the economy that developed rapidly after the passage of the North American Free Trade Agreement (NAFTA) in 1992—a trade agreement between Mexico, the United States, and Canada—were industry, trade, and tourism. About half of Guanajuato's cities produce goods for export. Between 1999 and 2002 Guanajuato's foreign trade doubled.

13 ▪ Industry

Industry is centered in cities such as León, Salamanca, and Irapuato. The main industries are silver and gold mining, oil, manufacturing of shoes in León, manufacturing of fabrics and clothing, and tourism. Guanajuato has an export rate three times the national average

14 ▪ Labor

Guanajuato has the lowest unemployment rate in Mexico. Workers are engaged in mining, agriculture, manufacturing, and tourism.

The US Bureau of Labor Statistics reported that Mexican workers saw their wages increase 17%, from $2.09 per hour in 1999 to $2.46 per hour in 2000. (The average US worker earned $19.86 per hour in 2000.) After one year, workers are entitled by law to six days paid vacation.

15 ▪ Agriculture

Guanajuato is a fertile agricultural state, producing strawberries, mangoes, bananas, oats, sorghum, chilies, onions, cauliflower, broccoli, asparagus, peas, tomatoes, and alfalfa. Farmers also grow flowers such as roses, and cempasúchil, a special flower used in the celebration for the Day of the Dead (or All Souls Day, a Catholic holiday that falls on November 2, the day after All Saints Day).

In some parts of the state, cattle, pigs, sheep, goats, and poultry are raised.

16 ▪ Natural Resources

Mexico is the largest silver producer in the world. Silver has been mined in the state since the 1500s. Guanajuato ranks fourth among the country's silver-producing states (after Zacatecas, Chihuahua, and Durango). Together the four states produce three-fourths of Mexico's silver output. The Los Torres mine is a major producer.

17 ▪ Energy and Power

The government-run Federal Electricity Commission (Comision Federal de Electricidad—CFE) supplies almost all of Mexico's power. Energy consumption in Guanajuato has been increasing by about 4% per year.

18 ▪ Health

The state of Guanajuato has 30 general hospitals, 593 outpatient centers, and 87 surgical centers. Most of the Mexican population is covered under a government health plan. The IMSS (Instituto Mexicano de Seguro Social) covers the general population. The ISSSTE (Instituto de Seguridad y Servicios Sociales de Trabajadores del Estado) covers state workers.

19 ▪ Housing

The population is growing by almost 2% per year. In some cities, the housing available cannot meet the demand. Over one-third of the housing in Guanajuato requires upgrading or replacement, and about 10% (mostly in rural areas) have no running water or electricity.

20 ▪ Education

The system of public education was first started by President Benito Juárez in 1867. Public education in Mexico is free for students from ages six to sixteen. According to the 2000 census, there were more than 1.1 million school-age students in the state. Many students elect to go to private schools. The thirty-one states of Mexico all have at least one state university. The Universidad de Guanajuato (University of Guanajuato) is located in the capital.

21 ▪ Arts

The state of Guanajuato sponsors the Ballet Folklórico of Guanajuato. The Universidad de Guanajuato (University of Guanajuato) has a symphony orchestra. There is also a choir called the Voces of Guanajuato. The theatrical group, Cornisa 20,

© Robert Frerck/Woodfin Camp

Homes on a hillside near the capital, Guanajuato.

participates in many cultural fairs. There is also the more formal Ludus Teatro.

22 ■ Libraries and Museums

The state of Guanajuato has 114 branches of the national library system. There are thirty museums. In Celaya, there is a mummy museum. In the capital, Guanajuato, there is a museum dedicated to Spanish novelist Miguel de Cervantes's work *Don Quijote* (Don Quixote).

23 ■ Media

The newspaper, *Corréo*, is published in the capital, Guanajuato. Celaya has *El Sol de Bajio*, while Irapuato has *El Sol de Irapuato*. León has two papers: *El Heraldo de León* and *El Sol de León*. San Miguel de Allende has a bilingual newspaper, *Atención*, published in Spanish and English.

24 ■ Tourism, Travel, and Recreation

Guanajuato means "hills of frogs" in the native language. The capital is best-known as a colonial silver mining town, where visitors can tour the silver mines. Two main museums, a mummy museum and the museum of famous muralist and painter Diego Rivera (1886–1957), are ma-

© Robert Frerck/Woodfin Camp

The Hidalgo Market in the capital, Guanajuato, was built in the late 1800s.

jor tourist attractions. In mid-October, the Festival Cervantina honoring the works of Miguel de Cervantes (1547–1616), who wrote *Don Quixote*, is a huge tourist attraction requiring reservations in advance.

25 ■ Sports

Irapuato has a soccer team that plays in the Sergio León Chavez stadium, which holds 30,712 spectators. There is also a 15,000-seat Plaza de Toros (bullfighting ring) at the Plaza Revolución. Celaya has a soccer team, Atlético Celaya, which plays in the 25,000-seat Miguel Aleman stadium.

26 ■ Famous People

Famous people from the state include Miquel Hidalgo y Costilla (1753–1811), a priest and revolutionary who fought for the rights of native peoples and published the *Grito de Dolores* (Cry of Pain), a pamphlet that helped to trigger the fight for independence in 1810. Diego Rivera (1886–1957) was a world-famous painter and muralist. His works include the fresco *The Great City of Tenochtitlán,* at the National Palace in Mexico City; *The Allegory of California* at the San Francisco Stock Exchange; and a series of murals at the Detroit Institute of Art. Vicente Fox (1942–) was born in Mexico City but moved with his family to Guanajuato early in his childhood. He was governor of the state before being elected president of Mexico in 2000.

27 ■ Bibliography

Books

DeAngelis, Gina. *Mexico.* Mankato, MN: Blue Earth Books, 2003.

Gaines, Ann. *Vicente Fox: The Road to the Mexican Presidency.* Chanhassen, MN: Child's World, 2003.

Supples, Kevin. *Mexico.* Washington, DC: National Geographic Society, 2002.

Web Sites

Mexico for Kids. http://www.elbalero.gob.mx/index_kids.html (accessed on June 15, 2004).

Surfing & Adventure Travel in Mexico: Guanajuato State. http://www.surf-mexico.com/states/GTO/ (accessed on June 17, 2004).

Guerrero

Pronunciation: geh-REH-roh.

Origin of state name: Honors the memory of Vicente Guerrero Saldaña (1783–1831) who took part in the independence movement.

Capital: Chilpancingo de los Bravo (typically called Chilpancingo).

Entered country: 1849.

Coat of Arms: The upper section is formed by a headdress with eleven colored feathers. The central blue background represents the sky and water. A warrior displays a mace (clublike weapon) horizontally with his right hand. In his left hand, he holds a shield, which is a Náhuatl (language of the Aztec Indians) symbol for power, decorated in red, green, purple, and yellow. The warrior wears a tiger skin with spots denoting the stars that represent Tezcatlipoca, Lord of the Night. In the lower part of the shield, nine feathers form a fan.

Holidays: Año Nuevo (New Year's Day—January 1); Día de la Constitución (Constitution Day—February 5); Benito Juárez's birthday (March 21); Primero de Mayo (Labor Day—May 1); Revolution Day, 1910 (November 20); and Navidad (Christmas—December 25).

Flag: There is no official flag.

Time: 6 AM = noon Greenwich Mean Time (GMT).

1 ▪ Location and Size

Guerrero is located in southern Mexico. It covers an area of 64,586 square kilometers (24,937 square miles), slightly larger than the US state of West Virginia. It is bordered on the north by the Mexican states of Michoacán, México, and Morelos; on the east by the states of Puebla and Oaxaca; and on the south by the Pacific Ocean. Guerrero has seventy-six municipalities. The capital, Chilpancingo de los Bravos (typically called Chilpancingo), is located approximately in the center of the state.

Guerrero is one of the most mountainous states in Mexico. Its mountain ranges (*sierras*) include the Sierra Madre del Sur and the Sierras del Norte. Between these two mountain ranges is the warm and dry region surrounding the Río Balsas (Balsas River). The state is also known for its coastal plain, which stretches along the coastline of the Pacific Ocean. Agriculture and livestock thrive in the interior valleys.

© Kal Muller/Woodfin Camp

Acapulco was one of Mexico's first resort towns.

The basin of the Río Balsas is formed by small rivers (tributaries) that rise in the Sierras del Norte and in the Sierra Madre del Sur and eventually flow into the Río Balsas. Acapulco, established in 1550 by Spanish settlers, is one of Mexico's oldest resorts. The natural Pacific coast harbor there is surrounded by cliffs. The El Veladero National Park protects the natural areas in the mountains around Acapulco.

2 ■ Climate

Acapulco on the coast is generally hot and fairly humid. Most of the rain falls from June to October, when there are light showers each day, with occasional tropical storms. A damaging hurricane, Hurricane Pauline, caused several hundred deaths when it struck Guerrero and Oaxaca in October 1997. The winter months (December to April) are slightly cooler with less rainfall. The average winter temperature ranges from 25°C to 27°C (77°F to 81°F). The average summer temperature ranges from 28°C to 29°C (82°F to 84°F).

3 ■ Plants and Animals

There are tropical forests and mangroves along the Pacific Ocean. Oak and pine forests are found in the mountain areas. The valley around the Río Balsas has small, scrubby shrubs. Exotic tropical trees like the amate (umbrella plant), organ cactus, and many varieties of palm trees are common.

Native animals include iguanas and other lizards, snakes, rabbits, and coyotes.

Animals that are endangered or whose habitat is threatened by development include jaguar, eagle, turtle, and iguana. There are many lizard and snake species, and rabbits and coyotes are plentiful.

4 ■ Environmental Protection

Acapulco and Ixtapa are two of Mexico's most important tourist sites. The El Veladero National Park, in the mountain range that surrounds Acapulco Bay, is home to many tropical trees and some wildlife.

5 ■ Population, Ethnic Groups, Languages

Guerrero had a total population of 3,079,649 in 2000; of the total, 1,491,287

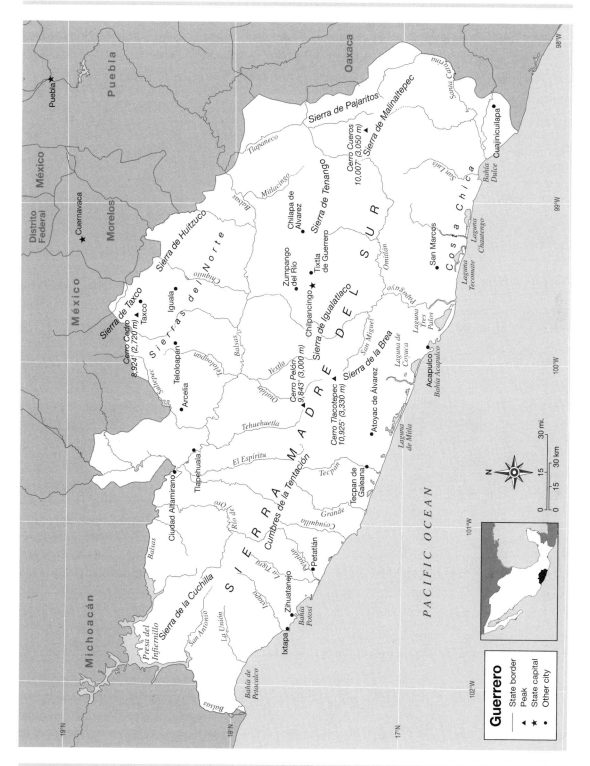

Puebla

Oaxaca

México

Distrito
Federal

Morelos

México

Michoacán

PACIFIC OCEAN

Sierra de Pajaritos

Sierra de Malinaltepec

Costa Chica

Cerro Cueros
10,007' (3,050 m)

Sierra de Tenango

Chilapa de
Álvarez

Sierra de Huitzuco

Sierra del Norte

Chiquito

Zumpango
del Río

Tixtla
de Guerrero

Chilpancingo

Sierra de Igualatlaco

San Marcos

Laguna
Tecomate

Laguna
Chautengo

Cuajiniculapa

Bahía
Dulce

Santa Catarin

San Luis

Omitlán

Papagayo

Sierra de Taxco

Taxco

Iguala

Cerro Cedro
8,924' (2,720 m)

Teloloapan

Arcelia

Balsas

Tlapehuala

Ciudad Altamirano

Sultepec

Teloloapan

Cerro Pelón
9,843' (3,000 m)

Yextla

Cerro Tlacotepec
10,925' (3,330 m)

Sierra de la Brea

Atoyac de Álvarez

Laguna
Tres
Palos

Laguna de
Coyuca

Acapulco
Bahía Acapulco

San Miguel

Laguna
de Mitla

El Espíritu

Cumbres de la Tentación

Tecpan

Tecpan de
Galeana

Grande

Coyuquilla

Tepehua

Petatlán

Zihuatanejo

Ixtapa

Bahía
Potosí

Bahía de
Petacalco

Balsas

Presa del
Infiernillo

Sierra de la Cuchilla

La Tigra

San Antonio

La Unión

Río de Oro

SIERRA MADRE DEL SUR

Tlapaneco

Mitlacingo

Balsas

Puebla

Cuernavaca

30 mi.

30 km

15

15

N

0

0

101°W

100°W

99°W

98°W

102°W

19°N

18°N

17°N

Guerrero

— State border

▲ Peak

★ State capital

• Other city

were men and 1,588,362 were women. The population density was 48 people per square kilometer (124 people per square mile). In 2000, the capital of Chilpancingo had a population of 192,509. Almost everyone speaks Spanish, and about 14% of the population speaks one of the indigenous languages as their first language. Guerrero has a relatively large indigenous population.

6 ▪ Religions

According to the 2000 census, 77% of the population, or 2.4 million people, were Roman Catholic; about 4%, or 117,511 people, were Protestant. That year there were also 43,320 Jehovah's Witnesses and 875 Jews. Over 100,000 people reported no religion.

7 ▪ Transportation

There are 8,146 kilometers (5,091 miles) of paved roads and 94 kilometers (58 miles) of railroad in the state. A four-lane highway connects Mexico City and Acapulco. International airports in Zihuatanejo and Acapulco, both near the Pacific coast, provide flights to and from Guerrero.

8 ▪ History

The oldest evidence of human presence in Guerrero dates back to 300 B.C., when the Olmec inhabited central and southern Mexico. In the 10th century, Teotihuacan groups built pyramids in Texmelincan and Teloloapan. Human settlements were also built on the Pacific coast by Tepaneca Indians and others. Náhuatl (Aztec) groups eventually invaded the well-populated region in the 11th century. When the Aztecs conquered central Mexico, they divided

© Robert Frerck/Woodfin Camp

Santa Prisa Catholic Church was built in 1748.

the region that constitutes modern-day Guerrero into seven entities. Tax collection mechanisms were introduced, and centralized Aztec government exerted influence over the local natives.

When the Spanish arrived, they conquered the Aztec. The Spanish then replaced the Aztec in dominating the indigenous populations. In 1523, Juan Rodríguez led an expedition to the region. In 1527, Alonso de Saavedra Cerón sailed off the Pacific coast towards the Molucas Islands but his expedition never returned.

© Robert Frerck/Woodfin Camp

Laguna de Coyuca bird sanctuary in Acapulco.

In 1534, Spanish expeditions discovered silver in Taxco. Mineral production attracted more Spanish settlers. This radically changed the lives of indigenous communities. Trade with Asia was possible because the natural harbor at Acapulco made a great Pacific coast port. The tough and dangerous trip between Acapulco and Mexico City required twelve days to complete. But the prospects of lucrative trade routes with Asia converted it into one of the busiest colonial roads in Mexico.

Slave trade was also practiced in Acapulco during that period. Runaway slave communities formed in the mountain region and remained active until the mid-19th century. Modern-day descendants of African slaves live along the southern Pacific coast.

During the movement to gain independence for Mexico from imperialist Spain, José Morelos (1765–1815) was commissioned by Mexican priest and revolutionary Miguel Hidalgo (1753–1811) to form an independence army in Guerrero. More than three thousand soldiers joined Morelos. They liberated Chilpancingo from Spanish control and declared it the nation's capital in 1813 after the Anahuac Congress (the meeting at which regional leaders decided to fight for Mexican independence). After Morelos's death, the struggle for independence continued. Vicente Guerrero (1783–1831) emerged

© Mireille Vautier/Woodfin Camp

Masks used for religious festivals.

as the strongest independence leader and the movement eventually succeeded with the implementation of the Plan of Iguala in 1821, which freed Mexico from Spanish control.

Guerrero was appointed as chief of the southern region of Mexico, where he fiercely fought for the establishment of a federal republic. The political instability in the country led Guerrero to undertake a number of armed battles. He eventually became president of Mexico in 1829 but was assassinated nine months after taking office.

Indigenous rebellions and discontent with Antonio Lopez de Santa Anna (1794–1876), who served as president of Mexico from 1833 to 1836, helped worsen the po-

litical and military instability of the region. Many constitutionalist and liberal leaders sought refuge in Guerrero and attempted to reorganize their opposition to French emperor Maximilian (1832–1867). (France had conquered and ruled parts of Mexico from 1864 to 1866.) During the Porfiriato period, when Porfirio Diáz was in power (1877–1880 and 1884–1911), conflicts between caudillo (politically powerful) leaders and military strongmen made it difficult for Guerrero to be fully controlled by the state authorities. The presence of militias and the weak state government made it easier for the Mexican Revolution to take hold in Guerrero starting in 1910.

When the revolution came to an end, the Institutional Revolutionary Party (PRI) emerged as the national political force. Allegiance to the PRI helped reduced old conflicts between local caudillo families in Guerrero. The presidency of Miguel Alemán from 1946 to 1952 helped promote economic development, particularly in Acapulco.

Widespread poverty and inequality helped fuel support for different guerrilla groups in the 1960s and 1970s. Economic development in the 1980s and the consolidation of Acapulco, Ixtapa, and Taxco as tourism attractions have benefited the economy of the state. Rural violence by insurgent groups continues in the early years of the 21st century. Guerrero is among the states with high numbers of insurgent groups operating in the countryside. Insurgents are small groups that rebel against the government, but who are not large enough or well-organized enough to carry out a revolution.

9 ▪ State and Local Government

A powerful state governor is democratically elected every six years. All governors since the end of the Mexican Revolution (1910–1920) have belonged to the Institutional Revolutionary Party (PRI). Rene Juárez Cisneros won the 1999 gubernatorial election, defeating a Party of the Democratic Revolution (PRD) challenger. The dominance of one political party, the PRI, has made it difficult to implement separation of power and check-and-balance provisions. A unicameral (one chamber) state congress is comprised of a forty-six-member assembly. Twenty-eight representatives are elected in single member districts and eighteen by proportional representation.

Guerrero is comprised of seventy-five municipalities. Local governments in Guerrero have varying powers and attributions. Larger and more populated municipalities are more autonomous and independent of the state government. Municipal presidents and council members are elected for three-year nonrenewable terms.

10 ▪ Political Parties

The three main political parties in all of Mexico are the Institutional Revolutionary Party (PRI), the National Action Party (PAN), and the Party of the Democratic Revolution (PRD). The PRI has dominated politics in Guerrero since after the end of the Mexican Revolution. PRI governors from Guerrero have been important actors at the national level. Guerrero is one of the most populated states and a PRI stronghold. Candidates for president of Mexico seek the active support of the Guerrero governor. The PRD traces its roots to revolutionary activities of the 1960s.

11 ▪ Judicial System

A Superior Tribunal of Justice is the state's highest court. Comprised of sixteen members appointed by the governor with congressional approval, the justices can be re-appointed after their six-year terms expire. There is a mandatory retirement provision for all those age sixty-five or older. In addition, there are local and state level appeals courts as well as an electoral tribunal.

12 ▪ Economy

The state of Guerrero has diverse and abundant natural resources. Active economic sectors are farming, commerce, and

© Robert Frerck/Woodfin Camp

Storefronts on the Plaza Borda in Taxco.

transportation. Tourism is also an important segment of the economy. Manufacturing, mining, and energy production are growing. Following the passage of the North American Free Trade Agreement (NAFTA) in 1992, a trade agreement between Mexico, the United States, and Canada, export values increased (between 1997 and 1998 alone exports increased 15.6%).

13 ■ Industry

Historically, Guerrero did not have much large-scale industry. The state has many small establishments, such as blacksmith shops, carpenter shops, and hat factories,

all of which provide products and services to a local market. There are some manufacturing facilities that process products made from palm leaves and fibers. There are also a few assembly plants that produce clothing for export. Following the passage of the North American Free Trade Agreement (NAFTA) in 1992, many new *maquiladoras* assembly plants were established, especially in the northern region of the state.

14 ■ Labor

The US Bureau of Labor Statistics reported that Mexican workers saw their wages increase 17%, from $2.09 per hour in 1999 to $2.46 per hour in 2000. (The average US worker earned $19.86 per hour in 2000.) After one year, workers are entitled by law to six days paid vacation.

15 ▪ Agriculture

The main economic activities in the valleys in the center of the state are agriculture and livestock breeding. The main agricultural products are maize (corn), beans, sorghum, rice, sesame, tomato, melon, lemon, coffee, coconuts, and bananas. Guerrero produces more than 3% of beef consumed in Mexico.

Only 10% of the cultivated land in Guerrero is irrigated.

16 ▪ Natural Resources

Taxco is in the center of the silver mining region of Mexico. Many of the forests in the inland regions have been cut down by international timber companies. In 2003, the World Bank invested in a program to help indigenous people manage the forests on their lands in Guerrero.

17 ▪ Energy and Power

The government-run Federal Electricity Commission (CFE) supplies most of Mexico's power. Unlike many states to the north where demand for power is increasing, the demand for electricity in Guerrero declined during the late 1990s, reflecting the lack of growth in population.

18 ▪ Health

There are 27 general hospitals, 1,016 outpatient centers, and 71 surgical centers in the state.

Most of the Mexican population is covered under a government health plan.

The IMSS (Instituto Mexicano de Seguro Social) covers the general population. The ISSSTE (Instituto de Seguridad y Servicios Sociales de Trabajadores del Estado) covers state workers.

19 ▪ Housing

Only about one-fourth of the housing available in Guerrero is in good repair. More than 40% is in need of significant upgrading. Many homes do not have running water or access to electricity.

20 ▪ Education

The system of public education was first started by President Benito Juárez (1806–1872) in 1867. Public education in Mexico is free for students from ages six to sixteen. According to the 2000 census, there were approximately 900,000 school-age students in the state. Many students elect to go to private schools. The thirty-one states of Mexico all have at least one state university. Universidad Autonoma de Guerrero (Independent University of Guerrero) is in the capital, Chilpancingo.

21 ▪ Arts

Acapulco and Taxco both have several theaters. Many craft galleries and artisans' workshops are open to the public throughout the state.

22 ▪ Libraries and Museums

Guerrero has 145 branches of the national library system. There are forty-one museums in the state. Acapulco has a naval museum and Cuajinicuilapa has a museum of Afro-Indian (Afromestizo) culture, reflecting the culture of the state's population who trace their ancestry to former slaves. Taxco, located in the center of a silver mining region, has a museum devoted to the history of silver mining and jewelry making.

23 ▥ Media

Acapulco has three daily newspapers, including *El Sol de Acapulco, El Sur,* and *Novedades Acapulco.* An English-language daily, *Acapulco Newspaper,* is published for tourists, with information on shopping, dining, and other tourist attractions. In Puerto Vallarta, the newspapers are the *PV Tribune* and *Vallarta Today.*

24 ▥ Tourism, Travel, and Recreation

Acapulco is one of Mexico's oldest and best known resort areas. The city lies around the spectacular Acapulco Bay. Visitors enjoy water sports, beaches, deep-sea fishing, and golf. A tourist attraction are the cliff divers, who plunge from high rocky cliffs into deep water pools. San Diego Fort, built to defend the area against pirates, dates from 1616. Other cities that attract tourists are Ixtapa and Zihuanatejo, both of which lie on the ocean coast that become known as the Mexican Riviera (after the resort area on the south coast of France). Taxco, a colonial city located in the mountains at an altitude of 3,000 me-

ters (6,000 feet), is famous for its hundreds of small shops that sell silver jewelry.

25 ▥ Sports

Acapulco has a bullfighting ring at the Plaza Caletilla. Acapulco's professional baseball team plays in the 13,000-seat Universidad Deportiva stadium.

26 ▥ Famous People

The state is named for Vicente Guerrero Saldaña (1783–1831), a leader in the independence movement. Poet and playwright Juan Ruiz de Alarcón (c. 1580–1639) was born in Taxco. Cuauhtémoc (c. 1495–1522), the last Aztec ruler, was hung by order of Spanish conqueror Hernán Cortés (1485–1547) and is buried in Ixcateopan.

27 ▥ Bibliography

Books

DeAngelis, Gina. *Mexico.* Mankato, MN: Blue Earth Books, 2003.

Supples, Kevin. *Mexico.* Washington, DC: National Geographic Society, 2002.

Vincent, Theodore G. *The Legacy of Vicente Guerrero: Mexico's First Black Indian President.* Gainesville, FL: University Press of Florida, 2001.

Web Sites

Mexico for Kids. http://www.elbalero.gob.mx/index_kids.html (accessed on June 11, 2004).

Surfing & Adventure Travel in Mexico: The State of Guerrero. http://www.surf-mexico.com/states/Guerrero/ (accessed on June 17, 2004).

Hidalgo

Pronunciation: ee-DAHL-goh.

Origin of state name: Named for the priest, Father Miguel Hidalgo y Costilla (1753–1811), who launched the movement for independence from Spanish rule.

Capital: Pachuca de Soto (often shortened to Pachuca).

Entered country: 1862.

Coat of Arms: The upper half of the seal symbolizes the landscape before the arrival of the Spaniards. The bell on the left represents the call for independence made in 1810. The red cap signifies Hidalgo's status as a free and independent state. The lower half of the seal symbolizes military actions. Flanking the seal on the left is the banner of the Virgin of Guadalupe and on the right is the national flag of Mexico.

Holidays: Año Nuevo (New Year's Day—January 1); Día de la Constitución (Constitution Day—February 5); Benito Juárez's birthday (March 21); Primero de Mayo (Labor Day—May 1); Revolution Day, 1910 (November 20); and Navidad (Christmas—December 25).

Flag: There is no official flag.

Time: 6 AM = noon Greenwich Mean Time (GMT).

1 ▌ Location and Size

Hidalgo lies in the center of Mexico. It covers an area of 20,502 square kilometers (7,916 square miles), about the same size as the US state of New Jersey. Hidalgo is bordered on the north by the Mexican state of San Luis Potosí; on the east by the Mexican states of Veracruz and Puebla; on the south by México state and Tlaxcala; and on the west by the state of Querétaro. Hidalgo has eighty-four municipalities. The capital is Pachuca.

Hidalgo has three principal landscapes. The Huasteca, a fertile lowland area, lies in the north. The center of the state has mountain ranges (*sierras*). The largest region is the nearly flat southern highland plateau. The Huasteca region is crossed by the Calabozos, Amajac, Candelaria, and Hules Rivers, which reach the Pánuco River and flow into the Gulf of Mexico.

There are many rivers in the sierras. The Moctezuma flows along the border with Querétaro. The Tula River crosses the Mezquital valley.

2 ■ Climate

The average temperature is 16°C (61°F). The temperature ranges from a high of 32°C (90°F) and a low of 9°C (48°F). Average annual rainfall at elevations around 2,000 meters (660 feet) is 578 millimeters (23 inches).

3 ■ Plants and Animals

In the mountains, the trees include fir, pine, oak, and juniper. There are also exotic hardwood trees, such as mahogany, ebony, rosewood, and mesquite. Coffee also grows in the mountains.

Native animals include the white-tailed deer, jaguar, coyote, porcupine, and skunk. Rattlesnakes are native to the state, along with several species of lizard.

4 ■ Environmental Protection

El Chico National Park, about 20 kilometers (12.5 miles) from the capital, was one of the first forests to be protected in the country.

5 ■ Population, Ethnic Groups, Languages

Hidalgo had a total population of 2,235,591 in 2000; of the total, 1,081,993 were men and 1,153,598 were women. The population density was 107 people per square kilometer (277 people per square mile). In 2000, the capital Pachuca had a population of 244,688.

6 ■ Religions

According to the 2000 census, 80% of the population, or 1.8 million people, were Roman Catholic; about 5%, or 102,748 people, were Protestant. That year there were also 16,767 Jehovah's Witnesses and 391 Jews. About 45,000 people reported no religion.

7 ■ Transportation

The state has about 4,858 miles (7,822 kilometers) of roads and 546 miles (879 kilometers) of railroads. There is one international airport and one domestic airport.

8 ■ History

There is evidence in Huapalcalco of a human presence in Hidalgo as early as 7000 B.C. Ruins from the Tehotihuacano period (150 B.C.–750 A.D.) are scattered throughout the region. The Mixcóatl settled in the region around 900 A.D. Indigenous Toltec leader Topiltzin, also known as Quetzalcóatl, assumed power in 977. He promoted architecture and the arts and banned human sacrifices. Defeated later, Quetzalcóatl escaped towards the north and is believed to have founded the Aztec empire. Toltecs escaped attacks from other indigenous groups and eventually abandoned the city of Tula in 1156. The Mexicas crossed Hidalgo before founding and settling in Mexico-Tenochtitlán. With the emergence of the Aztec empire, Hidalgo was conquered by the Aztecs, but some parts of the region remained independent.

Because of its geographical location in the central valley of Mexico, Hidalgo became an integral part of the Aztec empire and a central access route to the capital city from the Caribbean coast and northern Mexico. Hidalgo's strategic location made it a prized trophy for all those who sought to control the central valley of Mexico. From the Aztec empire until the Mexican Revolution of

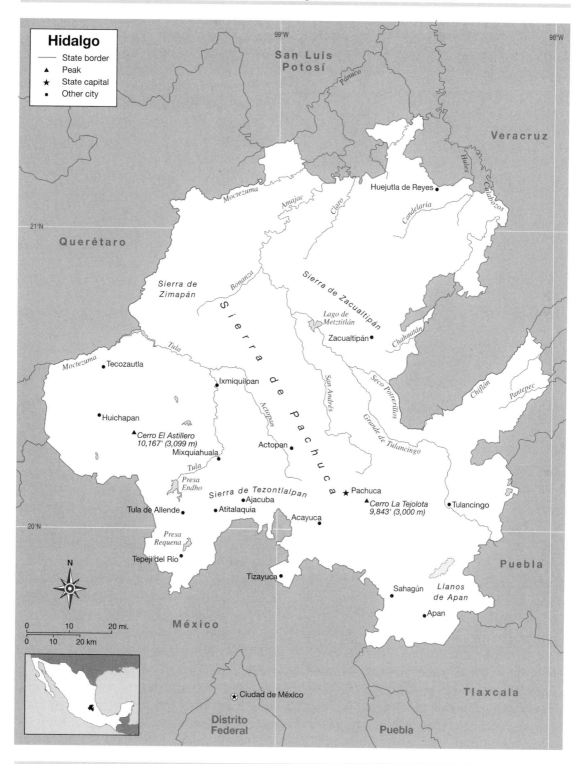

Hidalgo

- —— State border
- ▲ Peak
- ★ State capital
- • Other city

San Luis Potosí

Veracruz

99°W

98°W

Querétaro

21°N

Moctezuma

Pánuco

Amajac

Claro

Candelaria

Huites

Calabozos

• Huejutla de Reyes

Sierra de Zimapán

Bonanza

Sierra de Zacualtipán

Lago de Metztitlán

Zacualtipán •

Chahuatán

Tula

Moctezuma

• Tecozautla

• Ixmiquilpan

Seco Potrerillos

Chiflón

Pantepec

S i e r r a d e P a c h u c a

• Huichapan

Actopan

San Andrés

Grande de Tulancingo

▲ Cerro El Astillero
10,167' (3,099 m)

Actopan •

Mixquiahuala •

Tula

Presa Endho

Sierra de Tezontlalpan

Ajacuba •

★ Pachuca

▲ Cerro La Tejolota
9,843' (3,000 m)

• Tulancingo

Tula de Allende •

• Atitalaquia

Acayuca •

20°N

Presa Requena

Tepeji del Río •

Tizayuca •

Sahagún •

Llanos de Apan

Puebla

• Apan

N

México

Tlaxcala

0   10   20 mi.

0   10   20 km

⊛ Ciudad de México

Distrito Federal

Puebla

© Robert Frerck/Woodfin Camp

Aqueduct, Los Arcos del Padre.

1917, Hidalgo was a prime battleground for the control of access to the central valley of Mexico.

Spanish conqueror Hernán Cortés (1485–1547) traveled through Hidalgo on his way to conquer the Aztec empire in 1519. Spanish settlements in the region first introduced cattle and some agricultural crops in the mid-16th century. Franciscan (an order of the Roman Catholic Church) missions were established to convert the indigenous populations. Large silver mines and other minerals were discovered in the late 16th century. Mining activity eventually facilitated the development of an early working-class movement. Miners organized a group in the late 18th century to demand better wages and better working conditions.

The independence movement was pushed for by patriots and priests loyal to Miguel Hidalgo. An army of more than six thousand was formed in Hidalgo and headed by two priests. Indigenous revolts also added fuel to the political instability that characterized Mexico during the 1810s. Eventually, independence leaders prevailed, but personal disputes remained and political instability characterized much of 19th-century life in Hidalgo. During the Mexican-American War (1846–48), US troops occupied Hidalgo and defeated a Mexican loyalist army from Tampico in the Mexican state of Tamaulipas.

When the Mexican Republic was restored, Hidalgo was converted into a state in 1869.

Political conflicts did not disappear, but peace was more common during the Porfiriato period, when Porfirio Diaz (1830–1915; president from 1877 to 1880 and again from 1884 to 1911) took power, Agriculture and mineral production remained central to the state's economy. When opposition leader Francisco Madero (1873–1913) announced his presidential campaign in 1908, Hidalgo leaders supported him. When Porfirio Díaz (1830–1915) decided to run for reelection in 1910, Hidalgo joined the revolutionary forces. Madero's troops occupied Pachuca in 1911. A number of battles occurred in Hidalgo until years after the 1917 constitution was approved and passed into law for Mexico. The revolution ended in Hidalgo years after the rest of the country was pacified. In the 1920s and 1930s, the Roman Catholic Church and the Mexican government struggled over who would control the people and the economy of the country. This conflict, known as the Cristero War, reached Hidalgo. Some Roman Catholic loyalists attempted to oppose the revolutionary government's effort to restrict the power of the church.

9 ■ State and Local Government

A state governor is elected every six years for a nonrenewable term. A legislature comprised of a twenty-nine-seat congress, eighteen elected in single member districts and eleven by proportional representation, serve for nonrenewable three-year terms and have formal check-and-balance powers. However, existing separation of power provisions have not been enforced since the state legislature and state governorship have always been controlled by the Institutional Revolutionary Party (PRI).

The eighty-four municipalities that exist in the state have limited but considerable formal attributions and powers. Municipal presidents and council members are elected for nonrenewable three-year terms. Some opposition party candidates have won a number of municipal presidencies in recent years.

10 ■ Political Parties

The three main political parties in all of Mexico are the Institutional Revolutionary Party (PRI), the National Action Party (PAN), and Party of the Democratic Revolution (PRD). The PRI has controlled the state governorship since the early 1900s. Manuel Ángel Nuñez won the 1999 elections, and new gubernatorial elections are scheduled for 2005. The conservative PAN and left-wing PRD have grown in recent years, but only the PAN has a statewide organization capable of challenging the PRI.

11 ■ Judicial System

A Superior Tribunal of Justice is the state's highest court. Its members are appointed by the president with legislative approval. If they are ratified after their six-year terms expire, they serve until the mandatory retirement age of sixty-five. The president of the Superior Tribunal is appointed by its members. Membership in the Superior Tribunal is restricted to qualified attorneys. In addition, the judicial system is comprised of an electoral tribunal and lower courts.

12 ■ Economy

Most industry is centered around the municipalities along the western border, including Tepeji del Rio and Tula. Industries in these areas produce textiles and assemble industrial products. Agriculture is also an important segment of the economy.

13 ■ Industry

Textiles and cement are two primary industries.

14 ■ Labor

The US Bureau of Labor Statistics reported that Mexican workers saw their wages increase 17%, from $2.09 per hour in 1999 to $2.46 per hour in 2000. (The average US worker earned $19.86 per hour in 2000.) After one year, workers are entitled by law to six days paid vacation.

15 ■ Agriculture

La Huasteca, a lowland region that covers the northern part of the state, has fertile soil and adequate rain for agriculture. Sugarcane, corn, oats, barley, wheat, beans, chilies, coffee, and fruits are grown there. There are also pastures for raising livestock.

In arid and rocky areas where there is no irrigation for crops, a hardy plant, the maguey, is grown. A liquid, called *agua miel* (honey water), accumulates in the center of the plant. This liquid is collected and fermented to make a popular drink known as *pulque*. The plant also produces grubs (*chinicuiles*) that are gathered, cooked, and eaten. Residents of Hidalgo also eat ants' eggs (*escamoles*) as part of their diets.

16 ■ Natural Resources

Hidalgo is rich in mineral deposits, including lead, iron, manganese, and zinc. There is also production of precious metals and minerals, such as gold, silver, and opals. Stone and marble, used to decorate churches and other buildings, is quarried in the state. There are thermal springs that attract tourists.

17 ■ Energy and Power

The government-run Federal Electricity Commission (CFE) supplies most of Mexico's power. Unlike many states to the north where demand for power is increasing, the demand for electricity in Hidalgo remained fairly constant during the late 1990s. There is an electrical plant and an oil refinery in Tula.

18 ■ Health

The state of Hidalgo has 25 general hospitals, 722 outpatient centers, and 37 surgical centers. Most of the Mexican population is covered under a government health plan. The IMSS (Instituto Mexicano de Seguro Social) covers the general population. The ISSSTE (Instituto de Seguridad y Servicios Sociales de Trabajadores del Estado) covers state workers.

19 ■ Housing

Only about one-half of the housing available in Hidalgo is in good repair. More than 30% is in need of significant upgrading. Many homes do not have running water or access to electricity.

20 ■ Education

The system of public education was first started by President Benito Juárez (1806–1872) in 1867. Public education in Mexico is free for students from ages six to sixteen. According to the 2000 census, there were approximately 550,000 school-age students in the state. Many students elect

© Kal Muller/Woodfin Camp

La Huasteca, a lowland region that covers the northern part of the state, has fertile soil and adequate rain for agriculture.

to go to private schools. The thirty-one states of Mexico all have at least one state university. The Universidad Autónoma de Hidalgo (Independent University of Hidalgo) is located in the capital.

21 ■ Arts

Hidalgo has six local cultural centers, including one at the Universidad Autónoma de Hidalgo. There are also eight theaters, including El Teatro de la Ciudad de San Francisco. Handicrafts produced by the artisans of Hidalgo include wool and cotton textiles, pottery, mats, and other items made from ixtle fiber of the maguey plant.

22 ■ Libraries and Museums

There are 235 libraries and twenty-five museums in the state. Pachuca, the capital, has a museum that commemorates the history of the Spanish colonial period. There is also a mining museum, where rocks and minerals of the state are displayed. The city of Tulancingo has a railroad museum.

23 ■ Media

The capital city, Pachuca, has one daily newspaper, *El Sol de Hidalgo.* A high-

© Robert Frerck/Woodfin Camp

Toltecs abandoned the city of Tula in 1156.

powered antenna is located in Tulancingo. It provides satellite communications, connecting Mexico to many other parts of the world.

24 ■ Tourism, Travel, and Recreation

Pachuca, the capital, has a cathedral and many marketplaces. The main fairs are the San Francisco Fair (October 4) and the Virgin de Guadalupe (December 12). In Tula, there is an archeological site, Huapalcalco. El Chico National Park near Pachuca offers mountain climbing.

25 ■ Sports

Pachuca, the capital, claims to be the first city in Mexico where soccer was played. Pachuca has a soccer team that plays in the 25,000-seat Hidalgo stadium. Pachuca's basketball team is the Garzas Plata.

26 ■ Famous People

The state was named for Miguel Hidalgo y Costilla (1753–1811), who is known for issuing the call for independence on September 16, 1810. Manuel Ángel Nuñez (1951–) was elected governor in 1999.

27 ■ Bibliography

Books

Carew-Miller, Anna. *Famous People of Mexico.* Philadelphia: Mason Crest Publishers, 2003.

DeAngelis, Gina. *Mexico.* Mankato, MN: Blue Earth Books, 2003.

Supples, Kevin. *Mexico.* Washington, DC: National Geographic Society, 2002.

Web Sites

Mexico for Kids. http://www.elbalero.gob.mx/index_kids.html (accessed on June 11, 2004).

Visit Mexico: State of Hidalgo. http://www.visitmexico.com/destinations/r_cen/s_hil/ (accessed on June 17, 2004).

Jalisco

Pronunciation: hah-LEES-koh.

Origin of state name: The name Jalisco comes from the Náhuatl words *xali ixco* (sandy surface).

Capital: Guadalajara.

Entered country: 1824.

Coat of Arms: At the center is a dark blue shield with gold borders, accented with red x-shapes. Two golden lions face a tree in the center. Above the shield, there is a helmet with a red pennant flying from its top.

Holidays: Año Nuevo (New Year's Day—January 1); Día de la Constitución (Constitution Day—February 5); Benito Juárez's birthday (March 21); Primero de Mayo (Labor Day—May 1); Revolution Day, 1910 (November 20); and Navidad (Christmas—December 25).

Flag: There is no official flag.

Time: 6 AM = noon Greenwich Mean Time (GMT).

1 ▪ Location and Size

Jalisco is located in the center of Mexico. It has an area of 80,137 square kilometers (30,941 square miles), which is a little smaller than the U.S. state of South Carolina. Jalisco is bordered to the northwest by the Mexican state of Nayarit; to the north by the Mexican states of Zacatecas, Aguascalientes, and San Luis Potosí; to the east by the Mexican states of Guanajuato and Colima; and to the west by the Pacific Ocean. Jalisco has 124 municipalities. Its capital is Guadalajara.

Jalisco has large mountain ranges (*sierras*) including the Sierra Madre Occidental, with plateaus. The Los Huicholes, Los Guajalotes, and San Isidro Mountains, El Gordo Hill, and the Tequila volcano all form part of the Sierra Madre Occidental. Other mountains include the Cacoma, Manantlán, Tapalpa, and Lalo. In the southern part of the state lie the Nevado de Colima and Colima volcanoes.

Nuevo Vallarta is only about 7 miles (11 kilometers) from the Puerto Vallarta Airport in the neighboring state of Jalisco.

There are large valleys in the state. The most important rivers in Jalisco include the Lerma-Santiago, which crosses the central part of the state. The Lerma River begins in México state and runs into Lake Chapala. The San Juan de los Lagos and San Miguel Rivers cross the Los Altos zone of Jalisco.

Lake Chapala is the largest lake in Mexico. The San Marcos, Cajititlán, Atotonilco, Zacoalco, and Sayula lagoons are also found in Jalisco.

2 ■ Climate

In the capital, Guadalajara, the January temperature averages 16°C (60°F). In June, the average is 23°C (74°F). Rainfall is heaviest between June and September. Average annual rainfall is 134 centimeters (53 inches). Puerto Vallarta on the Pacific Ocean is warmer, with average January temperatures of 22°C (71°F) and June average temperatures 28°C (82°F).

3 ■ Plants and Animals

There are tropical forests with mahogany, rosewood, and cedar trees, mosses, and orchids. There are also lemon, coconut, and banana trees. In the cooler regions, there are white pine (and other species of pine), oak, fir, birch, and hazelnut trees. Native

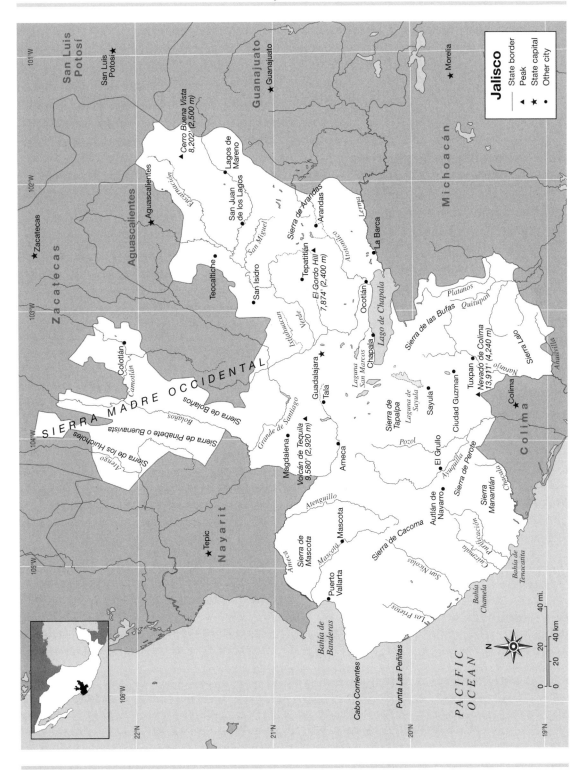

Jalisco
- State border
- ▲ Peak
- ★ State capital
- • Other city

San Luis Potosí

★ San Luis Potosí

Guanajuato

★ Guanajuato

▲ Morelia

Michoacán

★ Zacatecas

Zacatecas

Aguascalientes

★ Aguascalientes

▲ Cerro Buena Vista 8,202' (2,500 m)

Lagos de Mareno

San Juan de los Lagos

Sierra de Arandas

Arandas

Lerma

La Barca

Encarnación

San Miguel

Teocaltiche

• San Isidro

Tepatitlán

El Gordo Hill 7,874' (2,400 m)

Ocotlán

Chapala

Lago de Chapala

Atotonilco

Verde

Ixtlahuacán

Laguna San Marcos

Sierra de las Bufas

Platanos

Quitupan

Sierra Lalo

Colotlán

Camotlán

SIERRA MADRE OCCIDENTAL

Sierra de Bolaños

Bolaños

Grande de Santiago

Guadalajara

Tala

Laguna de Sayula

Sayula

Sierra de Tapalpa

Tuxpan

Nevado de Colima 13,911' (4,240 m)

Naranjo

Colima

Colima

Ahuijulla

Sierra de Pinabete o Buenavista

Sierra de los Huicholes

Atengo

Magdalena

Volcán de Tequila 9,580' (2,920 m)

Ameca

Pozol

El Grullo

Ciudad Guzman

Ayuquila

Sierra de Perote

Autlán de Navarro

Sierra Manantlán

Chacala

Purificación

Calzada

▲ Tepic

Nayarit

Ameca

Sierra de Mascota

Mascota

Mascota

Atenguillo

Sierra de Cacoma

San Nicolás

Bahía de Tenacatita

Puerto Vallarta

Bahía de Banderas

Los Pretios

Bahía Chamela

Bahía de Tenacatita

Cabo Corrientes

Punta Las Peñitas

PACIFIC OCEAN

N

40 mi.

40 km

20

20

0

0

101°W

102°W

103°W

104°W

105°W

106°W

22°N

21°N

20°N

19°N

animals include pumas, jaguars, wolves, coyotes, wildcats, badgers, foxes, deer, eagles, doves, grouse, sparrow hawks, and many types of snakes. Small animals such as squirrels and raccoons also find habitat in Jalisco.

4 ▇ Environmental Protection

Sierra de Manantlan Biosphere Reserve is located between the states of Jalisco and Colima in west-central Mexico. The reserve, which protects the Jalisco dry forests, is one of the most important protected areas in North America for biodiversity. It shelters over 2,700 species of plants (40% of all plants native to Mexico). About 560 species of vertebrates are protected there, including 26% of all mammal and 33% of all bird species in Mexico.

5 ▇ Population, Ethnic Groups, Languages

Jalisco had a total population of 6,322,002 in 2000; of the total, 3,070,241 were men and 3,251,761 were women. The population density was 80 people per square kilometer (207 people per square mile). In 2000, the capital of Guadalajara, Mexico's second-largest city, had a population of 1,647,720. Almost all residents of Jalisco speak Spanish.

6 ▇ Religions

According to the 2000 census, 84% of the population, or 5.3 million people, were Roman Catholic; about 2%, or 110,413 people, were Protestant. That year there were also 40,646 Jehovah's Witnesses and 983 Jews. About 90,000 people reported no religion.

7 ▇ Transportation

Guadalajara-Don Miguel Hidalgo Airport and Puerto Vallarta International-Gustavo Diaz Ordaz Airport provide international flights to and from Jalisco. The Guadalajara airport is the second-busiest airport (after Mexico City) in Mexico.

8 ▇ History

The first human settlements date back to more than ten thousand years ago. In 300 A.D., the Mexican states of Nayarit, Colima, and Jalisco witnessed the emergence of a sedentary civilization near the Pacific Ocean. Towards the interior, more than a dozen different groups lived by the time the Spaniards first arrived in Mexico in 1519.

First invaded by Spaniard Alonso de Avalos in 1522, the area that now constitutes Jalisco, together with Aguascalientes and Zacatecas, was later named Nueva Galicia. Spanish conqueror Nuño de Guzmán (d. 1544) gained control of the region in 1536, but an indigenous rebellion in 1541 evolved into the Mixton War. Eventually, the Spaniards defeated the indigenous rebels and successfully incorporated the region into the colonial economy. Its capital city, Guadalajara, was founded in 1531. Many of the more than fifty Catholic churches in Guadalajara date from the colonial period, and its cathedral was finished in 1618. Indigenous revolts in 1593 and 1601 brought instability and generated a violent reprisal by the Spanish colonizers. A university was created in 1792, twenty-five years after the expulsion of the Jesuits (an order of the Roman Catholic Church). The first printing press was brought to Guadalajara in 1793.

In November of 1810, Guadalajara fell under the siege of the independence insurgents, who fought against Spanish control of Mexico. Father Miguel Hidalgo (1753–1811), one of the leaders of the independence movement, decreed the end of slavery there. Bishop Juan Cruz Ruiz de Cabañas y Creso, a priest who was a part of the independence movement, excommunicated (banned from the church) Hidalgo. After Hidalgo's assassination royalist forces moved to defeat the pro-independence insurgents and retake Guadalajara. Eventually, Jalisco joined other Mexican states in the formal declaration of independence under the Plan of Iguala agreement in 1821 and a new state constitution was passed into law in 1825. However, military uprisings and epidemic outbreaks hurt the economy and the consolidation of Jalisco as a powerful state during the mid-19th century.

Benito Juárez (1806–1872), the leader of the liberal faction that was seeking to establish a strong central government, was captured in Guadalajara in 1858 and almost killed. Eventually, Juárez and his allies emerged as the victor of the war between the liberals and the conservatives (who supported French colonial rule), but Jalisco initially supported the conservative forces and French emperor Maximilian (1832–1867). (France had conquered and ruled parts of Mexico from 1864 to 1866.) Eventually, the liberal forces gained control of Jalisco and Porfirio Díaz (1830–1915) governed with the acquiescence of the Jalisco elite until the Mexican Revolution broke out in 1910. Split among the different factions, Jalisco militias loyal to Díaz overpowered the revolutionaries early on in the Mexican Revolution. Later, revolutionary leader Francisco "Pancho" Villa (1878–1923) entered Guadalajara with

© Peter Langer/EPD Photos

Iglesia del Carmen (del Carmen Church) in Guadalajara, one of the more than 50 Roman Catholic churches in Guadalajara.

his legendary Northern Division. Villa demanded land distribution and recognition of the peasants as legitimate actors in Mexican politics. After peace was mostly achieved in 1917, the revolutionary victors did not easily control Jalisco. Conflict raged between the Roman Catholic Church and the new government throughout the 1920s and 1930s. This conflict, known as the Cristero War, was launched by conservative Roman Catholics who opposed the anti-clerical positions of the new government. The conflict originated in Jalisco, where most of the fierce battles were fought.

Eventually, the revolutionary government made peace with the Roman Catholic Church. Conservative Jalisco leaders coexisted with revolutionary governors. Jalisco soon evolved to become a major industrial center.

Beginning in the 1930s, the Institutional Revolutionary Party (PRI) exercised control in Jalisco. Many believed the PRI maintained control of the country by discouraging debate. The late 1960s and early 1970s were characterized by unrest and demands for government reforms throughout Mexico. Several guerrilla groups (radical political groups) were operating in Jalisco during this period. In 1973, they kidnapped the father-in-law of then Mexican president Luis Echeverría (1970–1976) and former Jalisco governor José Guadalupe Zuno. As in the rest of the country, guerilla activity decreased in the late 1970s. In the 1980s, the conservative National Action Party (PAN) emerged as the main threat to the control that the PRI had successfully achieved over Jalisco. PAN continued to grow in influence through the 1980s, 1990s, and 2000s.

9 ■ State and Local Government

A state governor is democratically elected for a nonrenewable six-year term. The state congress is comprised of forty deputies. Twenty are elected in single member districts, and twenty are elected by proportional representation, all for nonrenewable three-year terms. Separation of power and check-and-balance provisions were first fully exercised after PAN candidate Alberto Cárdenas became state governor in 1995.

There are 124 municipal governments in Jalisco. They have varying degrees of informal independence. The larger municipalities have more control over their own budgets. Municipal presidents and council members are elected for nonrenewable three-year terms.

10 ■ Political Parties

The three main political parties in all of Mexico are the Institutional Revolutionary Party (PRI), the National Action Party (PAN), and the Party of the Democratic Revolution (PRD). As in most other Mexican states, the PRI exercised absolute control of state level politics since the end of the Mexican Revolution until the late 1980s. PAN victories in local elections prepared the way for an impressive PAN triumph at the gubernatorial race in 1995. The PAN again won the 2001 gubernatorial election with former Guadalajara mayor Francisco Ramírez Acuña. The PRD has limited presence in the state.

11 ■ Judicial System

The Supreme Tribunal of Justice is the highest court in Jalisco. Its members are appointed by a two-thirds majority in congress from a list presented by the judiciary. Members are appointed for seven-year terms. If ratified, the second and last term is ten years of service. Appointees must meet strict qualification requirements. Strict separation of power between the executive, legislative, and judicial is provided for in detail in the state constitution. In addition, Jalisco has an electoral tribunal and local courts.

© Peter Langer/EPD Photos

Fountain in Guadalajara.

12 ■ Economy

Jalisco's economy ranks third among the Mexican states. Tourism along the Pacific Ocean coastline, especially around the resort of Puerto Vallarta, is an important segment of the economy. Jalisco produces tequila, an alcoholic beverage sold in Mexico and also exported. Petróleos Mexicanos, the state petroleum company, is exploring for oil in the southeast part of the state. Along the southern coast, fishing and mining are important. The state is a major producer of sugar.

13 ■ Industry

Over thirty of Mexico's largest companies are based in Jalisco. The state manufactures 60% of all computers produced in Mexico. Many industries produce agricultural products. Crops that are processed include peanuts and agave (for the production of tequila). Embroidery, formerly done by hand, is now mechanized. Embroidered garments are produced for export, especially to Asia through the port of Manzanillo in the neighboring state of Colima. Jalisco beekeepers produce commercial quantities of honey.

14 ▦ Labor

The US Bureau of Labor Statistics reported that Mexican workers saw their wages increase 17%, from $2.09 per hour in 1999 to $2.46 per hour in 2000. (The average US worker earned $19.86 per hour in 2000.) After one year, workers are entitled by law to six days paid vacation.

15 ▦ Agriculture

Jalisco is the country's leading producer of corn and sugar. Jalisco also has large, modern dairy and poultry farms. Crops grown in the state include beans, oats, alfalfa, chilies, sorghum, onions, and chickpeas. Farmers also raise cattle, pigs, sheep, and goats.

16 ▦ Natural Resources

Along the coast there is a thriving fishing industry. There are silver and gold mines in northern Jalisco. The dry forests thrive in regions where there is rain during four or five months of the year. During the dry periods, the trees of the dry forests lose their leaves. Jalisco's dry forests grow in the region around the Colima volcano.

17 ▦ Energy and Power

Almost all of the energy in Mexico is provided by the Federal Electricity Commission (CFE). In February 2002, the CFE introduced new electric rates. For households that use less than 140 kilowatt hours per month, there was no rate increase. (This is about 75% of all Mexican households, according to CFE). After the rate increased in 2002, about 44% of Jalisco residents were charged higher rates because they used more than the minimum electricity.

18 ▦ Health

The state of Jalisco has 45 general hospitals, 999 outpatient centers, and 219 surgical centers. The Hospital San Javier in Guadalajara is the only center for gamma knife surgery in Mexico. There is also an AmeriMed hospital in Puerto Vallarta.

Most of the Mexican population is covered under a government health plan. The IMSS (Instituto Mexicano de Seguro Social) covers the general population. The ISSSTE (Instituto de Seguridad y Servicios Sociales de Trabajadores del Estado) covers state workers.

19 ▦ Housing

Over three-fourths of the housing available in Jalisco is in good repair. Only 5% is in need of significant upgrading. These homes may not have running water or access to electricity.

20 ▦ Education

The system of public education was first started by President Benito Juárez in 1867. Public education in Mexico is funded by the state and is free for all students ages six to sixteen. According to the 2000 census, there were approximately 1.4 million school-age students in the state. However, many students elect to go to private schools. The thirty-one states of Mexico all have at least one state university. The Universidad de Guadalajara (University of Guadalajara) is located in the capital.

21 ▦ Arts

Jalisco has almost seventy local cultural institutions. There are also twenty-seven theaters, including the Lakeside Little Theater, which sponsors works in English.

© Peter Langer/EPD Photos

Cathedral in Guadalajara. Many Roman Catholic churches in Guadalajara date from the colonial period, and its cathedral was finished in 1618.

Jalisco also has a philharmonic orchestra. The Teatro Degollado in Guadalajara, which presents musical and theater productions, opened in 1866 with an opera production.

22 ▨ Libraries and Museums
There are 226 branches of the national library system in Jalisco. There are also sixty-six museums. Cocula has a museum dedicated to the art of the *mariachi* (traditional Mexican music). The Museo Tonal-lán (Tonalá Museum) features paintings and traditional pottery and masks. The Instituto de las Artesanías Jaliscienses (Arts and Crafts Institute of Jalisco) is in the capital, Guadalajara. The capital also has a wax museum, a museum of paleontology (the study of fossils), a popular art museum, an archeological museum, a museum of science and technology that includes a planetarium, and a museum of the army and air force.

23 ▨ Media
The capital, Guadalajara, has five daily newspapers: *Guadalajara Reporter, El Informador, El Occidental,* the English-language *Guadalajara Colony Reporter,* and *Mural.*

24 ▨ Tourism, Travel, and Recreation
The capital, Guadalajara, is known as the Pearl of the West because of its beautiful architecture and geographic location. It is also the home of many festive *mariachi* bands that play at weddings and other festivals. Along with golf and tennis, Guadalajara also hosts *charro* (rodeos), where cowboys compete in roping and riding events. Zoológico Guadalajara is a major zoo in the capital. Puerto Vallarta is the state's best-known resort. Tourists enjoy sport fishing, rock climbing, and mountain biking. Zapopan has the Museo de Casa Albarrón, featuring taxidermy (stuffed and mounted animals) exhibits of the great hunters. The famous "Mexican hat dance" originated in the city of Guadalajara.

25 ▪ Sports

Soccer is extremely popular, and there are three soccer teams in the state—Guadalajara, Atlas, and Tapatio. Soccer matches are played in the 63,163-seat Estadio Jalisco (Jalisco Stadium). The university's soccer team in Guadalajara plays in the 30,000-seat 3 de Marzo stadium. There is also a 20,000-seat bullfighting ring in Guadalajara. Zapopan has a basketball team, the Tecos de la Universidad Autónoma de Guadalajara, which plays in the 40,000-seat Gimnasio Universitario.

26 ▪ Famous People

Notable Jalisco citizens include Bishop Juan Cruz Ruiz de Cabañas y Crespo (b. Spain, 1752–1824), who directed the construction of the Cabañas hospice for homeless people and orphans. The Cabañas became the headquarters for the state secretary of culture in 1992. Artist Gerardo Murillo (1875–1964) was born in Guadalajara and used the pseudonym Dr. Atl. Muralist José Clemente Orozco (1883–1949) was born in Ciudad Guzmán.

His *Man of Fire* may be seen in the Cabañas Institute in Guadalajara. Novelist Agustín Yáñez (1904–1980) wrote about myths of the indigenous people and the Spanish colonial era. His works include the novels *The Edge of the Storm* and *The Lean Lands*. Popular writer Juan Rulfo (1918–1986) is best-known for his works *The Burning Plain* and *Pedro Páramo*. Carlos Santana (b. 1947), whose band is Santana, is a famous Mexican rock-and-roll guitarist born in Autlan De Navarro.

27 ▪ Bibliography

Books

Carew-Miller, Anna. *Famous People of Mexico.* Philadelphia: Mason Crest Publishers, 2003.

DeAngelis, Gina. *Mexico.* Mankato, MN: Blue Earth Books, 2003.

Supples, Kevin. *Mexico.* Washington, DC: National Geographic Society, 2002.

Web Sites

Guadalajara Reporter. http://www.guadalajara reporter.com (accessed on June 15, 2004).

Mexico for Kids. http://www.elbalero.gob.mx/index_ kids.html (accessed on June 15, 2004).

México

Pronunciation: MEH-hee-koh.

Origin of state name: The state (and country) name comes from words in the language of the indigenous Náhuatl people: *metztli* (moon), *xictli* (center), and *co* (place).

Capital: Toluca.

Entered country: 1824.

Coat of Arms: A shield surrounded by gold trim, and a red border with the words "Libertad Travajo Cultura" (Spanish for "Freedom Work Culture"). In the upper left is a pyramid, representing the historic Aztec civilization; in the upper right, commemorating the Battle of Cross Mountain in the war for independence, two crosses rise above a green peak. A cannon is firing in front of the peak. The lower half of the shield features an open book with a pick and a spade, representing the rich ores found in the state. The yellow and brown rays in the background represent agriculture.

Holidays: Año Nuevo (New Year's Day—January 1); Día de la Constitución (Constitution Day—February 5); Benito Juárez's birthday (March 21); Primero de Mayo (Labor Day—May 1); Revolution Day, 1910 (November 20); and Navidad (Christmas—December 25).

Flag: There is no official state flag.

Time: 6 AM = noon Greenwich Mean Time (GMT).

1 ■ Location and Size

México state is one of the thirty-one states of Mexico. Its capital, Toluca, lies near the center of the state. México state is bordered on the north by the Mexican states of Querétaro and Hidalgo; on the east by the Mexican states of Tlaxcala and Puebla; on the south by Distrito Federal (Federal District) and the Mexican states of Morelos and Guerrero; and on the west by the Mexican state of Michoacán. It has an area of 21,196 square kilometers (8,184 square miles), about the same size as the US state of Massachusetts. México has 122 municipalities.

The state of México is crossed by three parallel volcanic chains. There are mountains in the west, the Monte Alto and Las Cruces Mountains in the center of the state, and the Sierra Nevada in the east.

The northern region consists of flatlands and hills; in the south, there are mountains, canyons, and ravines; in the east, there are mountains and volcanoes; in the west, there are plains, hills, and mountains; and in the central area, there are extensive broad valleys surrounded by hills. One of the largest volcanoes is Iztaccíhuatl (5,286 meters/17,343 feet).

The state of México's rivers include the Lerma, the Tula, the Moctezuma, and the Pánuco. Some areas of the state, such as the valley of Cuautitlán-Texcoco, have no water resources.

2 ▪ Climate

The climate varies considerably by region. In the valley regions, the climate is hot and dry. Around the capital, Toluca, the climate is cooler. The average annual temperature range in Toluca is 12 to 17°C (54 to 63°F). Rainfall in Toluca averages 800 to 900 millimeters (31 to 35 inches).

3 ▪ Plants and Animals

In the eastern part of the state, the mountains of the Sierra Nevada are covered with pine, oak, white cedar, and fir trees. Plants native to the valleys are cactus, nopal (similar to prickly pear), copal trees (a type of tree with heavy, thick resin), and gourds.

Native animals include coati (a raccoon-like animal) and deer. There are many bird species native to the state, including the sparrow hawk. The state of México and its southern neighbor, Michoacán, are winter home to hundreds of thousands of migrating monarch butterflies.

4 ▪ Environmental Protection

There is a reserve to protect the habitat of the migrating monarch butterflies. Its territory, which was expanded in 2001 to 54,000 hectares (133,400 acres), lies in both México and Michoacán. In 2003, the government of México was considering requiring its industrial plants to track pollutants. A national park, Parque Nacional Izta-Popo, covers the terrain around the volcanic peaks Iztacíhuatl and Popocatepetl. Popocatepetl, which lies in neighboring Puebla, is the highest active volcano in the Northern Hemisphere.

5 ▪ Population, Ethnic Groups, Languages

México had a total population of 13,096,686 in 2000; of the total, 6,407,213 were men and 6,689,473 were women. The population density was 586 people per square kilometer (1,517 people per square mile). In 2000, the capital of Toluca had a population of 665,617. About 97% of citizens speak Spanish as their first language; 3% speak one of the indigenous languages as their first language.

6 ▪ Religions

According to the 2000 census, 77% of the population, or ten million people, were Roman Catholic; 3%, or 423,068 people, were Protestant. That year there were also 12,354 Seventh-Day Adventists, 25,491 Mormons, 134,468 Jehovah's Witnesses, and 14,084 Jews. Over 280,000 people reported no religion.

7 ▪ Transportation

There are international airports in Toluca (Toluca-Alfonso Lopez Airport) and Mexico City that provide international flight service to México state. There are 1,227 kilometers (762 miles) of railroad tracks. A system of 9,510 kilometers (5,907 miles) of highways links the state with the rest of the country.

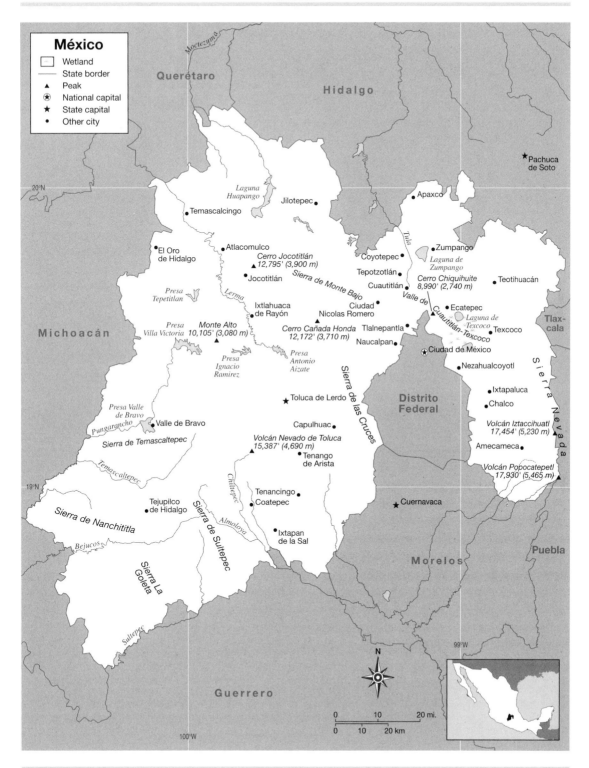

México

- ▢ Wetland
- State border
- ▲ Peak
- ✪ National capital
- ★ State capital
- • Other city

Querétaro

Hidalgo

Michoacán

Tlax-cala

Distrito Federal

Morelos

Puebla

Guerrero

★ Pachuca de Soto

Moctezuma

20°N

Laguna Huapango

• Jilotepec

• Apaxco

• Temascalcingo

• Atlacomulco

Cerro Jocotitlán ▲ 12,795' (3,900 m)

• Coyotepec

• Zumpango

Laguna de Zumpango

• El Oro de Hidalgo

• Jocotitlán

Sierra de Monte Bajo

• Tepotzotlán

Cerro Chiquihuite 8,990' (2,740 m)

• Teotihuacán

Presa Tepetitlan

Lerma

• Ixtlahuaca de Rayón

• Ciudad Nicolas Romero

• Cuautitlán

Valle de

• Ecatepec

Laguna de Texcoco

• Texcoco

Presa Villa Victoria

Monte Alto 10,105' (3,080 m) ▲

Cerro Cañada Honda ▲ 12,172' (3,710 m)

• Tlalnepantla

Cuautitlán-Texcoco

• Naucalpan

• Nezahualcoyotl

Presa Ignacio Ramirez

Presa Antonio Aizate

✪ Ciudad de México

Sierra Nevada

Presa Valle de Bravo

★ Toluca de Lerdo

Sierra de las Cruces

Distrito Federal

• Ixtapaluca

• Chalco

Pungarancho

• Valle de Bravo

• Capulhuac

Volcán Iztaccihuatl 17,454' (5,230 m)

Sierra de Temascaltepec

Volcán Nevado de Toluca ▲ 15,387' (4,690 m)

• Tenango de Arista

• Amecameca

Temascaltepec

19°N

Chiltepec

• Tenancingo

• Coatepec

★ Cuernavaca

Volcán Popocatepetl ▲ 17,930' (5,465 m)

• Tejupilco de Hidalgo

Sierra de Nanchititla

Sierra de Sultepec

Almoloya

• Ixtapan de la Sal

Morelos

Puebla

Bejucos

Sierra La Goleta

Sultepec

N

99°W

0   10   20 mi.

0   10   20 km

100°W

© Robert Frerck/Woodfin Camp

The Temple of the Moon at the head of the Street of the Dead in Michoacan de Ocampo includes ruins that date to 100 B.C.

8 ▊ History

First inhabited around 5000 B.C., the central valley of México was the home to several different civilizations before the Aztecs settled in the region around the 13th century. Among the early civilizations, Olmec and Toltec groups built towns and religious centers. Perhaps the most important pre-Aztec constructions, the pyramids of the Sun and the Moon, belong to the Teotihuacan culture (200 to 800 A.D.). By the time the Spaniards arrived, Toltec groups inhabited the valley surrounding the capital city Tenochtitlán, where the Aztecs ruled.

Spanish conqueror Hernán Cortés (1485–1547) organized in Texcoco the attack on México-Tenochtitlán in 1521. Dutch Franciscan priests (from an order of the Roman Catholic Church) first settled in the region in 1523 to convert the large indigenous population that inhabited the central valley of México. Jesuits, Agustines, and Dominican priests (from other orders of Catholicism) joined the Catholic conversion efforts starting in the 1530s. The Tepozotlán convent was one of the most important Jesuit centers in the entire continent during the Spanish conquest of Mexico.

Yet, the diseases brought by the Spaniards and the oppression imposed upon the indigenous communities brought the population down from two million at the time of the conquest to about two hundred thousand a century later. Agricultural production and services to the growing capital city of México, one of the most important centers of Spanish colonial presence in the Americas, represented the region's main economic activities during the 17th and 18th centuries.

The independence movement quickly reached the then Province of México. The independence army overpowered the royalists (loyal to Spain) in Toluca and then moved on to Mexico City. The royalist opposition to independence was defeated in a bloody battle at Las Cruces Mountain in 1810. After the execution of independence leader José Morelos (1765–1815), the region was once again controlled by the royalist forces. Yet, the new independence movement in 1821 was finally successful in freeing the province from Spanish colonial rule. In 1827, the separation of Mexico City as the nation's capital forced the province of México to establish Toluca as the new state capital.

US troops briefly occupied the state in 1847. Constant administrative and political reforms assigned former state of México territories to newly created provinces and states during much of the 19th century. The state became a central fighting ground for the civil war between liberals and conservatives in the 1860s. Yet, after the liberals were victorious, the state was peacefully controlled first by liberal president Benito Juárez (1806–1872) and later by President Porfirio Díaz (1830–1915). During the years that Porfírio Díaz was in power, roads, bridges, and other structures were built. He also consolidated the central government and made it strong enough to begin to challenge the influence

of the Roman Catholic Church and the large landowners. The years that Porfírio Díaz was in power (1877–1880 and 1884–1911) came to be known as the Porfiriato period.

Another revolution began in 1910 and became known as the Mexican Revolution. This new conflict caused friction in the state between large landowners and landless peasants. The creation of the Mexico Federal District (Mexico DF), as the nation's capital, at the end of the revolution in 1917, was the last time the state lost territory to newly created entities. Rapid urbanization and industrial development characterized the state's economy during most of the 20th century.

Although it is formally and legally a different state, with significant rural population, a significant share of the state's population inhabits the areas that surround Mexico DF and are thus considered today part of the larger metropolitan area of one of the most populated cities in the world.

9 ▨ State and Local Government

The powerful state governor is elected democratically every six years and cannot be immediately re-elected. The legislature is a unicameral (one) chamber comprised of forty-five members elected in single member districts and thirty members elected by proportional representation. Deputies serve for three-year terms and cannot be immediately re-elected. Because the Institutional Revolutionary Party (PRI) has dominated the executive and legislative branches throughout most of the 20th century, existing division of power and check-and-balances provisions have only been recently utilized as opposition parties have increased their presence in the legislature.

The 122 municipal governments that comprise the state of México hold municipal president and council member elections every three years. Immediate re-election is prohibited. Larger municipalities have more resources, especially those that border Mexico City.

10 ▪ Political Parties

The three main political parties in the country of Mexico are the Institutional Revolutionary Party (PRI), the National Action Party (PAN), and the Party of the Democratic Revolution (PRD). The PRI has controlled politics in the state of México since the end of the revolution. No other party has succeeded in winning a gubernatorial race in that state, although the PAN and the PRD have won important municipal presidencies. Governor Arturo Montiel Rojas was elected for a six-year term in 1999.

11 ▪ Judicial System

The Superior Tribunal of Justice is the highest court of the state of México. Its members are appointed by a special council of the judiciary and their nonrenewable term lasts for fifteen years. The renewal of justices is staggered to provide continuity to the high court. Only qualified and experienced attorneys can be appointed to the high court by the council of the judiciary. In addition, an electoral court and various local courts also constitute the state judicial system.

12 ▪ Economy

The state of México has a strong economy based in manufacturing and mining. It is also one of Mexico's major producers of staple crops. The Teotihuacan pyramids are an international tourist destination. The state of México's economic activity represents 10% of the national gross domestic product (GDP).

13 ▪ Industry

The state of México's chief industries are food processing, construction, motor vehicles, chemicals, textiles, paper, machinery and assembly industries, electric and electronic equipment and appliances. Twenty industrial parks are operating throughout the state with companies such as Chrysler, Ford, Nissan, Hoechst, Pfizer, and Motorola among them. Handicrafts, such as wooden carvings, pottery, metal, basketwork, and the paper lampshades, onyx, obsidian figures, and stone mortars of the Zumpango region are produced in México state.

14 ▪ Labor

The US Bureau of Labor Statistics reported that Mexican workers saw their wages increase 17%, from $2.09 per hour in 1999 to $2.46 per hour in 2000. (The average US worker earned $19.86 per hour in 2000.) After one year, workers are entitled by law to six days paid vacation.

15 ▪ Agriculture

Crops are grown in the state of México on large and small farms. Some of the farmland is irrigated while some is not. Cultivation of irrigated crops include the mango, avocado, orange, plum, nuts, mamey (similar to an apricot), and papaya. Non-irrigated crops are corn, wheat, alfalfa, maguey (cactus), lima beans, tomatoes, and beans.

16 ■ Natural Resources

There are nine national parks located in the state of México. Visitors to the state's national parks can enjoy mountain climbing, fishing, camping, or horseback riding. In Nevado de Toluca National Park, there is a volcanic crater with two deep lakes. Scuba divers and hikers enjoy the natural environment of these crater lakes. Bird watching, especially hummingbirds, is popular in Zoquiapan y Anexas National Park. Sacramonte National Park features views of the Popocatépetl and Iztacíhuatl volcanoes from the top of Sacramonte Hill.

17 ■ Energy and Power

Almost all of the energy in Mexico is provided by the Federal Electricity Commission (CFE). In February 2002, the CFE introduced new electric rates. For households that use less than 140 kilowatt hours per month, there was no rate increase. (This is about 75% of all households, according to CFE). After the rate increases in 2002, state of México residents were charged higher rates because they use more than the minimum electricity.

18 ■ Health

The state of México has 71 general hospitals; 1,192 outpatient centers; and 183 surgical centers.

Most of the Mexican population is covered under a government health plan. The IMSS (Instituto Mexicano de Seguro Social) covers the general population. The ISSSTE (Instituto de Seguridad y Servicios Sociales de Trabajadores del Estado) covers state workers.

19 ■ Housing

Over three-fourths of the housing available in the state of México is in good repair. Only 9% is in need of significant upgrading. These homes may not have running water or access to electricity.

20 ■ Education

The system of public education was first started by President Benito Juárez in 1867. Public education in Mexico is free for students from ages six to sixteen. According to the 2000 census, there were approximately 2.7 million school-age students in the state. Many students elect to go to private schools. The thirty-one states of Mexico all have at least one state university. Universidad Autónoma del Estado de México (Independent University of the State of México) is in Toluca.

21 ■ Arts

The state of México has its own Ballet Folklórico company. There are over fifteen theaters and thirty-nine cultural centers, located in Toluca and other cities. There are also several chapters of the French cultural society Alianza Francesa.

22 ■ Libraries and Museums

The state of México has 587 branches of the national library system. There are also seventy-four museums. The capital city, Toluca, has a museum devoted to watercolor paintings, a museum of modern art, a science museum, botanical gardens, a stamp museum, and a museum of anthropology. The city of Teotihuacán, an excavated ruin, showcases the pyramids and city structure of the Aztec civilization.

Popocatepetl volcano viewed from the east, from a site between Tlaxcala and Puebla.

23 ■ Media

The capital city, Toluca, has two daily newspapers, *El Diario* and *El Sol de Toluca.*

24 ■ Tourism, Travel, and Recreation

The capital city, Toluca, is mainly an industrial city. Tourists often stay in Toluca hotels when they travel to visit the ruins of the Aztec ceremonial city Teotihuacán. At Teotihuacán, the famous Pyramids of the Sun and the Moon are located. Teotihuacán means "the place where men become gods." Ixtapán de la Sal is famous for its spas and thermal baths. The Parque Nacional Izta-Popo (Izta-Popo National Park) is the home of México's two famous volcanoes, Popocatépetl and Iztacíhuatl.

25 ■ Sports

Toluca has a basketball team, La Ola, that plays in a 6,000-seat stadium. Nearby Mexico City has six soccer stadiums, including the 114,465-seat Estadio Azteca (Aztec Stadium). Toluca also has several minor league soccer teams, which play at the 26,000-seat Nemesio Diez stadium. Nezahualcoyotl has a professional soccer team, NEZA, which plays in the 37,075-seat Neza 86 stadium.

26 ▨ Famous People

Juana Inés de la Cruz (1651–1695) was a nun who became a well-known poet and outspoken supporter of women's rights.

27 ▨ Bibliography

Books

Carew-Miller, Anna. *Famous People of Mexico.* Philadelphia: Mason Crest Publishers, 2003.

DeAngelis, Gina. *Mexico.* Mankato, MN: Blue Earth Books, 2003.

Supples, Kevin. *Mexico.* Washington, DC: National Geographic Society, 2002.

Web Sites

Mexico for Kids. http://www.elbalero.gob.mx/index_kids.html (accessed on June 15, 2004).

Visit Mexico: State of Mexico. http://www.visitmexico.com/destinations/r_cen/s_mex/ (accessed on June 17, 2004).

Michoacán

Pronunciation: mee-CHO-ah-CAHN.

Origin of state name: Probably comes from the native word Mechoacan, which means "place of the fishermen."

Capital: Morelia (moh-REH-lee-ah).

Entered country: October 3, 1824.

Coat of Arms: The fish at the top of the state coat of arms refers to Michoacán as the "place of fishermen." The picture of a man on horseback represents Generalísimo José María Morelos y Pavón (1765–1815), for whom the capital city of Morelia was named. The three crowns symbolize the history of the region as part of the Purépecha empire. The buildings pictured are meant to represent industry and culture. Blue is used to depict the sky and water.

Holidays: Año Nuevo (New Year's Day—January 1); Día de la Constitución (Constitution Day—February 5); Benito Juárez's birthday (March 21); Primero de Mayo (Labor Day—May 1); Revolution Day, 1910 (November 20); and Navidad (Christmas—December 25).

Flag: There is no official state flag.

Time: 6 AM = noon Greenwich Mean Time (GMT).

1 ▦ Location and Size

Michoacán is located in west-central Mexico. It has an area of 59,865 square kilometers (23,114 square miles), which is a little smaller than the US state of West Virginia. Michoacán is bordered on the north and west by the Mexican state of Jalisco; on the north by the Mexican state of Guanajuato; on the northeast by the Mexican state of Querétaro; on the east by the Mexican states of México and Guerrero; on the west by the Mexican state of Colima and the Pacific Ocean; and on the south by Guerrero and the Pacific Ocean. Michoacán has 113 municipalities. Its capital is Morelia.

Michoacán is formed in part by two large mountain ranges, the Transversal Volcanic Sierra and the Sierra Madre del Sur. There are more than eighty volcanoes in the state, including Pico de Tancítaro (3,842 meters/12,605 feet) and Patamban (3,750 meters/12,303 feet). Other important volcanoes include Paricutín volcano (2,775 meters/9,100 feet) and the twenty-six volcanic craters in its vicinity. There are fifty-five volcanic craters near Pico de Tancítaro.

© Peter Langer/EPD Photos

This waterfall is found in Eduardo Ruiz National Park, named for historian Eduardo Ruiz. The park lies near Uruapan, about 120 kilometers (75 miles) from the capital, Morelia.

In the north, the land is generally flat; the Maravatío and Zamora valleys are located in this region.

Lake Chapala lies on the border with Jalisco. It is Mexico's largest lake. Lake Chapala has an area of about 1,686 square kilometers (651 square miles). Other lakes in the state include Cuitzeo, Pátzcuaro, and Zirahuén. The Río Lerma (Lerma River) rises in Mexico state and crosses Michoacán in the north. Other rivers flow into it, including the Angulo and Duero. The Balsas River runs along the border with Guerroro.

2 ■ Climate

The climate varies widely from place to place depending on altitude and prevailing winds. The coast enjoys a tropical climate with an average temperature of about 28°C (82°F). The central region has a milder climate, with an average temperature of about 22°C (71°F). The high-altitude regions can experience freezing temperatures.

The average temperature in the state ranges from a minimum of 18°C (64°F) to a maximum of 28°C (83°F). The average precipitation ranges from a minimum of 64

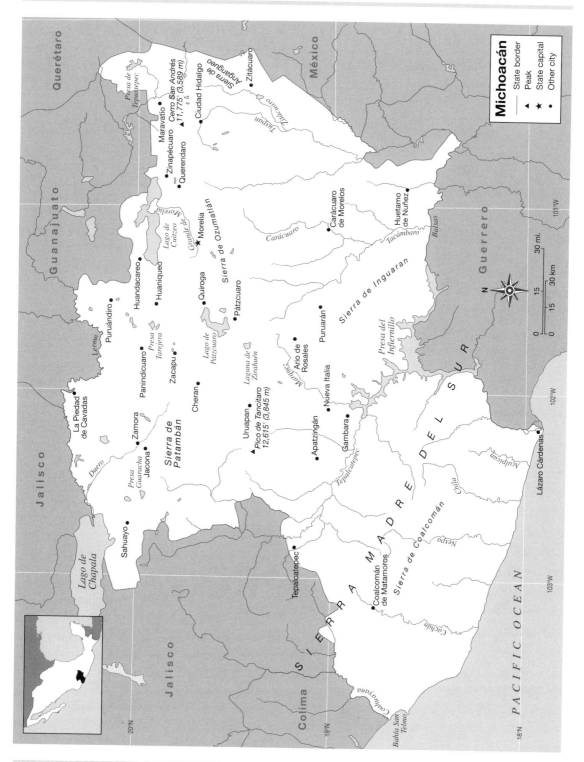

Michoacán

- —— State border
- ▲ Peak
- ★ State capital
- • Other city

Querétaro

México

Guanajuato

Presa de Tepaltepec

Maravatío
Zinapécuaro Cerro San Andrés ▲ 11,775' (3,589 m)
Querendaro
Ciudad Hidalgo
Zitácuaro
Zitácuaro

Sierra de Angangueo

Tuxpan

Zitácuaro

Morelia
Grande de Morelia
Lago de Cuitzeo
★ Morelia
Sierra de Ozumatlán

Carácuaro
de Morelos

Carácuaro

Huetamo
de Nuñez

Tacámbaro

Balsas

Guerrero

Huandacareo
Huaniqueo
Quiroga
Pátzcuaro

Puruándiro

Presa Tarejera

Lago de Pátzcuaro

Puruarán

Sierra de Inguaran

Presa del Infiernillo

101°W

N

30 mi.

30 km

15

15

0

Panindícuaro
Zacapu

Lerma

Cheran

Laguna de Zirahuén

Ario de
Rosales

Matanguez

Nueva Italia

Presa de Patamban

Uruapan
▲ Pico de Tancítaro
12,615' (3,845 m)

Apatzingán

Gambara

Sierra de

La Piedad
de Cavadas

Zamora
Jacona

Duero

Presa Guaracha

Sahuayo

Lago de Chapala

Jalisco

Tepalcatepec
Tepalcatepec

Coalcomán
de Matamoros

Sierra de Coalcomán

Chila

Nexpa

Aguililla

Lázaro Cárdenas

102°W

103°W

SIERRA MADRE DEL SUR

Cachán

PACIFIC OCEAN

Bahía San Telmo

Coahuayana

Colima

Jalisco

20°N

19°N

18°N

centimeters (25 inches) to a maximum of 162 centimeters (64 inches).

3 ▪ Plants and Animals

The state has a wide variety of tree species, including forests of oak, cedar, and pine. Mango trees can be found in the eastern and western regions. Common animals include coyotes, skunks, armadillos, squirrels, and lynxes. Eagles and parrots are found in the tropical regions. Sharks, whales, and porpoises inhabit the waters of the coast. There are more species of whales and porpoises here than in any other part of the world. Marine life includes about nine hundred fish species and thirty-four species of marine mammals.

4 ▪ Environmental Protection

In the eastern region of the state, there are five protected areas that serve as the winter home for the monarch butterflies of North American. Each year, tens of millions of monarch butterflies migrate to the high-altitude fir forests from Canada and the United States. In 2001, the governments of the states of México and Michoacán began a program to expand the reserve areas from 39,540 acres to a total of 133,400 acres.

There are seven other national parks in Michoacán, including Lago de Cuemécaro located in Tenancicuaro.

In 2003, Michoacán received a federal grant to establish a system requiring industries to track pollutants.

5 ▪ Population, Ethnic Groups, Languages

In 2000, Michoacán had a total population of 3,985,667. Of the total, 1,911,078 were men and 2,074,589 were women. The population density was 68 people per square kilometer (176 people per square mile). In 2000, the capital, Morelia, had a population of 619,958. Almost all citizens speak Spanish as their first language. About 3.5 percent of the population speaks an indigenous (native) language as their first language.

6 ▪ Religions

According to the 2000 census, 83% of the population, or 3.3 million people, were Roman Catholic; nearly 2%, or 63,726 people, were Protestant. That year there were also 31,787 Jehovah's Witnesses and over 75,000 people who reported no religion.

7 ▪ Transportation

Uruapan Airport provides international flights to and from Michoacán. There are about 8,618 kilometers (3,353 miles) of roads in the state and 1,275 kilometers (792 miles) of railroads.

8 ▪ History

Olmec and Nahuatl groups inhabited the region since 200 B.C. Indigenous Quechua groups migrated to the region around 500 A.D. and eventually dominated the other groups. The Quechua established the capital city in Páztcuaro, one of the oldest indigenous cities built in Mexico. Later, another indigenous leader, Tariácuri, conquered new land. He founded the Purépecha empire. His descendants estab-

© Peter Langer/EPD Photos

The aqueduct in the capital, Morelia, was built in 1785. It stretches for more than one mile (1.6 kilometers) through the city.

lished the capital city in Tzintzuntzán and expanded the empire. They challenged the influence of the Aztec empire in central Mexico before the arrival of the Spanish conquistadors (Spanish conquerors of the Americas).

Emperor Zuuangua defeated an invading Aztec army led by Montezuma II (Moctezuma II; 1466–1520). He secured his empire and kept out Aztec rule. Spanish conqueror Hernán Cortés (1485–1547) arrived in the region in 1519. Zuuangua later rejected a plea to fight the Spanish conquistadors. He tried to remain neutral. But he died of smallpox, a disease brought by the Spaniards.

Eventually, his empire was conquered by the Europeans.

In 1522, Spanish soldier Cristobal de Olid (1488–1524) peacefully conquered the Purépecha empire for the Spanish crown. The population was already decimated by diseases brought by the Spaniards. The military might of the conquistadors overpowered all indigenous resistance efforts. Spanish leader Nuño Beltrán de Guzmán summoned Purépecha emperor Tangáxoan to Mexico City for talks. But instead of talking, he kidnapped him. Beltrán de Guzmán asked for a large ransom of gold before he would set Tangáxoan free. Beltrán de Guzmán later

The picturesque town of Angangueo, the center of the area where monarch butterflies migrate each year.

launched a conquest of Michoacán in 1530. It ended with the torture and execution of Tangáxoan and the Spanish occupation of the region.

In 1533 Vasco de Quiroga initiated the conversion of the indigenous communities to the teachings of the Roman Catholic Church. He was made bishop of Michoacán in 1538. The city of Morelia was founded in 1541.

Agricultural activity characterized much of the colonial period (period of Spanish rule). Frequent volcanic eruptions caused the deaths of thousands of indigenous people.

When the independence movement began in Mexico (about 1810), Mexican priest and revolutionary Miguel Hildago y Costilla (1753–1811) entered Morelia without much resistance. Royalists (those loyal to Spain) had abandoned the city a few days earlier. During Hidalgo's stay in Morelia, the newly appointed governor declared the end of slavery. The independence fighters were eventually defeated by Royalists in 1811 at a battle at Calderón Bridge, however, and true independence was not achieved until 1821.

Political instability characterized much of the 19th century, until Mexican general and later president Porfirio Díaz

(1830–1915) brought peace to the country. He took control after the death of President Benito Juárez (1806–1872). Porfirio Díaz initiated a long period of liberal authoritarian rule known as "porfiriato." The revolution of 1910 brought an end to porfiriato. Michoacán became a central battleground for revolutionaries who wanted land reform. Several revolutionary leaders fought in Michoacán. Thousands of landless peasants joined armies and militias to win more rights and land for peasants.

The most important 20th-century Mexican president, Lázaro Cárdenas (1895–1970), was a native of Michoacán. Cárdenas was named president in 1934. He adopted land reforms and gave millions of peasants the right to farm on communal (shared) lands. Cárdenas also nationalized the oil companies. This provided the government with money for education, health care, and public services. Cárdenas also brought political stability and formed the Institutional Revolutionary Party (PRI). Cárdenas is known as the father of present-day Mexico. He is revered as the man who brought stability to the country. His land distribution policies improved the standards of living for a majority of Mexicans.

9 ■ State and Local Government

The state governor is elected every six years and cannot be immediately re-elected. In relative terms, the executive has enormous powers and attributions. The legislative assembly is comprised of a unicameral (single) chamber with forty deputies (twenty-four are elected from single member districts and sixteen are elected by proportional representation). Checks and balances and separation of powers provisions were not fully enforced until

2001, when the Party of the Democratic Revolution (PRD) won the state gubernatorial race and no party won absolute majority in the state legislature.

The 113 municipal governments in Michoacán democratically elect their municipal presidents and council members every three years. Immediate re-election is not allowed. Municipal governments in more populated cities have more influence, resources, and leverage than governments in largely rural areas.

10 ■ Political Parties

The three main political parties in all of Mexico are the Institutional Revolutionary Party (PRI), the National Action Party (PAN), and the Party of the Democratic Revolution (PRD). The PRI historically dominated Michoacán politics. The PRD has emerged as the strongest party in recent years. In 2002, the PRD's candidate, Lázaro Cárdenas Batel, was the first man to defeat a PRI candidate for governor. He is the grandson of Lázaro Cárdenas, the founder of the PRI and former president of Mexico, and the son of Cuauhtemoc Cárdenas, the founder of the PRD. Lázaro Cárdenas Batel capitalized on the strength of the left in Michoacán and his family name recognition.

11 ■ Judicial System

The Supreme Tribunal of Justice is the highest court in the state. Its seven members are elected for three-year terms and can be re-elected. Justices must retire when they reach the age of seventy. New appointments are made by the legislature from a three-person list submitted by the governor. Other judicial bodies are the electoral tribunal and local courts. Although judicial independence was nominally established in the state constitution, the excessive influence exerted by the PRI over local authorities in the past prevented the full autonomy of the state judicial system.

12 ▪ Economy

Finance and insurance companies account for the largest percentage of the economy (about 20%) in Michoacán. Service-based companies account for 18% of the economy, followed by agriculture, 17%; trade, 17%; manufacturing, 14%; transportation and communication, 8%; construction, 5%; and mining, 1%.

13 ▪ Industry

Handicrafts, oil, and iron and steel are the primary industries. The largest steel plant in Latin America is located in Michoacán.

14 ▪ Labor

Michoacán citizens have migrated in large numbers to work in the United States and elsewhere. The US Bureau of Labor Statistics reported that Mexican workers saw their wages increase 17%, from $2.09 an hour in 1999 to $2.46 an hour in 2000. (The average US worker earned $19.86 an hour in 2000.)

15 ▪ Agriculture

Michoacán is the largest producer of avocados in the country. The state also ranks third in the nation for production of chickpeas and lemons, and fourth for production of sesame and sorghum. Sugarcane, corn, and wheat are important staples. Mangoes, strawberries, papaya, and limes are grown as well.

The breeding of livestock is important in Michoacán. Pork, beef, and poultry are the main meat products. The state is also known for its production of milk, eggs, honey, and beeswax.

16 ▪ Natural Resources

Michoacán is Mexico's third-largest timber producer.

Mining has played a significant role in the state's economy. About thirty-two cities have substantial deposits of iron ore. The iron and steelworks facility at Lázaro Cádenas processes large quantities of iron, zinc, and steel. Gold has been found in Angangueo and Churumuco. Copper is produced in Coalcomán and Tingambato.

The fishing industry provides mojarra (small silvery fish), carp, red snapper, turtles, and oysters.

17 ▪ Energy and Power

Almost all of the energy in Mexico is provided by the Federal Electricity Commission (CFE). In February 2002, the CFE introduced new electric rates. For households that use less than 140 kilowatt hours per month, there was no rate increase. (This is about 75% of all households in Mexico, according to CFE).

18 ▪ Health

There are 43 general hospitals, 864 outpatient centers, and 89 surgical centers in Michoacán.

Most of the Mexican population is covered under a government health plan. The IMSS (Instituto Mexicano de Seguro Social) covers the general population. The

© Woodfin Camp

Fishers on Pátzcuaro Lake use butterfly-shaped nets.

ISSSTE (Instituto de Seguridad y Servicios Sociales de Trabajadores del Estado) covers state workers.

19 ■ Housing

Only about one-half of the housing available in Michoacán is in good repair. About 19% is in need of significant upgrading. Many homes do not have running water or access to electricity.

20 ■ Education

The system of public education was first started by President Benito Juárez in 1867. Public education in Mexico is free for students from ages six to sixteen. According to the 2000 census, there were approximately one million school-age students in the state. Many students elect to go to private schools. The thirty-one states of Mexico all have at least one state university. Both the El Colegio de Michoacán and the Universidad Michoacana are located in Michoacán. The oldest university on the American continent, Universidad Michoacana de San Nicolás de Hidalgo, was founded in 1540. (It was known as Colegio de San Nicolás Hidalgo at that time.)

© Kal Muller/Woodfin Camp

Janitzio Island lies in Pátzcuaro Lake. Its buildings have white walls and red-tiled roofs. A 40-meter (132-foot) monument of Mexican patriot José Morelos, sculpted from pink stone, stands on the island's highest point.

21 ■ Arts

Michoacán has a contemporary dance company and a musical group called Ensamble de las Rosas. There is a symphony orchestra in Morelia. A children's chorus, Niños Cantores de Morelia, is also based in Morelia. There are also eighteen theaters and sixteen auditoriums. Most communities have local cultural centers.

22 ■ Libraries and Museums

Michoacán has two hundred libraries. The capital, Morelia, has a mask museum and a museum of contemporary arts. The city of Aquila has a museum dedicated to sea turtles.

23 ■ Media

The capital city, Morelia, has four daily newspapers: *Diario de Morelia*, *El Sol de Morelia*, *La Extra*, and *La Voz de Michoacán*. The city of Zamora publishes *El Sol de Zamora*.

24 ■ Tourism, Travel, and Recreation

Morelia is a main tourist attraction. People living in Morelia enjoy spring-like temper-

© Kal Muller/Woodfin Camp

Masks made from vegetables are seen during a festival in Uruapan.

atures year-round. There are communities of retired American and Canadian citizens in Morelia. These communities sponsor courses for those who wish to study Spanish. Morelia is a beautiful colonial city offering museums and shopping. One of the main attractions is the planetarium.

25 ▪ Sports

Morelia has a basketball team, the Zorros. It also has a soccer team, which plays in the 38,384-seat Morelos stadium. The 15,000-seat Plaza Monumental in Morelia is a bullfighting ring. There is a smaller

ring, the Palacio del Arte, which holds four thousand people.

26 ▪ Famous People

José María Morelos y Pavón (1765–1815) was born in the city of Vallatoid, which has since been renamed Morelia in his honor. He was a priest and soldier who served as a popular revolutionary leader. Lázaro Cárdenas (1895–1970) was president of Mexico from 1934 to 1940 and became known as a champion for the working class. Alfonso García Robles (1911–1991) was a Mexican statesman. He received the

Noble Peace Prize in 1982 for his work toward nuclear disarmament.

27 ■ Bibliography

Books

Andrade, Mary J. *The Vigil of the Little Angels: Day of the Dead in Mexico.* San Jose, CA: La Oferta Review, 2001.

DeAngelis, Gina. *Mexico.* Mankato, MN: Blue Earth Books, 2003.

Supples, Kevin. *Mexico.* Washington, DC: National Geographic Society, 2002.

Web Sites

Mexico for Kids. http://www.elbalero.gob.mx/index_kids.html (accessed on June 15, 2004).

Surfing & Adventure Travel in Mexico: The State of Michoacán. http://www.surf-mexico.com/states/Michoacan/ (accessed June 17, 2004).

Morelos

Pronunciation: moe-RAY-lohss.

Origin of state name: Named for the military hero José María Morelos y Pavón (1765–1815), who fought in the war for Mexican independence.

Capital: Cuernavaca (kwair-nah-VAH-kah).

Entered country: April 1869.

Coat of Arms: The green field in the center features a cornstalk, symbolizing the fertility of the land. The silver banner above the cornstalk contains the Spanish words for land and freedom. Around the border is a slogan from revolutionary leader Emiliano Zapata (1879–1919): "The land will be returned to those who work it with their hands."

Holidays: Año Nuevo (New Year's Day—January 1); Día de la Constitución (Constitution Day—February 5); Benito Juárez's birthday (March 21); Commemoration of the Free and Sovereign State of Morelos (April 16); Primero de Mayo (Labor Day—May 1); Revolution Day, 1910 (November 20); and Navidad (Christmas—December 25).

Flag: There is no official state flag.

Time: 6 AM = noon Greenwich Mean Time (GMT).

1 ■ Location and Size

Morelos is located in south-central Mexico. The region is known as the "Central Breadbasket" because it is an important center for agriculture. The state has an area of about 4,942 square kilometers (1,908 square miles), about the same size as the US state of Delaware. It is bordered on the north by the Distrito Federal (Federal District); on the northwest and northeast by México state; on the southeast by the Mexican state of Puebla; and on the west and southwest by the Mexican state of Guerrero. Morelos has thirty-three municipalities. The capital is Cuernavaca.

The northern and eastern regions of Morelos are mountainous. The highest peaks are El Tezoyo, Tres Cumbres, El Palomito, La Corona, and La Herradura.

Most of the rivers of Morelos are formed by rainwater that runs off the northern mountains. The Amacuzac River crosses the southeastern part of the state. The Grande and Tepalcingo Rivers are found in the eastern part of the state.

Lagoons near Cuernavaca.

The largest lake is Laguna Tequesquitengo (teh-keh-kee-TEN-go), with an area of about 124 square kilometers (48 square miles). Many popular hunting and fishing resorts are found there.

2 ■ Climate

The country is divided into three basic climatic regions: Sierra Alta, Piedemonte, and Los Valles. Los Valles (the valleys) covers most of the state and has hotter temperatures. The small Sierra Alta and Piedemonte regions are in the higher elevations of the north, which generally have cooler temperatures.

Temperatures in the state range from a minimum of about 10°C (49°F) to a maximum of about 23°C (74°F). The capital city of Cuernavaca is known worldwide as "The City of Eternal Spring" because of its temperate climate. The average year-round temperature in Cuernavaca is 20°C (68°F). The main rainy season is from the end of May until September. Annual precipitation ranges from 87 centimeters (34 inches) in some regions to 183 centimeters (72 inches) in other areas.

3 ■ Plants and Animals

In the Sierra Alta region, there are forests of pine, fir, and oak. Other plants include

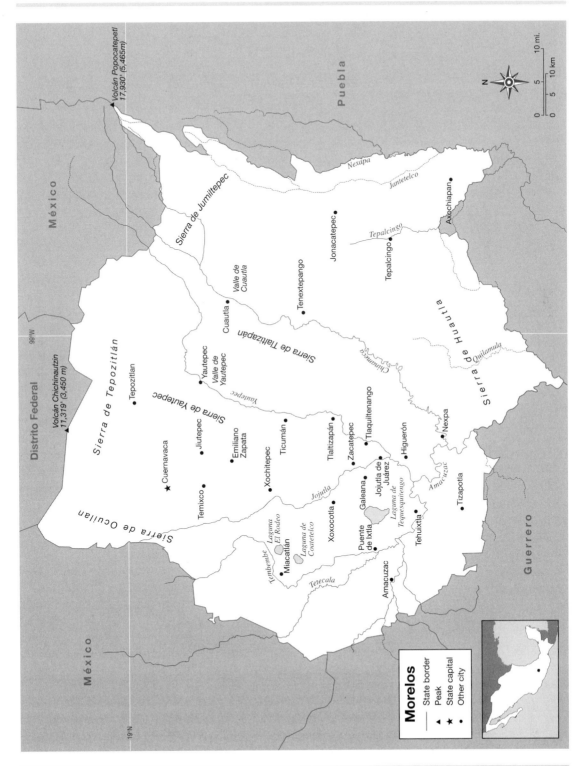

Morelos
- State border
- ▲ Peak
- ★ State capital
- • Other city

Cuernavaca Cathedral

madrona (a shrub with yellow berries) and ferns. Carnations, lilies, violets, and marigolds are common flowers. In the Piedemonte region, there are nopal (a type of cactus), cactus, mesquite, and maguey. In the valleys, there are willows and amates. Poinsettias, the official flower of Cuernavaca, are grown in some regions. Bougainvillea is common throughout the state.

Common bird species include quail, eagles, sparrow hawks, and doves. The gallina de monte, an endangered bird species, is found in Morelos as well. Coyotes, badgers, and tlacuaches (Mexican opossum) are found throughout state, as are chameleons and iguanas.

4 ▪ Environmental Protection

Lagunas de Zempoala National Park (lah-GOO-nahs dai zem-po-AH-lah) lies in northwest Morelos near the border with the state of México. It features three volcanic crater lakes. Cacahuamilpa National Park near the town of Taxco serves to protect a series of dramatic natural caverns with some chambers that are 82.2 meters (270 feet) high. There are six national parks in Morelos.

5 Population, Ethnic Groups, Languages

In 2000, Morelos had a total population of 1,555,296. Of the total, 750,799 were men and 804,497 were women. The population density was 318 people per square kilometer (823 people per square mile). In 2000, the capital, Cuernavaca, had a population of 337,966. Almost all citizens speak Spanish as their first language. About 2.3 percent of the population speaks an indigenous (native) language as their first language.

6 Religions

According to the 2000 census, 72% of the population, or 1.1 million people, were Roman Catholic; 6%, or 97,860 people, were Protestant. That year there were also 9,455 Seventh-Day Adventists, 4,719 Mormons, 27,084 Jehovah's Witnesses, and 1,788 Jews. Over 70,000 people reported no religion.

7 Transportation

Cuernavaca Airport provides international flights to and from Morelos. The state has about 1,819 kilometers (1,130 miles) of roads and 246 kilometers (153 miles) of railroads.

8 History

The first human settlements in Morelos date back to 2000 B.C. Toltec groups inhabited the land and started farms in the area. Around 600 A.D., the Xichicalco became the region's largest settlement. According to some historians, the worshiping of Quetzalcóatl (believed to be the father of civilization) was first started there. In the 12th century, the end of the Toltec empire allowed for the settlement of different groups in the region. In the 14th century, the Tlahuicas became the largest group in the region. In the late 1420s, the Tlahuicas were overpowered despite fierce resistance and were then absorbed by the Aztec empire.

When the Spaniards arrived, Spanish conqueror Hernán Cortés (1485–1547) sent Gonzalo de Sandoval to conquer the region in 1521. In 1523, Sandoval settled in the region. He established North America's first sugar cane mill at Tlaltenango. The first Franciscan priests arrived in 1529 to convert the indigenous people to the Roman Catholic faith. Diseases and mistreatment by Spanish settlers drastically reduced the indigenous population during the 16th and 17th centuries. Later in the 17th century, African slaves were brought to work on the sugar cane and other plantations. The region became an important route to connect the capital city of Mexico with the southern provinces during the colonial period.

The independence movement did not reach Morelos until 1811, a year after the historic uprising initiated by Mexican priest and revolutionary Miguel de Hidalgo y Costilla (1753–1811). Cuernavaca, the most important city in the region, became a center of independence revolt. Priest José Morelos (1765–1815) fought for independence in the state until he was killed in 1815. Yet, resistance against Spanish rule persisted in the region. When independence was finally achieved for the entire country in 1821, Cuernavaca joined in.

As in the rest of Mexico, political instability characterized much of the 19th century. Morelos continued to be one of the largest producers of sugar cane in the world. The large landowners and the plantation

© Peter Langer/EPD Photos

A street scene in the capital, Cuernavaca.

economy combined to create enormous inequalities between the wealthy and the working peasants. Morelos lies close to the capital of the country. Because of this, Morelos also became a strategic battleground for all those who sought to overthrow the national government during the 19th century. During this period, the region was given the name Morelos after independence leader José Morelos.

In 1910, when the Mexican Revolution began, several leaders who sought to promote land distribution revolted against the government. Emiliano Zapata (1879–1919) was among them. Together with revolutionary Francisco "Pancho" Villa (1878–1923),

Zapata is one of the best known heroes of the Mexican Revolution. Zapata was leader of the Southern Liberation Army. He fought fiercely alongside the ever-changing factions of the revolution to demand peasant rights and land reform. After the new constitution was approved in 1917, Zapata continued fighting to improve the lives of peasants. He was captured and killed in 1919.

Several uprisings demanding land reform and vindicating peasants' rights took place during the 20th century after the revolution. But the central government successfully maintained order and peace. A rapid industrialization process and ambitious development of the infrastructure helped Morelos become an industrial, agricultural, and tourist center in the decades after the end of the revolution.

9 ▪ State and Local Government

The governor is elected for a nonrenewable six-year term and exerts an enormous influence over state matters. The legislature is comprised of a thirty-member state congress. Deputies are elected for nonrenewable three-year terms—eighteen members are elected from single member districts, and twelve are elected for proportional representation. Formal provisions for separation of power and checks and balances have recently been tested. For the first time since the end of the revolution, a party other than the Institutional Revolutionary Party (PRI) won the gubernatorial race in 2000. Sergio Estrada Cajigal Ramírez, a member of the National Action Party (PAN), was elected for a six-year term ending in 2006.

The thirty-three municipalities that comprise the state of Morelos elect their municipal presidents and council members every three years, for nonrenewable terms. Larger municipalities have more leeway to decide their own budget and make administrative decisions.

10 ▪ Political Parties

The three main political parties in all of Mexico are the Institutional Revolutionary Party (PRI), the National Action Party (PAN), and the Party of the Democratic Revolution (PRD). Despite the historical predominance of the PRI in the state, the emergence of strong opposition in the 1990s in the rest of Mexico reached Morelos, too. The PAN is now the strongest party in the state, but the PRD has a growing presence as well. The PRI continues to exert influence in local governments.

11 ▪ Judicial System

The Superior Tribunal of Justice is comprised of justices appointed by the state congress from a three-person list presented by the Council of the Judiciary. Justices are elected for an initial six-year period. If they are ratified, they cannot be removed until they reach the mandatory retirement age of sixty-five. Only highly qualified attorneys familiar with state legislation can be included on the list presented by the Council of the Judiciary.

12 ▪ Economy

Service-based companies account for about 23% of the economy in the state. Manufacturing is the second largest economic group at about 19%. Trade accounts for about 17%, followed by finance and insurance companies at 14%, agriculture and livestock at 12%, transportation and communications at 9%, construction at 5%, and mining at 1%.

The main exports are motor vehicles, tomatoes, sugar cane, honey, and flowers.

13 ▪ Industry

Nissan Mexicana, Upjohn, Beecham de México, and Firestone all have large facilities in the state, mostly near Cuernavaca.

14 ▪ Labor

The US Bureau of Labor Statistics reported that Mexican workers saw their wages increase 17%, from $2.09 per hour in 1999 to $2.46 per hour in 2000. (The average US worker earned $19.86 an hour in 2000.)

© Peter Langer/EPD Photos

Coastline near Nuevo Vallarta, a resort city.

After one year, workers are entitled by law to six days paid vacation.

15 ■ Agriculture

Morelos is considered to be one of Mexico's most important agricultural regions. Flowers such as carnations, bird of paradise, and chrysanthemums are grown for export. Corn, tomatoes, and avocados are grown throughout the state. Sugar cane and peaches are also important crops. Livestock include sheep, cows, pigs, horses, goats, and poultry.

16 ■ Natural Resources

Morelos has rich archaeological sites.

17 ■ Energy and Power

Almost all of the energy in Mexico is provided by the Federal Electricity Commission (CFE). In February 2002, the CFE introduced new electric rates. For households that use less than 140 kilowatt hours per month, there was no rate increase. (This is about 75% of all households in Mexico, according to CFE). Electricity consumption declined in the mid-1990s in Morelos.

18 ■ Health

There are 12 general hospitals, 264 out-patient centers, and 33 surgical centers in Morelos.

Most of the Mexican population is covered under a government health plan. The IMSS (Instituto Mexicano de Seguro Social) covers the general population. The ISSSTE (Instituto de Seguridad y Servicios Sociales de Trabajadores del Estado) covers state workers.

19 ■ Housing

About two-thirds of the housing available in Morelos is in good repair. Only 10% is in need of significant upgrading. These homes do not have running water or access to electricity.

20 ■ Education

The system of public education was first started by President Benito Juárez (1806–1872) in 1867. Public education in Mexico is free for students from ages six to sixteen. According to the 2000 census, there were approximately 300,200 school-age students in the state. Many students elect to go to private schools. The thirty-one states of Mexico all have at least one state university. The Universidad Autonoma del Estado de Morelos (Independent University of Morelos) is located in Cuernavaca.

21 ■ Arts

Morelos has seventeen theaters, many of them open air. There is a French Alliance chapter in Cuernavaca. Also in Cuernavaca there is a cultural center named after the famous muralist David Alfaro Siqueiros (1896–1974). Two musical groups, Mitote Jazz and Banda de Música

Santamaría, are famous in Morelos. There are two puppet theaters: Artimañas and Groupo Gente (which cater to hospitals and social interaction groups).

22 ■ Libraries and Museums

There are 133 branches of the national library in Morelos. There are also thirty-eight museums. In Cuernavaca, there is a science museum and a museum of herbal medicine, which has a medicinal herb garden. Cuernavaca's Palacio de Cortes has some murals by Mexican artist Diego Rivera (1886–1957). The David Alfaro Siquieros museum also houses murals by muralist David Alfaro Siquieros.

23 ■ Media

The capital, Cuernavaca, has two daily newspapers: *El Sol de Cuernavaca* and *La Unión de Morelos.* The city of Cuautla has *El Sol de Cuautla.* There is also an English-language newspaper, *Cuernavaca Lookout.*

24 ■ Tourism, Travel, and Recreation

Morelos has a temperate climate. There are many golf courses, national parks, and spas catering to tourists. There are also many archeological sites, including Las Pilas at Chalcatzingo and the Pyramid of Tepozteco. A favorite site with tourists is the San Anton waterfall. Fairs and festivals include the Feast for Our Lady of the Miracles (late August–early September). Cuernavaca has many language schools catering to American and Canadian tourists wishing to study Spanish.

25 ■ Sports

There are no major stadiums or sports teams in Morelos. Spectators enjoy sports in Mexico City.

26 ■ Famous People

Emiliano Zapata (1879–1919) was a revolutionary who lead the native peoples of Morelos to fight for their right to own their own land. The troops who fought with him were called zapatistas.

27 ■ Bibliography

Books

Carew-Miller, Anna. *Famous People of Mexico.* Philadelphia: Mason Crest Publishers, 2003.

DeAngelis, Gina. *Mexico.* Mankato, MN: Blue Earth Books, 2003.

Supples, Kevin. *Mexico.* Washington, DC: National Geographic Society, 2002.

Web Sites

Mexico for Kids. http://www.elbalero.gob.mx/index_kids.html (accessed on June 11, 2004).

Morelos. http://www.tourbymexico.com/morelos/morprinc.htm (accessed June 17, 2004).

Nayarit

Pronunciation: nah-yah-REET.

Origin of state name: The state was named in honor of Nayar, a sixteenth-century governor of the Cora (Nayari) people, an indigenous group native to the state.

Capital: Tepic (teh-PEEK).

Entered country: February 5, 1917.

Coat of Arms: The coat of arms of Nayarit is made up of three sections. A corn stalk appears on the left, weapons appear on the right, and a mountain landscape lies across the lower section. In the center is a small shield surrounded by a white border with seven footprints, symbols of the seven tribes of the Nahuatl, or Aztecs. An illustration of the Eagle of Aztlan is in the center of the shield. Green, blue, and gold are used to represent the colors of the Nayarit landscape.

Holidays: Año Nuevo (New Year's Day—January 1); Día de la Constitución (Constitution Day—February 5); Benito Juárez's birthday (March 21); Primero de Mayo (Labor Day—May 1); Revolution Day, 1910 (November 20); and Navidad (Christmas—December 25).

Flag: There is no official state flag.

Time: 5 AM = noon Greenwich Mean Time (GMT).

1 ■ Location and Size

Nayarit is located on the western coast of Mexico. It covers an area of 27,620 square kilometers (10,664 square miles), which is a little larger than the US state of Maryland. Nayarit is bordered on the north by the Mexican states of Sinaloa and Durango; on the south by the Mexican state of Jalisco; on the east by the Mexican states of Zacatecas and Jalisco; and on the west by the Pacific Ocean. Nayarit has twenty municipalities. The capital is Tepic.

Most of the population lives in the broad valleys of the state. Tepic and Xalisco are located in the Matatipac valley, and Compostela lies in the Coatlán valley. In the mountainous eastern regions, the highest mountains include San Juan, Sanguangüey, El Ceboruco, Cumbre de Pajaritos, and Pichos.

Nayarit has 289 kilometers (181 miles) of Pacific coastline. There are clusters of islands in the Pacific Ocean that belong to Nayarit. These include Islas Marías, Isla Isabela, and Las Marietas.

The main rivers are the Santiago, San Pedro, and Acaponeta. The Ameca River forms the border with Jalisco. Las Cañas forms the border with Sinaloa. There are a number of lakes along the coast, including the Santa María del Oro, San Pedro Lagunillas, and Agua Brava.

2 ▪ Climate

The climate in the valley and coastal regions is typically warm. The average year-round temperature in Tepic is 20°C (68°F). However, there are cooler temperatures in the mountain regions. The statewide average high temperature is 27°C (80°F). The average low temperature statewide is 21°C (69°F). Annual rainfall ranges from a minimum of 77 centimeters (30 inches) in some regions to a maximum of 264 centimeters (104 inches) in other parts of the state.

3 ▪ Plants and Animals

There are mangrove trees along the coast and pastures across the valleys. Coconut palms and guava trees can be found in the state. Pine and oak trees grow in the mountain regions. Common animals include white-tailed deer, wildcats, pumas, and wild boars. Smaller mammals include skunks, badgers, rabbits, and armadillos. Mountain doves, cojólite (a kind of pheasant), and the bobo bird live in the state as well.

4 ▪ Environmental Protection

El Manglar is an organization that was formed in 1993 to protect the mangroves and rain forests. The forests were threatened by rapid growth of tourism and shrimp farming. Isla Isabel is the site of a national park.

5 ▪ Population, Ethnic Groups, Languages

In 2000, Nayarit had a total population of 920,185. Of the total, 456,105 were men and 464,080 were women. The population density was 33 people per square kilometer (85 people per square mile). In 2000, the capital, Tepic, had a population of 305,025.

Indigenous groups that live in the state are the Coras, Huicholes, Tepehuanos, and Mexicaneros. Almost all citizens speak Spanish as their first language. About 4.6% of the population speaks indigenous (native) languages as their first language.

6 ▪ Religions

According to the 2000 census, 81% of the population, or 748,579 people, were Roman Catholic; about 3%, or 24,313 people, were Protestant. That year there were also 8,686 Jehovah's Witnesses and about 30,000 people who reported no religion.

7 ▪ Transportation

Tepic Airport provides international flights to and from Nayarit. There are about 3,089 kilometers (1,919 miles) of roads and 245 miles (395 kilometers) of railroads in the state.

8 ▪ History

Although there is scattered evidence that

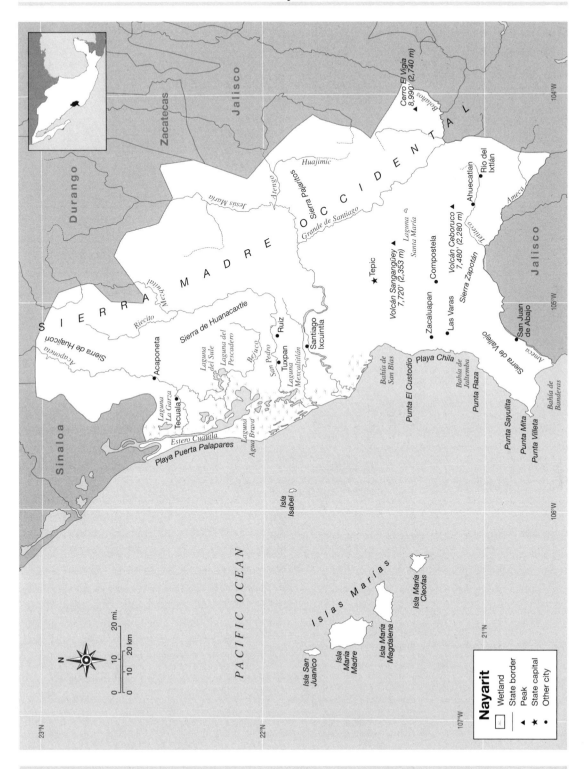

Jalisco

Zacatecas

Durango

Sinaloa

Cerro El Vigía
8,990' (2,740 m)

Bolaños

Huajimic

Atengo

Jesús María

Sierra Pajaritos

SIERRA MADRE OCCIDENTAL

Grande de Santiago

Río del
Ixtlán

Ahuecatlan

Ameca

Jalisco

Laguna
Santa María

Volcán Sangangüey ▲
7,720' (2,353 m)

Zacaluapan Compostela

Volcán Ceboruco ▲
7,480' (2,280 m)

★ Tepic

Las Varas

Sierra Zapotán

San Juan
de Abajo

Ameca

Bahía de
Banderas

Sierra de Vallejo

Mazatutul

Riecito

Sierra de Huanacaxtle

Ruiz

Santiago
Ixcuintla

Punta Raza

Bahía de
Jaltemba

Sierra de Huajicori

Acaponeta

Laguna
del Sule

Laguna del
Pescadero

San Pedro

Tuxpan

Laguna
Mexcaltitlán

Bejuco

Bahía de
San Blas

Playa Chila

Punta El Custodio

Laguna
La Garza

Tecuala

Estero Cuautla

Laguna
Agua Brava

Punta Sayulita

Punta Mita

Punta Villeta

Playa Puerta Palapares

Isla
Isabel

PACIFIC OCEAN

Islas Marías

Isla San
Juanico

Isla
María
Madre

Isla María
Magdalena

Isla María
Cleofas

20 mi.

20 km

10

10

0

0

N

23°N

22°N

22°N

21°N

107°W

106°W

105°W

104°W

Nayarit

Wetland

State border

▲ Peak

★ State capital

• Other city

© Kal Muller/Woodfin Camp

Isla Isabela is one of the islands in the Pacific Ocean that belongs to Nayarit.

Beltrán de Guzmán built the Espíritu Santo village on top of the ruins of the indigenous city of Tepic. Cortés visited Tepic in 1531 and attempted to take control of the region, but Beltrán de Guzmán successfully convinced the Spanish crown to name him governor of a newly created province for the territories conquered by Beltrán de Guzmán.

Beltrán de Guzmán was replaced in 1536 by Diego Pérez de la Torre, who died in 1538 fighting an indigenous revolt. The new governor, Cristobal de Oñate, changed the provincial capital to a valley near Tepic. Several indigenous revolts threatened the Spanish colonizers' control of the region. The most famous revolt was led by indigenous leader Tenamaxtli in 1548. During most of the 16th and 17th century, Franciscan priests (of the Roman Catholic Church) sought to convert the indigenous Cora, but many fiercely resisted Spanish occupation. Only in 1722 did the Spaniards succeed in conquering the indigenous rebels in the Nayar mountain range. Economic development was experienced in the 18th century primarily due to the region's strategic location for trade with California.

As an independence movement began to take shape in 1810, local priest and leader José María Mercado rose to control most of the region. But a royalist army (loyal to Spain) recaptured most of Nayarit a year later. A few years later, the independence movement had completely disappeared in the region.

National independence in 1821 did not bring many changes to Nayarit. The 1830s and 1840s were characterized by conflicts between centralists and federalists, whereas the 1850s and 1860s witnessed war between liberals and conservatives. The national victory of the liberals led by Benito

points to human settlements as early as 5000 B.C., it was only around 400 A.D. that the Cora civilization originated in the region. The Cora reached their most impressive level of development around 1200.

The first Spaniard to arrive in Nayarit was Hernán Cortés (1485–1547), who visited the region in an expedition in 1523. Five years later, Nuño Beltrán de Guzmán conquered the different villages that existed in the region. Famous for his ruthless behavior and his will to overpower indigenous leaders,

Juárez (1806–1872) first and by Porfirio Díaz (1830–1915) later brought peace and some economic development to Nayarit. The region was first made an autonomous entity in 1860.

During the Mexican Revolution, which started in 1910, different factions fought in Nayarit. Factions were loyal to Mexican revolutionaries Francisco Madero (1873–1913), Porfirio Díaz (1830–1915), Victoriano Huerta (1854–1916), and Venustiano Carranza (1859–1920). Some militias loyal to revolutionary Francisco "Pancho" Villa (1879–1923) also fought in the region. When the Carranza forces emerged as victorious, they quickly controlled Nayarit. The 1917 constitutional convention declared Nayarit as a federal state. A new state constitution was passed into law in 1918.

The revolutionary army was led by Lázaro Cárdenas (1895–1970) in Nayarit. Some battles were also fought in Nayarit during the Cristero war, where Roman Catholic loyalists revolted against the anti-clerical policies of the revolutionary government in the late 1920s.

There was some economic development resulting from ambitious agriculture promotion policies undertaken by the government in the 1950s and 1960s, but Nayarit has remained one of the poorest and least developed states in Mexico.

9 ■ State and Local Government

The legislature is comprised of a thirty-seat congress. Eighteen deputies are elected in single member districts and twelve are elected by proportional representation. Although historically Institutional Revolutionary Party (PRI) governors exercised overwhelming influence over the legislature, after the PRI lost the governorship to the National Action Party (PAN) in 1999, provisions for separation of powers and checks and balances have been generally enforced. Yet, the governor continues to enjoy much power and excessive influence, curtailing the oversight power of the legislature.

The twenty municipalities that comprise Nayarit hold regular democratic elections for municipal presidents and council members every three years. Immediate re-election is not allowed. Highly centralized budgetary and administrative decision making at the state level hinder the development and consolidation of local governments.

10 ■ Political Parties

The three main political parties in all of Mexico are the Institutional Revolutionary Party (PRI), the National Action Party (PAN), and the Party of the Democratic Revolution (PRD). The PRI controlled state level politics since the end of the Mexican Revolution (1910–20). All state governors were PRI members until Antonio Echevarría Domínguez, of the PAN, won the 1999 election. The PRD has a limited presence in larger town, but the PRI has survived as a strong opposition party.

11 ■ Judicial System

The Superior Tribunal of Justice is the highest court in the state. It is comprised of seven justices appointed for nonrenewable ten-year terms by the congress from a list submitted by the state governor. Only qualified and well-respected attorneys familiar with state laws and regulations can be appointed. In addition, an electoral tribunal and local courts also comprise the state's legal system. The historic influence of PRI governors over other authorities often reached the members of the Superior Tribunal, but the arrival of more competitive electoral politics has also had positive effects on the autonomy of the state judiciary.

12 ▪ Economy

Service-based companies account for about 24% of the state economy. Agriculture and livestock contribute about 20%, followed by finance and insurance companies at 17%, trade at 16%, manufacturing at 10%, transportation and communications at 9%, construction at 3%, and mining at 1%.

13 ▪ Industry

The tobacco industry has been one of the most significant contributors to the state economy. However, tourism and other service industries are becoming more important. Tepic is the site of a major cigarette factory. The headquarters for the two largest tobacco companies in the country are found in Nayarit. Other industries in the state include manufacturing activities linked to agriculture and food processing, woods, and textiles. In the south there are several small factories that produce tequila and leather goods. The sugarcane industry is also still prominent in the state.

14 ▪ Labor

The US Bureau of Labor Statistics reported that Mexican workers saw their wages increase 17%, from $2.09 per hour in 1999 to $2.46 per hour in 2000. (The average US worker earned $19.86 per hour in 2000.) After one year, workers are entitled by law to six days paid vacation.

15 ▪ Agriculture

Nayarit is the leading tobacco growing state of Mexico. Both tobacco and sugarcane are the primary export crops of the state. Fruit growing is a major part of agriculture and includes production of avocados, mango, papaya, bananas, and tamarind. Other major crops include corn, beans, peanuts, and squash. Cows, sheep, pigs, chickens, and goats, are the primary livestock animals; however, deer, iguana, raccoons, and rabbits are also used for meat. The southern region of the state is known for its honey production.

16 ▪ Natural Resources

The coastal lake zone has an abundant amount of shrimp. Tuna and red snapper are also part of the ocean catch. The main fishing center is at San Blas, which is also the site of an oyster research center. Coconut palms and oak trees are cut for commercial use. Gold, silver, and lead are found in the state and processed in two main facilities.

17 ▪ Energy and Power

Almost all of the energy in Mexico is provided by the Federal Electricity Commission (CFE). In February 2002, the CFE introduced new electric rates. For households that use less than 140 kilowatt hours per month, there was no rate increase. (This is about 75% of all households in the country, according to CFE.) As a small state whose economy has been based predominantly on agriculture, Nayarit's electricity consumption is among the lowest in Mexico.

18 ■ Health

The state of Nayarit has 12 general hospitals, 335 outpatient centers, and 29 surgical centers.

Most of the Mexican population is covered under a government health plan. The IMSS (Instituto Mexicano de Seguro Social) covers the general population. The ISSSTE (Instituto de Seguridad y Servicios Sociales de Trabajadores del Estado) covers state workers.

19 ■ Housing

About two-thirds of the housing available in the state of Nayarit is in good repair. Only about 13% is in need of significant upgrading. These homes do not have running water or access to electricity.

20 ■ Education

The system of public education was first started by President Benito Juárez in 1867. Public education in Mexico is free for students from ages six to sixteen. According to the 2000 census, there were approximately 210,000 school-age students in the state. Many students elect to go to private schools. The thirty-one states of Mexico all have at least one state university. The Universidad Auntónoma de Nayarit is located in Tepic.

21 ■ Arts

The state of Nayarit has a local ballet company, the Ballet de Cámara de Nayarit. The city of Tepic has two theaters. There are also over twenty-five auditoriums and public venues throughout the state.

22 ■ Libraries and Museums

There are seventy-four branches of the national library system. There are also twenty-six museums. In the capital, Tepic, there is a regional museum, a museum of visual arts, and a museum of popular arts, such as papier mâché, ironworks, masks, and embroidery. Tepic also houses a museum dedicated to the poet Amado Nervo (1870–1919).

23 ■ Media

The capital city, Tepic, publishes a daily newspaper, *Meridiano*.

24 ■ Tourism, Travel, and Recreation

Nayarit hosts festivals for *charros* (horsemen) and rodeos. Main celebrations in Tepic are those during Holy Week (the week before the Christian holiday Easter) and for Independence Day (mid-September).

25 ■ Sports

Swimming, surfing, and fishing are popular water sports for residents and tourists alike. Soccer is a popular sport, particularly among school children. The Nicolas Alvarez Ortega Stadium (soccer) is located in Tepic.

26 ■ Famous People

The poet Amado Nervo (1870–1919) was born in Nayarit. Antonio Echevarría Domínguez was elected governor in 1999.

27 ▓ Bibliography

Books

DeAngelis, Gina. *Mexico.* Mankato, MN: Blue Earth Books, 2003.

Supples, Kevin. *Mexico.* Washington, DC: National Geographic Society, 2002.

Web Sites

Mexico for Kids. http://www.elbalero.gob.mx/index_kids.html (accessed on June 15, 2004).

Surfing & Adventure Travel in Mexico: Nayarit. http://www.surf-mexico.com/states/Nayarit/ (accessed on June 17, 2004).

Nuevo León

Pronunciation: noo-WAY-voh-lay-OWN.

Origin of state name: Nuevo León was named in honor of the Spanish kingdom of León.

Capital: Monterrey (mohn-teh-REH-ee).

Entered country: 1824.

Coat of Arms: The coat of arms of Nuevo León is made up by four squares. At the top, six bees represent the hard-working nature of the local citizens. The upper left square features a picture of the sun over La Silla Hill (a landmark that often symbolizes the state), with an orange tree. In the upper right-hand square, a crowned lion is ready to attack. In the lower left, there is a picture of the San Francisco convent. On the lower-right, five smoking chimneys represent industry. The weapons around the border represent both native warriors and Spanish conquerors. The banner displays the state motto, *Sempre Ascendens,* which means "always rising."

Holidays: Año Nuevo (New Year's Day—January 1); Día de la Constitución (Constitution Day—February 5); Benito Juárez's birthday (March 21); Primero de Mayo (Labor Day—May 1); Revolution Day, 1910 (November 20); and Navidad (Christmas—December 25).

Flag: There is no official state flag.

Time: 6 AM = noon Greenwich Mean Time (GMT).

1 ▪ Location and Size

Nuevo León is located in northern Mexico. It covers an area of 64,556 square kilometers (24,925 square miles), or about half the size of the US state of New York. It is bordered on the north and east by the Mexican state of Tamaulipas. The Río Bravo (or Río Bravo del Norte) separates the northern tip of Nuevo León from the US state of Texas. This river is known as the Río Grande in the United States. On the south, the state is bordered by the Mexican states of Tamaulipas and San Luis Potosí, and on the west by the Mexican states of Coahuila, Zacatecas, and San Luis Potosí. Nuevo León has fifty-one municipalities. The capital is Monterrey.

The Sierra Madre Oriental, one of Mexico's major mountain ranges, crosses the state. A series of caves near Monterrey known as Grutas de García are accessible to the public.

The most important river in Nuevo León is the San Juan, which flows 121 kilometers (75 miles) northeast into Tamaulipas.

© Robert Frerck/Woodfin Camp

The Río Bravo (or Río Bravo del Norte) separates the northern tip of Nuevo León from the US state of Texas. This river is known as the Río Grande in the United States.

The Río Salado flows from Coahuila through Nuevo León to join the Río Bravo.

2 ■ Climate

The state has an extreme range of temperatures, but for most of the year the climate is generally hot. In the north, the climate is hot and dry. In the central region, by the Sierra Madre, temperatures are cooler. In the south, the climate is dry and desert-like.

In Monterrey, the lowest recorded temperature was about 0°C (32°F) and the highest was 44°C (111°F). On average, the temperature in Monterrey is above 26°C (80°F) for about 238 days each year. The average temperatures for the entire state are a minimum of about 17°C (62°F) and a maximum of 23°C (74°F). Average precipitation for the state ranges from a minimum of 20 centimeters (8 inches) to a maximum of 100 centimeters (39 inches).

3 ■ Plants and Animals

Natural pastures and thickets cover some of the dry, low-altitude regions of the state. Forests of pine and oak trees can be found in areas with a greater level of

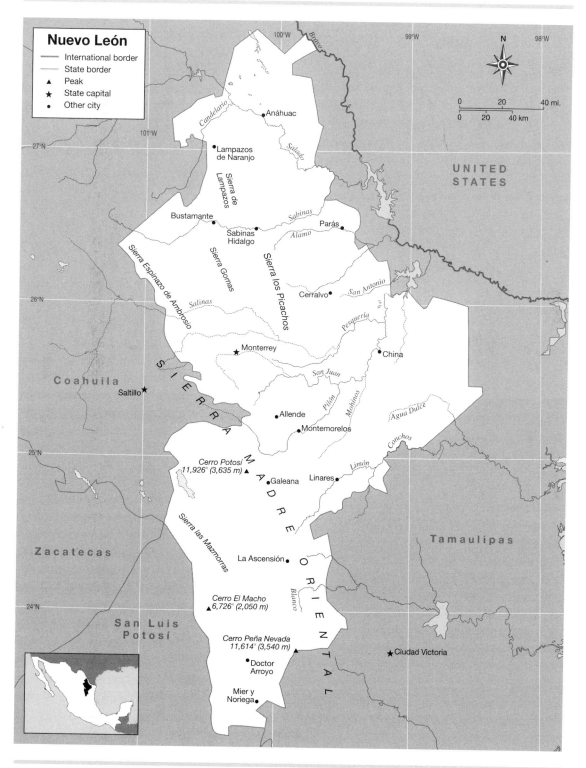

Nuevo León

— International border
— State border
▲ Peak
★ State capital
• Other city

N

| 0 | 20 | 40 mi. |
| 0 | 20 | 40 km |

100°W   99°W   98°W

UNITED STATES

27°N   101°W

Candelario

•Anáhuac

•Lampazos de Naranjo

Sierra de Lampazos

Salado

Sabinas

Bustamante•   •Sabinas Hidalgo   Alamo   Parás•

Sierra Gomas   Sierra los Picachos

26°N   Salinas

•Cerralvo   San Antonio

Pesquería

★Monterrey   •China

Coahuila

Saltillo★   San Juan

Pilón   Mohinos   Agua Dulce

•Allende
•Montemorelos   Conchos

25°N

Cerro Potosí
11,926' (3,635 m) ▲
•Galeana   Linares•   Limón

Sierra las Mazmorras   Tamaulipas

Zacatecas

La Ascensión•

Cerro El Macho
▲ 6,726' (2,050 m)   Blanco

24°N

San Luis Potosí

Cerro Peña Nevada
11,614' (3,540 m) ▲

★Ciudad Victoria

•Doctor Arroyo

Mier y Noriega•

Sierra Espinazo de Ambrosio

S I E R R A   M A D R E   O R I E N T A L

humidity. Common animals in the state include tlacuaches (Mexican opossum), rabbits, coyotes, pumas, wild boar, and white-tailed deer.

4 Environmental Protection
Environmental concerns for the state include maintaining an adequate safe water supply and properly managing hazardous waste materials. There are four national parks in the state, including the Cumbres de Monterrey National Park.

5 Population, Ethnic Groups, Languages
In 2000, Nuevo León had a total population of 3,834,141; of the total, 1,907,939 were men and 1,926,202 were women. The population density was 60 people per square kilometer (155 people per square mile). In 2000, the capital, Monterrey, had a population of 1,108,499. Almost all citizens speak Spanish as their first language. Less than 1% of the population speaks indigenous (native) languages.

6 Religions
According to the 2000 census, 78% of the population, or about three million people, were Roman Catholic; about 6%, or 211,402 people, were Protestant. That year there were also 10,403 Seventh-Day Adventists, 10,563 Mormons, 46,150 Jehovah's Witnesses, and 665 Jews. Almost 100,000 people reported no religion.

7 Transportation
Monterrey Airport provides international flights to and from Nuevo León. The state has about 8,664 kilometers (5,381 miles) of roads and 1,096 kilometers (681 miles) of railroads.

8 History
There is scattered anthropological and archeological evidence of early nomad and hunter and gatherer indigenous groups during the first centuries of the Christian era. Yet, when the Spaniards arrived, there were no large human settlements in the region. Most of the native population was comprised of nomadic groups that traveled through the unfriendly Nuevo León terrain.

The first conquistadors (those who sought to conqueror Mexico for the Spanish crown) to visit the region were Alvar Nuñez Cabeza de Vaca (c. 1490-c. 1560) around 1535 and Andrés de Olmos around 1545. In 1575, Alberto del Canto found a valley that he called Extremadura, where the city of Monterrey was later founded. Further north, he found the mineral deposits of San Gregorio. In 1579, King Felipe II (1527–1598) of Spain granted Luis Carvajal y de la Cueva the authorization to conquer those territories. Three years later, Carvajal initiated his expedition and founded the San Luis de Francia settlement. In the early 16th century, Diego de Montemayor was named governor of the region and he led a new colonization effort. Franciscan priests joined Montemayor with the intention of converting the indigenous population to Catholic faith. However, colonization efforts were mostly abandoned by the late 16th century.

During the 16th century, Tlaxacala Indians were sent to help the colonization efforts and to help nomadic tribes learn the advantages of permanent settlements. Because of the lack of accessible cheap labor and the vast territorial extensions, cattle ranching became the most important economic activity in the region during the colonial period. The need to combat nomadic tribes, however, made it costly for cattle ranchers to consolidate their businesses. In the mid 1700s there was a short-lived mining fever resulting from the discovery of gold and silver mines. The mines were rapidly exploited to their limits and the fever subsided. During the late 1700s, Catholic convents and seminaries were built in the region, taking advantage of the large land entitlements given to the church and because population density remained low.

The independence movement caught on for a short period of time in Nuevo León in 1811. But after the execution of the extremely popular and powerful priest and revolutionary Miguel de Hidalgo y Costilla (1753–1811), the independence revolts were brought to a halt. Royalist forces, loyal to Spain, then regained control of the entire region. After the adoption of the Plan of Iguala in 1821, Nuevo León became a province of independent Mexico. Starting in 1824 it was made into a federal state, and a new state constitution was promulgated.

Political instability characterized much of the 19th century. First, conflicts between centralists and federalists, and later, civil war between liberals and conservatives, prevented the economic development of the region. These continuing conflicts regularly threw social order into turmoil in Monterrey and other towns. The consolidation of a liberal regime after Mexico ceded its northern territories, including Texas, to the United States helped bring about much needed economic development. However, low population density remained a problem for Nuevo León. A new railroad between Mexico City and Monterrey helped bring

© Kal Muller/Woodfin Camp

A series of caves near Monterrey, known as Grutas de García, are accessible to the public.

about industrialization towards the end of the 19th century.

The Mexican Revolution started early in Nuevo León. Mexican revolutionist Fransciso Indalécio Madero (1873–1913) was arrested in Monterrey in 1910 during his failed presidential campaign. Accusations of fraud by incumbent president Porfirio Díaz (1830–1915) triggered the call for a revolution later that year. Eventually, the revolutionary victors controlled Nuevo León. The state participated in the writing and promulgation of the Mexican Constitution of 1917.

© Kal Muller/Woodfin Camp

Waterfalls in Nuevo León.

After the end of the revolution, Nuevo León consolidated as a cattle ranching state. In addition, Monterrey consolidated its position as the most important industrial and financial center of northern Mexico.

9 ■ State and Local Government

The state governor is elected for a nonrenewable six-year term. The legislature is comprised of a forty-two-seat unicameral (one chamber) congress. Twenty-six deputies are elected from single member districts, and sixteen deputies are elected by proportional representation. Until 1997, the Institutional Revolutionary Party (PRI) had exercised absolute control over the legislature and state governorship. That year, a National Action Party (PAN) candidate won the gubernatorial race. The PRI regained control of the governorship in 2003. But, the alternation in power and the strength of the PAN and PRI have called into play the implementation of separation-of-power and checks-and-balances provisions previously existing in the constitution.

The fifty-one municipalities that comprise Nuevo León hold democratic elections for municipal presidents and council members every three years. Immediate re-election is not allowed. Although some decentralization initiatives are producing positive results, the state still has a long way to go to achieve successful decentralization.

10 ▪ Political Parties
The three main political parties in all of Mexico are the Institutional Revolutionary Party (PRI), the National Action Party (PAN), and the Party of the Democratic Revolution (PRD). Although the PRI dominated state politics since the end of the Mexican Revolution, the PAN consolidated as a strong local party in Nuevo León since the mid 1950s. PAN candidates regularly won several municipal government elections. Since Fernando Canales Clariond won the 1997 gubernatorial elections, the PAN consolidated as the largest state party. The PRI gubernatorial victory in 2003 with José Natividad González shows the consolidation of a two party system in the state.

11 ▪ Judicial System
The Superior Tribunal of Justice is the highest court in the state. Its members are appointed by the congress from a three-person list submitted by the state governor. The term of appointment is ten years and justices can be re-elected only for an additional ten-year term. Only highly qualified attorneys can be appointed to the high court. A judicial council also plays a role in fostering the development of a high quality justice system. An electoral tribunal and other lower courts are also part of the Nuevo León judicial system.

12 ▪ Economy
Nuevo León is the third most industrialized state of Mexico and most residents enjoy a good standard of living. One of its municipalities, San Pedro Garza García, has the highest per capita income in Latin America. Manufacturing accounts for the greatest percentage of the economy at 27%. Service-based companies account for 22% of the economy, followed by trade at 19%, finance and insurance at 15%, transportation and communication at 11%, construction at 3%, agriculture and livestock at 2%, and mining at 1%.

13 ▪ Industry
Nuevo León has a diversified industrial structure, which includes oil refining and heavy and light manufacturing. Nuevo León is a leading national producer of iron, steel, and chemicals. There are many large companies manufacturing products in Nuevo León. Cemex (the world's fourth-largest cement company), Bimbo (bakery and pastry), Maseca (food and grains), Banorte (a bank wholly owned by Mexicans), Alestra (telecommunications), Vitro (glass), Hylsa (aluminum), FEMSA (Coca-Cola in Latin America), and Cervecería Cuauhtémoc-Moctezuma (brewers of five beer brands) are all located in Monterrey.

14 ▪ Labor
The US Bureau of Labor Statistics reported that Mexican workers saw their wages increase 17%, from $2.09 per hour in 1999 to $2.46 per hour in 2000. (The average US worker earned $19.86 per hour in 2000.) After one year, workers are entitled by law to six days paid vacation. Because of the industry in Nuevo León, workers earn relatively high wages.

15 ▪ Agriculture

Nuevo León has three distinct growing regions, the Northern Gulf Coastal Plain, the Sierra Madre Oriental region, and the Highland region. Agricultural products vary by region. The Northern Gulf Coastal Plain produces watermelon, pears, melons, squash, corn, beans, chili peppers, cotton, and avocado. The Sierra Madre Oriental region and the Highland region both produce corn, wheat, avocado, carrots, beans, and potatoes. The Sierra Madre Oriental region also produces green tomatoes, while the Highland region produces onion, squash, and chili peppers.

In the Northern Gulf Coastal Plain the primary livestock are cattle, goats, pigs, sheep, and horses. In the Sierra Madre Oriental region, livestock is predominantly goats and horses. In the Highland region livestock consists mainly of goats.

16 ▪ Natural Resources

Mining products include zinc, copper, lime, coal, iron, silver, and barite (used for drilling oil wells).

17 ▪ Energy and Power

Almost all of the energy in Mexico is provided by the Federal Electricity Commission (CFE). In February 2002, the CFE introduced new electric rates. For households that use less than 140 kilowatt hours per month, there was no rate increase. (This is about 75% of all households in Mexico, according to CFE). However, in Nuevo León eight major dams in the state provide hydroelectric power and water for irrigation. El Cuchillo Dam on the San Juan provides hydroelectric power to Monterrey.

18 ▪ Health

Nuevo Leon has 31 general hospitals, 532 outpatient centers, and 121 surgical centers.

Most of the Mexican population is covered under a government health plan. The IMSS (Instituto Mexicano de Seguro Social) covers the general population. The ISSSTE (Instituto de Seguridad y Servicios Sociales de Trabajadores del Estado) covers state workers.

19 ▪ Housing

Over four-fifths of the housing available in the state of Nuevo León is in good repair. Only about 4% is in need of significant upgrading. These homes may not have running water or access to electricity.

20 ▪ Education

The system of public education was first started by President Benito Juárez (1806–1872) in 1867. Public education in Mexico is free for students from ages six to sixteen. According to the 2000 census, there were approximately 730,000 school-age students in the state. Many students elect to go to private schools. The thirty-one states of Mexico all have at least one state university. The Universidad de Monterrey is in the capital, Monterrey.

21 ▪ Arts

The state of Nuevo León has over twenty-five theaters. A theater group, Teatro Saltimbanque, and a musical group, Música Maestra, perform throughout the state. There are also cultural centers in most cities.

22 ■ Libraries and Museums

There are 282 branches of the national library system in Nuevo León. In the city of Allende, there is a museum of anthropology. In the capital, Monterrey, there is a baseball hall of fame and a tennis hall of fame, which honors Mexican players. Monterrey also has a glass museum, a natural history museum, a railroad museum, a police museum, and a museum of contemporary art.

23 ■ Media

The capital, Monterrey, has four daily newspapers: *Diario de Monterrey*, *El Norte*, *El Porvenir*, and *Milenio*.

24 ■ Tourism, Travel, and Recreation

There is a park based on the television series *Sesame Street*. Birds and butterflies native to the Western Sierra Madre region thrive in the habitat of Chipinque Park. Visitor can also hike and go rock climbing there.

25 ■ Sports

Monterrey's basketball team, the Fuerza Regia, plays in the 4,200-seat Gimnasio Nuevo León. The minor league baseball team, Sultanes de Monterrey, plays in the 27,000-seat Estadio Monterrey. There are two soccer teams in the state. The Reyados Monterrey, play in the 38,622-seat Tecnológico. The Tigres play in the 45,000-seat Universitario stadium. The León soccer team plays in the 33,943-seat Nou Camp stadium.

26 ■ Famous People

Alfonso Reyes (1889–1959) was born in Monterrey. He was a diplomat and a teacher and was considered to be one of the greatest Spanish American writers of his time. One of his most famous prose poems was *Visión de Anáhuac*.

27 ■ Bibliography

Books

DeAngelis, Gina. *Mexico*. Mankato, MN: Blue Earth Books, 2003.

Hernández, Marie Theresa. *Delirio—The Fantastic, the Demonic, and the Reél: The Buried History of Nuevo León*. Austin: University of Texas Press, 2002.

Mora-Torres, Juan. *The Making of the Mexican Border*. Austin: University of Texas Press, 2001.

Supples, Kevin. *Mexico*. Washington, DC: National Geographic Society, 2002.

Web Sites

Mexico for Kids. http://www.elbalero.gob.mx/index_kids.html (accessed on June 15, 2004).

Nuevo Léon. http://www.tourbymexico.com/nvoleon/nvoleon.htm (accessed June 17, 2004).

Oaxaca

Pronunciation: wah-HAH-kah.

Origin of state name: The name of the state comes from the Náhuatl (the language of the Aztecs) word *Hauxyacac,* which means "on the top of the guaje tree." The guaje tree is common throughout the state.

Capital: Oaxaca de Juárez (wah-HAH-kah deh HWAH-rehs), named for the former president Benito Juárez (1806–1872).

Entered country: October 13, 1824.

Coat of Arms: An eagle perched on a cactus with a snake in its beak forms the top of the symbol. The shield below contains an oval encircled by the motto "El Respeto Al Derecho Ajeno es La Paz", with symbols of the state's archeology.

Holidays: Año Nuevo (New Year's Day—January 1); Día de la Constitución (Constitution Day—February 5); Benito Juárez's birthday (March 21); Primero de Mayo (Labor Day—May 1); Revolution Day, 1910 (November 20); and Navidad (Christmas—December 25).

Flag: There is no official state flag.

Time: 6 AM = noon Greenwich Mean Time (GMT).

1 ▪ Location and Size

Oaxaca is located on the southern coast of Mexico. It is the fifth-largest state with an area of 95,364 square kilometers (36,820 square miles), which is a little larger than the US state of Indiana. Oaxaca is bordered on the north by the Mexican states of Puebla and Veracruz; on the east by the Mexican state of Chiapas; on the south by the Pacific Ocean; and on the west by the Mexican state of Guerrero. Oaxaca is divided into 570 municipalities. Its capital is Oaxaca de Juárez.

In the central Oaxaca Valley, in the west on the Isthmus of Tehuantepec (an isthmus is a narrow strip of land that connects two larger areas, in this case the Bay of Campeche on the north and the Gulf of Tehuantepec on the south), and along the coast, the land is flat. But Oaxaca is also one of the most mountainous states in Mexico. The state is crossed by three great mountain ranges (*sierras*): the Sierra Madre del Sur, the Sierra Madre Oriental (also known as the Sierra de Oaxaca), and the Sierra Atravesada. Canyons and caves also are found throughout the state.

Panoramic view of the capital.

The largest river is the Río Papaloapan, which forms when several small rivers join near the border with Veracruz.

In Oaxaca, the most beautiful waterfalls are the Salto de Conejo, Cabdadihui, Yatao, Salto de Fraile, and Apaola. The largest lagoons are found near the Pacific coast. They are the Chacahua and Manialtepec lagoons in the coastal region, and the Superior and Inferior lagoons on the Isthmus of Tehuantepec.

2 ▊ Climate

The climate is moderate all year. The average winter temperature is 17°C (63°F) in November, December, and January. From May to August, the average temperature is 22°C (72°F). The average rainfall in Oaxaca de Juárez is 69.5 centimeters (27.4 inches) per year. Rainfall for the entire state ranges from a minimum average of about 42.7 centimeters (16.8 inches) to a maximum average of about 375 centimeters (147 inches). Oaxaca occasionally is struck by damaging hurricanes, such as Hurricane Pauline in October 1997.

3 ▊ Plants and Animals

Oaxaca has about thirty thousand different plant species. Some of the most common trees are oyamel trees, ahuehuete (cypress), cedar, mahogany, ash, oak, and

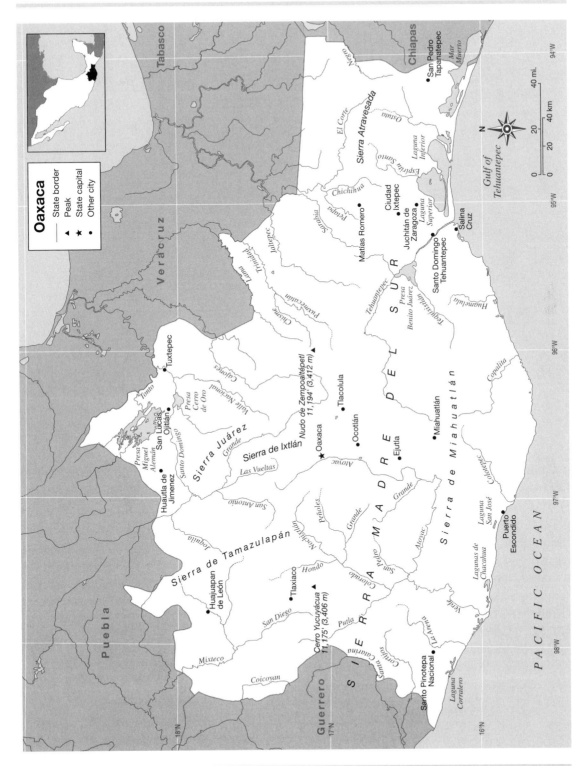

Oaxaca

— State border
▲ Peak
★ State capital
• Other city

Tabasco

Chiapas

San Pedro
Tapanatepec

Mar
Muerto

40 mi.

40 km

Sierra Atravesada

El Corte

Negro

Ostua

Laguna
Inferior

Espíritu Santo

N

20

20

0

0

Gulf of
Tehuantepec

Chichihua

Ciudad
Ixtepec

Laguna
Superior

Matías Romero

Juchitán de
Zaragoza

Salina
Cruz

Veracruz

Jaltepec

Santa Elena

Peludo

Tehuantepec

Presa
Benito Juárez

Santo Domingo
Tehuantepec

Huamelula

Trinidad

Chisme

Putla

Tuxtepec

Ixuan

Cajones

Valle Nacional

Presa
Cerro
de Oro

Nudo de Zempoaltépetl
11,194' (3,412 m)

Tlacolula

Sierra de Miahuatlán

Copalita

Tonto

San Lucas
Ojitlán

Santo Domingo

Grande

Sierra de Ixtlán

Oaxaca

Ocotlán

Miahuatlán

Presa
Miguel
Alemán

Sierra Juárez

Las Vueltas

Atoyac

Ejutla

Huautla de
Jimenez

San Antonio

Peñoles

Grande

Grande

Atoyac

Laguna
San José

Puerto
Escondido

Jaquila

Nochixtlán

San Pedro

Coloyepec

Laguna
de
Chacahua

Sierra de Tamazulapán

Hondo

Colorado

Santa Catarina

La Arena

Verde

Puebla

Huajuapan
de León

Tlaxiaco

Cerro Yucuyácua
11,175' (3,406 m)

San Diego

Putla

Cortijos

Mixteco

Coicoyan

Santo Pinotepa
Nacional

Laguna
Corralero

Guerrero

SIERRA

MADRE

DEL

SUR

Tehuantepec

PACIFIC OCEAN

94°W

95°W

96°W

97°W

98°W

18°N

17°N

16°N

A woman with her pottery.

juniper. Coconut palms and mangroves (a tropical evergreen) are also found. Fennel, thyme, and laurel are common plants. Small animals include squirrels, tlacuaches (Mexican possums), and armadillos. Larger mammals include deer, wildcats, leopards, wild boar, tapirs, and spider monkeys. Some common birds include tzentzontles (the bird of a thousand voices), goldfinches, sparrows, hawks, and eagles. Fish species include lisa, red snapper, sailfish, carp, shrimp, and lobster.

4 ▪ Environmental Protection

The Lagunas de Chacahua National Park (lah-GOO-nahs dai chah-KAH-wah) is a protected area on the coast with many bamboo groves and mangrove swamps. In 2002, eight communities in Oaxaca began local conservation efforts as part of a Community Protected Areas program. These new Community Protected Areas are focused on efforts to preserve the Mexican dry forest on the Pacific coast and the Mesoamerican Pine-Oak forest in Sierra Norte.

5 ▪ Population, Ethnic Groups, Languages

Oaxaca had a total population of 3,438,765 in 2000; of the total, 1,657,406 were men and 1,781,359 were women. The population density was 37 people per square kilometer (96 people per square mile). In 2000, the capital, Oaxaca de Juárez, had a population of 256,848.

There are sixteen different indigenous (native) groups that are formally registered within the state. They include the Zapotec, Amuzgos, Chochos, Huaves, and others. There is also a group known as the Afromixtecas, who represent an ethnic mix of the Mixteca and the African slaves who were brought to Mexico by the Spanish. Most citizens speak Spanish as their first language. About 37.2% of the population speaks indigenous languages. This is the second highest percentage in the country (after Yucatan).

6 ▦ Religions

According to the 2000 census, 74% of the population, or about 2.6 million people, were Roman Catholic; about 7%, or 234,150 people, were Protestant. That year there were also 25,986 Seventh-Day Adventists, 37,504 Jehovah's Witnesses, and 1,199 Jews. Almost 150,000 people reported no religion.

7 ▦ Transportation

Oaxaca Airport provides international flights to and from Oaxaca. The state has about 15,569 kilometers (9,670 miles) of roads and 651 kilometers (450 miles) of railroads.

8 ▦ History

Some archeological ruins that date back to more than 11,000 B.C. make Oaxaca the first place where human settlements occurred in Mexico. Olmec culture developed in the region around 3,000 B.C.

Quiché culture first emerged around 2,000 B.C. The archeological ruins of Monte Albán were built around 800 B.C. Zapoteca Indians built large irrigation systems in the Oaxaca Valley around 800 A.D. during the early centuries of the Christian era. Mexica Indians populated the region starting around 1200 A.D. The Aztecs founded the city of Oaxaca and dominated the other indigenous groups and cultures in the mid-14th century.

When the Spaniards first arrived and Spanish conqueror Hernan Cortés (1485–1547) sought to defeat the Aztec empire in Tenochtitlán-Mexico (ancient name of Mexico City), some of Cortés's envoys went to the region and made peace with the Chinanteco Indians. Mexica Indians, however, continued to resist Spanish occupation until 1522. At that time Francisco de Orozco and Pedro de Alvarado (c. 1485–1541) completed the conquest of the region for the Spanish crown. Attempts to convert the native Oaxaca Indians to Christianity had begun in 1521. In 1529, Cortés, seeking to protect territories that he hoped to retain for himself, ordered the destruction of many villages that were founded by Spanish soldiers and conquistadors (those who sought to take control of Mexico for Spain). Internal land conflicts among the Spanish colonizers and the resistance of several indigenous groups made the region somewhat unstable for a few years after the conquest. Cortés introduced sugarcane and wheat to his vast territories. Agricultural production soon consolidated as the main economic engine in the region.

By the 16th century, the indigenous population had been decimated. Diseases brought by the Europeans, overexploitation for agricultural purposes, and widespread famine brought defeat. Yet, agricultural pro-

© Catherine Karnow/Woodfin Camp

Examples of radish art displayed during El Festival de los Rábanos (Festival of the Radishes) held in December each year.

duction flourished as Oaxaca traded with Puebla and Mexico City. Silk was widely produced in the region. Silk production helped Oaxaca establish trade relations with places as distant as Peru through the Pacific ports of Huatulco and Tehuantepec. The capital city of the region, Antequera (later renamed Oaxaca), had more than six thousand inhabitants.

Mexican priest and revolutionist José María Morelos y Pávon (1765–1815) brought the independence movement to Oaxaca in 1812. A later attempt by a Spanish royalist army sent from Guatemala to regain control of Oaxaca failed. Defeat was at the hands of a militia army led by another Mexican priest and patriot Mariano Matamoros (1770–1814). Later, after Morelos's downfall, Spanish royalists regained control of Oaxaca until the region joined the rest of Mexico in declaring independence with the Plan of Iguala in 1821. Oaxaca became a federal state of Mexico in 1824.

The unstable period that marked the reign of Antonio López de Santa Anna (1794–1876), who was in and out of power from the early 1830s to the mid 1850s, ended when Benito Juárez (1806–1872), Oaxaca's most revered son, emerged as a local and national leader in the 1850s. (Juárez officially became president of Mexico in 1858). Another Oaxaca notable leader, Porfirio Díaz (1830–1915), successfully resisted the efforts by French troops to take control of Oaxaca. (The French, under the leadership of Emperor Maximilian [1832–1867], briefly controlled parts of Mexico from 1863 to 1867.) With the triumph of the Reforma movement led by Juárez, Oaxaca joined the rest of Mexico in supporting the liberal government that brought about radical and profound reforms. Juárez, a native indigenous himself, died in 1872 while serving as president. Porfirio Díaz, Juárez's former ally and political opponent when Juárez last served as president, eventually became president himself in 1877. His rule came to an end with the Mexican Revolution of 1910.

During Juárez's and Díaz's tenures, Oaxaca developed as an agricultural, financial, and commercial center. Díaz extended the railroads well into the state and brought telegraph lines to the major cities. Toward the end of Díaz's reign, many of the leaders in Oaxaca supported him against the revolutionaries who were opposed to the aging president taking on yet another presidential term. However, a few revolutionary revolts sparked throughout the state. After Díaz abandoned the presidency and left Mexico, military conflicts reached Oaxaca as well.

After the revolution, Oaxaca evolved as a tourist, commercial, and agricultural center. Because of its extremely rich archeological heritage and numerous ancient religious and historic sites, Oaxaca is also considered the birthplace of much of Mexico's legendary history and traditions.

9 ▦ State and Local Government
The state governor is democratically elected every six years. Immediate re-election is not allowed. The legislature is comprised of a forty-two-member unicameral (single chamber) congress. Twenty-five deputies are elected in single member districts, and seventeen deputies are elected by proportional representation, all for three-year periods. Immediate re-election is not allowed. The Institutional Revolutionary Party (PRI) continues to dominate the state government.

The 570 municipalities that comprise Oaxaca hold democratic elections for municipal presidents and council members every three years. Immediate re-election is not allowed. Because of the widely varying size and financial resources of the different municipalities, decentralization efforts have produced mixed results in recent years.

10 ▦ Political Parties
The three main political parties in all of Mexico are the Institutional Revolutionary Party (PRI), the National Action Party (PAN), and the Party of the Democratic Revolution (PRD). The PRI has been the historically dominant party in state politics throughout the 20th century. After the Mexican Revolution, only PRI candidates have won the gubernatorial races. Most recently, José Murat won the 1998 gubernatorial race, defeating PAN and PRD candidates. PAN and PRD have gained electoral strength in recent years and have successfully captured important municipal governments.

11 ▦ Judicial System
The Superior Tribunal of Justice is the highest court in the state. The governor appoints members for renewable fifteen-year terms, with legislative approval. Jus-

© Robert Frerck/Woodfin Camp

Alameda Park in the capital surrounds the cathedral. Each December, it is filled with market stalls during El Festival de los Rábanos (Festival of the Radishes).

tices are not accountable to the executive or legislative branches, but they must pursue justice and defend the autonomy of the judiciary. The appointees must possess a number of stringent attorney qualifications. In addition, the state judicial system also is made up of lower courts and an electoral tribunal.

12 ■ Economy

Most of the people in Oaxaca work in agriculture. However, service-based industries are growing in importance. Agriculture accounts for about 15% of the state economy. However, finance and insurance companies account for 20% of the economy and general service-based companies account for 22%. Trade accounts for 16% of the economy, followed by manufacturing at 14%, transportation and communications at 8%, construction at 4%, and mining at 1%.

13 ■ Industry

Most manufacturing companies are located in the central valley regions, the Tuxtepec region, and on the Tehuantepec Isthmus. Industry is only a small part of the nation's total economy. There is, however, a large oil refinery at Salina Cruz that

196

© Peter Langer/EPD Photos

A flower vendor wears her inventory on her hat.

supplies most of the oil and oil byproducts that are used by the Pacific coastal region.

Oaxaca is well-known for its handicrafts. These include clothing, pottery, and wood and leather items. Handicrafts are usually produced by individual artists. Some communities have small-scale production of handicrafts by groups of workers.

14 ▪ Labor

The US Bureau of Labor Statistics reported that Mexican workers saw their wages increase 17%, from $2.09 per hour in 1999 to $2.46 per hour in 2000. (The average US worker earned $19.86 per hour in 2000.)

After one year, workers are entitled by law to six days paid vacation.

15 ▪ Agriculture

Most of the citizens of Oaxaca are farmers. The most important crops are mangoes and coffee. Oaxaca produces more mangoes than any other Mexican state. Oaxaca is the third largest producer of coffee. Corn and beans are the major crops for local consumption. Other important crops include squash, avocado, oranges, sugarcane, and tobacco. Most of the livestock are beef and dairy cattle. A festival every December celebrates the radish, which

© Robert Frerck/Woodfin Camp

This 2,000-year-old ahuehuete (cypress) tree is known as El Tule. It is believed to be the world's largest tree, with a circumference of nearly 140 feet (42 meters).

was introduced to Mexico by the Spanish in the late 1500s.

16 ■ Natural Resources

Though Oaxaca has a wide variety of fish, the fishing industry has not been developed to its full potential. Shrimp are a popular catch. Forests cover about half of the land area in the state, with most forest areas belonging to local communities. Wood is cut primarily for fuel and building material, but there are some small businesses that produce furniture, ply-

wood, and paper. Gold, silver, lead, copper, and zinc are all found in state mines.

17 ■ Energy and Power

Almost all of the energy in Mexico is provided by the Federal Electricity Commission (CFE). In February 2002, the CFE introduced new electric rates. For households that use less than 140 kilowatt hours per month, there was no rate increase. (This is about 75% of all households in Mexico, according to CFE). There is a small project to generate electricity using wind power.

18 ■ Health

The state of Oaxaca has 40 general hospitals, 1,218 outpatient centers, and 65 surgical centers.

Most of the Mexican population is covered under a government health plan. The IMSS (Instituto Mexicano de Seguro Social) covers the general population. The ISSSTE (Instituto de Seguridad y Servicios Sociales de Trabajadores del Estado) covers state workers.

19 ■ Housing

Only about one-fourth of the housing available in the state of Oaxaca is in good repair. More than 47% is in need of significant upgrading. Many homes do not have running water or access to electricity.

20 ■ Education

The system of public education was first started by President Benito Juárez in 1867. Public education in Mexico is free for students from ages six to sixteen. According to the 2000 census, there were approximately 885,000 school-age students in the state. Many students elect to go to private schools. The thirty-one states of Mexico all have at least one state university. The Benito Juárez University of Oaxaca is located in the state.

21 ■ Arts

Oaxaca has three local performing companies: the Contemporary Dance Company of Oaxaca; Mírame, a musical group; and Pasatono, a group performing indigenous music. There are also seven theaters and dozens of local cultural centers. Oaxaca is also famous for its painted animals made of copal wood, native to the area. Also black clay pottery is a native craft.

22 ■ Libraries and Museums

Oaxaca has 413 branches of the national public library. Among the thirty museums in the state, the best known is the archeological site of Monte Albán, a pre-Columbian settlement. Oaxaca also has a stamp museum, a museum of graphic arts, a museum of contemporary arts, and a cultural museum.

23 ■ Media

In the capital, Oaxaca, there are two daily newspapers: *El Impartial* and *Noticias.*

24 ■ Tourism, Travel, and Recreation

The beaches of Huatulco, forty-minutes by airplane trip from the capital, Oaxaca, are clean and natural. Tangolunda Bay draws tourists interested in the environment. Visitors to the Huatulco area enjoy water sports, scuba diving, snorkeling, and fishing. The coastal village of Puerto Escondido is a main tourist resort. The city of Oaxaca features beautiful colonial architecture. Oaxaca is famous for its black clay pottery artifacts. The Fiestas of Lunes del Cerro is held during the last two weeks of July each year. The streets of the cities and towns are filled with music and performers in this festival celebrating the state's heritage. The Festival de los Rábanos in December features specially grown oversized radishes, carved into works of art. Some of the radishes reach over seven pounds (15 kilograms) in weight, 18 inches (50 centimeters) in length, and 5 inches (12 centimeters) in width.

25 ■ Sports

Oaxaca has a baseball team, the Guerreros, which plays in the 8,000-seat L. E. Vasconcelos stadium.

26 ■ Famous People

Benito Juárez (1806–1872) was a Zapotec Indian who was born on March 21, 1806, in the Oaxaca village of San Pablo Guelatao. He served as president of Mexico for two terms. He is considered to be one of the most beloved Mexican leaders. His birthday is a national holiday. Porfirio Díaz (1830–1915) was a dictator who ruled Mexico from 1877 until 1911. Juana Inés de la Cruz (1651–1695), a 17th-century feminist writer, and Rufino Tamayo (1899–1991), a renowned Mexican painter, were also natives of Oaxaca.

27 ■ Bibliography

Books

Carew-Miller, Anna. *Famous People of Mexico.* Philadelphia: Mason Crest Publishers, 2003.

DeAngelis, Gina. *Mexico.* Mankato, MN: Blue Earth Books, 2003.

Sacks, Oliver W. *Oaxaca Journal.* Washington, DC: National Geographic Society, 2002.

Supples, Kevin. *Mexico.* Washington, DC: National Geographic Society, 2002.

Web Sites

Mexico for Kids. http://www.elbalero.gob.mx/index_kids.html (accessed June 15, 2004).

Surfing & Adventure Travel in Mexico: The State of Oaxaca. http://www.surf-mexico.com/states/Oaxaca/ (accessed June 17, 2004).

Puebla

Pronunciation: PWEH-blah.

Origin of state name: The state of Puebla was named for its capital city, which was established by the Spaniards. New settlements were often called pueblas.

Capital: Puebla. The formal name, Heroica Puebla de Zaragoza, honors Ignacio Zaragoza who led the Mexican army to defeat the French.

Entered country: October 13, 1824.

Coat of Arms: The coat of arms is a shield divided into four squares: one depicts a factory, representing progress; the hydroelectric dam represents Puebla's contribution to the supply of electricity; the rifle commemorates the Civil War that began November 20, 1910; the human hand holding a plant with farm land in the background represents agriculture. The smaller shield in the center features a mountain landscape with a rising sun, marked 5 Mayo 1862. (This is the date that the Mexican army defeated the French.) At the top of the shield is a native symbol for the sun. The snakes along the sides are symbols of the Tolteca culture. Around the shield is the state motto *unidos en el tiempo en el esfuerzo en la justicia y en la esperanza* (United in time, in effort, in justice and in hope).

Holidays: Año Nuevo (New Year's Day—January 1); Día de la Constitución (Constitution Day—February 5); Benito Juárez's birthday (March 21); Primero de Mayo (Labor Day—May 1); Revolution Day, 1910 (November 20); and Navidad (Christmas—December 25).

Flag: There is no official state flag.

Time: 6 AM = noon Greenwich Mean Time (GMT).

1 ■ Location and Size

Puebla is part of the central region of the country that is known as the breadbasket of Mexico. The state has an area of 33,919 square kilometers (13,096 square miles), which is twice the size of the US state of Hawaii. It is bordered by the Mexican states of México, Morelos, Guerrero, Oaxaca, Veracruz, Hidalgo, and Tlaxcala.

Puebla is divided into 217 municipalities. Its capital city is also called Puebla.

The landscape is mountainous. Wide valleys, such as the one where the capital is located, lie at high elevations.

Three of the highest volcanoes are Citlaltépetl (also called Pico de Orizaba), which lies on the border with Veracruz and has an elevation of 5,700 meters (18,700 feet); Popocatépetl, which lies about 48 kilometers

(30 miles) west of the capital and has an elevation of 5,450 meters (17,887 feet); and Malinche (also called Matlalcueyatl), which lies on the border with Tlaxcala and has an elevation of 4,461 meters (14,636 feet).

There are dozens of small rivers in Puebla. The Necaxa River flows for about 200 kilometers (125 miles) through Puebla and Veracruz to the Gulf of Mexico. It provides water for irrigation and hydroelectric power. Near the Veracruz border, the Necaxa Falls cascade over 165 meters (540 feet). There are several reservoirs in the state. The mineral waters of the state's natural springs are believed to have healing properties.

2 ■ Climate

Temperatures are fairly constant year-round, with variation depending on elevation. The daytime temperatures range from 21°C to 27°C (70°F to 80°F). At night, the temperature drops to around 4°C (45°F). There is little rainfall from November to March, but from April through October heavy afternoon rains are common.

3 ■ Plants and Animals

Pine, willow, and oak trees are common throughout the state. There are large forest areas in the Huachinango region. Animals common to the state include hares, raccoons, rabbits, and eagles. The quetzal, a green-feathered bird, is found in the Tezuitlán region.

4 ■ Environmental Protection

La Malinche National Park (lah mah-LEEN-chay) is a protected area on the border with the state of Tlaxcala. The park is located at the base of the Malinche volcano (4,461 meters/14,636 feet). The

Tehuacán-Cuicatlán Biosphere Reserve, with protected pine and oak forests, lies on the border with Oaxaca.

5 ■ Population, Ethnic Groups, Languages

Puebla had a total population of 5,076,686 in 2000; of the total, 2,448,801 were men and 2,627,885 were women. The population density was 148 people per square kilometer (383 people per square mile). The capital, Puebla, Mexico's fourth-largest city, had a 2000 population of 1,346,176. Almost all citizens speak Spanish as their first language. About 13.1% of the population speaks indigenous (native) languages, a number that is almost twice as high as the national average of about 7%.

6 ■ Religions

According to the 2000 census, 78% of the population, or about four million people, were Roman Catholic; about 4%, or 188,586 people, were Protestant. That year there were also 42,415 Jehovah's Witnesses and 2,251 Jews. Almost 95,000 people reported no religion.

7 ■ Transportation

Puebla-Huejotsingo Airport provides international flights to and from Puebla. The state has about 8,046 kilometers (4,998 miles) of roads and 709 kilometers (440 miles) of railroads.

8 ■ History

Archeological evidence points to a civilization that developed agriculture and established sedentary human settlements in the region around 6000 B.C. Olmec influence was clear in Puebla starting in 1000

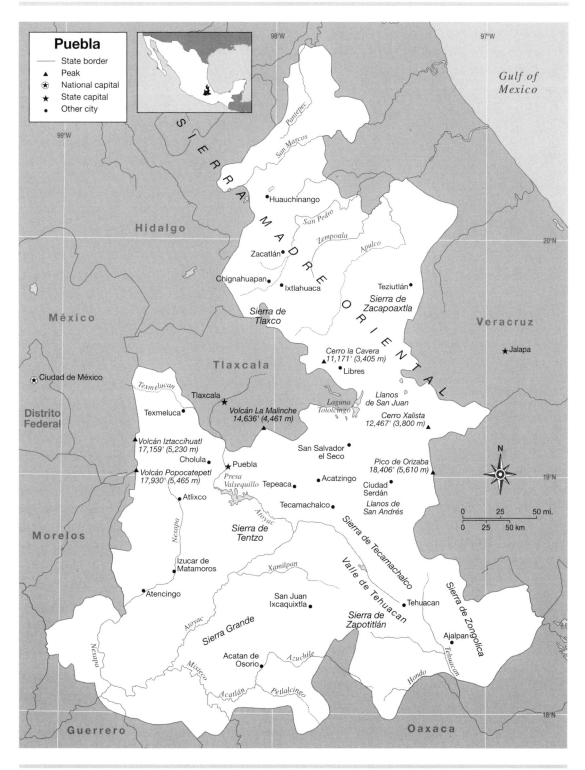

Puebla

- State border
- ▲ Peak
- ⊛ National capital
- ★ State capital
- • Other city

Gulf of Mexico

98°W

97°W

99°W

SIERRA MADRE ORIENTAL

Panepec

San Marcos

• Huauchinango

San Pedro

Hidalgo

Zempoala

Apulco

20°N

Zacatlán•

Chignahuapan•

•Ixtlahuaca

Teziutlán•

México

Sierra de Tlaxco

Sierra de Zacapoaxtla

Veracruz

Cerro la Cavera
▲11,171' (3,405 m)

★Jalapa

•Libres

Tlaxcala

Llanos de San Juan

Laguna Totolcingo

Tlaxcala★

⊛ Ciudad de México

Texmelucan

Volcán La Malinche
14,636' (4,461 m)

Cerro Xalista
12,467' (3,800 m) ▲

Texmeluca•

▲Volcán Iztaccíhuatl
17,159' (5,230 m)

Distrito
Federal

Cholula•

San Salvador
el Seco•

Pico de Orizaba
18,406' (5,610 m) ▲

N

19°N

•Puebla

▲Volcán Popocatepetl
17,930' (5,465 m)

Presa
Valsequillo

Tepeaca•

•Acatzingo

Ciudad
Serdán•

•Atlixco

Tecamachalco•

Llanos de
San Andrés

Atoyac

0   25   50 mi.

0   25   50 km

Morelos

Nexapa

Sierra de
Tentzo

Sierra de Tecamachalco

Izucar de
Matamoros•

Xamilpan

Valle de Tehuacan

Sierra de Zongolica

•Atencingo

San Juan
Ixcaquixtla•

Sierra Grande

Atoyac

Tehuacan•

Sierra de
Zapotitlán

Tehuacan

•Ajalpan

Nexapa

Acatan de
Osorio•

Mixteco

Azuchile

Hondo

Acatlán

Petlalcingo

18°N

Guerrero

Oaxaca

© Robert Frerck/Woodfin Camp

The El Parian market in the capital, Puebla.

B.C. Around 300 A.D. Teotihuacán culture was present in the region, especially in Cholula. The Totonaca culture developed in the northern part of Puebla. Mixteco Indians occupied Choloula starting in 900 A.D. In the 12th century, an exiled Toltec-Chichimec group from Tula occupied the region. Mexicas occupied most of the region starting in the 14th century.

In 1519, on their way to Tenochtitlán -Mexico (present-day Mexico City), Spanish conqueror Hernán Cortés's (1485–1547) troops occupied Huejotzingo and Cholula. They killed most of the native people living there. In 1520, the Spanish conquistadors (those who sought to conqueror Mexico for Spain) controlled most important villages and human settlements in the region. After the fall of the Aztec empire, the Spaniards moved on to conquer the remaining indigenous territories in Puebla. In 1524, massive land grants, known as encomiendas, were assigned by the Spanish crown to the conquistadors. The purpose of the encomiendas was to promote the exploitation of the land for agricultural and mining. Cattle ranching and sugarcane and silk production were developed during the late 16th century. Franciscan priests initiated the conversion of indigenous groups to the Roman Catholic faith starting in 1524.

During the early 17th century, the most important textile factories of the Spanish American colonies were situated in the city of Puebla. A printing press brought in 1640 reflected Puebla's importance as a commercial, agricultural, and industrial center in Mexico. Yet, the indigenous population was decimated rapidly. They died from poor living conditions forced on them by the Spanish colonizers. They also died from diseases brought by the Spaniards to the new continent.

The independence movement came to Puebla in 1811. But fierce resistance from Spanish royalists (people loyal to Spain) prevented a decisive victory by the pro-independence fighters. The independence fighters were led by José Morelos (1765–1815). Neither side exercised definitive control of the state until Agustín de Iturbide (1783–1824) led his army into Puebla and declared independence in 1821.

Between the late 1820s and 1867, Puebla was characterized by constant conflicts between different factions and internal power disputes. First, federalists against centralists and later, liberals against conservatives faced off in confusing and often bloody battles for the control of one of the most economically and strategically important states in the federation. The Battle of Puebla was one of the most symbolically important battles. It took place on May 5, 1862, when French troops invaded Mexico. They faced fierce resistance by Mexican patriots loyal to constitutional president Benito Juárez (1806–1872).

Porfirio Díaz (1830–1915) followed Juárez as president of Mexico, and Díaz reign in power is often referred to as the porfiriato period. Puebla experienced healthy and sustained economic growth resulting from agriculture, cattle production, and textiles. As in the rest of the country, growth of the infrastructure was central to the economic development plan pushed for by authoritarian leader Porfirio Díaz.

The Mexican Revolution, which began in 1910, was fiercely fought in Puebla. Revolutionary leader Emiliano Zapata (1879–1919) fought against those opposed to land redistribution and peasants' rights. Eventually, the winners of the revolution imposed their more moderate views and the revolts were pacified.

After the revolution, Puebla evolved to become an industrial center, but its large rural population remained largely impoverished. People in rural areas had limited access to the benefits of economic development.

9 ▪ State and Local Government

The state governor is democratically elected every six years. Immediate re-election is not allowed. The legislature is comprised of a unicameral (single chamber) congress elected every three years, with no immediate re-election provisions. Its forty-one members are made up of twenty-six legislators elected from single member districts and fifteen elected by proportional representation. Because the Institutional Revolutionary Party (PRI) continues to dominate the executive and legislative branches, constitutional provisions for separation of power have not been fully implemented.

The 217 municipalities that comprise Puebla hold democratic elections for municipal presidents and council members every three years. Immediate re-election is not allowed. Because of the widely varying size and financial resources of the different

© Kal Muller/Woodfin Camp

The voladores (people who fly) perform during the October feria (festival) in Cuetzalan.

municipalities, decentralization efforts have produced mixed results in recent years.

10 ■ Political Parties

The three main political parties in all of Mexico are the Institutional Revolutionary Party (PRI), the National Action Party (PAN), and the Party of the Democratic Revolution (PRD). The PRI has historically dominated power in Puebla since the end of the Mexican Revolution. Puebla is one of the PRI strongholds. Governor Manuel Bartlett (1993–1999) unsuccess-

fully sought the PRI presidential nomination in 2000. Most recently, PRI's Melquiades Morales became the governor in 1999. Although they have made electoral gains in the larger urban areas, the PAN and the PRD remain largely minority parties in Puebla.

11 ■ Judicial System

The Superior Tribunal of Justice is the highest court in the state. Its members are appointed by the legislature from a three-person list presented to it by the state governor. Only highly qualified attorneys can be appointed to the highest court. Because Puebla has been ruled exclusively by the PRI since the end of the revolution, the judiciary has historically exercised little independence and autonomy.

12 ■ Economy

Manufacturing companies account for the largest percentage of the economy, at about 24%. General service-based companies account for about 19% of the economy, followed by trade activities at 18%, finance and insurance companies at 18%, transportation and communication companies at 8%, agriculture and livestock production at 8%, construction at 4%, and mining at 1%.

13 ■ Industry

Puebla's manufacturing activity centers on the automotive and textile industries. Volkswagen is one of the major companies with facilities in the state. The textile industry is centered in the capital city of Puebla. Handicrafts are popular products in some regions.

14 ■ Labor

The US Bureau of Labor Statistics reported that Mexican workers saw their wages increase 17%, from $2.09 per hour in 1999 to $2.46 per hour, in 2000. (The average US worker earned $19.86 per hour in 2000.) After one year, workers are entitled by law to six days paid vacation. People living in rural areas of the state earn much less than the national average hourly rate.

15 ■ Agriculture

The main agricultural crops throughout the state are corn, coffee, avocados, beans, and alfalfa. Apples are another important crop, and the Huachinango region even hosts an annual apple fair. Other fruit crops produced in the state include mangos, grapes, oranges, lemons, and peaches. Potatoes are an important crop in the Ciudad Serdán region, which also hosts a regional fair to celebrate this crop.

Livestock includes cattle (for both meat and dairy products), pigs, and poultry. In some areas, donkeys are raised as well. The San Pedro Cholula region is known for its honey, milk, and cream cheese production. The Tehuacán region is one of the nation's most important producers of poultry and eggs.

16 ■ Natural Resources

The silver mines in Puebla are known for their rich deposits of ore and a high-quality silver product. Deposits of gold, copper, and lead are also found in the state.

17 ■ Energy and Power

Almost all of the energy in Mexico is provided by the Federal Electricity Commission (CFE). In February 2002, the CFE introduced new electric rates. For households that use less than 140 kilowatt hours per month, there was no rate increase. (This is about 75% of all households in Mexico, according to CFE).

18 ■ Health

There are 50 general hospitals, 939 outpatient centers, and 106 surgical centers in the state of Puebla.

Most of the Mexican population is covered under a government health plan. The IMSS (Instituto Mexicano de Seguro Social) covers the general population. The ISSSTE (Instituto de Seguridad y Servicios Sociales de Trabajadores del Estado) covers state workers.

19 ■ Housing

Only about one-half of the housing available in Puebla is in good repair. More than 25% is in need of significant upgrading. Many homes in rural areas do not have running water or access to electricity.

20 ■ Education

The system of public education was first started by President Benito Juárez in 1867. Public education in Mexico is free for students from ages six to sixteen. According to the 2000 census, there were approximately 912,000 school-age students in the state. Many students elect to go to private schools. The thirty-one states of Mexico all have at least one state university. The Universidad de las Américas, Puebla (University of the Americas, Puebla) is found in the state.

21 ■ Arts

Puebla has many cultural centers and theaters. The Teatro Carpa Carlos Ancira is a theater for the blind. The folk ballet company, Ballet Folklórico of Puebla, performs regularly. Local artisans produce handicrafts, including clay pottery, wooden masks, and fiber works.

22 ■ Libraries and Museums

There are 566 libraries in Puebla. The capital, Puebla, has a museum displaying the many species of snakes found in the state. There are several other museums in the capital, including a puppet museum, a railroad museum, a science museum with an IMAX theater, a natural history museum, and an auto museum.

23 ■ Media

The capital city, Puebla, has three daily newspapers: *AL de Puebla, El Sol de Puebla,* and *La Jornada de Oriente.*

24 ■ Tourism, Travel, and Recreation

Puebla is a large commercial state. Buildings and ruins from the colonial and pre-Columbian period may be found in the city of Cholula, where there is a site with pre-Columbian pyramids and a church built in the 18th century. Tourists enjoy visiting the cathedral and the El Parian marketplace, both in the capital, Puebla. Tourists also enjoy sampling foods that originated in the state, including mole sauce (spicy chocolate sauce of Aztec origin) and chalupas. Tourists also are drawn to the mineral springs of Tehuacan and the thermal baths of Chignahuapan.

In October Cuetzalan, about four hours by bus from the capital, hosts a feria (festival) that features *voladores* (people who fly). The *voladores* dress in colorful costumes, and climb to the top of a pole 150 feet (45 meters) tall. The *voladores* then tie their ankles to ropes wound around the pole, and leap away from the pole. They fly around and around the pole as the rope unwinds. Their flight is accompanied by flute music.

25 ■ Sports

The capital, Puebla, has a soccer team that plays in the 42,649-seat Cuahutehmoc stadium. Two minor league baseball teams, Los Pericos and Los Tigres, play in the Estadio Hermanos Serdán.

26 ■ Famous People

The ceramic artist Herón Martinez Mendozo is from Acatlán, Puebla. His work is included in the Nelson A. Rockefeller collection of Mexican art at California's Mexican Museum. His relatives in Acatlán continue to produce ceramic works from his designs.

27 ■ Bibliography

Books

LaFrance, David G. *Revolution in Mexico's Heartland: Politics, War, and State Building in Puebla, 1913–1920.* Wilmington, DE: SR Books, 2003.

Supples, Kevin. *Mexico.* Washington, DC: National Geographic Society, 2002.

Web Sites

Mexico for Kids. http://www.elbalero.gob.mx/index_kids.html (accessed on June 15, 2004).

Puebla, Mexico. http://www.sipuebla.com/travel.htm (accessed June 15, 2004).

Querétaro

Pronunciation: keh-REH-taw-rwo.

Origin of state name: The name comes from the native word *queréndaro,* which means "the place of the crags" (rocky terrain).

Capital: Santiago de Querétaro (The name was officially changed to Santiago de Querétaro from Querétaro in July 1996, but it is still commonly known as Querétaro.)

Entered country: October 3, 1824.

Coat of Arms: The coat of arms features a shield divided into three sections. A picture of the Sun with a human face is at the top of the shield, underneath the symbol of the cross. A horseman carrying a flag is pictured next to a picture of a tree. The flags that surround the shield are Mexican flags. The figure on top of the shield is the Mexican coat of arms.

Holidays: Año Nuevo (New Year's Day—January 1); Día de la Constitución (Constitution Day—February 5); Benito Juárez's birthday (March 21); Primero de Mayo (Labor Day—May 1); Revolution Day, 1910 (November 20); and Navidad (Christmas—December 25).

Flag: There is no official state flag.

Time: 6 AM = noon Greenwich Mean Time (GMT).

1 ▪ Location and Size

Querétaro is located in the central region of the country known as the breadbasket of Mexico. It covers an area of 11,769 square kilometers (4,544 square miles), which is about half the size of the US state of New Hampshire. Querétaro is bordered on the north by the Mexican state of San Luis Potosí; on the east by the Mexican states of México and Michoacán; and on the west by the Mexican state of Guanajuato. Querétaro has eighteen municipalities. The capital is Santiago de Querétaro.

The landscape is marked by the central highland plateau and two large mountain ranges (*sierras*). The Sierra Gorda in the north is part of the Sierra Madre Oriental; it is made up of high peaks, small valleys, and deep canyons. In the south, there are mountains of volcanic origin including the Sierra Queretana.

In addition to plateau, the central highland plateau region has high mountainous regions such as the Pinal de Zamorano, which lies between Querétaro and Guanajuato.

The Pánuco River flows into the Gulf of Mexico. The Lerma River becomes the Santiago River, and flows into the Pacific Ocean.

2 ▪ Climate

The climate in the south is usually cool and humid, with abundant rain in the summer, hail, and frequent frosts. In the central part of the state, the climate is dry or semi-dry, with very little rainfall. The northern region is sometimes referred to as the Querétaro desert zone because it is so dry. In the capital city of Santiago de Querétaro, the average year-round temperature is 18°C (64°F). The temperature rarely goes below 10°C (50°F). Average rainfall is about 60 centimeters (24 inches) per year.

3 ▪ Plants and Animals

Thorny, sturdy plants grow in the dry regions of the state. These include ocotillo (a woody, thorny shrub) and nopal cactus (prickly pear). Pine and oak forests cover some of the highland region. White-tailed deer are common. Smaller mammals include raccoons, weasels, squirrels, skunks, and tlacuaches (Mexican opossum). Hawks, woodpeckers, sparrows, and doves are common birds.

4 ▪ Environmental Protection

The Sierra Gorda Biosphere Reserve covers about 383,000 hectares (946,400 acres) in Querétaro. The reserve is home to several endangered and threatened species, including black bears, jaguars, the green toucan, and the Humboldt butterfly. Other national parks in the state include Cerro de las Campanas and El Cimatario.

5 ▪ Population, Ethnic Groups, Languages

Querétaro had a total population of 1,404,306 in 2000; of the total, 680,966 were men and 723,340 were women. The population density was 120 people per square kilometer (310 people per square mile). In 2000, the capital, Santiago de Querétaro, had a population of 639,839. Almost all citizens speak Spanish as their first language. A small number, about 2.1% of the population, speaks indigenous (native) languages.

6 ▪ Religions

According to the 2000 census, 83% of the population, or 1.2 million people, were Roman Catholic; about 2%, or 23,461 people, were Protestant. That year there were also 7,764 Jehovah's Witnesses and over 20,000 people who reported no religion.

7 ▪ Transportation

Querétaro Airport provides international flights to and from the state. The state has about 7,822 kilometers (4,858 miles) of roads and 879 kilometers (546 miles) of railroads.

8 ▪ History

The first human settlements date back to around 400 A.D. The Teotihuacán culture populated the area for several centuries. Later inhabited by the Otomi civilizations, the Mexicas conquered the region a couple of centuries before the arrival of the Spanish conquistadors (explorers and soldiers who sought to claim Mexico for Spain). The Otomi people became allies of the Spanish conquerors and joined forces to defeat the Mexicas in the Querétaro region. Cristóbal de Olid was the first Spaniard to visit the region in 1522.

Between 1522 and 1526, two Otomi leaders had converted to Roman Catholi-

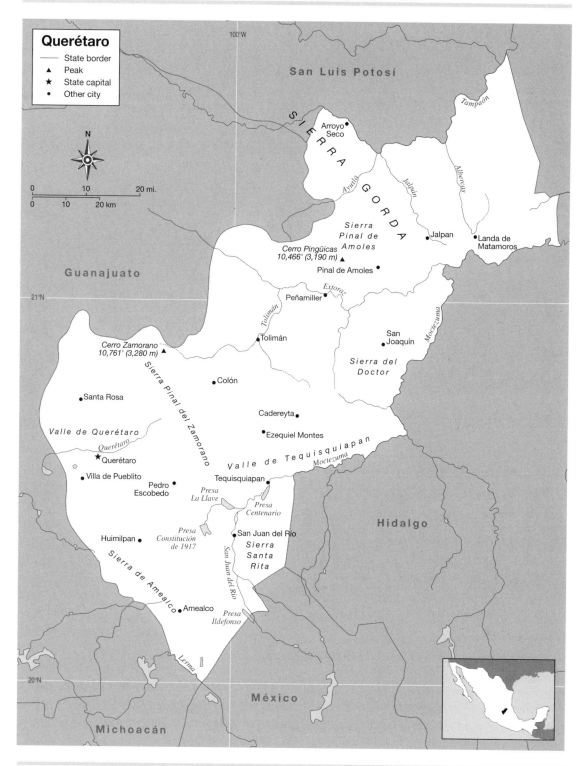

Querétaro

- —— State border
- ▲ Peak
- ★ State capital
- ● Other city

N

| 0 | 10 | 20 mi. |
| 0 | 10 | 20 km |

San Luis Potosí

SIERRA GORDA

Tampaón

Arroyo Seco ●

Ayutla

Jalpán

Alberces

Sierra Pinal de Amoles

Jalpan ●

● Landa de Matamoros

Cerro Pingüicas 10,466' (3,190 m) ▲

● Pinal de Amoles

Guanajuato

21°N

Extoraz

Peñamiller ●

Tolimán

San Joaquín ●

Cerro Zamorano 10,761' (3,280 m) ▲

● Tolimán

Sierra del Doctor

Moctezuma

Sierra Pinal del Zamorano

● Colón

● Santa Rosa

Cadereyta ●

Valle de Querétaro

● Ezequiel Montes

Querétaro

★ Querétaro

Valle de Tequisquiapan

Moctezuma

● Villa de Pueblito

Tequisquiapan ●

Presa La Llave

Pedro Escobedo ●

Presa Centenario

Hidalgo

Huimilpan ●

Presa Constitución de 1917

San Juan del Río ●

Sierra Santa Rita

San Juan del Río

Sierra de Amealco

● Amealco

Presa Ildefonso

Lerma

20°N

México

Michoacán

A famous and impressive aqueduct was built in Querétaro between 1726 and 1739.

cism. They changed their names to Fernando de Tapia and Nicolás de San Luis Montañez. They founded the city of Santiago de Querétaro. The city grew and consolidated as an agricultural and commercial center during the 16th and 17th centuries. It was officially named the third city of the viceroyalty of Mexico in 1671. A famous and impressive aqueduct was built in Querétaro between 1726 and 1739.

National heroes Miguel Hidalgo y Costilla (1753–1811) and Mariano Matamoros (1770–1814) were priests in the region when they initiated the independence movement against Spanish rule in 1810. With the defeat of the independence forces two years

later, the region was brought back into royalist rule, although some pro-independence militias remained active throughout the 1810s. With the formal declaration of independence in 1821, Querétaro was made a province. It achieved the status of federal state in 1824. The first state constitution dates back to 1825.

During the federalist-centralist and liberal-conservative conflicts of most of the 19th century, Querétaro experienced political and social instability. Different leaders revolted against state and national authorities, with varying levels of success. For a short period of time (from 1863 to 1867), Querétaro and much of Mexico was under French occupation and the rule of Emperor Maximilian (1832–1867). When Maximilian was forced to abandon Mexico City in 1867, he sought refuge in Querétaro. He was later defeated and arrested there. Monarchical rule was abolished. Emperor Maximilian was tried and sentenced to death. He was executed in Querétaro on June 19, 1867.

When the liberals, under the leadership of Benito Juárez (1806–1872), regained control of the country, Querétaro was occupied by liberal loyal troops. During the Porfiriato period (the years that Porfirio Díaz [1830–1872] was in power [1877–1880 and 1884–1911]), Querétaro experienced economic and infrastructural development. Some Protestant churches, most notably the Methodist Church, also established a presence in the region during Porfirio Díaz's rule.

A strike by the railroad workers was violently repressed by the government in 1909. This growing tension between workers and the government partially led to the Mexican Revolution in 1910. Different factions fought for control of Querétaro during the first years of the revolution, which lasted from 1910 to 1917. When the Mexican Constitution was promulgated in 1917, Querétaro was under the rule of the revolutionary victors.

The Cristero War was a conflict between those loyal to the Roman Catholic Church leadership and the revolutionary government. It affected Querétaro to a small degree. Its violence mostly ended with the end of the revolution in 1917. During the post-revolutionary decades, Querétaro evolved as an industrial center. It benefited from its proximity to the capital city of Mexico. Querétaro's economy was largely industrial. The Institutional Revolutionary

Party (PRI) was powerful in rural Mexico, but it was not as effective in Querétaro. The National Action Party (PAN) emerged as a viable political alternative in Querétaro in 1997. Three years later, in 2000, the PAN candidate defeated the PRI candidate in the national presidential election for the first time.

9 ■ State and Local Government

The state governor is elected for a non-renewable six-year term. The state legislature is a unicameral (single chamber) assembly comprised of twenty-five members. Fifteen members are elected in single member districts and ten are elected by proportional representation. Legislators serve for three-year terms and immediate re-election is not allowed. The Institutional Revolutionary Party (PRI) does not hold the governorship, but it maintains a strong presence in the legislature. Because no one party controls the executive and legislative branches of government, constitutional provisions for separation of power are put to work.

The eighteen municipalities that comprise Querétaro hold democratic elections for municipal presidents and council members every three years. Immediate re-election is not allowed. Although some decentralization initiatives are producing positive results, the state still has a long way to go to achieve successful decentralization.

10 ■ Political Parties

The three main political parties in all of Mexico are the Institutional Revolutionary Party (PRI), the National Action Party (PAN), and the Party of the Democratic Revolution (PRD). Although the PRI tightly dominated state politics through-

© Peter Langer/EPD Photos

Tequisquiapan, about two hours' drive from Mexico City, is a popular weekend destination for residents of the congested city. Tequisquiapan has a central plaza with a church with a single bell tower on one side and shops and restaurants on the other three sides.

out most of the 20th century, the PAN emerged as a powerful party after the wave of democratization of the late 1980s. The PAN first won a gubernatorial election in 1997. The PAN won its second consecutive gubernatorial election in 2003 when Francisco Garrido Patrón became state governor.

11 Judicial System

The Superior Tribunal of Justice is the highest court in the state. Its ten members are elected by the legislature from a three-person list presented to it by the governor. After their three-year terms expire, they can be re-appointed. Only qualified attorneys can be appointed to the highest court. In addition, an electoral tribunal court and lower courts also comprise the state's judicial system.

12 Economy

Manufacturing accounts for the largest percentage of the economy at about 32%. Trade activities account for about 19% of the economy, followed by service-based companies at 18%, transportation and communications at 11%, finance and insurance at 11%, agriculture and livestock at 4%, construction at 4%, and mining at 1%.

13 ■ Industry

Food processing industries in the state include such well-known companies as Carnation and Purina. The textile industry includes the manufacturing of fabrics from wool, cotton, and henequen (a type of tropical plant). Most manufacturing companies are in or around the capital city. The auto parts company Tremac is one of the biggest employers in Santiago de Querétaro. Handicrafts such as furniture, baskets, pottery, and jewelry are important industries on a smaller scale.

14 ■ Labor

The US Bureau of Labor Statistics reported that Mexican workers saw their wages increase 17%, from $2.09 per hour in 1999 to $2.46 per hour in 2000. (The average US worker earned $19.86 per hour in 2000.) After one year, workers are entitled by law to six days paid vacation.

15 ■ Agriculture

Agriculture is one of the main economic activities. Primary crops include beans, cabbage, alfalfa, onions, lettuce, and sorghum. Livestock breeding, especially of dairy cows, is important in the pasturelands. The state of Querétaro is one of the leading milk producers in the country.

16 ■ Natural Resources

Mineral resources include silver, iron, copper, and mercury. The state is also well-known for its opals. The chief mining districts are in Cadereyta and Toliman.

17 ■ Energy and Power

Almost all of the energy in Mexico is provided by the Federal Electricity Commission (CFE). In February 2002, the CFE introduced new electric rates. For households that use less than 140 kilowatt hours per month, there was no rate increase. (This is about 75% of all households in Mexico, according to CFE). Querétaro's electricity consumption in the 1990s was low compared to the rest of Mexico. After the passage of the North American Free Trade Agreement (NAFTA)—a trade agreement between Mexico, the United States, and Canada—electricity consumption grew because of the manufacturing facilities that were built in the state.

18 ■ Health

There are 8 general hospitals, 293 outpatient centers, and 27 surgical centers in the state of Querétaro.

Most of the Mexican population is covered under a government health plan. The IMSS (Instituto Mexicano de Seguro Social) covers the general population. The ISSSTE (Instituto de Seguridad y Servicios Sociales de Trabajadores del Estado) covers state workers.

19 ■ Housing

More than one-half of the housing available in the state of Querétaro is in good repair. About 15% is in need of significant upgrading. These homes may not have running water or access to electricity.

20 ■ Education

The system of public education was first started by President Benito Juárez in 1867. Public education in Mexico is free for students from ages six to sixteen. According to the 2000 census, there were approximately 239,000 school-age students in the state. Many students elect to go to private schools. The thirty-one states of Mexico all have at least one state university. The Universidad Autónoma de Querétaro (Independent University of Querétaro) is located in the capital.

21 ▪ Arts
Querétaro has nine local cultural centers and thirteen theaters, including those located at the Universidad Autónoma de Querétaro. Querétaro also hosts many musical, art, and dance presentations. The Escuela de Danza Nijinsky is a school of ballet.

22 ▪ Libraries and Museums
The state of Querétaro has fifty-four libraries. There are eighteen museums including a museum of art and a museum of mathematics.

23 ▪ Media
The daily newspaper *El Diario de Querétaro* is published in the capital. *El Sol de San Juan del Río* is published in the city of San Juan del Río.

24 ▪ Tourism, Travel, and Recreation
San Miguel de Allende attracts many foreign tourists. The city is home to many artists and writers. The San Miguel music festival in December is famous. There is also a festival on September 29 each year to honor San Miguel Arcángel, the city's patron saint. There are many churches and many religious festivals held year-round. San Miguel is also known for its excellent restaurants. Two points of interest in this colonial city are La Parroquia (a pink Gothic-style church) and El Chorro, a natural spring where women of the town still do laundry. The capital city, Santiago de Querétaro, has an archeological zone known as El Cerrito; ruins from pre-Hispanic civilizations dating from the first century may be viewed there. The city also has an aqueduct that was built in 1743.

25 ▪ Sports
The city of Santiago de Querétaro has a basketball team, Las Cometas, and a soccer team, which plays in the 50,000-seat La Corregidora stadium. There is a 12,000-seat bullfighting ring in the Plaza Santa María.

26 ▪ Famous People
Francisco Garrido Patrón became governor in 2003.

27 ▪ Bibliography
Books

Supples, Kevin. *Mexico.* Washington, DC: National Geographic Society, 2002.

Web Sites

Mexico for Kids. http://www.elbalero.gob.mx/index_ kids.html (accessed on June 15, 2004).

Quintana Roo

Pronunciation: keen-TAH-nah ROH-oh.

Origin of state name: The state was named after Andrés de Quintana Roo (1787–1851), who fought for Mexican independence.

Capital: Chetumal (cheh-too-MAHL).

Entered country: 1974.

Coat of Arms: A rising sun with seven rays represents the first seven municipalities of Quintana Roo. The symbol in the upper left represents a marine shell marking the state's position on the Caribbean. The five-pointed star symbolizes the "morning star," representing the planet Venus. It can generally be seen in the eastern sky just before sunrise and represents the state's position as the easternmost point of Mexico. The three triangles represent the forests of Quintana Roo. Red is the Mayan color to represent the east, yellow represents the south, white is the north, and black is the west. Green is a sacred color.

Holidays: Año Nuevo (New Year's Day—January 1); Día de la Constitución (Constitution Day—February 5); Benito Juárez's birthday (March 21); Primero de Mayo (Labor Day—May 1); Revolution Day, 1910 (November 20); and Navidad (Christmas—December 25).

Flag: There is no official state flag.

Time: 6 AM = noon Greenwich Mean Time (GMT).

1 ▇ Location and Size

Quintana Roo is the easternmost state at the tip of the Yucatán Peninsula. Quintana Roo covers an area of 42,030 square kilometers (16,228 square miles), which is a little less than half the size of the US state of Maine. It borders the Mexican states of Yucatán to the northwest, Campeche to the west, the Central American countries of Belize and Guatemala to the south, and the Gulf of Mexico and the Caribbean Sea to the east and north. The state has eight municipalities. Its capital is Chetumal.

Quintana Roo is situated on the Yucatán Peninsula, which is low and flat. The southwestern region of the peninsula is the highest, reaching an altitude of more than 200 meters (660 feet) above sea level. The Caribbean coastline is long and beautiful, with fine beaches. One important feature of this coastline is the coral reef.

The most important river is the Hondo River, which forms the border with Belize.

© Robert Frerck/Woodfin Camp

Mayan ruins.

The state also has many lagoons. There are also underground caves filled with water that has filtered through the porous rocks. These caves are known as cenotés.

2 ▪ Climate

The warm waters of the Caribbean Sea contribute to the climate, which is generally warm and humid. The average temperature range is 25.5°C to 26.5°C (78°F to 80°F), with maximum high temperatures between 36°C and 38°C (97°F and 100°F) and low temperatures ranging from 12°C to 14°C (54°F to 57°F). The highest monthly average rainfall, 17 centimeters (6.7 inches), occurs in September. Annual rainfall ranges from 1,100 to 1,500 millimeters (43 to 59 inches), with the average being 1,200 millimeters (47 inches). The region is also frequently affected by tropical storms and hurricanes. In September 1989 Hurricane Hugo struck Cancún with 320-kilometer-per-hour (200-mile-per-hour) winds, causing major damage to the resort hotels there.

3 ▪ Plants and Animals

There are four basic ecosystems, or natural environments, found in the state: forests, savanna, mangroves, and reefs. The forests contain mahogany, cedars, East Indian rosewoods, and palm trees. Common animals in this ecosystem are anteaters, spider monkeys, white-tailed deer, and tepezcuintles (a type of dog). Birds found here include turkeys, parrots, doves, and nightingales. The savanna region features pastureland and bushes. Mangroves are tropical evergreen trees that generally grow along the coast and have large, tangled root systems. Animals found in the mangroves include herons, pelicans, and ducks. Manatees and alligators are also found in the nearby waters. The limestone reef that lies along the coast is the home of lobsters, shrimp, sea snails, and other fish.

4 ▪ Environmental Protection

There are several protected areas that are meant to preserve and sustain the diverse ecosystems of the state. These areas include Tulum National Park, the Yum Balam Protected Area, Sian Ka'an Biosphere Reserve, and El Eden Ecological Reserve.

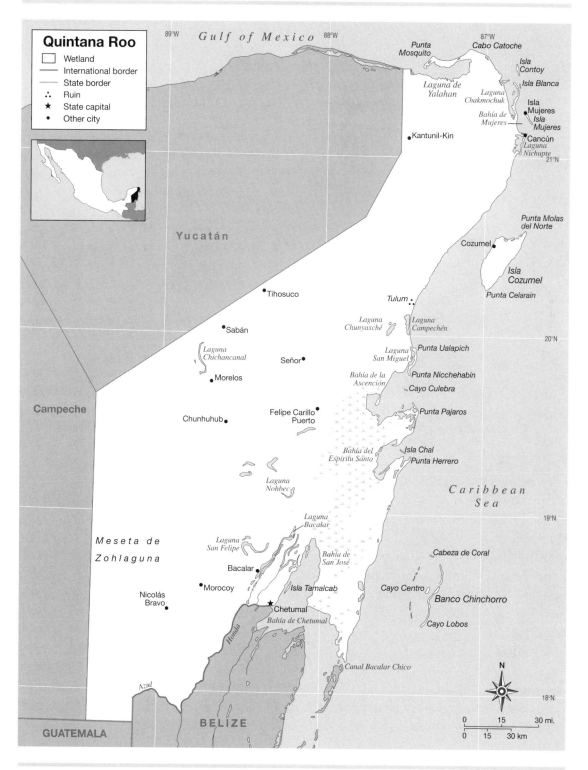

Quintana Roo

- ▢ Wetland
- ── International border
- ⋯⋯ State border
- ∴ Ruin
- ★ State capital
- • Other city

Gulf of Mexico

89°W
88°W
87°W

Punta Mosquito

Cabo Catoche

Isla Contoy

Laguna de Yalahan

Isla Blanca

Laguna Chakmochuk

Isla Mujeres

Bahía de Mujeres

Isla Mujeres

Kantunil-Kin

Cancún

Laguna Nichupte

21°N

Yucatán

Punta Molas del Norte

Cozumel

Isla Cozumel

Tihosuco

Tulum

Punta Celarain

Laguna Chunyaxché

Laguna Campechén

Sabán

20°N

Laguna Chichancanal

Señor

Laguna San Miguel

Punta Ualapich

Morelos

Punta Nicchehabin

Bahía de la Ascención

Cayo Culebra

Campeche

Chunhuhub

Felipe Carillo Puerto

Punta Pajaros

Isla Chal

Bahía del Espíritu Santo

Punta Herrero

Laguna Nohbec

Caribbean Sea

19°N

Laguna Bacalar

Laguna San Felipe

Cabeza de Coral

Bahía de San José

Meseta de Zohlaguna

Bacalar

Isla Tamalcab

Cayo Centro

Banco Chinchorro

Morocoy

Nicolás Bravo

Chetumal

Bahía de Chetumal

Cayo Lobos

Hondo

Canal Bacalar Chico

N

18°N

Azul

GUATEMALA

BELIZE

0   15   30 mi.

0   15   30 km

© Robert Frerck/Woodfin Camp

The Labna Arch was the entrance to the city of Labna, which flourished around 700–800 A.D.

5 ▪ Population, Ethnic Groups, Languages

Quintana Roo had a total population of 874,963 in 2000; of the total, 448,308 were men and 426,655 were women. The population density was 21 people per square kilometer (54 people per square mile). In 2000, the capital, Chetumal, had a population of 121,602.

Most citizens speak Spanish as a first language. However, about 23% of the population speaks indigenous (native) languages. This is the fourth-highest percentage in the country (following Yucatan, Oaxaca, and Chiapas).

6 ▪ Religions

According to the 2000 census, 63% of the population, or 552,745 people, were Roman Catholic; 10%, or 84,319 people, were Protestant. That year there were also 14,285 Seventh-Day Adventists, 16,919 Jehovah's Witnesses, and 587 Jews. Over 80,000 people reported no religion.

7 ▪ Transportation

Cancún International Airport, Chetumal International Airport, and Cozumel Airport provide international flights to and from Quintana Roo. The state has about 5,302 kilometers (3,293 miles) of roads.

8 ■ History

Around 3000 B.C. proto-Mayan groups first populated the region. During the 10th century, a Mayan group known as the Itzáes built the cities of Chichén-Itzá and Champotón, two of the most impressive Mayan ruins that still exist in Mexico. Together with other groups influenced by the Toltec and Chichimec cultures, the Itzáes formed the Mayapan League, a sort of lose coalition of Mayan cities. In 1194, the Itzáes abandoned Chichén-Itzá. They founded the city of Petén, another celebrated Mayan architectural wonder.

In 1502, the first contact with Spanish conquistadors (Spanish explorers who sought to conquer Mexico for Spain) took place off the coast of Quintana Roo, where some of the members of Christopher Columbus's (1451–1506) last expedition discovered native fishing boats. In 1511, a Spanish ship from Darien (Panama) was stranded near the coast. Several survivors were captured and executed in the region with the exception of Gonzalo Guerrero and Jerónimo de Aguilar, who were accepted and assimilated into Mayan culture.

In 1517, the Hernández de Córdoba expedition arrived in Cabo Catoche and later Juan de Grijalba (c. 1489–1527) arrived in Cozumel. In 1519, Spanish conqueror Hernán Cortés (1485–1547) arrived in Chetumal and rescued Jerónimo de Aguilar. In 1526, Francisco de Montejo (c. 1479–1553) proposed to Spanish king Carlos V (1500–1558) the conquest of the Yucatán province. The conquest was started in 1527 and completed in 1546 by Montejo's son, Francisco Montejo y León.

During the 16th and 17th centuries, pirates operating in the Caribbean constantly attacked the coastal regions. In 1652, the city of Salamanca de Balacar was attacked by buccaneers and then abandoned. Efforts were made to prevent a possible English invasion from the Belize territories. Catholic conversion efforts were first launched in the 18th century, allowing for the Maya population to retain much of its original cultural heritage well into the independence period.

After independence, in 1823, Guatemala annexed much of the Petén-Itzá territory. In 1841, an effort by large landowners to declare the independence of the Yucatán Peninsula from Mexico failed because of the lack of international recognition. In 1847, an ethnic war brought instability and destruction to the region. Mexico and Britain signed the Marshal Saint John Treaty that established the Belize-Mexico border on the Hondo River.

In 1901, the last indigenous rebels were subdued. In 1902, Quintana Roo was made an independent territory, autonomous of the Yucatán state. After being incorporated with Yucatán and Campeche during different phases of the Mexican Revolution, Quintana Roo was made an independent entity by President Lázaro Cárdenas (1895–1970), who served as president of Mexico from 1934 to 1940. The region became a federal state only in 1974.

Because of its innumerable natural beauties and its rich archeological and anthropological heritage, UNESCO incorporated the region into its Man and Biosphere Program in 1986. Aside from its growing and consolidating tourism industry, Quintana Roo remains a scarcely populated state with little industrial and non-tourism related economic activities. Two major factors have influenced Quintana Roo's slow growth: tourism has been widely promoted by the central national government and its late

© Robert Frerck/Woodfin Camp

The ruins at Tulum are preserved as part of Tulum National Park.

achievement of federal statehood. Quintana Roo has yet to develop a strong local economy and vibrant civil society.

9 ■ State and Local Government

The state governor is elected for a six-year nonrenewable term. The state legislature is comprised of twenty-five deputies elected for nonrenewable three-year terms. Fifteen deputies are elected in single member districts and ten are elected by proportional representation. Although the constitution includes separation of power provisions, the governor exercises enormous influence over the legislature, reflecting the tight control the Institutional Revolution-

ary Party (PRI) has wielded over state politics since its beginning.

The eight municipalities that make up Quintana Roo hold democratic elections for municipal presidents and council members every three years. Immediate re-election is not allowed. Because the PRI continues to exercise strong power at the gubernatorial level, decentralization efforts have lagged behind in Quintana Roo.

10 ■ Political Parties

The three main political parties in all of Mexico are the Institutional Revolutionary Party (PRI), the National Action Party (PAN), and the Party of the Democratic

Revolution (PRD). The PRI has continued to dominate state politics, as it has in much of the country since the end of the Mexican Revolution. Although the PAN and PRD have received a considerable share of the vote in recent elections, the PRI remains as the strongest party in the state. There has yet to be a non-PRI governor in Quintana Roo since it became a federal state.

11 ▪ Judicial System

The Superior Tribunal of Justice is the highest court in the state. Its members are appointed by the legislature from a three-person list submitted to them by the Superior Tribunal. Only qualified attorneys can be included in the list. There is a mandatory retirement age of sixty-five. In addition, an electoral tribunal court and local courts complete the state's judicial system.

12 ▪ Economy

Tourism is the most important economic activity in Quintana Roo accounting for 80% to 90% of the economy. Cancún, once an uninhabited island, has grown to be one of the world's leading tourist destinations. Cancún secures 25% to 28% of all Mexican tourism. The number of hotel rooms and visitors has far exceeded projections. Agriculture, livestock breeding, forestry exploitation, apiculture (beekeeping), and fishing follow in importance. Industrial activities have barely gained footing in the economy. Exports are chicle (a chief ingredient of chewing gum), honey, seafood, and fruit.

13 ▪ Industry

Industrial activity in Quintana Roo is related to the tourism industry. Large-scale industry is in sugar and construction materials. Small-scale industry is in tortillas, bread, purified water, and ice. Otherwise, other activities have barely begun.

14 ▪ Labor

The US Bureau of Labor Statistics reported that Mexican workers saw their wages increase 17%, from $2.09 per hour in 1999 to $2.46 per hour in 2000. (The average US worker earned $19.86 per hour in 2000.) After one year, workers are entitled by law to six days paid vacation.

15 ▪ Agriculture

Agricultural products are corn, beans, rice, sugarcane, jalapeño chilies, and watermelon. Beekeeping products are honey and wax. Cattle, pigs, and sheep are the livestock bred.

16 ▪ Natural Resources

There is fishing for shrimp, lobster, and sea snails. Mahogany and cedar are forested. Chicle, a sticky white sap that may be used as the raw material for chewing gum and other products, is another forestry product found in both the high and low stature semi-evergreen forests of Quintana Roo.

17 ▪ Energy and Power

Almost all of the energy in Mexico is provided by the Federal Electricity Commission (CFE). In February 2002, the CFE introduced new electric rates. For households that use less than 140 kilowatt hours per month, there was no rate increase.

© Robert Frerck/Woodfin Camp

Cancun is a popular resort destination.

(This is about 75% of all households in Mexico, according to CFE.)

18 ■ Health

The state of Quintana Roo has 15 general hospitals, 196 outpatient centers, and 28 surgical centers. There is also an Amer-iMed center, an American hospital, in Cancún geared towards tourists and their families.

Most of the Mexican population is covered under a government health plan. The IMSS (Instituto Mexicano de Seguro Social) covers the general population. The ISSSTE (Instituto de Seguridad y Servicios Sociales de Trabajadores del Estado) covers state workers.

19 ■ Housing

Only about one-half of the housing available in the state of Quintana Roo is in good repair. More than 26% is in need of significant upgrading. Many homes do not have running water or access to electricity. Population growth was more than double the national average in the mid 1990s, resulting in not enough housing to meet demands.

20 ■ Education

The system of public education was first started by President Benito Juárez (1806–1872) in 1867. Public education in Mexico is free for students from ages six to sixteen. According to the 2000 census, there were approximately 139,600 school-age students in the state. Many students elect to go to private schools. The thirty-one states of Mexico all have at least one state university. The Universidad de Quintana Roo is located in the capital, Chetumal.

21 ■ Arts

Quintana Roo has seven theaters and cultural centers. A principal cultural center is the Centro Cultural de Bellas Artes. There are displays of archeological artifacts from the city of Chetumal.

22 ■ Libraries and Museums

There are forty-four branches of the library system in Quintana Roo. There is an archeological museum and a museum of popular art in Cancún. Cozumel also has a museum.

23 ■ Media

Cancún, has one daily newspaper, *Novedades Quintana Roo*.

24 ■ Tourism, Travel, and Recreation

The two main tourist attractions are the cities of Cancún and Cozumel. These are primarily tourist destinations, but they are also places from which people take off to visit famous archeological sites, such as Chichén-Itzá. Cozumel, a small island with excellent beaches, has many Mayan archeological ruins at San Gervasio. The Chankanaab Lagoon is a natural aquarium popular with snorkelers. The archeological city of Tulum is one of the main tourist attractions of Quintana Roo. Tulum was a Mayan site built on a cliff overlooking the Caribbean. Isla Mujeres (Isle of Women) offers diving and snorkeling. There is a large stone cross in the water dedicated to those who lost their lives there. Quintana Roo was also the site of the pirate trade.

25 ■ Sports

Water sports are popular for both residents and tourists, who are drawn to the Caribbean beaches of the state.

26 ■ Famous People

Quintana Roo was named after Andrés Quintana Roo (1787–1851), an early patriot of the Mexican Republic. Joaquín Ernesto Hendricks Díaz was elected governor of Quintana Roo in 1999, for a six-year term.

27 ■ Bibliography

Books

Cancun and the Yucatan. London, Eng.: Dorling Kindersley, 2003.

DeAngelis, Gina. *Mexico.* Mankato, MN: Blue Earth Books, 2003.

Supples, Kevin. *Mexico.* Washington, DC: National Geographic Society, 2002.

Web Sites

Mexico for Kids. http://www.elbalero.gob.mx/index_kids.html (accessed on June 15, 2004).

San Luis Potosí

Pronunciation: sahn-loo-ees poh-toh-SEE.

Origin of state name: The Spaniards originally named the region Valle de San Luis, a name that was soon shortened to San Luis. After discovering large amounts of gold and silver, the Spaniards added the word Potosí (hill), which was a name they were applying to rich mining regions.

Capital: San Luis Potosí.

Entered country: 1824.

Coat of Arms: The coat of arms features San Luis Rey, the patron saint of the state, standing on top of San Pedro Hill, which has cave-like openings representing the mines of the state. Blue and yellow are used to represent night and day. Two silver and two gold bars represent the mining activities of the state.

Holidays: Año Nuevo (New Year's Day—January 1); Día de la Constitución (Constitution Day—February 5); Benito Juárez's birthday (March 21); Primero de Mayo (Labor Day—May 1); Revolution Day, 1910 (November 20); and Navidad (Christmas—December 25).

Flag: There is no official state flag.

Time: 6 AM = noon Greenwich Mean Time (GMT).

Location and Size

San Luis Potosí covers an area of 62,849 square kilometers (24,266 square miles), which is slightly larger than the US state of West Virginia. It is surrounded by nine Mexican states, thereby being the state with the most states bordering on it. To the north are the states of Coahuila and Nuevo León; on the northeast, Tamaulipas; on the east, Veracruz; on the south, Hidalgo, Querétaro, and Guanajuato; on the southwest, Jalisco; and on the west, Zacatecas. San Luis Potosí is divided into fifty-eight municipalities. The capital city is also called San Luis Potosí.

The Sierra Madre Oriental mountain range runs along the eastern portion of San Luis Potosí.

The longest river system is the Santa María, which joins the Moctezuma River to form the Pánuco River. There are spectacular waterfalls at Tamul and Micos.

2 ▪ Climate

In regions of higher altitude, the climate is dry and desert-like. In the central re-

© Kal Muller/Woodfin Camp

Most farms are found in the Huasteca region of the state, which is a fertile lowland area in the east.

gion of the state, the climate may vary from cool to hot, but the lower regions of the state are generally hot and humid. In the capital city of San Luis Potosí, the average year-round temperature is about 18°C (64°F). The average precipitation in the capital is 35 centimeters (13.9 inches) per year.

3 ■ Plants and Animals

Some of the most common plants in the state are Chinese palm and yucca trees, organ cactus, nopal (prickly pear), and various ferns and mosses. Sapodilla, papaya, and banana trees are also found. Large mammals include wildcats and deer. Small mammals include prairie dogs, hares, tlacuaches (Mexican opossums), and tepezcuintles (small dogs). Rattlesnakes and armadillos can also be found. Hawks and eagles are common birds.

4 ■ Environmental Protection

In 2003, San Luis Potosí received federal monies to assist the state in efforts to develop systems for tracking industrial pollutants. Protected areas in the state include El Potosí National Park and Gogorrón National Park.

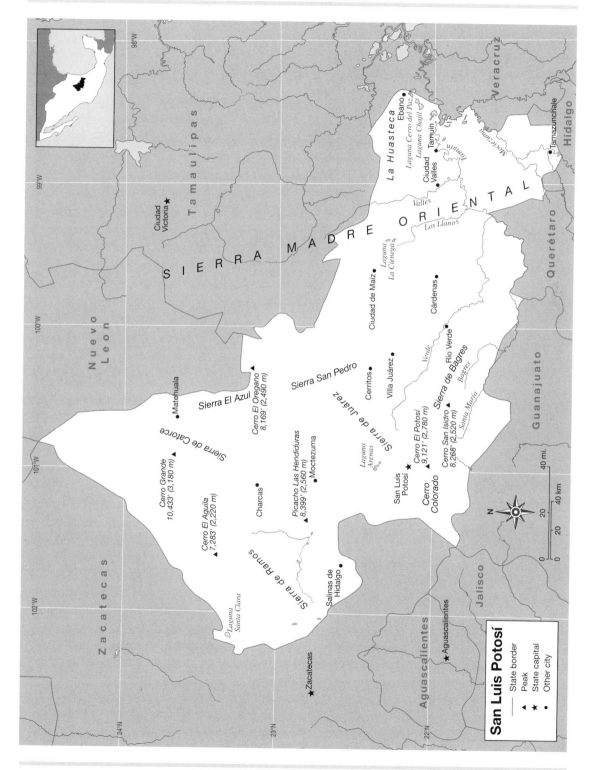

Tamaulipas

Veracruz

Hidalgo

La Huasteca

Ebano

Laguna Cerro del Paz

Laguna Chajil

Tamuín

Ciudad Valles

Tamazunchale

Valles

Los Llanos

S I E R R A   M A D R E   O R I E N T A L

Ciudad Victoria ★

Tamaulipas

Nuevo León

Laguna
La Cienega

Ciudad de Maíz

Cárdenas

Querétaro

Verde

Sierra San Pedro

Cerritos

Villa Juárez

Sierra de Bagres

Bagres

Sierra El Azul

▲ Cerro El Oregano
8,169' (2,490 m)

Santa María

Matehuala

Sierra de Río Verde

Cerro San Isidro
8,268' (2,520 m) ▲

Guanajuato

Sierra de Catorce

Sierra de Juárez

Cerro El Potosí
9,121' (2,780 m)

Laguna
Arenas

San Luis
Potosí ★

Cerro
Colorado ▲

Cerro Grande
10,433 (3,180 m) ▲

Cerro El Aguila
▲ 7,283' (2,220 m)

Charcas •

Picacho Las Hendiduras
▲ 8,399 (2,560 m)

Moctezuma •

*Laguna
Santa Clara*

Sierra de Ramos

Salinas de
Hidalgo •

Zacatecas

Aguascalientes

Aguascalientes ★

Jalisco

Zacatecas ★

40 mi.

N

40 km

20

20

0

0

San Luis Potosí

State border
▲ Peak
★ State capital
• Other city

24°N

23°N

22°N

102°W

101°W

100°W

99°W

98°W

© Mireille Vautier/Woodfin Camp

An example of the masks on display in the Museum of the Mask, found in the capital, San Luis Potosí.

5 ■ Population, Ethnic Groups, Languages

San Luis Potosí had a total population of 2,299,360 in 2000; of the total, 1,120,837 were men and 1,178,523 were women. The population density was 38 people per square kilometer (98 people per square mile). In 2000, the capital, San Luis Potosí, had a population of 669,353.

Almost all citizens speak Spanish as their first language. About 11.7% of the population speaks indigenous (native) languages.

6 ■ Religions

According to the 2000 census, 80% of the population, or 1.8 million people, were Roman Catholic; 4 %, or 93,257 people, were Protestant. That year there were also 14,365 Jehovah's Witnesses and over 45,000 people who reported no religion.

7 ■ Transportation

The state has about 8,293 kilometers (5,151 miles) of roads and 1,280 kilometers (795 miles) of railroads. There are two airports in the state, mostly for domestic flights.

8 ■ History

Around 10,000 B.C. hunter and gatherer groups first visited the San Luis Potosí region. There are some archeological ruins that date back to 1200 B.C. in the region. Before the arrival of the Spanish conquistadors (those who sought to conqueror Mexico for Spain), Chichimeco and Huasteco groups inhabited the area. In October 1522, Spanish conqueror Hernán Cortés (1485–1547) initiated the conquest of the region. In 1524, Nuño Beltrán de Guzmán took possession of the territory as the crown-appointed governor. Another Spaniard, Beltrán de Guzmán, kidnapped thousands of native Indians. He sold them as slaves in other parts of Mexico. Around 1539, Franciscan priests Antonio de Roa and Juan Sevilla initiated a campaign to convert the Indians in the region to Roman Catholicism. The discovery of mineral deposits in San Luis Potosí and Zacatecas in 1546 attracted new settlers. The Chichimec Indians revolted against increased colonial presence and launched a military offensive known as the Chichimec War toward the end of the 1500s.

Franciscan priest Diego de la Magdalena established a hospice for Indians in what later became the town of San Luis Potosí. In 1583, Mestizo (mixed Spanish and Indigenous) military leader Miguel Caldera sought to bring an end to the Chichimec War. Viceroy Luis de Velasco (1511–1564) sent four hundred indigenous families who had converted to Catholicism to live among the Chichimec starting in 1591. In 1592, the discovery of new mineral deposits created a gold rush. The town of San Luis Potosí was formally founded in late 1592. Toward the turn of the century, new cattle ranches and agricultural fields emerged to service the growing mining industry. The Chichimec War ended in the 17th century. The indigenous populations were overpowered by the Spanish population's growth and the power of the colonizers. San Luis Potosí consolidated as a major mining center in Mexico during the 17th and 18th century.

The independence movement reached San Luis Potosí in 1810. Despite a number of bloody uprisings, the royalist forces (loyal to Spain) successfully maintained control of the region until 1821, when end to Spanish rule in the entire country came with a formal declaration of independence. San Luis Potosí became a federal state in 1824. Its new constitution was written in 1826.

A period of instability characterized much of Mexico between 1830 and 1870. After this period, forces loyal to President Porfirio Díaz (1830–1915) controlled San Luis Potosí. Economic development and improvements in infrastructure characterized much of the period. But indigenous insurrections continued. Different groups and different movements revolted demanding land distribution and improvements in the living conditions of peasants. A precursor of the Mexican Revolution was the first Liberal Congress organized in San Luis Potosí in 1901.

Revolutionary leader Francisco Indalécio Madero (1873–1913) was arrested in July 1910 and sent to San Luis Potosí. He successfully escaped. He then issued the Plan of San Luis on October 5th, which encouraged Mexicans to take up arms against the government and marked the beginning of the Mexican Revolution (1910–1920). Near the end of the revolution in 1917, the Cristero War, where Catholic loyalists revolted against the secular nature of the new government, made it more difficult for revolutionary violence to be subdued.

During the period of Institutional Revolutionary Party (PRI) rule, which lasted from 1934 to 2003 (when Marcelo Santos of the National Action Party was elected governor), San Luis Potosí emerged as one of the most troubled states in the union. A revolt against the land distribution programs championed by President Lázaro Cárdenas (1895–1970) in 1939 was violently repressed. The civic movement led by rightwing physician Salvador Nava generated political instability. This popular and relentless democratic leader challenged the domination of the PRI.

9 ■ State and Local Government

The state governor is democratically elected for a nonrenewable six-year term. The state legislature is comprised of twenty-seven deputies elected for nonrenewable three-year terms. Fifteen deputies are elected in single member districts and twelve are elected by proportional representation. Because of strong competition from the National Action Party (PAN) since the mid 1960s, militant legislative power have been exercised as PAN leaders have employed check-and-balance provisions against the governor.

The fifty-eight municipalities that comprise San Luis Potosí hold democratic elections for municipal presidents and council members every three years. Immediate re-election is not allowed. Although some decentralization initiatives are producing positive results, the state still has a long way to go to achieve successful decentralization.

10 ■ Political Parties

The three main political parties in all of Mexico are the Institutional Revolutionary Party (PRI), the National Action Party (PAN), and the Party of the Democratic Revolution (PRD). Although the PRI dominated state politics since the end of the Mexican Revolution in 1917, a charismatic conservative leader, Salvador Nava, became mayor of San Luis Potosí in 1959. In 1991, Nava ran for governor and lost to the PRI amid accusations of massive fraud. Finally, the PRI control came to an end in 2003, when PAN's Marcelo Santos was elected governor.

11 ■ Judicial System

The Supreme Tribunal of Justice is the state's highest court. Its thirteen members are appointed by the legislature from a three-person list presented to them by the governor. Only qualified attorneys can be nominated. After their six-year terms expire, justices can be re-elected. Because of a strong self-governing legislature, an independent judiciary enforces formal separation of powers between the various branches of the government. In addition, an electoral tribunal court and lower courts are also components of the state's judicial system.

12 ■ Economy

Manufacturing is the largest economic activity in San Luis Potosí, accounting for about 26% of the economy. General service-based companies accounts for 18% of the economy, followed by trade activities at 17%, finance and insurance at 15%, agriculture and livestock at 9%, transportation and communications at 9%, construction at 5%, and mining at 1%.

13 ■ Industry

Most of the industrial activities take place in or around the capital city. The primary industries are food processing, automobile manufacturing, mining, and textiles.

Some large foreign companies have facilities in San Luis Potosí, including Bendix (auto parts), Sandoz (pharmaceuticals), Union Carbide (chemicals), and Bimbo (food products).

14 ■ Labor

The US Bureau of Labor Statistics reported that Mexican workers saw their wages increase 17%, from $2.09 in 1999 to $2.46 in 2000. (The average US worker earned $19.86 in 2000.) Mexican law has established six paid vacation days per year for all workers.

15 ■ Agriculture

Most farms are found in the Huasteca region of the state, which is a fertile lowland area in the east. Fruit crops such as

© Mireille Vautier/Woodfin Camp

This Roman Catholic cathedral in San Luis Potosí dates from the 18th century.

oranges, mangos, bananas, and guavas are important in this region. Corn and beans are primary crops throughout the state. Goats, sheep, and cattle are the primary livestock.

16 ▨ Natural Resources

The state has rich mineral resources, particularly silver, gold, and fluorite.

17 ▨ Energy and Power

Almost all of the energy in Mexico is provided by the Federal Electricity Commission (CFE). In February 2002, the CFE introduced new electric rates. For house-holds that use less than 140 kilowatt hours per month, there was no rate increase. (This is about 75% of all households in Mexico, according to CFE).

18 ▨ Health

The state of San Luis Potosí has 20 general hospitals, 532 outpatient centers, and 46 surgical centers.

Most of the Mexican population is covered under a government health plan. The IMSS (Instituto Mexicano de Seguro Social) covers the general population. The ISSSTE (Instituto de Seguridad y Servicios Sociales de Trabajadores del Estado) covers state workers.

19 ▦ Housing

More than one-half of the housing available in the state of San Luis Potosí is in good repair. More than 26% is in need of significant upgrading. Many homes do not have running water or access to electricity.

20 ▦ Education

The system of public education was first started by President Benito Juárez (1806–1872) in 1867. Public education in Mexico is free for students from ages six to sixteen. According to the 2000 census, there were approximately 562,000 school-age students in the state. Many students elect to go to private schools. The thirty-one states of Mexico all have at least one state university. Universidad Autónoma de San Luis Potosí (Independent University of San Luis Potosí) is located in the capital.

21 ▦ Arts

The capital city is home to three local dance companies: the Ballet Provincial de San Luis Potosí, the Grupo de Danza Folklórica, and the Danza Contemporánea. Musical groups include La Banda de Música del Gobierno de San Luis Potosí and the San Luis Potosí Symphony Orchestra. San Luis Potosí also has nine theaters, including open air theaters. Most cities and towns have cultural centers.

22 ▦ Libraries and Museums

There are 103 branches of the public library. San Luis Potosí has eighteen museums including a bullfighting museum, the Museum of the Mask, a cultural arts museum, and a museum dedicated to comic book heroes (both Mexican and American).

23 ▦ Media

The capital city, San Luis Potosí, has two daily newspapers: *El Sol de San Luis Potosí* and *Pulso.*

24 ▦ Tourism, Travel, and Recreation

In the capital, San Luis Potosí, tourists often visit the Church of Nuestra Senora del Carmen because of its tiled domes and famous altars. The national fair of San Luis Potosí is celebrated in August. Santa María del Río has an ancient aqueduct that forms a waterfall. There is a spa with thermal baths nearby. The area around Santa María del Río is a popular resort area.

25 ▦ Sports

The capital, San Luis Potosí, hosts a basketball team, Santos, and a soccer team, the Real San Luís. Soccer is played in the 24,000-seat Alfonso Lastras stadium.

26 ▦ Famous People

C. Marcelo de los Santos Fraga was elected governor in 2003.

27 ▦ Bibliography

Books

DeAngelis, Gina. *Mexico.* Mankato, MN: Blue Earth Books, 2003.

Supples, Kevin. *Mexico.* Washington, DC: National Geographic Society, 2002.

Web Sites

Mexico for Kids. Online http://www.elbalero.gob.mx/index_kids.html (accessed on June 15, 2004).

Sinaloa

Pronunciation: see-nah-LOH-ah.

Origin of state name: The name Sinaloa comes from the Cahita language. It is a combination of the words *sina,* which means *pithaya* (a plant with thorny stalks), and *lobola,* which means rounded. The pithaya is a common plant throughout the region.

Capital: Culiacán (coo-lee-ah-CAHN).

Entered country: 1830.

Coat of Arms: The state coat of arms is an oval shield set on top of a solid rock base and crowned with a variation of the national emblem. There are five footprints in the border of the shield. Pictures inside the shield include a castle, anchors, and a deer head.

Holidays: Año Nuevo (New Year's Day—January 1); Día de la Constitución (Constitution Day—February 5); Benito Juárez's birthday (March 21); Primero de Mayo (Labor Day—May 1); Revolution Day, 1910 (November 20); and Navidad (Christmas—December 25).

Flag: There is no official state flag.

Time: 5 AM = noon Greenwich Mean Time (GMT).

1 ▪ Location and Size

Sinaloa lies along the coast of the Gulfo de California. It covers an area of 58,091 square kilometers (22,429 square miles), which is a little smaller than the US state of West Virginia. The state is bordered on the north by the Mexican states of Sonora and Chihuahua; on the south by the Mexican state of Nayarit; and on the east by the Mexican state of Durango. Sinaloa has eighteen municipalities; its capital is Culiacán.

In Sinaloa, there are three types of landscape: a coastal plan in the west, mountains (*sierras*) in the east, and valleys between them. In the eastern part of the state Sierra Madre Occidental is known by different names. Valleys lie between the ranges of mountains and the coastal plain, where the land is flat with few hills.

The rivers rise in the Sierra Madre Occidental and cross the state to flow into the Gulfo de California and the Pacific Ocean. Major rivers are the Fuerte and Sinaloa.

2 Climate

The state features a wide variety of climates. The climate along the coastal plains is generally hot. In the valleys, the climate can range from temperate to hot, while in the mountain regions temperatures range from temperate to cold.

In the summer months of June, July, and August, the daytime temperature averages 32°C (90°F); in the winter months of December, January, and February, the daytime temperature averages 27°C (80°F). Most of the rainfall occurs during July, August, and September. In the capital city of Culiacán, the average year-round temperature is 24°C (76°F) and the average rainfall is 54 centimeters (21.3 inches) per year.

3 Plants and Animals

Some of the most common trees in the state include oaks, poplars, ceiba, and mangroves (a tropical evergreen that usually grows along the coast). The pithaya (for which the state is named) is common throughout the state, as are laurels and bougainvilleas. Fruit trees such as lemons, peaches, and pears are found as well.

Some common mammals include deer, wildcats, badgers, wild boar, coyotes, and tlacuaches (Mexican possums). There are also many rabbits, squirrels, and raccoons. Sparrow hawks, buzzards, ducks, and swallows are common birds. Turtles, iguanas, and alligators also can be found.

4 Environmental Protection

Through the North American Commission for Environmental Cooperation (CEC), the state of Sinaloa has formed a partnership with the US state of Alaska in a project called the Western Hemisphere

Shorebird Reserve Network. The Sinaloan wetlands serve as the winter home of over 30% of the Pacific Flyway shorebirds that breed in Alaska, Canada, and other West Coast regions of the United States. The Bahia Santa Maria (Santa Maria Bay) is one of several protected areas in the state.

5 Population, Ethnic Groups, Languages

Sinaloa had a total population of 2,536,844 in 2000; of the total, 1,264,143 were men and 1,272,701 were women. The population density was 44 people per square kilometer (114 people per square mile). In 2000, the capital, Culiacán, had a population of 744,859.

Almost all citizens speak Spanish as their first language. A small number, about 2.2%, of the population speaks indigenous (native) languages.

6 Religions

According to the 2000 census, 77% of the population, or about two million people, were Roman Catholic; almost 3%, or 65,346 people, were Protestant. That year there were also 32,783 Jehovah's Witnesses and over 180,000 people who reported no religion.

7 Transportation

Sinaloa has three international airports: Mazatlán, Culiacán, and Los Mochis. There are 16,335 kilometers (10,146 miles) of roads. Culiacán has a highly developed highway network, including a four-lane highway direct to the United States. The railroad network links Sinaloa with the rest of Mexico and with key cities in the United States. There are about 1,234

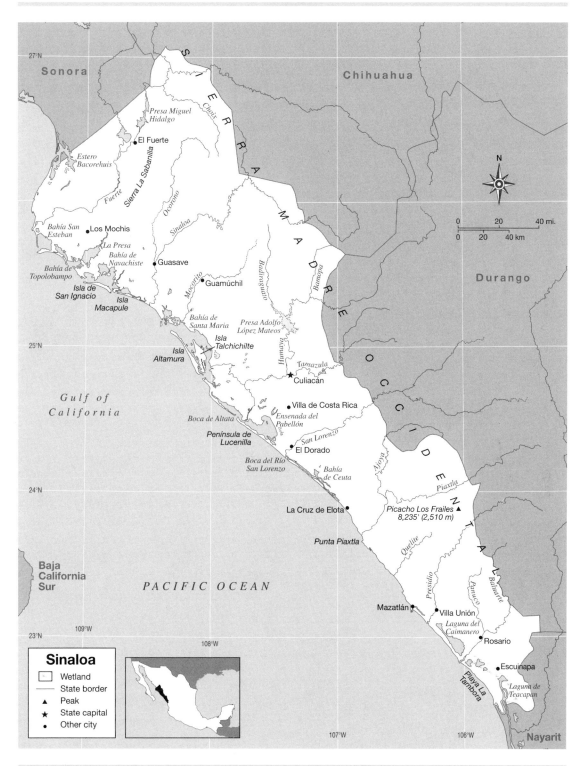

Sonora

Chihuahua

27°N

S
I
E
R
R
A

Presa Miguel
Hidalgo

● El Fuerte

Estero
Bacorehuis

Choix

M

Fuerte

Sierra La Sabanilla

Ocorono

A

Sinaloa

Bahía San
Esteban Los Mochis ●

D

La Presa
Bahía de
Navachiste ● Guasave

Mocorito

Badiraguato

R

Bahía de
Topolobampo

Isla de
San Ignacio

Isla
Macapule

● Guamúchil

E

Bamopa

Durango

Bahía de
Santa Maria

Presa Adolfo
López Mateos

Humaya

25°N

Isla
Talchichilte

Isla
Altamura

Tamazula

★ Culiacán

O

Gulf of
California

● Villa de Costa Rica

C

Boca de Altata

Ensenada del
Pabellón

C

Península de
Lucenilla

San Lorenzo

● El Dorado

I

Ajoya

Boca del Río
San Lorenzo

Bahía
de Ceuta

D

Piaxtla

24°N

E

Picacho Los Frailes ▲
8,235' (2,510 m)

● La Cruz de Elota

Quelite

N

Punta Piaxtla

Presidio

Pánuco

Baltarte

T

Baja
California
Sur

PACIFIC OCEAN

A

Mazatlán ●

● Villa Unión

L

23°N

109°W

Laguna del
Caimanero

● Rosario

108°W

● Escuinapa

107°W

106°W

Playa La
Tambora

Laguna de
Teacapan

Nayarit

N

0   20   40 mi.
0   20   40 km

Sinaloa

- ⬡ Wetland
- — State border
- ▲ Peak
- ★ State capital
- ● Other city

© Robert Frerck/Woodfin Camp

Copala was an busy mining town.

kilometers (766 miles) of railway. There are major ports at Mazatlán and Topolobampo. The commercial route, CANMEX, that runs north and south from Alberta, Canada, through the United States to Mexico City, runs through the state. This is one of the most important routes for international trade in North America.

8 ■ History

Some nomadic tribes regularly visited the region as early as 12,000 B.C. Yet, the first permanent settlements emerged around 250 B.C. around the Baluarte River area. A Yuto-Aztec cultural renaissance took

place at the northern end of the state around 900 A.D. in the settlements of Culiacán and Guasave. When the Spanish conquistadors (explorers who sought to claim Mexico for Spain) arrived, the region was inhabited by six different groups of sedentary and nomadic indigenous peoples. In 1529, Nuño Beltrán de Guzmán initiated the conquest of northern Mexico.

The slave trade of native Indians provoked revolts and uprisings that forced the Spaniards to relocate their main settlements. Indigenous leader Ayapín led one of the most notorious uprisings that forced Spaniards to request military support from neighboring Nueva Galicia (a former Spanish administrative region). Although that uprising was defeated, other indigenous uprisings forced the Spanish to abandon some settlements. Indigenous rebels executed Spanish conqueror Pedro de Montoya in 1583 when he attempted to colonize the area. Starting in 1591, a number of Jesuit missions won the sympathy of the otherwise resistant indigenous population. During most of the 17th century, colonial penetration was possible because of the successful Catholic conversion efforts by Jesuit priests. The province of Sinaloa was created in 1732 by royal decree. In 1767, a royal decree was issued to remove the Jesuits from Spanish America. This caused more problems for Sinaloa. Missions were abandoned and the indigenous people were robbed of their communal lands and forced to become feudal peasants and miners.

Although some independence leaders sought to provoke an uprising in the region, royalist forces (those loyal to Spain) soon controlled the revolts in 1810. During the decade-long independence quest, Sinaloa became a major center for contraband and illicit traffic. The states of Sonora and Sinaloa were initially part of the same federal entity, but they were formally separated into two different states in 1830. Local land-owning elites controlled state politics for much of the remaining 19th century, with little influence or authority from central Mexico.

During the liberal-conservative conflict of the 1860s, British and US troops attempted to invade the city of Mazatlán to protect the interest of foreign nationals. But conservative elites successfully subdued the challenge of those liberals loyal to President Benito Juárez (1806–1872). As a result, most local leaders fought against the presence of foreign troops on nationalist grounds. After being occupied by French troops during the reign of Emperor Maximilian (1832–1867)—France briefly controlled parts of Mexico from 1863 to 1867—Sinaloa was freed. It was later controlled by the federal troops loyal to president Juárez.

During the porfiriato period, from 1876 to 1910, when Porfirio Díaz (1830–1915) was in power as president of Mexico, Sinaloa experienced economic growth, but its small population hindered economic development and consolidation. Different factions fought in Sinaloa during the Mexican Revolution, which started in 1910, with some Francisco "Pancho" Villa (revolutionary leader; 1878–1923) loyalists claiming control of significant portions of the state. Yet, by 1917, forces loyal to the newly established constitutional government controlled the state. Some conflicts arose with the land reform initiatives promoted by the dominating political party, the Institutional Revolutionary Party (PRI), which affected large land estates owned by US companies. However, Sinaloa's scarce population prevented large land-related conflicts from emerging in the post-revolutionary period. The state's proximity to the United States, where there is a large market for illegal drugs, made it a prime candidate for the illegal production of the poppy, the plant used to produce opium.

9 ▮ State and Local Government

The state governor is democratically elected for six-year terms and cannot be re-elected when the term expires. The legislature is comprised of a forty member unicameral (single chamber) congress. Twenty-four members are elected in single member districts and sixteen are elected by proportional representation. Congres-

© Robert Frerck/Woodfin Camp

Corn is one of the crops grown by farmers in Sinaloa.

sional elections occur every three years and immediate re-election is not allowed. The Institutional Revolutionary Party (PRI) has exercised tight control of the state executive and legislative powers.

The eighteen municipalities that comprise Sinaloa hold democratic elections for municipal presidents and council members every three years. Immediate re-election is not allowed. Some decentralization initiatives are producing positive results. However, the fact that the PRI continues to control state level politics has prevented impor-

tant decentralization initiatives from being implemented.

10 ■ Political Parties

The three main political parties in all of Mexico are the Institutional Revolutionary Party (PRI), the National Action Party (PAN), and the Party of the Democratic Revolution (PRD). The PRI continues to exercise strong control of state level politics. That party has never lost a gubernatorial election since the end of the Mexican Revolution in 1917. The conservative PAN has shown a growing and consolidating electoral strength. Yet, alternation of power at the state level has yet to occur.

11 ■ Judicial System

The Supreme Tribunal of Justice is the highest court in the state. Its eleven members are appointed for fifteen-year terms with no re-election provisions. There is a mandatory retirement age of seventy. In addition, an electoral tribunal and local courts also comprise the state judicial system. The lack of alternation in power at the gubernatorial level has made it difficult for the Supreme Tribunal to become fully autonomous.

12 ■ Economy

The main economic activities of Sinaloa are agriculture, fishing, livestock breeding, commerce, and industry. Agriculture is the dominant economic activity. Crops are mainly under irrigation. The state is the leader in rice and vegetable production and second in wheat and bean production in the country. Fishing is the second most important economic activity.

Agriculture and livestock account for about 21% of the economy. Service-based companies account for another 21% of the economy, followed by trade activities at 19%, finance and insurance at 16%, transportation and communications at 11%, manufacturing at 8%, construction at 3%, and mining at 1%.

13 ■ Industry

Industrial parks are scattered throughout the state. They are linked to agriculture production and the fishing industry, including canning, packing, and frozen food plants. Industrial trained workers are primarily in the textile and agriculture industries. Industrial products produced in Sinaloa are tomato purée, flour, sugar, beer, edible oil, and chilorio (pork cooked in chili). The city of Los Mochis has developed a special ecological industrial park dedicated to housing nonpolluting industries.

14 ■ Labor

The US Bureau of Labor Statistics reported that Mexican workers saw their wages increase 17%, from $2.09 per hour in 1999 to $2.46 per hour in 2000. (The average US worker earned $19.86 per hour in 2000.) After one year, workers are entitled by law to six days paid vacation.

15 ■ Agriculture

Agriculture products coming from Sinaloa include tomatoes, beans, corn, wheat, sorghum, potatoes, soybeans, sugarcane, and squash. Crops are grown near sea level under irrigation in large fields using mechanized methods. Sinaloa is one of Mexico's leading sugarcane producers; sugarcane is one Mexico's main sources of income.

The beekeeping industry that contributes to the pollination of these crops was devastated by the arrival of the Africanized honeybee (AHB) in Sinaloa around 1990. Eighteen deaths resulted and many beekeeping businesses closed.

Products that come from livestock breeding in Sinaloa are meat, sausage, cheese, and milk.

16 ■ Natural Resources

Fishing harvests include shrimp, tuna, sea bass, sardines, and marlin. Mineral resources include gold, silver, lead, and zinc.

Nonmetallic minerals include limestone, talc, and salt.

17 ▪ Energy and Power

Almost all of the energy in Mexico is provided by the Federal Electricity Commission (CFE). In February 2002, the CFE introduced new electric rates. For households that use less than 140 kilowatt hours per month, there was no rate increase. (This is about 75% of all households in Mexico, according to CFE).

Sinaloa has six hydroelectric plants, two thermoelectric plants, and one turbo gas plant with a total generating capacity of 1,800 megawatts. The hydrological (water system) infrastructure is one of the most advanced in Mexico.

18 ▪ Health

There are 31 general hospitals, 432 outpatient centers, and 86 surgical centers in Sinaloa.

Most of the Mexican population is covered under a government health plan. The IMSS (Instituto Mexicano de Seguro Social) covers the general population. The ISSSTE (Instituto de Seguridad y Servicios Sociales de Trabajadores del Estado) covers state workers.

19 ▪ Housing

About two-thirds of the housing available in the state of Sinaloa is in good repair. Only about 13% is in need of significant upgrading. These homes do not have running water or access to electricity.

20 ▪ Education

The system of public education was first started by President Benito Juárez in 1867. Public education in Mexico is free for students from ages six to sixteen. According to the 2000 census, there were approximately 573,000 school-age students in the state. Many students elect to go to private schools. Sinaloa has twenty-five universities and technical schools with sixty-two campuses distributed throughout the state and 106 technical training facilities. The Sinaloa Science Center was opened in 1993 to provide interactive educational activities for children and adults. English is taught in most private and public schools.

21 ▪ Arts

The state of Sinaloa has many performing musical groups. There is Ballet Folklórico (a contemporary dance group), an opera chorus, a percussion ensemble, and an orchestra. Sinaloa has twelve theaters including a Greek theater, seventeen auditoriums, and various local cultural centers.

22 ▪ Libraries and Museums

The state of Sinaloa has 140 libraries. There are over twenty museums in the state, including a museum of art and science in Culiacán, the capital. Mazatlán has an aquarium, an art museum, and an archeological museum.

23 ▪ Media

The capital, Culiacán, has three daily newspapers: *El Debate, El Sol,* and *Noroeste.* Los Mochis publishes the daily newspaper *El Sol.* In Mazatlán, there are two daily newspapers: *Adelante* and *El Sol del Pacífico.*

24 ▢ Tourism, Travel, and Recreation

Founded in 1531, Culiacán is one of the oldest cities in Mexico. The city offers sport hunting and fishing for tourists. Many hunters come to shoot white-winged pigeon when in season. Los Mochis is the point of origin of the railroad that connects the Sinaloan Coast with the Sierra Tarahumara.

25 ▢ Sports

The capital, Culiacán, has a professional baseball team, the Tomateros, which plays in the 16,000-seat General Angel Flores stadium. Mazatlán has a baseball team, the Venados, which plays in the 12,000-seat Teodoro Mariscal stadium. Mazatlán also has an 8,000-seat bullring. Guasave has a baseball team, the Algodoneros, which plays in the 8,000-seat Francisco Carranza Limón stadium.

26 ▢ Famous People

Juan S. Millán was elected as governor of Sinaloa in 1999 and is expected to hold office until December 2004. Mexican singer and songwriter Chalino Sanchez died in Sinaloa in 1992.

27 ▢ Bibliography

Books

DeAngelis, Gina. *Mexico.* Mankato, MN: Blue Earth Books, 2003.

Supples, Kevin. *Mexico.* Washington, DC: National Geographic Society, 2002.

Web Sites

El Portal del Gobienero de Sinaloa (English version). http://www.sinaloa.gob.mx/english/index.html (accessed on June 17, 2004).

Mexico for Kids. http://www.elbalero.gob.mx/index_kids.html (accessed on June 15, 2004).

Sonora

Pronunciation: soh-NOH-rah.

Origin of state name: There are conflicting stories about the origin of the state name. The name is probably from the word Señora (Our Lady), which refers to the Virgin Mary of Roman Catholicism brought to Mexico by Spanish explorers.

Capital: Hermosillo (her-moh-SEE-yoh).

Entered country: 1830.

Coat of Arms: The upper section is divided into three triangles. The center triangle depicts a picture of a Yaquí tribesman performing the Dance of the Deer. The left triangle represents the mining industry, and the right triangle represents agriculture. The two squares at the bottom depict livestock and fish, representing other important industries in the state.

Holidays: Año Nuevo (New Year's Day—January 1); Día de la Constitución (Constitution Day—February 5); Benito Juárez's birthday (March 21); Primero de Mayo (Labor Day—May 1); Revolution Day, 1910 (November 20); and Navidad (Christmas—December 25).

Flag: There is no official state flag.

Time: 5 AM = noon Greenwich Mean Time (GMT).

1 ▪ Location and Size

Sonora, Mexico's second largest state after Chihuahua, is located in the North Pacific region of the country. It covers an area of 184,934 square kilometers (71,403 square miles), which is a little larger than the US state of North Dakota. Sonora borders the Mexican states of Sinaloa to the south, Chihuahua to the east, and Baja California to the northwest. The Sea of Cortés, or the Gulfo de California, is located to the east. The US state of Arizona lies to the north. Sonora has seventy-two municipalities. The capital is Hermosillo.

The mountain region of the Sierra Madre Occidental, which is known by different names as it crosses Sonora, begins near the border with the state of Chihuahua.

The western part of the state is an extensive plain that is wide in the north and narrows in the south. In the southern region, the mountain ranges (*sierras*) are found. A low coastal plain stretches along the Gulfo de California.

Sonora's rivers run into the Gulfo de California. The Yaquí, which is the largest river in the state, and its Bavispe, Sahuaripa, and Moctezuma tributaries, begins near the

Blooming cactus.

US border and flows southwest to the Gulfo de California. The Mayo River, which is located in the southern part of the state, is about 400 kilometers (250 miles) and flows through Chihuahua and Sonora to the Gulfo de California. The Colorado forms the natural border between Sonora and the Mexican state of Baja California.

2 ■ Climate

The coastal regions of the state are generally warm and dry with a year-round average temperature of about 23°C (75°F). The northern part of the state is temperate and dry with an average year-round temperature of about 16°C (61°F). In the mountain

regions, temperatures can be much cooler. In Hermosillo, the average year-round temperature is about 23°C (75°F). The average rainfall in the capital is about 24 centimeters (9.5 inches) per year. In the northern city of Nogales, average rainfall is about 42 centimeters (16.9 inches) per year. The average snowfall in Nogales is 11 centimeters (4.5 inches) per year.

3 ■ Plants and Animals

Palmilla, jojoba, pitahaya, and desert ironwood are plants common to the coastal regions of the state. In the mountain regions, forests of pine and oak are more common. Larger mammals found in the

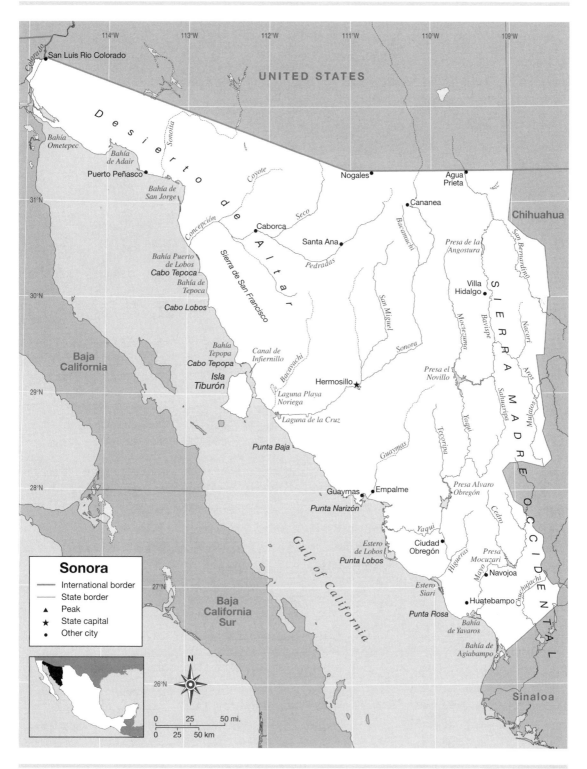

Sonora

- —— International border
- —— State border
- ▲ Peak
- ★ State capital
- • Other city

© Peter Langer/EPD Photos

Adobe brick manufacturer.

state include deer, wild boar, coyotes, pumas, wild rams, and bears. Smaller mammals include rabbits, hares, and squirrels. Chameleons, iguanas, and tarantulas are also found. Common birds include hawks and buzzards.

4 ■ Environmental Protection

The state has experienced air pollution problems due to dusty roads, wood burning for fuel, and automobile emissions. Maintaining an adequate, safe supply of drinking water is also a concern in some areas. National parks in Sonora include the El Pinacate Biosphere Reserve and the Cajon del Diablo.

5 ■ Population, Ethnic Groups, Languages

Sonora had a total population of 2,216,969 in 2000; of the total, 1,110,590 were men and 1,106,379 were women. The population density was 12 people per square kilometer (31 people per square mile). In 2000, the capital, Hermosillo, had a population of 608,697.

Almost all citizens speak Spanish as a first language. A small number, about 2.9%

of the population, speaks indigenous (native) languages.

6 ▊ Religions

According to the 2000 census, 78% of the population, or 1.7 million people, were Roman Catholic; 4%, or 94,467 people, were Protestant. That year there were also 7,290 Mormons, 22,231 Jehovah's Witnesses, and over 106,000 people who reported no religion.

7 ▊ Transportation

Ciudad Obregón Airport, Guaymas-General Jose Maria Yanez International Airport, and Nogales International Airport provide international flights to and from Sonora. The state has about 24,016 kilometers (14,917 miles) of roads and 1,958 kilometers (1,216 miles) of railroads.

8 ▊ History

First human presence in the state dates back to 30,000 B.C. when nomadic tribes of hunters and gatherers inhabited the region. The Pinacate Mountain region holds some ruins of settlements that are around fifteen thousand years old. Yet, more permanent human settlements first emerged around 1500 B.C. in the more fertile parts of the state, while the dessert continued to house nomadic tribes. The Hohokam culture (originally from Arizona), the Mogollón culture (from New Mexico), and the Casas Grandes and Paquime cultures (from Chihuahua) influenced the region. Influence from Mesoamerican cultures that reached the region with trade and commercial interests were also strong during the first centuries A.D. A massive

migration from the Casa Grande region to the mountainous region gave birth to the Ópata tribes in 1340. At the arrival of the Spanish conquistadors (explorers who sough to claim Mexico for Spain), the different indigenous groups belonged to the Yuto-Náhuatl and Hokana linguistic families.

In 1531, Nuño Beltrán de Guzmán founded the city of San Miguel de Culiacán in what is now the neighboring state of Sinaloa. Sinaloa is where the Spanish initiated the search for mineral deposits, promoted slave trade, and fostered new colonization efforts in the region. In 1533, Diego Guzmán became the first Spaniard to enter what is now Sonora. He found resistance from indigenous populations near the Yaquí River and soon abandoned the region. In 1536, Spanish explorer Alvar Nuñez Cabeza de Vaca (c. 1490-c. 1560) and three other survivors of the failed Pánfilo de Narváez expedition passed through the region. In *Shipwreck,* his account of the years they wandered through indigenous territories before finding a Spanish settlement, Cabeza de Vaca, referred to two marvelous indigenous cities, Cíbola and Quivira. Several expeditions were launched to find those cities, but they apparently did not exist.

Because the region was slowly populated, it did not evolve into a major economic center in colonial Mexico. A prison was built in Sonora in 1586. New efforts to conquer indigenous territories drastically decimated the native population during the 17th century. The efforts by Jesuit priests to convert the indigenous population to Roman Catholicism and create sedentary settlements helped integrate the remaining native population to the colonial economy. The Jesuits created settlements where Indians could work the land

and provide labor for mining enterprises. However, some Yaquí indigenous uprisings continued throughout the 17th century.

In 1810, Sonoran independence leaders revolted in an effort to join the independence movement launched elsewhere in Mexico. However, most landowners in Sonora were more concerned with keeping the attacks by the Apache Indians at bay.

It was only in 1821 that Sonora became incorporated into independent Mexico. Two years later, Sonora and Sinaloa were separated into two different states. After a period of political instability that characterized much of 19th century Mexico, Sonora was occupied by US troops in 1847. The Treaty of Hidalgo, where Mexico ceded territory to the United States, achieved peace between the two countries. This allowed for the exit of foreign troops. Yet, instability remained the dominant political culture in the region until the end of the Mexican Revolution in 1917.

Having consolidated as a cattle ranching and agricultural economy, Sonora remains a scarcely populated state with vast stretches of unpopulated desert areas. Its proximity to the United States has made the state an attractive port of entry for illicit drugs. Additionally, its location fosters a growing number of *maquiladoras* (manufacturing assembly plants) since the adoption of the North American Free Trade Agreement (NAFTA), a trade agreement between Mexico, the United States, and Canada, in 1994.

9 ■ State and Local Government

A state governor is democratically elected every six years. No immediate re-election is allowed. The legislature is comprised of a unicameral (one chamber) state congress with twenty-seven members who serve nonrenewable three-year terms. Eighteen members are elected in single member districts and nine are elected by proportional representation. Because the state has been ruled exclusively by the Institutional Revolutionary Party (PRI) since the end of the Mexican Revolution, formal separation of power provisions have not been effectively enforced. To this end, the PRI governor has exercised excessive influence over the PRI-controlled legislature.

The seventy-two municipalities that comprise Sonora hold democratic elections for municipal presidents and council members every three years. Immediate re-election is not allowed. Although some decentralization initiatives are producing positive results, the state still has a long way to go to achieve successful decentralization.

10 ■ Political Parties

The three main political parties in all of Mexico are the Institutional Revolutionary Party (PRI), the National Action Party (PAN), and the Party of the Democratic Revolution (PRD). The PRI has been the dominant party in the state since the end of the Mexican Revolution. All governors in Sonora the last seventy-five years have belonged to that party. In 1994, Sonora's favorite rising politician, Luis Donaldo Colosio (1948–1994), was appointed PRI presidential candidate but was assassinated before the election was held. The PAN is the second largest party in the state.

11 ■ Judicial System

The Supreme Tribunal of Justice is the highest court in the state. The state governor, with legislative approval, appoints seven members for renewable six-year terms. Only highly qualified attorneys

© Robert Frerck/Woodfin Camp

Cerro Colorado, seen in the distance, is a volcanic cone about one-half mile (1,000 meters) in diameter. It lies in Pinacate National Park, a nearly 800-square-mile (2,000-square-kilometer) park in northwest Sonora.

with proven experience can be appointed to the Supreme Tribunal. Because the state has not experienced alternation in power since the Mexican Revolution, the formal autonomy and independence of the judiciary has not been enforced. In addition, an electoral tribunal and local courts also comprise the state's judicial system.

12 ■ Economy

General service-based companies accounts for about 19% of the economy. Trade activities also account for about 19% of the economy, followed by manufacturing at 18%, finance and insurance

at 15%, agriculture and livestock at 15%, transportation and communications at 9%, construction at 3%, and mining at 2%.

13 ■ Industry

The state has many *maquiladoras,* or assembly plants, that produce items for companies such as Ford and Sara Lee. Most *maquiladoras* make electrical appliances and electronic equipment such as computer circuits and vacuum cleaners.

14 ■ Labor

The US Bureau of Labor Statistics reported that Mexican workers saw their wages

Desert sunset.

increase 17%, from $2.09 per hour in 1999 to $2.46 per hour in 2000. (The average US worker earned $19.86 in 2000.) After one year, workers are entitled by law to six days paid vacation.

15 ■ Agriculture

Agricultural plays an important role in the economy of the state. In the north and northeast, where the climate is dry, irrigation systems are used and farmers produce alfalfa, vegetables, fodder, grapes, dates, and olives. The main crops in the central region include wheat, barley, alfalfa, and safflower. The main crops in the east include corn, beans, apples, and peaches. In the south and southeast, the main crops are wheat, corn, and beans. A special regional cheese is produced in the southeast. It is spiced with chiltepín (piquín chile), which grows in the desert.

The primary types of livestock are cattle, pigs, poultry, and goats. Horses, mules, and donkeys are also raised in the east.

16 ■ Natural Resources

Mineral resources in the state include copper, graphite, silver, gold, lead, and tungsten. Sonora has the fourth largest mining industry in the country. Fish species caught in the coastal and river waters of the state include shrimp, lobina, barge, and mojarra.

17 ░ Energy and Power

The Federal Electricity Commission (CFE) provides almost all of the energy in Mexico. In February 2002, the CFE introduced new electric rates. For households that use less than 140 kilowatt hours per month, there was no rate increase. (This is about 75% of all households in Mexico, according to CFE). After the rate increases in 2002, Sonora residents were charged higher rates because they use more than the minimum electricity.

18 ░ Health

Sonora has 44 general hospitals, 336 outpatient centers, and 90 surgical centers.

Most of the Mexican population is covered under a government health plan. The IMSS (Instituto Mexicano de Seguro Social) covers the general population. The ISSSTE (Instituto de Seguridad y Servicios Sociales de Trabajadores del Estado) covers state workers.

19 ░ Housing

About three-fourths of the housing available in the state of Sonora is in good repair. Only about 9% is in need of significant upgrading. These homes may not have running water or access to electricity.

20 ░ Education

President Benito Juárez (1806–1872) first started the system of public education in 1867. Public education in Mexico is free for students from ages six to sixteen. According to the 2000 census, there were approximately 469,500 school-age students in the state. Many students elect to go to private schools. The thirty-one states of Mexico all have at least one state university. The main campus of the Universidad de Sonora is located in the capital, Hermosillo.

21 ░ Arts

Sonora has twenty-six local cultural centers including a French Alliance center in Ciudad Obregón. Three types of local music can be heard in towns throughout Sonora: *rancheras* recount lost loves, *corridos* are long narrative poems, and *huapangos* are rhythmic songs often heard at bullfights. Most activities are connected to Sonora's beautiful beaches.

22 ░ Libraries and Museums

The state of Sonora has 121 libraries. There are also twenty-six museums. The capital city, Hermosillo, has a children's bubble museum. The city of Huatabampo has a Mayan museum, and the city of Cajeme has a museum of the Yaquí Indians.

23 ░ Media

The capital city, Hermosillo, has two daily newspapers: *El Imparcial* and *El Independiente.* Ciudad Obregón publishes *Tribuna.* The city of San Luís Río Colorado has *Tribuna de San Luís.*

24 ░ Tourism, Travel, and Recreation

The city of Hermosillo is on the Sea of Cortés, which has many beautiful beaches. Bahía Kino, in the town of Kino, is a great beach for snorkeling and swimming. Isla Tiburon (Shark Island) is a wildlife preserve. Puerto Peñasco (Rocky Point) also has beautiful beaches. Ciudad Obregón is surrounded by many settlements of the Yaquí Indians, such as Torim and Vicam. Often authentic dances are performed for tourists.

25 ▦ Sports

The capital, Hermosillo, has a professional baseball team, the Naranjeros, which plays in the 13,000-seat Hector Espino stadium. Navojoa also has a baseball team, the Mayos, which plays in the 12,000-seat Manuel "Ciclón" Echeverria stadium.

26 ▦ Famous People

Álvaro Obregón (1880–1928) was a revolutionary general who also served as president from 1920 to 1924. Fernando Valenzuela (1960-), was a pitcher for the Los Angeles Dodgers. In 1986, he became the first rookie to win the Cy Young Award, an award given to the best pitcher in major league baseball.

27 ▦ Bibliography

Books

Brown, John. *Journey into the Desert.* New York: Oxford University Press, 2002.

DeAngelis, Gina. *Mexico.* Mankato, MN: Blue Earth Books, 2003.

Heisey, Adriel. *Under the Sun: A Sonoran Desert Odyssey.* Tucson, AZ: Rio Nuevo, 2000.

Patent, Dorothy Hinshaw. *Life in a Desert.* Minneapolis, MN: Lerner, 2003.

Supples, Kevin. *Mexico.* Washington, DC: National Geographic Society, 2002.

Web Sites

Mexico for Kids. http://www.elbalero.gob.mx/index_kids.html (accessed on June 15, 2004).

Sonora, Mexico. http://www.sonora-mexico.com/portada2.htm (accessed on June 17, 2004).

Tabasco

Pronunciation: tah-BAHS-koh.

Origin of state name: May have originated from the native Aztec word *tlapaco,* which means "humid land." May also have originated with the first Spaniards, who thought the native leader was Tabasco, but his name was more likely Taabs-Coob.

Capital: Villahermosa (vee-ah-hair-MOH-sah).

Entered country: 1824.

Coat of Arms: Four squares depict castles, a shield and sword, a crowned lion ready to attack, and a native warrior. In the center, an oval features a representation of the Virgin Mary.

Holidays: Año Nuevo (New Year's Day—January 1); Día de la Constitución (Constitution Day—February 5); Benito Juárez's birthday (March 21); Primero de Mayo (Labor Day—May 1); Revolution Day, 1910 (November 20); and Navidad (Christmas—December 25).

Flag: There is no official state flag.

Time: 6 AM = noon Greenwich Mean Time (GMT).

1 ■ Location and Size

Tabasco is located on the Isthmus of Tehuantepec (an isthmus is a narrow strip of land that connects two larger areas, in this case the Bay of Campeche on the north and the Gulf of Tehuantepec on the south). Tabasco covers an area of 24,662 square kilometers (9,522 square miles), which is a little smaller than the US state of Vermont. The state is bordered on the north by the Gulf of Mexico; on the south by the Mexican state of Chiapas; on the east by the Central American country of Guatemala and the Mexican state of Campeche; and on the west by the Mexican state of Veracruz. It has seventeen municipalities, and its capital is Villahermosa.

Almost all the territory of Tabasco is low and flat. The only exception is the region bordering the state of Chiapas, where the hilly region of the Chiapas Sierra begins.

This state has almost a third of all Mexico's water resources. Tabasco's major rivers are the Grijalva and the Usumacinta. The Usumacinta, Mexico's largest river, forms a natural border between Mexico and Guatemala. Other noteworthy rivers include the Palizada, San Pedro, San Pablo, Tonalá, and

Mezcalapa. In Tabasco, the largest lagoons are the Rosario, Las Ilusiones, Pomposú, Machona, and Canitzán.

2 Climate
The warm waters of the Gulf of Mexico contribute to the climate, which is generally warm and humid. The average temperatures is 24°C to 28°C (76°F to 82°F). The highest monthly average rainfall occurs in August and September. Up to 30 centimeters (12 inches) of rain often falls during September alone.

3 Plants and Animals
The mountain region of the state has rain forest conditions that are well suited for the growth of exotic trees (including mahogany, cedar, ceiba, palo, tinto, barí, and rubber trees) and various species of ferns. Fruit trees such as tamarind, orange, and sapodilla (the source of chicle, the base for chewing gum and other products) are also found. Mangroves (tropical evergreens with a tangled root system) are found along the coast.

Deer, ocelots, spider monkeys, and jaguars are a few of the larger mammals found in the state. Smaller mammals include squirrels, anteaters, and rabbits. Alligators and a wide variety of poisonous and non-poisonous snakes can be found in the state. Common birds include macaws, quetzals, toucans, and hummingbirds.

4 Environmental Protection
Protected areas in the state include the Biosphere Reserve of the Wetlands of Centla, which has been designated as a Wetland of International Importance by the international conservation group

known as the Ramsar Convention. This area has been threatened by the activities of the petroleum exploration and production company Petróleos Mexicanos (PEMAX).

5 Population, Ethnic Groups, Languages
Tabasco had a total population of 1,891,829 in 2000; of the total, 934,515 were men and 957,314 were women. The population density was 76 people per square kilometer (197 people per square mile). In 2000, the capital, Villahermosa, had a population of 545,433.

Almost all citizens speak Spanish as their first language. A small number, about 3.7%, of the population, speaks indigenous (native) languages.

6 Religions
According to the 2000 census, 62% of the population, or about 1.2 million people, were Roman Catholic; 12%, or 226,683 people, were Protestant. That year there were also 58,701 Seventh-Day Adventists, 20,734 Jehovah's Witnesses, and over 180,000 people who reported no religion.

7 Transportation
Tabasco has one international airport. The state also has about 7,912 kilometers (4,914 miles) of roads and 315 kilometers (196 miles) of railroads.

8 History
The Olmec civilization developed in Tabasco starting in 1500 B.C. It was around 500 B.C. that the Olmec reached its cultural and economic peak. The Maya emerged as the dominant culture in the region

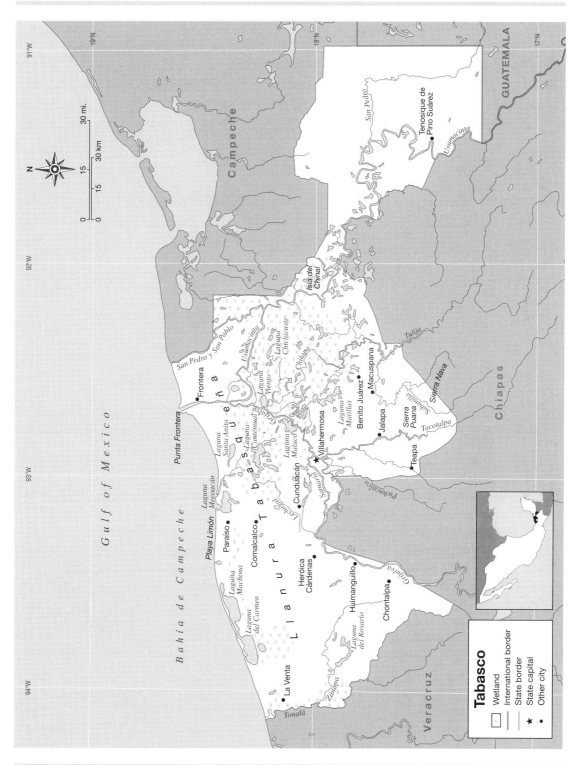

The Olmec civilization reached its peak in Tabasco around 500 B.C. This Olmec tomb, constructed of basalt, a dark-colored rock, is part of the archaeological site at La Venta.

between 100 and 1000 A.D. Toltec culture became dominant in the 13th century, and the Chontales began to grow in the 14th century. Commerce between Nahuas and Maya facilitated the development and rise of sizeable cities, like Cimatán and Teapa. Some 135,000 native indigenous people inhabited the area around 1500.

In 1518, Spanish explorer Juan de Grijalva's (c. 1489–1527) five-ship expedition in the Caribbean first reached Tabasco territory. Soon, the Spaniards entered into contact with the Chontales natives who gave them utensils made of gold as gifts. This sparked interest among the Spaniards to explore the territory in search of gold mines. Spanish explorer Hernán Cortés (1485–1547) reached the region a year later and successfully fought against the Chontales. The Spanish military might convinced a local indigenous leader, called Tabasco, to present Cortés with a present of twenty native women. Among them was Malinche, who later became Cortés's mistress and mother of his son Martín. Malinche is often unjustly accused of providing Cortés with vital information to defeat the Aztecs. Her ability to learn Spanish and communicate with Cortés is the reason for those unfounded claims.

Indigenous uprisings and the Spanish preoccupation with dominating the central valley of Mexico delayed the conquest of Tabasco until the late 16th century. For a brief period, Tabasco was put under the authority of the province of Guatemala. By the end of the 16th century, the indigenous population was barely around 7,500, and there were no more than one hundred Spanish colonizers. To promote agricultural activity, the Spanish began introducing African slaves. Its geographic location and the growing trade that existed in the region made Tabasco a prime target of British, French, and Dutch pirates. The pillage by pirates and the uprisings by the indigenous population and African slaves hindered the economic development and population growth in the region. Those uprisings also reflected the deplorable living conditions of the indigenous and enslaved populations. New uprisings during the 18th century provoked the Spaniards to increase the slave trade and promote new settlements by colonizers.

The 1810 independence movement did not reach Tabasco. It was only in 1821 that the region became independent of Spanish colonial rule. In 1824 Tabasco became a federal state. Political instability and confrontations between local military leaders characterized much of the 19th century. For a brief period of time, US troops occupied the region during the Mexican-American War (1846–48). In 1863, French invading troops occupied the region to enforce the monarchial rule of Emperor Maximilian (1832–1867).

Liberal forces successfully brought an end to monarchical rule in 1867. Tabasco was soon brought under control, first by Mexican president Benito Juárez (1806–1872) loyalists, and later by forces loyal to Porfirio Díaz (1830–1915), the man who ruled Mexico between 1876 and 1910.

The Mexican Revolution, which started in 1910, had limited impact in this scarcely populated region. The revolutionary victors quickly obtained the support of the local elites before the new constitution of Mexico was written in 1917. The Institutional Revolutionary Party (PRI), the dominant political party in the country for many years, exercised overwhelming power in Tabasco during most of the 20th century, especially after large oil fields were discovered in the state.

9 State and Local Government

The state governor is democratically elected every six years for a nonrenewable term. There are twenty-one legislators in the state's unicameral (single chamber) Chamber of Deputies. Fourteen members are elected from single member districts and seven are elected by proportional representation for nonrenewable three-year terms. Although there are formal provisions for separation of power, the governor has historically exercised enormous prerogatives and attributions. Accusations of electoral fraud have questioned the legitimacy of the democratic system in the state in recent years.

The seventeen municipalities that comprise Tabasco hold democratic elections for municipal presidents and council members every three years. Immediate re-election is not allowed. Although some decentralization initiatives are producing positive results, the state still has a long way to go to achieve successful decentralization. More effective decentralization has consolidated in the more populous municipalities.

© Peter Langer/EPD Photos

Rural habitat in Tabasco.

10 ▌ Political Parties

The three main political parties in all of Mexico are the Institutional Revolutionary Party (PRI), the National Action Party (PAN), and the Party of the Democratic Revolution (PRD). The PRI has dominated politics in Tabasco. Roberto Madrazo, the current president of the PRI, was a former governor of Tabasco (1995–2000). Madrazo's election as governor was marked by accusations of massive fraud against Andrés Manuel López Obrador, who was then the PRD candidate and as of 2004 was the mayor of Mexico City. The PRD is the second most important party in the state.

11 ▌ Judicial System

The Supreme Tribunal of Justice is the state's highest court. Its nineteen members are appointed by a two-thirds majority vote in the legislature from a three-person list submitted by the state governor. Only highly qualified attorneys, approved by a Council of the Judiciary, can be nominated to serve in the highest court. There has not been alternation in power in Tabasco, and the PRI has exercised enormous influence and power in the oil-rich state. As a result, the judicial system has not traditionally shown evidence of independence and autonomy.

12 ■ Economy

General service-based companies account for about 21% of the state economy. Trade activities account for about 18% of the economy, followed by mining at 16%, finance and insurance at 15%, construction at 9%, transportation and communications at 8%, agriculture and livestock at 8%, and manufacturing at 5%.

13 ■ Industry

Villahermosa is the commercial and manufacturing center of the state. Manufacturing companies include food processing plants and companies producing wood products, cigars, soap, and clothing. The oil industry continues to play an important role in the state economy and in the nation as a whole. There is some small-scale handicraft manufacturing, particularly in items made with alligator skin.

14 ■ Labor

The US Bureau of Labor Statistics reported that Mexican workers saw their wages increase 17%, from $2.09 per hour in 1999 to $2.46 per hour in 2000. (The average US worker earned $19.86 per hour in 2000.) After one year, workers are entitled by law to six days paid vacation.

15 ■ Agriculture

Most residents are employed in agriculture. Major crops include corn, beans, yucca, and rice. These crops are generally used for local consumption. Export crops include cacao (cocoa beans), sugarcane, bananas, and coconuts. Cattle, pigs, sheep, and goats are the primary livestock animals.

16 ■ Natural Resources

Oil and cement are among the most important natural mineral resources of the state.

17 ■ Energy and Power

Mexico's existing natural gas reserves are located primarily in the southwestern states of Tabasco and Chiapas. Almost all of the energy in Mexico is provided by the Federal Electricity Commission (CFE). In February 2002, the CFE introduced new electric rates. For households that use less than 140 kilowatt hours per month, there was no rate increase. (This is about 75% of all households in Mexico, according to CFE).

18 ■ Health

The state of Tabasco has 25 general hospitals, 586 outpatient centers, and 61 surgical centers.

Most of the Mexican population is covered under a government health plan. The IMSS (Instituto Mexicano de Seguro Social) covers the general population. The ISSSTE (Instituto de Seguridad y Servicios Sociales de Trabajadores del Estado) covers state workers.

19 ■ Housing

Only about one-half of the housing available in the state of Tabasco is in good repair. More than 18% is in need of significant upgrading. Many homes do not have running water or access to electricity.

20 ■ Education

The system of public education was first started by President Benito Juárez in 1867. Public education in Mexico is free for students from ages six to sixteen. According to the 2000 census, there were approximately 457,100 school-age students in the state. Many students elect to go to private schools. The thirty-one states of Mexico all have at least one state university. The Universidad Juarez Autonoma de Tabasco is located in Villahermosa.

21 ▌ Arts

Many cultural events take place in the Palacio del Gobierno, the Sala de Arte Antonio Ramírez, and the Teatro de Seguro Social in the capital, Villahermosa. Most cities have a cultural center, where local performing arts troupes perform.

22 ▌ Libraries and Museums

There are 556 libraries and eighteen museums in the state. Centro has a museum of anthropology. El Museo de la Venta in Villahermosa is a combination zoo and archeological museum. Its collections include large heads sculpted from basalt rock by the indigenous Olmec people. The Carlos Pellicer Museum in Villahermosa is a regional museum of anthropology.

23 ▌ Media

Villahermosa, the capital, has four daily newspapers: *Diario Olmeca, El Sureste de Tabasco, Novedades de Tabasco,* and *Tabasco Hoy.*

24 ▌ Tourism, Travel, and Recreation

There are natural regions of interest to tourists in the state. There is whitewater rafting at Usumacinta. Archeological sites are found at La Venta (Olmeca culture) and at Comacalco and Ponomá (Mayan culture). The beaches along the Gulf of Mexico attract tourists to the resorts there. Festivals are regularly held in the capital, Villahermosa. La Polvora Lagoon is a park with waterfalls and hiking and activities for children.

25 ▌ Sports

Villahermosa's baseball team, Olmecas de Tabasco, plays in the 10,500-seat Centenario 27 de Febrero stadium.

26 ▌ Famous People

La Malinche was the daughter of an Aztec ruler who became the mistress of the Spanish conqueror, Hernán Cortés. Roberto Madrazo was governor of Tabasco from 1995 to 2000, and he was the president of the Institutional Revolutionary Party (PRI) as of 2004.

27 ▌ Bibliography

Books

DeAngelis, Gina. *Mexico.* Mankato, MN: Blue Earth Books, 2003.

Supples, Kevin. *Mexico.* Washington, DC: National Geographic Society, 2002.

Web Sites

Mexico for Kids. http://www.elbalero.gob.mx/index_ kids.html (accessed on June 15, 2004).

Naturally Tabasco. http://www.mexonline.com/ tabasco-tourism.htm (accessed June 17, 2004).

Tamaulipas

Pronunciation: tah-mah-ooh-LEE-pahs.

Origin of state name: Name comes from the Huasteca word *tamaholipa*. It means either "where people pray" or "high mountains."

Capital: Ciudad Victoria (see-oo-DAHD veek-TOH-ree-ah).

Entered country: October 3, 1824.

Coat of Arms: The images on the coat of arms represent the economic activities of the state. Cornstalks and animals represent agriculture and livestock. The boat and the dock that appear on the lower half of the coat of arms represent fishing and industry. Cerro de Bernal, a well-known natural peak, is also shown in the lower part of the shield. The smaller shield in the top section represents the family coat of arms of José Escandón y Helguera, Count of Sierra Gorda, who colonized the state.

Holidays: Año Nuevo (New Year's Day—January 1); Día de la Constitución (Constitution Day—February 5); Benito Juárez's birthday (March 21); Primero de Mayo (Labor Day—May 1); Revolution Day, 1910 (November 20); and Navidad (Christmas—December 25).

Flag: There is no official state flag.

Time: 6 AM = noon Greenwich Mean Time (GMT).

1 ▌ Location and Size

Tamaulipas covers an area of 79,829 square kilometers (30,822 square miles), which is a little smaller than the US state of South Carolina. It lies in the northeast corner of Mexico in the region known as the Independent North. It is bordered on the north by the US state of Texas, on the south by the Mexican states of San Luis Potosí and Veracruz, on the east by the Gulf of Mexico, and on the west by the Mexican state of Nuevo León. Tamaulipas has forty-three municipalities. Its capital is Ciudad Victoria.

Tamaulipas has hills and plains in the northern, central, eastern, and southeastern regions. There are large mountain ranges (*sierras*) in the western and southwestern regions. These include the Sierra Madre Oriental, where the highest mountains in the state

People enjoy a refreshing swim in one of the state's rivers. All rivers rise in the mountains and run into the Gulf of Mexico.

are located, and the San Carlos, Tamaulipas, Maratines, Pamoranes, and San José de las Rucias sierras.

The most important rivers are the Bravo (or Grande), Conchos, Soto la Marina, Guayalejo, and Pánuco. All of these rivers rise in the mountains and run into the Gulf of Mexico. There are also lagoons, which are separated from the ocean by sand banks, all along the coast. The largest lagoon in Tamaulipas is the Laguna Madre.

2 ▪ Climate

The warm waters of the Gulf of Mexico contribute to the climate, which is gener-ally warm and humid. The average temperatures is 24°C to 28°C (76°F to 82°F). The highest monthly average rainfall occurs in August and September. In Ciudad Victoria, the average year-round temperature is 24°C (75°F). The average rainfall in this city is 70 centimeters (28 inches) per year.

3 ▪ Plants and Animals

Trees found in the state include mesquite, pine, and oak forests. Cacti, orchids, and bromeliads are found in some areas. Large mammals found in the state include white-tailed deer, wildcats, jaguars, and bears.

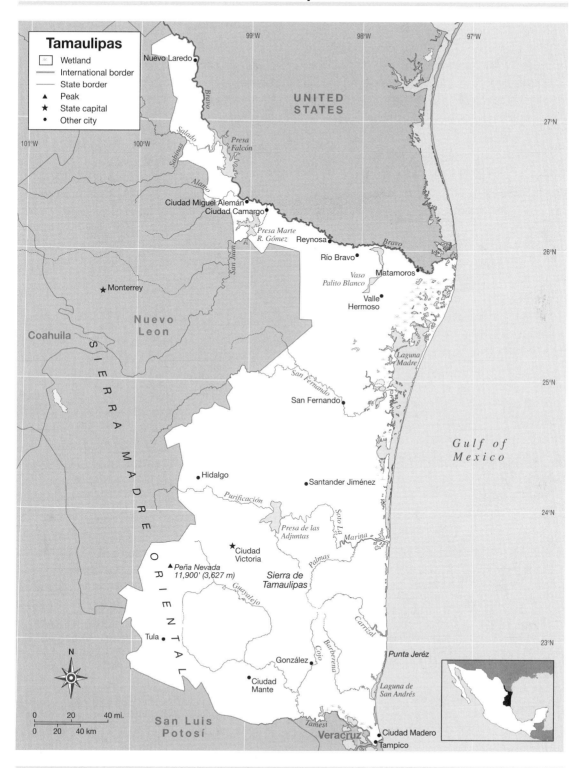

Tamaulipas

- Wetland
- International border
- State border
- ▲ Peak
- ★ State capital
- • Other city

99°W 98°W 97°W

Nuevo Laredo

UNITED STATES

27°N

101°W 100°W

Bravo

Salado

Sabinas

Alamo

Presa Falcón

Ciudad Miguel Alemán
Ciudad Camargo

San Juan

Presa Marte R. Gómez Reynosa

Río Bravo Matamoros

Vaso Palito Blanco

26°N

Bravo

Valle Hermoso

★ Monterrey

Nuevo León

Coahuila

S I E R R A
San Fernando

Laguna Madre

25°N

San Fernando

M A D R E

Gulf of Mexico

Hidalgo

• Santander Jiménez

Purificación

24°N

O R I E N T A L

Presa de las Adjuntas

La Soto

Marina

★ Ciudad Victoria

▲ *Peña Nevada* 11,900' (3,627 m)

Palmas

Sierra de Tamaulipas

Guayalejo

Carrisal

Tula

23°N

González

Cojo

Barberena

• Punta Jeréz

Ciudad Mante

Laguna de San Andrés

N

0 20 40 mi.
0 20 40 km

San Luis Potosí

Tamesí

Veracruz

Ciudad Madero
Tampico

Smaller mammals include hares, moles, and armadillos. Birds found in the state include turkeys, roadrunners, cockatoos, and pelicans. Tarantulas, chameleons, and several species of snakes and lizards are also found.

4 ▨ Environmental Protection

Environmental issues such as hazardous waste disposal and safe water supplies are concerns within the state. In 2003, the state government was considering setting up a system that would require industries to monitor their environmental pollutants. The El Cielo Biosphere Reserve is a protected cloud forest, which is a tropical rain forest in the mountains that has nearly constant cloud cover. Playa Tortuguera Rancho Nuevo is a wildlife reserve that has been designated as a Wetland of International Importance by the international conservation group known as the Ramsar Convention.

5 ▨ Population, Ethnic Groups, Languages

Tamaulipas had a total population of 2,753,222 in 2000; of the total, 1,359,874 were men and 1,393,348 were women. The population density was 34 people per square kilometer (88 people per square mile). In 2000, the capital, Ciudad Victoria, had a population of 262,686.

Almost all citizens speak Spanish as their first language. Less than 1% of the population speaks indigenous (native) languages.

6 ▨ Religions

According to the 2000 census, 73% of the population, or two million people, were

Roman Catholic; 8%, or 210,021 people, were Protestant. That year there were also 8,148 Seventh-Day Adventists, 10,094 Mormons, 39,461 Jehovah's Witnesses, and over 140,000 people who reported no religion.

7 ▨ Transportation

Ciudad Victoria Airport, Matamoros International Airport, and Nuevo Laredo-Qetzalcoatl International Airport provide international flights to and from Tamaulipas. The state has about 7,056 kilometers (4,383 miles) of roads and about 968 kilometers (601 miles) of railroads.

8 ▨ History

Archeological findings in the Cueva del Diablo caves point to human presence in the region as early as 6000 B.C. However, sedentary settlements date back to about 4000 B.C. First populated by Olmec groups, Tamaulipas was then populated by Chichimec and Huasteco groups. Between 1445 and 1466, Mexica armies commanded by Moctezuma Ilhuicamina conquered much of the territory and transformed it into a tributary region for the Mexica empire. Yet, Comanche, Apache, and other indigenous groups remained in rebellion against the invaders from central Mexico and were never conquered.

The first Spaniards to arrive were led by Francisco Hernández de Córdoba in 1517. Huasteco Indians defeated them. A new expedition led by Francisco de Garay was defeated a year later. In 1522, Hernán Cortés (1485–1547) defeated the rebel Indians and took control of the city of Chila. The lack of mineral deposits and the hostility of the indigenous people discouraged the Spaniards from attempting to expand their control to the northern end of the region. A number of efforts to convert the Indians to Catholicism also failed during most of the 16th century.

Early in the 17th century, Franciscan priests established missions in the region and began converting some of the sedentary populations. Cattle and sheep ranching brought increased economic activity to the region. Ranching also caused massive displacement of native populations from their original lands. Occasional indigenous revolts weakened colonial interest in the region. The presence of French colonizers in what would become the US state of Louisiana provoked concern among Spanish authorities in the 18th century. This French presence motivated a number of initiatives to populate the region and promote new economic activities. However, the reduced population and the lack of efficient transportation to the rest of Mexico hindered the economic development of the region.

Although some insurgent efforts were made to expand the independence movement to the region in 1810, Spanish royalist troops succeeded in preventing their success. The Plan of Iguala in 1821 ultimately incorporated Tamaulipas, which was made into a federal state in 1824. In 1836, nationalist troops from Tamaulipas fought against Texas secession. After the Mexican-American War (1846–48), Tamaulipas lost all of its territories north of the Rio Grande River to the United States. Political instability characterized much of the remaining 19th century, until the state began to experience economic development during the "Porfiriato era" (1876–1910), when president Porfirio Díaz (1830–1915) was in power.

The Mexican Revolution, which began in 1910, also reached Tamaulipas. As in the rest of Mexico, once the victors successfully agreed on a new national constitution, Tamaulipas was quickly brought into compliance. Emilio Portes Gil (1890–1978), governor of Tamaulipas during the 1920s, later went on to serve as president of Mexico between 1928 and 1930. During the rest of the 20th century, Tamaulipas consolidated its economy thanks to commerce with the United States. Since the adoption of the North American Free Trade Agreement (NAFTA)—a trade agreement between Mexico, the United States, and Canada—Tamaulipas has emerged as a manufacturing region for products exported to the United States. As one of the fastest growing states in the federation, Tamaulipas has benefited from the free trade reforms promoted by Mexico since the mid 1980s.

9 ■ State and Local Government

The state governor is democratically elected for a nonrenewable six-year term. There is a unicameral (single chamber) legislature called the state congress. Nineteen of its twenty-six deputies are elected from single member districts and seven deputies are elected by proportional representation. All serve three-year terms without an option for immediate reelection. Because the Institutional Revolutionary Party (PRI), the dominant political party throughout the country since the end of the Mexican Revolution, has not faced sufficiently strong competition from other parties in the state, formal separation of powers provisions have not been actually enforced. Under these conditions, the governor exercises more powers and recognition than mandated in the constitution.

The forty-three municipalities that comprise Tamaulipas hold democratic elec-

© Peter Langer/EPD Photos

Boats on a river in southern Tamaulipas.

tions for municipal presidents and council members every three years. Immediate re-election is not allowed. Although some decentralization initiatives are producing positive results, the state still has a long way to go to achieve successful decentralization.

10 ▪ Political Parties

The three main political parties in all of Mexico are the Institutional Revolutionary Party (PRI), the National Action Party (PAN), and the Party of the Democratic Revolution (PRD). The PRI has dominated politics in Tamaulipas since the end of the Mexican Revolution in 1917. All governors elected in the state have belonged to that party. Tomás Yarrington was elected governor in 1999 for a six-year term. The PAN has emerged as the second strongest party in the state, but its strength is primarily located in urban areas.

11 ▪ Judicial System

The Supreme Tribunal of Justice is the highest court in the state. Its seven members are appointed by a two-thirds majority of the legislature from among a pool of highly qualified attorneys with demonstrated experience and competence. If justices are ratified after their initial three-year appointments, they serve until their voluntary retirement. In addition, an electoral court and lower local courts also constitute the state's judicial system. Despite formal provisions that guarantee its independence, the overwhelming influence of the state governor has prevented the state judiciary from being more independent.

12 ■ Economy

Agriculture, fishing, and tourism are primary economic activities. However, manufacturing accounts for about 21% of the economy. Trade activities account for about 19% of the economy, followed by service-based companies at 17%, transportation and communications at 14%, finance and insurance at 13%, agriculture and livestock at 9%, construction at 6%, and mining at 1%.

13 ■ Industry

About 350 assembly plants (*maquiladoras*) are located along the border with the United States. Over 150,000 workers are employed in maquiladoras. In the southern part of the state, chemical and oil production facilities manufacture acrylic fiber, plastic resins, synthetic rubber, and polymers.

14 ■ Labor

The US Bureau of Labor Statistics reported that Mexican workers saw their wages increase 17%, from $2.09 per hour in 1999 to $2.46 per hour in 2000. (The average US worker earned $19.86 per hour in 2000.) After one year, workers are entitled by law to six days paid vacation.

15 ■ Agriculture

Part of the fertile lowland area known as La Huasteca, Tamaulipas has the climate and conditions for agriculture. It is the main producer of sorghum in Mexico. Other major crops include corn, cotton, and wheat. More than half the state's land area is devoted to livestock. About 4.6 million hectares of pastures and meadows support over one million cattle, 250,000 goats, 200,000 pigs, and 110,000 sheep.

16 ■ Natural Resources

The fishing industry is well developed because of the state's location on the Gulf of Mexico. The primary catch includes shrimp, crayfish, oysters, and crabs. Freshwater fish such as tilapia and catfish are also found in the state. There is also a thriving sport fishing industry serving tourists to the state. Oil is the primary mineral resource.

17 ■ Energy and Power

Almost all of the energy in Mexico is provided by the Federal Electricity Commission (CFE). In February 2002, the CFE introduced new electric rates. For households that use less than 140 kilowatt hours per month, there was no rate increase. (This is about 75% of all households in Mexico, according to CFE).

18 ■ Health

There are 36 general hospitals, 472 outpatient centers, and 90 surgical centers in Tamaulipas.

Most of the Mexican population is covered under a government health plan. The IMSS (Instituto Mexicano de Seguro Social) covers the general population. The

© Peter Langer/EPD Photos

Typical dance from Tamaulipas.

ISSSTE (Instituto de Seguridad y Servicios Sociales de Trabajadores del Estado) covers state workers.

19 ▪ Housing

More than one-half of the housing available in Tamaulipas is in good repair. More than 12% is in need of significant upgrading. Many homes do not have running water or access to electricity.

20 ▪ Education

The system of public education was first started by President Benito Juárez (1806–1872) in 1867. Public education in Mexico is free for students from ages six to sixteen. According to the 2000 census, there were approximately 556,000 school-age students in the state. Many students elect to go to private schools. The thirty-one states of Mexico all have at least one state university. Universidad Autónoma de Tamaulipas is located in Matamoros.

21 ▪ Arts

Tamaulipas has four major theater groups, including a mime theater. Most cities have a cultural center where local arts festivals and performing arts groups are showcased. There are also fifteen auditoriums located in various cities throughout the state. The International Festival of Tamaulipas, an arts festival, has attracted over one million attendees. The Centro Metropolitano de Tampico is a modern structure hosting experimental theater. A chorus made up of young people, Coro Meced Chimalli, presents concerts in the Palacio de Bellas Artes in the capital.

22 ▨ Libraries and Museums
There are one hundred branches of the national library system and seventeen museums in Tamaulipas. Matamoros has a museum of contemporary art. The capital, Ciudad Victoria, has an archeological museum. The Casamata Museum in Matamoros is a war museum.

23 ▨ Media
The capital, Ciudad Victoria, publishes the daily newspaper, *El Mercurio de Tamaulipas.* Nuevo Lardeo has two daily newspapers, *El Diario* and *El Mañana.* Reynosa also has two dailies: *El Mañana de Reynosa* and *Hora Cero.* Tampico's two newspapers are *El Diario de Tampico* and *El Sol de Tampico.*

24 ▨ Tourism, Travel, and Recreation
Matamoros lies on the border with the United States and attracts many tourists, many of whom like to shop in the marketplace. It is the official sister city to Brownsville, Texas. Many people come to shop in the Juarez marketplace. Playa Bagdad is also a popular beach getaway. Reynosa, a center for arts and crafts, also features a beach area, Las Playas, which is attractive

to tourists. In Nuevo Laredo, there is a greyhound racetrack and a market where hand-blown glass is sold. The Nuevo Laredo Fair is held in early September each year. Tampico has a marketplace where beach and ocean-related handicrafts are sold. Sport fishing enthusiasts visit the state each year for the Golden Sea Bass tournament, held the week before Easter. Near Tampico in Madero, one can go to Miramar Beach.

25 ▨ Sports
Two cities in Tamaulipas have basketball teams. Matamoros hosts the Correcaminos de la Universidad Autónoma de Tamaulipas, while the city of Victoria hosts a team called the Correcaminos de Victoria. The city of Matamoros also has a Plaza de Toros, which can hold 7,000 spectators. The city of Nuevo Laredo hosts a professional baseball team called the Tecolotes Dos Laredos. They play at the Parque La Junta, which seats 6,000 people. Another baseball team in Reynosa is called the Broncos. There is also a soccer team in Nuevo Laredo called the Gavilanes. Reynosa has a 5,000-seat bullfighting ring, Plaza de Toros. Tampico has a soccer team that plays in the 25,000-seat Tampaulipas stadium.

26 ▨ Famous People
Emilio Portes Gil (1890–1978) was born in the state and served as governor before becoming president of Mexico in 1928. Tomás Yarrington was elected governor in 1999.

27 ■ Bibliography

Books

DeAngelis, Gina. *Mexico.* Mankato, MN: Blue Earth Books, 2003.

Supples, Kevin. *Mexico.* Washington, DC: National Geographic Society, 2002.

Web Sites

Mexico for Kids. http://www.elbalero.gob.mx/index_ kids.html (accessed on June 15, 2004).

Tamaulipas State Government Web Site. http://www.tamaulipas.gob.mx/ (accessed June 17, 2004).

Tlaxcala

Pronunciation: teh-lawx-KAH-lah

Origin of state name: Probably based on the Náhuatl word *tlaxcallan,* which means "place of corn" or "place of corn bread (tortilla)."

Capital: Tlaxcala.

Entered country: 1824.

Coat of Arms: The coat of arms features a castle, which is meant to represent the state's link to Castile, Spain. The letters I, K, and F and the crowns in the border represent Queen Isabel, King Karolus (Charles I), and King Ferdinand, all of Spain. The skull and crossbones at the bottom represent those who died in the Spanish conquest of Mexico.

Holidays: Año Nuevo (New Year's Day—January 1); Día de la Constitución (Constitution Day—February 5); Benito Juárez's birthday (March 21); Primero de Mayo (Labor Day—May 1); Revolution Day, 1910 (November 20); and Navidad (Christmas—December 25).

Flag: There is no official state flag.

Time: 6 AM = noon Greenwich Mean Time (GMT).

1 Location and Size

Tlaxcala is Mexico's smallest state. It is located in the region of the country that is known as the Central Breadbasket. It is bordered on the north, east, and south by the Mexican state of Puebla; on the west by México state; and on the north and west by the Mexican state of Hidalgo. Tlaxcala covers an area of 3,913 square kilometers (1,511 square miles), which is just a little larger than the US state of Rhode Island. Only the Distrito Federal (Federal District) is smaller. Tlaxcala has sixty municipalities. The capital is Tlaxcala.

Tlaxcala has three mountain ranges. The Tlaxco mountains (*sierra*) are located in the north and are known for its El Peñón Hill. Another sierra serves as the natural border between Puebla and Tlaxcala. It is given different names according to the location: it is known as the Tlaxco Sierra in the north, where it is also called the Caldera Sierra; and towards the southeast, it is known as the Huamantla Sierra. The Huintépetl volcano forms part of this sierra. A volcanic mountain range, the highest peak of which is the extinct volcano known as Malinche, or Malintzi (4,451 meters/14,636 feet), lies near the

The Cathedral of Nuestra Señora de la Asuncion (Our Lady of the Assumption) in the capital, Tlaxcala, dates to the colonial period in the 1500s.

border with Puebla. The indigenous people call this volcano Matlalcueyatl.

There are plains located to the south of the Tlaxco Sierra and surrounding the volcanic range on the border with Puebla.

Tlaxcalan rivers, while small, play an important role because they feed the Balsas River, one of the largest rivers in Mexico. The main rivers in the state are the Zahuapan and Atoyac. The Zahuapan River rises in the Tlaxco Sierra and runs southward down the mountain slopes, where it joins the Apizaco River and forms the Atlihutzía waterfall. Upon reaching the border with Puebla, it runs into the Atoyac River; the Zahuapan River also receives water from the Amomoloc and Rojano Rivers.

2 ■ Climate

The climate throughout the state is generally cool. The average year-round temperature is about 16°C (60°F). Temperatures are usually under 21°C (70°F). Average rainfall in the capital city is about 79 centimeters (31 inches) per year.

3 ■ Plants and Animals

Pine, fir, and oak are the most common trees. Savin shrubs are found in several regions. Pastures cover some of the plains

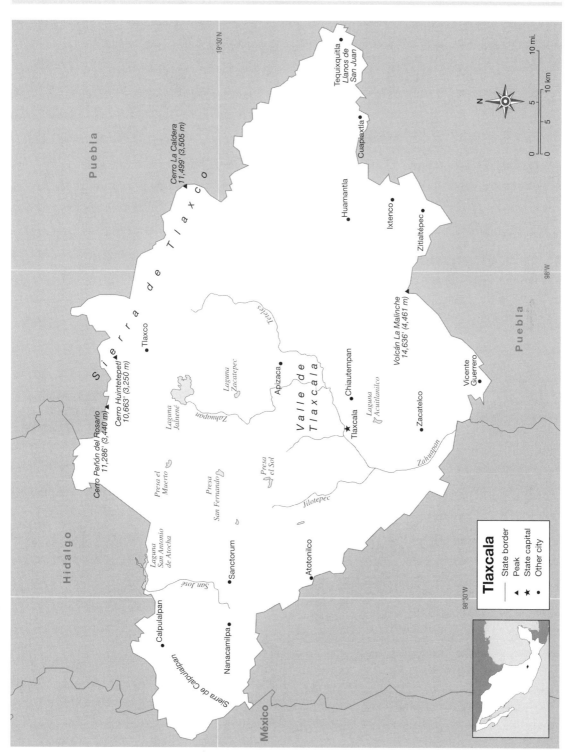

Tlaxcala

- — State border
- ▲ Peak
- ★ State capital
- • Other city

Puebla

Cerro La Caldera
11,499' (3,505 m)

Sierra de Tlaxco

Tlaxco

Cerro Peñón del Rosario
11,286' (3,440 m)

Cerro Huintetepetl
10,663' (3,250 m)

Laguna
Juhené

Laguna
Zacatepec

Zahuapan

Apizaca

Valle de
Tlaxcala

Chiautempan

★ Tlaxcala

Laguna
Acuitlanilco

Zacatelco

Vicente
Guerrero

Volcán La Malinche
14,636' (4,461 m)

Puebla

Huamantla

Ixtenco

Zitlaltépec

Tequixquitla
Llanos de
San Juan

Cuapiaxtla

Presa el
Muerto

Presa
San Fernando

Presa
el Sol

Jilotepec

Zahuapan

Hidalgo

Laguna
San Antonio
de Atocha

Sanctorum

Atotonilco

San José

Calpulalpan

Nanacamilpa

Sierra de Calpulalpan

México

19°30'N

98°W

98°30'W

N

10 mi.

10 km

and valley areas. Common mammals include hares, shrews, squirrels, and tlacuaches (Mexican possums). Sparrow hawks, eagles, and quail are found in the state. Rattlesnakes are also found in some areas.

4 ▪ Environmental Protection

In 2003, the state received a federal grant to establish a monitoring system for industrial pollution. Malinche National Park is a protected area surrounding a dormant volcano.

5 ▪ Population, Ethnic Groups, Languages

Tlaxcala had a total population of 962,646 in 2000; of the total, 469,948 were men and 492,698 were women. The population density was 241 people per square kilometer (624 people per square mile). In 2000, the capital, Tlaxcala, had a population of 73,184.

Almost all citizens speak Spanish as their first language. A small number, about 3.2% of the population, speaks indigenous (native) languages.

6 ▪ Religions

According to the 2000 census, 82% of the population, or 791,284 people, were Roman Catholic; over 2%, or 24,200 people, were Protestant. That year there were also 1,088 Seventh-Day Adventists, 1,140 Mormons, 9,875 Jehovah's Witnesses, and over 15,000 people who reported no religion.

7 ▪ Transportation

There is one domestic airport in the state. There are also about 1,843 kilometers (1,145 miles) of roads and about 308 kilometers (191 miles) of railroads.

© Mireille Vautier/Woodfin Camp

Located just over one half of a mile from the town center, this site commemorates Juan Diego Bernandino, the man who reported the apparition of the Virgin Mary at this site in 1541. The architecture and interior are in a Baroque style, and the interior includes decorations of carved figures and curling gilded wood that dates back to the 1700s, attributed to Francisco Miguel Tlayotehuanitzin, an Indian sculptor who worked for more than 20 years to create them.

8 ▪ History

Although the first evidence of human life in the state dates back to nomadic hunters and gatherers around 10,000 B.C., the indigenous Quinametin were the first to permanently settle in the region. With

Otomi and Teotihuacan influence, the Quinametin were later overpowered by the Olmec-Xicalanca whose Maya ancestry is evident. One of the most important archeological pieces from that period, the Chac-Mool sculpture housed in the National Museum of Anthropology in Mexico City, has clear Maya influence. The Olmec-Xicalanca built several cities and left numerous pieces of religious and cultural artifacts that have survived to this day.

In the 10th century, the Toltec-Chichimec exercised control of the area, but around 1330 A.D., the Tlaxcalteca permanently settled in the area after overpowering several other groups that inhabited the region. In 1348, they founded Tepectícpac, the first city of the Tlaxcallan empire. Between 1418 and 1430, the Tlaxcalteca Indians provided support and protection to Nezahualcóyotl, who later rose to be the philosopher king of Texcoco and an ally of the Mexico-Tenochtitlan Aztecs. Threats from powerful neighbors forced the Tlaxcalteca to develop their famous military might and organization. When Spanish conquistador Hernán Cortés (1485–1547) learned of the conflicts between Aztecs and Tlaxcaltecas, he invited the latter to join him in defeating the rulers of Mexico-Tenochtitlan. After an initial refusal, Cortés overpowered the Tlaxcaltecas and subdued them into an alliance against the Aztecs. With their support, Cortés overpowered the Aztecs. Tlaxcaltecas were later used to fight along with the Spaniards in new conquest efforts elsewhere in Mexico and Central America and to populate new territories conquered by the Spaniards.

During most of the 16th century, the Spanish conquistadors (those who sought to conquer Mexico for Spain) respected the agreement made between Cortés and the Tlaxcaltecas. As a result they did not levy taxes on them nor did they confiscate the land occupied by the native population in the region. However, toward the end of the 16th century, new Spanish authorities began to levy taxes and occupy the native's land. Although there were a few insurrections during the 17th and 18th centuries, the Tlaxcaltecas were successfully subdued by the Spanish colonizers. Different Catholic orders also promoted aggressive conversion efforts that permitted the consolidation of the Roman Catholic faith in the region.

Although there was an active pro-independence group in the state, the forces loyal to the Spanish crown successfully controlled the state between 1810 and 1821. When the Plan of Iguala secured Mexico's independence in 1821, Tlaxcala was incorporated into the newly independent country. However, it was only declared a federal state in 1824.

Political and social instability characterized much of the 19th century. Federalist-centralist and conservative-liberal conflicts hindered economic development and caused military confrontations. After peace was finally achieved with the victory of liberals led by Benito Juárez (1806–1872) in 1867, Tlaxcala became a commercial and textile center. These developments were especially prominent during the Porfirio Díaz government (1876–1910).

The Mexican Revolution, which began in 1910, brought about several peasant uprisings and military confrontations between different factions. However, the revolution victors were in control of the state when the new Mexican Constitution was introduced in 1917. During the rest of the 20th century, the small but densely populated state evolved as a regional commercial and textile center in Mexico.

9 ■ State and Local Government

The governor is democratically elected every six years for a nonrenewable term. The legislature is comprised of a unicameral (single chamber) congress. Nine of its twelve members are elected from single member districts and three are elected by proportional representation for three-year nonrenewable periods. Because the Institutional Revolutionary Party (PRI), the dominant political party in the country since the Mexican Revolution, only lost the gubernatorial chair in the 1999 elections, formal provisions for separation of power between the executive and legislative branches have only been enforced for the last few years. Yet, state democratic practices have improved.

The sixty municipalities that comprise Tlaxcala hold democratic elections for municipal presidents and council members every three years. Immediate re-election is not allowed. Although some decentralization initiatives are producing positive results, the state still has a long way to go to achieve successful decentralization.

10 ■ Political Parties

The three main political parties in all of Mexico are the Institutional Revolutionary Party (PRI), the National Action Party (PAN), and the Party of the Democratic Revolution (PRD). Although the PRI historically dominated state politics since the end of the Mexican Revolution in 1917, the 1999 gubernatorial elections produced the first alternation of power at the governor's desk. PRD militant, Alfonso

Abraham Sánchez, won a six-year term as governor. At the time, he was only the third PRD militant to win a state gubernatorial race. The PRI remains strong, as the second largest party in the state.

11 ■ Judicial System

The Superior Tribunal of Justice is the highest court in the state. Its members are elected by a simple majority vote of the legislature for renewable six-year terms. Because of the reduced size and small population of the state, the influence that the PRI exercised over the state judiciary significantly hindered its independence before 1999. When the PRD first won the governorship, the independence and autonomy of the judiciary were also automatically strengthened.

12 ■ Economy

Though agriculture is an important economic activity, manufacturing companies account for about 28% of the economy. Service-based companies account for about 21% of the economy, followed by finance and insurance at 16%, trade activities at 12%, transportation and communications at 9%, agriculture and livestock at 8%, construction at 5%, and mining at 1%.

13 ■ Industry

Textiles, chemicals, and pharmaceuticals are primary industries. The textile industries are primarily centered around Santa Ana Chiauhtempan, where both threads, fabrics, and finished clothing are made. Other textile facilities are located in the four industrial parks of the state in Ciudad Xicotencatl, Xiloxoxotla, Ixtacuixtla, and Calpulalpan. Other industries include machinery, automotive parts, and handicrafts of wood and clay.

14 ▪ Labor

The US Bureau of Labor Statistics reported that Mexican workers saw their wages increase 17%, from $2.09 per hour in 1999 to $2.46 per hour in 2000. (The average US worker earned $19.86 per hour in 2000.) After one year, workers are entitled by law to six days paid vacation.

15 ▪ Agriculture

Agriculture is important to the local food supply, but not as important as an export industry. The primary crop is corn. Others include alfalfa, barley, and wheat. Maquey is a crop used to produce syrup and vinegar. It is also used to produce *pulque,* an alcoholic beverage. Cattle, pigs, sheep, and goats are the primary livestock animals.

16 ▪ Natural Resources

Tlaxcala experiences frequent droughts. The largest challenge in natural resources is water conservation. The government has established programs to help the citizens learn how to conserve water.

17 ▪ Energy and Power

Almost all of the energy in Mexico is provided by the Federal Electricity Commission (CFE). In February 2002, the CFE introduced new electric rates. For households that use less than 140 kilowatt hours per month, there was no rate increase. (This is about 75% of all households in Mexico, according to CFE). As the smallest Mexican state, Tlaxcala's electricity consumption was the lowest in the early 1990s. However, the recent impact of the North American Free Trade Agreement (NAFTA)—a trade agreement between Mexico, the United States, and Canada—is reflected in Tlaxcala's energy consumption.

18 ▪ Health

The state of Tlaxcala has 9 general hospitals, 189 outpatient centers, and 21 surgical centers.

Most of the Mexican population is covered under a government health plan. The IMSS (Instituto Mexicano de Seguro Social) covers the general population. The ISSSTE (Instituto de Seguridad y Servicios Sociales de Trabajadores del Estado) covers state workers.

19 ▪ Housing

More than one-half of the housing available in the state of Tlaxcala is in good repair. More than 13% is in need of significant upgrading. Many homes do not have running water or access to electricity.

20 ▪ Education

The system of public education was first started by President Benito Juárez in 1867. Public education in Mexico is free for students from ages six to sixteen. According to the 2000 census, there were approximately 223,000 school-age students in the state. Many students elect to go to private schools. The thirty-one states of Mexico all have at least one state university. Tlaxcala's university is named the Universidad Autónoma de Tlaxcala, or the Autonomous University of Tlaxcala.

21 ■ Arts

The state of Tlaxcala has thirteen cultural centers and eleven auditoriums. There are three theaters, all located in the city of Tlaxcala. The city of Huamantla has a festival that takes place in August, during which all of the streets are decorated with paint, colored sand, or flowers to look like carpeting.

22 ■ Libraries and Museums

There are 118 branches of the national library system in Tlaxcala. There are fifteen museums. In the city of Huamantla there is a bullfighting museum and a puppet museum. In Tlaxcala, there is a museum of pre-Columbian cultures and a museum of local artistic crafts, the Museo de Artesanías.

23 ■ Media

The capital, Tlaxcala, publishes the daily newspaper *El Sol de Tlaxcala.*

24 ■ Tourism, Travel, and Recreation

The capital city, Tlaxcala, is sometimes called the Red City because of the ochre color of the buildings. The Governor's Palace has beautiful murals by a local artist, Desiderio Hernandez Xochitiotzin, who has been working on them since the 1960s. They depict the history of Tlaxcala. There are also local churches and museums featuring the pre-colonial history of Tlaxcala.

25 ■ Sports

Garzas Guerreras de Tlaxcala, the basketball team, is based in the state. There is a soccer field in Tlaxco.

26 ■ Famous People

Alfonso Abraham Sánchez Anaya was elected governor in 1998.

27 ■ Bibliography

Books

Supples, Kevin. *Mexico.* Washington, DC: National Geographic Society, 2002.

Web Sites

Mexico for Kids. http://www.elbalero.gob.mx/index_kids.html (accessed on June 15, 2004).

Visit Mexico. http://www.visitmexico.com/destinations/ (accessed June 17, 2004).

Veracruz

Pronunciation: vair-ah-KROOS

Origin of state name: Spanish explorer Hernán Cortés (1485- 1547) landed at Chalchihuecan in Veracruz on April 22, 1519, which was Good Friday, the Friday before Easter. Good Friday is also known as Vera Cruz (True Cross). Cortés called the settlement Villa Rica de la Vera Cruz.

Capital: Jalapa (hah-LAH-pah); sometimes spelled Xalapa

Entered country: October 3, 1824

Coat of Arms: A red cross at the top is inscribed with the word *vera* (cross), representing the name of the state. The castle represents the original settlement of Villa de La Vera Cruz. It is supported by the Columns of Hercules, which are also found on the Spanish coat of arms. The blue field represents the ocean. The columns and the blue field represent the fact that the original colony belonged to Spain, even though it was located across the Atlantic Ocean.

Holidays: Año Nuevo (New Year's Day—January 1); Día de la Constitución (Constitution Day—February 5); Benito Juárez's birthday (March 21); Primero de Mayo (Labor Day—May 1); Revolution Day, 1910 (November 20); and Navidad (Christmas—December 25).

Flag: There is no official state flag.

Time: 6 AM = noon Greenwich Mean Time (GMT).

1 ■ Location and Size

Veracruz is located in eastern Mexico in a region known as the Oil Basin and Gulf Lowlands. It is bordered on the north by the Mexican state of Tamaulipas; on the south by the Mexican states of Oaxaca, Chiapas, and Tabasco; on the east by the Gulf of Mexico; and on the west by the Mexican states of San Luis Potosí, Hidalgo, and Puebla. Veracruz covers an area of 72,815 square kilometers (28,114 square miles), which is about half the size of the US state of Illinois. The state is divided into 210 municipalities. The capital is Jalapa.

There are coastal plains along the coast of the Gulf of Mexico. Beyond the coastal plains, hills and canyons are found. Further inland there is the Sierra Madre Oriental, which has different names according to the region it occupies: Sierra de Huayacocotla, Zomelahuacan, Chiconquiaco, Huatusco,

Papaloapan, Coatzacoalcos, and Tonalá Rivers in the south.

2 ▌ Climate

The warm waters of the Gulf of Mexico contribute to the climate, which is generally warm and humid. The average temperature is 24°C to 28°C (76°F to 82°F). The highest monthly average rainfall occurs in August and September. Average rainfall in the city of Veracruz is about 173 centimeters (68.3 inches) per year. In Coatzacoalcos, the average rainfall is about 261 centimeters (102 inches) per year.

3 ▌ Plants and Animals

Cedar, mahogany, and ceiba trees are found in several regions of the country. Palm trees and mangroves grow in coastal regions. In the city of Papantla, vanilla pods are harvested from an orchid-type plant called tlixochitl. Wild boar, coyotes, ocelots, spider monkeys, and pumas live in various parts of the state. Iguanas and manatees are found in coastal regions. Alligators live in the Tuxtlas region. Birds found in the state include toucans, owls, woodpeckers, and buzzards.

4 ▌ Environmental Protection

The Sierra de los Tuxtlas ecoregion contains one of the largest moist forests in Mexico. Many plant and animal species found are unique to Mexico and cannot be found anywhere else in the world. The ecosystem includes seven volcanoes and several lakes, lagoons, and marshlands.

5 ▌ Population, Ethnic Groups, Languages

Veracruz had a total population of

Henk Sierdsema/Saxifraga/EPD Photos

An aerial view of Veracruz.

and Zongolica. The Otontepec, or Tantima, Sierra is found in the north. The Los Tuxtlas mountain range, which is not linked to the Sierra Madre Oriental, is found in the south.

The highest mountains in the state are the Pico de Orizaba (5,610 meters/18,500 feet above sea level) and the Cofre de Perote (4,200 meters/13,860 feet).

The most important rivers in Veracruz include the Pánuco, Tuxpan, and Cazones Rivers in the north; the Tecolutla, Actopan, La Antigua, Jamapa, Nautla, and Blanco Rivers in the central region; and the

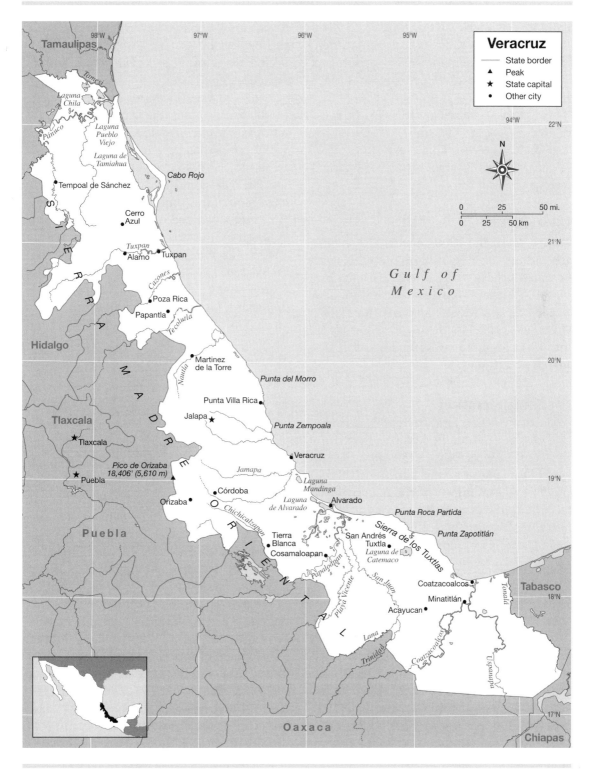

Veracruz
— State border
▲ Peak
★ State capital
• Other city

Tamaulipas

Laguna Chila

Laguna Pueblo Viejo

Laguna de Tamiahua

Pánuco

Tempoal de Sánchez

Cabo Rojo

Cerro Azul

Tuxpan
Álamo • Tuxpan

Cazones

Poza Rica

Papantla

Tecolutla

Hidalgo

Nautla

Martinez de la Torre

Punta del Morro

Punta Villa Rica

Jalapa ★

Punta Zempoala

Tlaxcala

Tlaxcala ★

Pico de Orizaba
18,406' (5,610 m)

Puebla ★

Jamapa

Veracruz

Laguna Mandinga

Orizaba •

Córdoba •

Laguna de Alvarado

Alvarado

Punta Roca Partida

Chichicatzapan

Puebla

Tierra Blanca

Cosamaloapan

San Andrés Tuxtla

Sierra de los Tuxtlas

Punta Zapotitlán

Laguna de Catemaco

Papaloapan

Playa Vicente

San Juan

Coatzacoalcos

Minatitlán

Acayucan

Tabasco

Lana

Trinidad

Coatzacoalcos

Uspanapa

Tonalá

Oaxaca

Chiapas

Gulf of Mexico

98°W 97°W 96°W 95°W 94°W

22°N
21°N
20°N
19°N
18°N
17°N

N

0   25   50 mi.
0   25   50 km

6,908,975 in 2000; of the total, 3,355,164 were men and 3,553,811 were women. The population density was 96 people per square kilometer (249 people per square mile).

Almost all citizens speak Spanish as their first language. About 10.4% of the state population speaks indigenous (native) languages, which is higher than the national average of about 7%.

6 ▪ Religions
According to the 2000 census, 73% of the population, or five million people, were Roman Catholic; 6%, or 422,973 people, were Protestant. That year there were also 80,266 Seventh-Day Adventists, 18,581 Mormons, 102,346 Jehovah's Witnesses, and 1,334 Jews. Over 410,000 people reported no religion.

7 ▪ Transportation
Poza Rica Airport and Tehuacán Airport provide international flights to and from Veracruz-Llave airport in the city of Veracruz Llave. The state has about 10,727 kilometers (6,663 miles) of roads and about 1,176 kilometers (730 miles) of railroads. The three major ports are at Coatzacoalcos, Alvarado, and Tuxpan.

8 ▪ History
Three important pre-Spanish civilizations evolved in this vast and extended coastal state. They were the Huasteca in the northern region, the Totonac culture in the middle region, and the late Olmec culture in southern Veracruz. The Triple Alliance formed in central Mexico, which included the Aztecs in Mexico-Tenochtitlan, the Texcoco, and the Tacuba, who dominated the entire Veracruz region at the beginning of the 15th century. They levied taxes on the numerous sedentary agricultural villages of the region.

The first Spaniards to arrive in Veracruz were under the command of Juan de Grijalva (c. 1489–1527) in 1518. Other members of the expedition were Pedro de Alvarado, Francisco de Montejo, and Bernal Diaz del Castillo, who later became a champion of indigenous rights. A second expedition, motivated by the presence of gold detected by the first expedition, was sent in 1519 under the command of Hernán Cortés (1485–1547). Cortés founded the city of Vera Cruz where he disembarked. Cortés and his lieutenant, Gonzalo Sandoval, overpowered an initial Huasteca rebellion. Because of the oppression by the Triple Alliance, the Totonac readily joined Hernán Cortés when he disembarked in Veracruz with the intention of defeating the Aztecs in their capital, Tenochtitlan (now Mexico City).

During the first years after the Spanish arrived, diseases brought by the Europeans and unknown to the indigenous people decimated the population. This devastation was helped by the massive enslavement to which most village inhabitants were subjected after being conquered. Sugarcane production made heavy demands on indigenous labor. As the indigenous population decreased, African slaves were brought to work in the plantations. The port city of Veracruz became the most important port of entry for all of Mexico. In 1601, the city was relocated to its present position. Several attacks by pirates in the 17th century demonstrated the economic and military importance of Veracruz for the Spanish crown. Massive slave trade converted Veracruz into the city with the largest enslaved population in Mexico. A

This Veracruz fort was the setting for the 1984 film, Romancing the Stone.

slave revolt in 1609, led by an African slave named Yanga, ended up in the formation of a runaway slave colony in a town known as San Lorenzo de los Negros.

Several insurgency efforts against Spanish rule surfaced after 1810, with Guadalupe Victoria (1789–1843) emerging as the most important independence leader in the region. When the Plan of Iguala came into effect in 1821, securing independence for the entire country of Mexico, the insurgent leader in Veracruz was Antonio López de Santa Anna (1794–1876). López de Santa Anna would become the most important military leader of Mexico during the 19th century. The on and off president allied with conser-

vative and liberal leaders alike with the sole objective of retaining power. Santa Anna lost the Mexican-American War (1846–48) and negotiated the Treaty of Guadalupe, where Mexico ceded large amounts of land to the United States. Veracruz became a federal state in 1824. A new state constitution was created in 1825.

Veracruz, as with the rest of Mexico, experienced political and social instability during much of the 19th century. Conflicts between centralists and federalists and between liberals and conservatives hindered economic development and provoked continuous revolts. Mexican president Benito Juárez (1806–1872) governed from Veracruz when his liberal government was attacked in Mexico City in 1857. A few years later, French emperor Maximilian (1832–1867) arrived in Veracruz in 1863 to assume the position of emperor of Mexico. (France had conquered and ruled parts of Mexico from 1864 to 1866.)

During the Mexican Revolution (1910–1920), Veracruz became a battleground for different factions. With the end of the revolution, its victors brought peace and stability to the region, which has consolidated as one of the most populated and economically active states of the Mexican union.

9 ▌ State and Local Government

The state governor is democratically elected for a six-year nonrenewable term. There is a unicameral (single chamber) legislature whose deputies are elected for nonrenewable three-year terms. Some deputies are elected both in single member districts and some deputies are elected at large. There can be no more than 60 deputies in total. Although the Institutional Revolutionary Party (PRI), the most powerful political party in the country since the end of the Mexican Revolution, historically exercised tight control over the state government, the rise of the National Action Party (PAN) and the Party of the Democratic Revolution (PRD) in large urban areas has made state politics more competitive. Formal separation of powers established in the constitution has been more effectively enforced since opposition parties have successfully won enough seats in the legislature to block unilateral actions by the PRI.

The 212 municipalities that comprise Veracruz hold democratic elections for municipal presidents and council members every three years. Immediate re-election is not allowed. The widely different sizes and wealth of the municipalities in the state makes it difficult for decentralization initiatives to work well across the state.

10 ▌ Political Parties

The three main political parties in all of Mexico are the Institutional Revolutionary Party (PRI), the National Action Party (PAN), and the Party of the Democratic Revolution (PRD). The PRI has continued to dominate politics at the state level. Two former state governors went on to become presidents of Mexico, Miguel Alemán Valdés (president from 1946 to 1952) and Adolfo Ruiz Cortines (president from 1952 to 1958). Longtime influential PRI leader, Fernando Gutierrez Barrios, was governor of the state between 1986 and 1988. The PAN and PRD have successfully won municipal races in local elections, but the PRI's strength in rural areas allows that party to remain the dominant force in the state.

11 ▌ Judicial System

The Superior Tribunal of Justice is the highest court in the state. The governor appoints its sixteen members for three-year terms with the approval of the legislature. If justices are ratified after their first term, they serve indefinitely. Only highly qualified attorneys can be appointed to the Superior Tribunal. Justices cannot publicly participate in any religious creed. In addition, there is an electoral court and a number of lower courts distributed throughout this large state.

12 ■ Economy

Manufacturing accounts for about 20% of the state economy. Service-based companies account for about 18% of the economy, followed by trade activities at 17%, finance and insurance at 17%, transportation and communications at 10%, agriculture and livestock at 10%, construction at 6%, and mining at 2%.

13 ■ Industry

Veracruz is one of the most important oil producing regions in the country. The Coatzacoalcos-Miniatitlan petrochemical plant is one of the state's most important industrial facilities. Other industrial centers can be found in Córdoba and Orizaba. Textile manufacturing is important in Rio Blanco.

14 ■ Labor

The U.S. Bureau of Labor Statistics reported that Mexican workers saw their wages increase 17%, from $2.09 per hour in 1999 to $2.46 per hour in 2000. (The average US worker earned $19.86 per hour in 2000.) After one year, workers are entitled by law to six days paid vacation.

15 ■ Agriculture

The most important agriculture crops in the state are corn, sugarcane, citrus fruits, and tobacco. Coffee is an important crop in the areas surrounding the capital city of Jalapa. Cattle, pigs, goats, and sheep are the main livestock animals. Poultry and bees are also raised.

16 ■ Natural Resources

Oil is the most important natural resource in the state.

17 ■ Energy and Power

Almost all of the energy in Mexico is provided by the Federal Electricity Commission (CFE). There is only one nuclear power plant in the country. It is located in Laguna Verde; its first reactor began operation in April 1989 and the second in November 1994. Laguna Verde generates over 5% of Mexico's total electricity output. In February 2002, the CFE introduced new electric rates. For households that use less than 140 kilowatt hours per month, there was no rate increase. (This is about 75% of all households in Mexico, according to CFE). After the rate increases in 2002, Veracruz residents were charged higher rates because they use more than the minimum amount of electricity.

18 ■ Health

The state of Veracruz has 77 general hospitals, 1,515 outpatient centers, and 182 surgical centers. There is also an American hospital in the city of Jalapa.

Most of the Mexican population is covered under a government health plan. The IMSS (Instituto Mexicano de Seguro Social) covers the general population. The ISSSTE (Instituto de Seguridad y Servicios Sociales de Trabajadores del Estado) covers state workers.

19 ■ Housing

Less than one-half of the housing available in the state of Veracruz is in good repair. More than 30% is in need of significant upgrading. Many homes do not have running water or access to electricity.

20 Education

The system of public education was first started by President Benito Juárez in 1867. Public education in Mexico is free for students from ages six to sixteen. According to the 2000 census, there were approximately 1.6 million school-age students in the state. Many students elect to go to private schools. The thirty-one states of Mexico all have at least one state university. The Universidad Veracruzana is located in the capital, Jalapa.

21 Arts

The state of Veracruz has fourteen theaters. The Universidad de Veracruz hosts the Ballet Folklórico de Veracruz. There are four local musical groups including an orchestra of popular music. The Groupo Chuchumbe performs a traditional fandango (a Spanish dance that is usually performed by a couple to the accompaniment of guitars and castanets), while the Groupo Mono Blanco plays traditional music from the south of Veracruz. Veracruz has two theater groups, one of which is located at the University of Veracruz.

22 Libraries and Museums

The state of Veracruz has 453 branches of the national library system. There are also thirty-seven museums. In Córdoba there is a museum of whimsical art and an archeological museum. In Texistepec there is a museum of the ancient city of Tenochtitlan. In the city of Tuxpan there is a museum dedicated to the friendship between Cuba and Mexico. The capital city of Veracruz has a local history museum. Jalapa has a museum of science and technology, a museum of local animal life, and a museum of anthropology.

23 Media

Five cities publish newspapers in the state of Veracruz. Coatzacoalcos has two daily papers: *Diario del Istmo* and *Diario Liberal del Sur*. Córdoba has *El Sol del Centro*. Veracruz has two daily newspapers: *El Dictamén* and *Negocios de Veracruz*. The city of Jalapa (Xalapa) publishes *Diario de Xalapa*.

24 Tourism, Travel, and Recreation

Veracruz is noted for its beautiful beaches. The Chacalacas sandbar (about 35 miles along the coast) features many aquatic sports. There is also an aquarium in the city of Veracruz. Veracruz is famous for its Carnival (like Mardi Gras). The city of Jalapa has a museum of anthropology housing over 25,000 artifacts. The Xalapeno Stadium is known for its unique architectural design. The Botanical Gardens and the Paseo de Los Lagos are other attractions.

25 Sports

Jalapa's basketball team is the Halcones. Córdoba also has a professional baseball team, the Cafeteros de Córdoba, which plays in the 8,000-seat Estadio Beisborama 72. The city of Veracruz has a soccer team that plays in the 43,154-seat Luis Pirata Fuentes stadium. Veracruz's baseball team, Rojos de Aguila, plays in the 7,782-seat Beta Avila stadium. The city of Orizaba has a soccer team, which plays in the 7,000-seat Plaza de Toros stadium.

26 ■ Famous People

Guadalupe Victoria (1789–1843) was an important leader in the region that is now Veracruz. Political and military figures from Veracruz include Antonio López de Santa Anna (1794–1876) and Ignacio de la Llave, who was governor of Veracruz state from 1857 to 1860. Two former state governors went on to become presidents of Mexico: Miguel Alemán Valdés (president from 1946 to 1952) and Adolfo Ruiz Cortines (president from 1952 to 1958). Fernando Gutiérrez Barrios, a long-time PRI leader, was governor of Veracruz from 1986 to 1988. Miguel Alemán Velazco, son of Miguel Alemán Valdés, took office as governor of Veracruz in 1998.

27 ■ Bibliography

Books

DeAngelis, Gina. *Mexico.* Mankato, MN: Blue Earth Books, 2003.

Supples, Kevin. *Mexico.* Washington, DC: National Geographic Society, 2002.

Web Sites

Mexico for Kids. http://www.elbalero.gob.mx/index_kids.html (accessed on June 15, 2004).

Surfing & Adventure Travel in Mexico: The State of Veracruz. http://www.surf-mexico.com/states/veracruz/index.html (accessed June 17, 2004).

YUCATAN

Yucatán

Pronunciation: yoo-kah-THAN

Origin of state name: The name reflects a translation error. The Spaniards misunderstood the native Mayas when they gave the name of their land. The Spaniards thought the Mayas said Yucatán, so that is the name they gave to the land.

Capital: Mérida (MEH-ree-dah)

Entered country: 1824.

Coat of Arms: A deer, representing the native Mayan people, leaps over an agave plant, once an important crop in the region. Representing the shared Mayan and Spanish heritage of the state, the symbols at the top and bottom of the border are Mayan arches and the symbols on the left and right are Spanish bell towers.

Holidays: Año Nuevo (New Year's Day—January 1); Día de la Constitución (Constitution Day—February 5); Benito Juárez's birthday (March 21); Primero de Mayo (Labor Day—May 1); Revolution Day, 1910 (November 20); and Navidad (Christmas—December 25).

Flag: There is no official state flag.

Time: 6 AM = noon Greenwich Mean Time (GMT).

1 ■ Location and Size

Yucatán is bordered on the north by the Gulf of Mexico, on the east and southeast by the Mexican state of Quintana Roo, and in the southwest by the Mexican state of Campeche. It covers an area of 43,380 square kilometers (16,749 square miles), about half the size of the US state of Maine.

Yucatán consists mainly of lowland areas, with the driest lands in the northwest. It sits on a horizontal bed of limestone, parts of which have been dissolved by rainwater, forming underground lakes. Its coastal regions feature white sand beaches and mangrove forests a few miles inland. To the south near Campeche are some rainforest areas, but most of the land is dry and does not support much vegetation.

2 ■ Climate

The warm waters of the Caribbean Sea contribute to the climate, which is generally warm and humid. It has an aver-

Pyramid of the Magician, Uxmal, Yucatan.

age temperature of 25°C to 27°C (77°F to 81°F), rarely dropping below 16°C (61°F) or rising above 49°C (120°F). The heaviest rainfall occurs in the summer months. Average annual rainfall in this area is 115 centimeters (45 inches).

3 ▪ Plants and Animals

Cedar, ceiba, pich, and poak trees are found throughout the region. Some of the most common animals include anteaters, porcupines, and raccoons. Pumas, jaguars, and long-tailed monkeys are found in some regions. Common birds include parrots, macaws, cardinals, and bluebirds.

Octopus and dolphins can be found in the coastal waters.

4 ▪ Environmental Protection

In 2003, the state government was considering the establishment of a new program to monitor industrial pollution. Isla Contoy is an uninhabited island off the coast that is a protected national park. Pelicans and egrets live on the island, along with other endangered species of birds. The Sian Ka'an Biosphere Reserve is a protected area of tropical rainforests, mangroves, and marshes. The Celestun Biosphere Reserve is another important protected area. The Reserve Estatal El Palmar is a state

Yucatán

State border
Ruin
★ State capital
● Other city

Quintana Roo

Gulf of Mexico

Campeche

Chemax

Tizimin

Espita

Valladolid

Buctzotz

Chichén-Itzá

Temax

Peto

Izamal

Sotuta

Dzidzantún

Cansahcab
Motul
Tekantó

Hoctún

Homún

Seyé

Tekit

Tekax
Oxkutzcab
Akil

Tzucacab

Baca
Conkal
Tixkokob
Kanasín

Acanceh

Tecoh

Mayapán

Chacmultún
Salpacal
Sayil
Labná
Kom

Yakaldzib

Progreso

Dzibilchaltún

Mérida ★

Muna

La Sierrita

Ticul

Kabah

Uxmal

Umán

Hunucmá

Maxcanó

Halachó

Estero de
Río Lagartos

Punta Yalkubul

Estero
El Islote

Playa San Bruno

Laguna
Rosada

Estero
Yukalpetén

Estero
Celestún

Punta Baz

Punta
Boxcahua

20 mi.
20 km

N

21°N

20°N

88°W

89°W

90°W

Campeche

park that is known as a wetland of international importance.

5 ■ Population, Ethnic Groups, Languages

Yucatán had a total population of 1,658,210 in 2000; of the total, 818,205 were men and 840,005 were women. The population density was 42 people per square kilometer (109 people per square mile). The capital, Mérida, is the most populous city, with 680,000 inhabitants.

Most citizens speak Spanish as their first language. A large number of people, about 37% of the population, speak indigenous (native) languages. This is the highest percentage of indigenous speakers in the country.

6 ■ Religions

According to the 2000 census, 75% of the population, or seven million people, were Roman Catholic; 7%, or 123,162 people, were Protestant. That year there were also 12,416 Seventh-Day Adventists, 24,553 Jehovah's Witnesses, and over 60,000 people who reported no religion.

7 ■ Transportation

Federal highways, roads, and rail lines connect Yucatán with its neighboring states. There are almost 9,000 kilometers (5,625 miles) of highways and over 600 kilometers (375 miles) of railway in the state. A four-lane toll road crosses the peninsula from Cancún (in the state of Quintana Roo) through Mérida toward the state of Campeche. Drivers traveling the full length of the road will pass through several toll booths (*casetas de cobro*) to pay tolls that total about US$24.

Common road hazards are speed bumps (*topes*) in villages and rural areas. Most topes are marked by signs.

Public transportation via city bus systems is available in Mérida and other cities. The town of Progreso, located about 40 kilometers (25 miles) from Mérida, is an important port for state commerce. Travel to major Mexican cities and international destinations is made possible by the Mérida Licenciado-Manuel Crescencio Rejon International Airport.

8 ■ History

The Mayan civilization, one of the most advanced Amerindian cultures of the ancient Americas, began in the Yucatán near 2500 B.C. Between 300 and 900 A.D., the Maya built several cities in the Yucatán region. The Toltec culture arrived in 987 A.D. led by its leader, Quetzalcóatl. Although the Toltec groups mixed with the Maya and other groups that inhabited the region, Toltec culture eventually emerged as the predominating culture in the region before the arrival of the Spanish. During the 12th century, the Maya city-state of Mayapán waged war against Chichen-Itzá. After a military victory, Mayapán expanded its influence over the rest of the area. The so-called Cocom dynasty (named after the Mayan Cocom tribe and kingly family) ruled until the mid-13th century. The post-classic Maya period ended around 1250 A.D. Most cities were abandoned, but those that remained continued their inter-city military conflicts.

The first Spaniards to visit the region were the survivors of the Pedro de Valdivia (c. 1498–1553) expedition that left the Central American country of Panama in 1511 toward Santo Domingo in the West Indies, but

The observatory at Chichen Itza.

shipwrecked near Yucatán before reaching its final destination. Two survivors, Jerónimo de Aguilar and Gonzalo Guerrero, became incorporated into Maya civilization. Guerrero married the daughter of the Chetumal chief and their son was the first officially recorded Mestizo (mixed Indian and Spanish) in Mexico. Jerónimo de Aguilar was later rescued by Spanish conqueror Hernán Cortés's (1485–1547) expedition.

In 1513, on his expedition to Florida, Juan Ponce de León (1460–1521) sailed near Yucatán but never disembarked in the region. In 1517, Francisco Fernández de Córdoba set foot in Cozumel, off the coast of the modern-day state of Quintana Roo, but was expelled by the Indians. He returned to Cuba. There he was informed of the existence of the region that was initially considered an island. The Hernán Cortés expedition that sailed off Cuba in 1519 briefly stopped by Yucatán, where Jerónimo de Aguilar was rescued, and then went north and disembarked in Veracruz.

Francisco de Montejo (c. 1479–1553) initiated the conquest of Yucatán in 1527 but was so fiercely fought against by the Indians that he fled. He returned three years later with his son Francisco de Montejo y León but was again unsuccessful in his effort to overpower the native Indians. A third attempt in 1537 proved successful. De

Montejo founded the cities of Campeche in 1540 and Mérida in 1542. Gaspar Pecheco, known for his cruel treatment of the Indians, completed the conquest on the western end of the region. Franciscan priests built more than thirty convents in an effort to convert the indigenous people to the Catholic faith. Spanish oppression and the diseases brought by the conquistadors (Spanish conquerors) significantly reduced the Amerindian population from an estimated 5 million in 1500 to 3.5 million a century later.

An indigenous rebellion led by Jacinto Canek in 1761 resulted in the deaths of thousands of Indians and the execution of Canek in the city of Mérida. Other indigenous revolts during the colonial period consolidated Yucatán's reputation as a region whose fierce Indians would not easily surrender to Spanish rule.

Yucatán did not participate in the independence movement of 1810. The Spanish authorities controlled the region and prevented any insurgencies. In 1821, with the Plan of Iguala, Yucatán was made a part of independent Mexico. Yucatán was formally made a state in 1824 and a new constitution was written in 1825. In addition to the federalist-centralist and liberal-conservative conflicts that characterized much of 19th century Mexico, Yucatán also experienced a number of indigenous rebellions during those decades.

After the Mexican Revolution in 1917, where different factions fought for control of the peninsula, the revolutionary victors brought peace to the region. In 1931, the territory of Quintana Roo was separated from Yucatán and made into an autonomous state. A new indigenous revolt in 1937 led Mexican president Lázaro Cárdenas (1895–1970) to adopt an aggressive land reform program in the state where Indians were given communal lands.

9 ▪ State and Local Government

The highest authority is the state governor, democratically elected for a nonrenewable six-year term. A unicameral (single chamber) legislature, the state congress, is elected every three years. Its twenty-five members include fifteen legislators elected from single member districts and ten legislators elected by proportional representation. All are elected for nonrenewable three-year terms. The legislature generally meets once a year, but extra sessions can be called by the governor or by a permanent committee if the need arises. State services receive funding from the federal government. Although formal provisions for separation of powers exist in the constitution, the overwhelming power historically exercised by the dominant Institutional Revolutionary Party (PRI) prevented many of those provisions from being effectively enforced.

The 106 municipalities that comprise Yucatán hold democratic elections for municipal presidents and council members every three years. Immediate re-election is not allowed. Although some decentralization initiatives are producing positive results, the state still has a long way to go to achieve successful decentralization.

10 ▪ Political Parties

The three main political parties in all of Mexico are the Institutional Revolutionary Party (PRI), the National Action Party (PAN), and the Party of the Democratic Revolution (PRD). The PRI is composed only of civilians and embraces all sorts of

© Peter Langer/EPD Photos

The Roman Catholic cathedral in the capital, Mérida, lies on one side of the Plaza Mayor, a wide square with trees and park benches.

political opinion. There are three significant pressure groups working within the PRI: labor, the peasantry, and the "popular" sector, which includes bureaucrats, teachers, and small business people. Although the PRI dominated politics in the state since the end of the Mexican Revolution in 1917, the 2001 gubernatorial elections gave the governorship to the conservative PAN. Patricio Patrón became the first non-PRI governor of the state. The PRI remains very powerful in rural areas, but the PAN has consolidated its presence in large urban areas.

11 Judicial System

The Superior Tribunal of Justice is the highest court in the state. Its six members are appointed by the state congress for nonrenewable four-year terms. Only qualified and experienced attorneys can be appointed to the highest state court. Because of the excessive power and influence of the governor during the years of PRI rule, the judiciary exercised limited autonomy. In addition, an electoral tribunal and local courts are also part of the state judiciary.

12 ▪ Economy

Service-based companies account for about 23% of the state economy. Trade activities (such as agribusiness, the textile and apparel industries, and furniture) account for about 21% of the economy, followed by finance and insurance at 19%, manufacturing at 13%, transportation and communications at 10%, agriculture and livestock at 7%, construction at 6%, and mining at 1%.

13 ▪ Industry

Most of the state's industry is focused on food processing and textiles. There are some electronics manufacturing plants within the state as well. The state has some assembly plants owned by US companies.

14 ▪ Labor

The US Bureau of Labor Statistics reported that Mexican workers saw their wages increase 17%, from $2.09 per hour in 1999 to $2.46 per hour in 2000. (The average US worker earned $19.86 per hour in 2000.) After one year, workers are entitled by law to six days paid vacation.

15 ▪ Agriculture

Agriculture is very important to the economy of the region. Major crops include corn, beans, sorghum, oranges, mangoes, and lemons. Cattle, pigs, and horses are the primary livestock animals. The state is well-known as a major supplier of honey.

16 ▪ Natural Resources

Fishing is an important economic activity along the coast. The catch includes sea bass, octopus, and shark. Oil is the most important mineral resource, but sand, gravel, clay, and salt are also mined, primarily for the production of construction materials.

17 ▪ Energy and Power

Almost all of the energy in Mexico is provided by the Federal Electricity Commission (CFE). In February 2002, the CFE introduced new electric rates. For households that use less than 140 kilowatt hours per month, there was no rate increase. (This is about 75% of all households in Mexico, according to CFE).

18 ▪ Health

The state of Yucatán has 18 general hospitals, 317 outpatient centers, and 44 surgical centers.

Most of the Mexican population is covered under a government health plan. The IMSS (Instituto Mexicano de Seguro Social) covers the general population. The ISSSTE (Instituto de Seguridad y Servicios Sociales de Trabajadores del Estado) covers state workers.

19 ▪ Housing

About one-half of the housing available in the state of Yucatán is in good repair. More than 19% is in need of significant upgrading. Many homes do not have running water or access to electricity.

20 ▪ Education

The system of public education was first started by President Benito Juárez (1806–1872) in 1867. Public education in Mexico is free for students from ages six to sixteen. According to the 2000 census, there were approximately 369,000 school-age students in the state. Many students elect

© Kal Muller/Woodfin Camp

A Mayan woman weaves a hammock.

to go to private schools. The thirty-one states of Mexico all have at least one state university. The Universidad Autónoma de Yucatán (Independent University of Yucatán) is in Mérida.

21 ▪ Arts

Yucatán has fifteen auditoriums and twelve theaters. There are thirty-one local cultural centers in cities and towns in the state. Research on the Mayan calendar is carried out at the Maya World Studies Center in Mérida. The calendar is used for astronomical calculations, date calculations, and markers for ceremonial dates.

22 ▪ Libraries and Museums

Yucatán has 144 libraries and fifty-five museums. The capital, Mérida, has a coin museum, a planetarium, the Museum of Anthropology and History, an Olympic museum, a museum of sacred art, and a contemporary art museum.

23 ▪ Media

The capital city, Mérida, publishes four daily newspapers: *Diario de Yucatán, Diario del Sureste, Por Esto,* and *La Revista Peninsular.*

24 ■ Tourism, Travel, and Recreation

Mérida was founded on ancient Mayan ruins. The cathedral of San Ildefonso was built over Mayan ruins, using some of the Mayan stones. Hidalgo Park and the marketplaces, Lucas de Galvez and the Portal de Granos, are popular sites for tourists to visit in Mérida. El Centenario Zoo is also found in the capital.

25 ■ Sports

The baseball season in Mexico is from April to August. The oldest league dates from 1925 and is called the Liga Mexicana. There is a Liga Mexicana team, Leones, in the state.

26 ■ Famous People

Agustin de Iturbide (1783–1824) was a Mexican revolutionary who helped win independence for Mexico and was the "Emperor of Mexico" from 1822 to 1823.

27 ■ Bibliography

Books

Cancun and the Yucatan. London, Eng.: Dorling Kindersley, 2003.

Carew-Miller, Anna. *Famous People of Mexico.* Philadelphia: Mason Crest Publishers, 2003.

DeAngelis, Gina. *Mexico.* Mankato, MN: Blue Earth Books, 2003.

Supples, Kevin. *Mexico.* Washington, DC: National Geographic Society, 2002.

Web Sites

Mexico for Kids. http://www.elbalero.gob.mx/index_kids.html (accessed on June 15, 2004).

State of Yucatan. http://www.yucatan.gob.mx (accessed on June 15, 2004).

Yucatan Today: The Tourist Guide. http://www.yucatantoday.com/ (accessed on June 15, 2004).

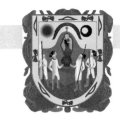

Zacatecas

Pronunciation: zah-kah-TEE-kahs

Origin of state name: Original inhabitants of the region were called *zacatecas* by their neighbors, which means "the people who live on the edge of the zacate (field)."

Capital: Zacatecas.

Entered country: 1823.

Coat of Arms: The city of Zacatecas was founded by the Spaniards, and the coat of arms depicts the arrival of the Spaniards, surrounded by weapons of the native inhabitants they found.

Holidays: Año Nuevo (New Year's Day—January 1); Día de la Constitución (Constitution Day—February 5); Benito Juárez's birthday (March 21); Primero de Mayo (Labor Day—May 1); Revolution Day, 1910 (November 20); and Navidad (Christmas—December 25).

Flag: There is no official state flag.

Time: 6 AM = noon Greenwich Mean Time (GMT).

1 Location and Size

Zacatecas is located in north-central Mexico. It covers an area of 75,040 square kilometers (28,973 square miles), which is smaller than the US state of South Carolina. It is bordered by the Mexican states of Aguascalientes, Coahuila, Durango, Guanajuato, San Luis Potosí, Jalisco, Nayarit, and Nuevo León. Zacatecas has 57 municipalities. The capital city is Zacatecas.

The deepest ravine in Zacatecas, Las Lecheras, measures 3,050 meters (10,000 feet) deep. It is surrounded by mountains (*sierras*), including the Las Bocas Sierra, the Sombrerete Sierra, Los Huacales, Los Alamos Sierra, Chapultepec Sierra, Pico de Teira, Grande Hill, Los García Plateau, and Zuldaca Sierra.

There are many hills in the state—some of them rise more than 2,500 meters (8,250 feet) above sea level. They form part of mountain ranges such as the Sierra Madre Occidental and the Sierra Madre Oriental.

The Sierra Madre Occidental is the main mountain range crossing the state.

There are two river basins: the Pacific and Interior Basins. The rivers of the Pacific Basin are very long and run through other states before reaching the Pacific Ocean. The main rivers are the San Pedro, Juchipila, Jerez, Tlaltenango, San Andrés, Atengo, and Valparaíso. The rivers of the Interior Basin do not reach the sea. They are the Calabacillas, Zaragoza, Los Lazos, San Francisco, and Aguanaval.

2 ■ Climate

The northern plateau location of the capital, Zacatecas, has a chilly climate in winter. In summer the climate is mild and dry, with the temperature averaging 17°C (62°F). The average annual rainfall is 28 centimeters (11 inches).

3 ■ Plants and Animals

The state can be divided into three natural regions: the Sierra Madre Oriental in the north, the Central Plateau, and the Sierra Madre Occidental in the south. The northern region has palm trees, nopal cactus, yucca, and huizache. The central region is mostly pastureland, and the south has oak forests as well as pastures and thickets.

Common animals include coyotes, wildcats, tlacuaches (Mexican opossums), deer, and wild boar. Common birds include wild turkeys, macaws, and eagles.

4 ■ Environmental Protection

The Sierra de Organos is a protected national park.

5 ■ Population, Ethnic Groups, Languages

Zacatecas had a total population of 1,353,610 in 2000; of the total, 653,583 were men and 700,027 were women. The population density was 18 people per square kilometer (46 people per square mile). In 2000, the capital, Zacatecas, had a population of 123,700.

Almost all citizens speak Spanish as their first language. Less than one percent of the population speaks indigenous (native) languages.

6 ■ Religions

According to the 2000 census, 84% of the population, or 1.1 million people, were Roman Catholic; about 2%, or 23,098 people, were Protestant. That year there were also 2,441 Seventh-Day Adventists, 7,861 Jehovah's Witnesses, and over 23,000 people who reported no religion.

7 ■ Transportation

The state has about 9,742 kilometers (6,051 miles) of roads and about 670 kilometers (416 miles) of railroads. There is one international airport.

8 ■ History

Before the arrival of Spanish settlers, Zacateco, Caxcán, and Guachichile groups inhabited the region. Although most were hunters and gatherers, a few settlements existed in the area when Spanish conquistadors (those who came to Mexico in order to claim it for Spain) Cristóbal de Oñate and Pedro Almendez Chirinos, lieutenants in the Nuño Beltrán de Guzmán expedition, organized a militia of Spanish soldiers and Mexica and Tlaxcaleca Indians

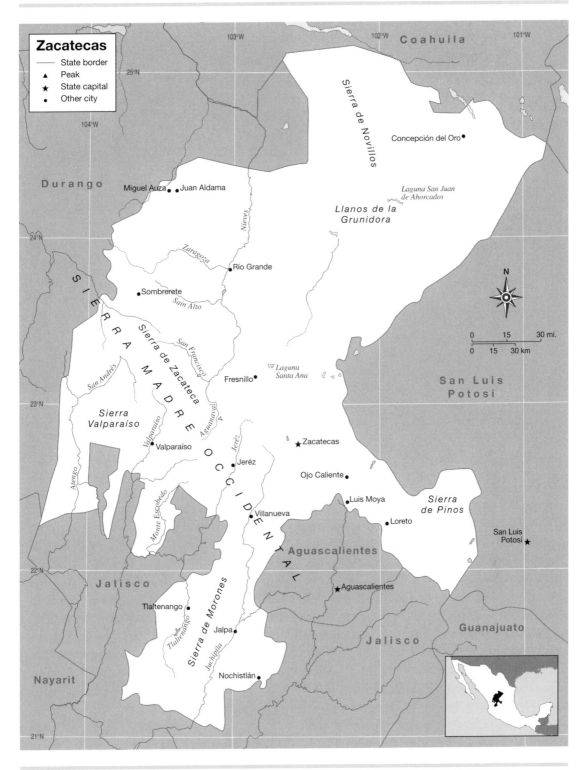

Zacatecas

— State border
▲ Peak
★ State capital
• Other city

Coahuila

Sierra de Novillos

Concepción del Oro •

Durango

Miguel Auza • • Juan Aldama

Nieves

Zaragoza

Laguna San Juan de Ahorcados

Llanos de la Grunidora

• Río Grande

• Sombrerete

Sain Alto

San Francisco

SIERRA

Sierra de Zacateca

San Andrés

Laguna Santa Ana

San Luis Potosí

Fresnillo •

MADRE

Aguanaval

Sierra Valparaíso

Valparaíso

Valparaíso •

Atengo

Jeréz

• Jeréz

★ Zacatecas

OCCIDENTAL

Ojo Caliente •

• Luis Moya

Monte Escobedo

Sierra de Pinos

Villanueva •

• Loreto

San Luis Potosí ★

Jalisco

Aguascalientes

Tlaltenango •

Sierra de Morones

★ Aguascalientes

Guanajuato

Tlaltenango

Jalpa •

Juchipila

Jalisco

Nayarit

Nochistlán •

N

0   15   30 mi.
0   15   30 km

© Robert Frerck/Woodfin Camp

Looking down Avenue Hidalgo in the capital, Zacatecas. The three-story building is the Theater Calderón, named in honor of Mexican playwright Fernando Calderón. The first performances were given there in May 1887.

to conquer the region. After founding the city of Zacatecas, Chirinos and his troops abandoned the region and returned to central Mexico. Administratively, Zacatecas was considered a part of the New Galicia region. Several insurrections by the Caxcán Indians caused severe damage to Spanish conquering troops. An indigenous leader, Tenamextle, also known as Diego the Aztec, mounted a rebellion that captured and executed Spanish conquistador Miguel de Ibarra in 1541. Another Spanish conquistador, Francisco de Ibarra, successfully retreated to neighboring Gua-

dalajara after failing to make peace with the indigenous rebels. The Spanish, under the command of Viceroy Antonio de Mendoza, ultimately succeeded in defeating the Caxcánes in the Mixtón War. Allied with Tlaxcalteca and Purepecha Indians, the Spanish troops defeated an army of twelve thousand warriors commanded by Tenamextle. More than ten thousand Caxcánes were killed, but Tenamextle escaped and continued to fiercely fight the Spaniards for eight more years.

After finding silver in the region in 1548, the Spanish stepped up their presence in Zacatecas. The city of Zacatecas, which had been destroyed, was rebuilt, and Zacatecas was made into a province of New Galicia. Several silver mines were put into operation. Indian rebels attacked the convoys that transported silver to Mexico City, reflecting the difficulties the Spaniards had in exercising control over the region. Known as the silver paths, the roads that led from Zacatecas to the rest of the country were the center of indigenous resistance and sabotage against mining and commercial activity. Mining activity continued to grow until the mid-17th century, when financial difficulties severely hindered silver production. Indian groups and runaway slaves brought from Africa continued to attack Spanish settlements and travelers who went from Zacatecas to neighboring Guadalajara in Jalisco.

Because mining activity had picked up again in the late 18th century, the independence movement sought support in Zacatecas in 1810, hoping to benefit from the silver production in the region. When troops loyal to the Spanish crown defeated the independence army of Miguel Hidalgo y Costilla (1753–1811), many pro-independence fighters escaped to Zacatecas until the royalist troops occupied the city in 1811. Zacatecas joined the new federal republic when national independence was finally achieved in 1821. The state was formally incorporated in 1823 and a new constitution was written in 1825.

Political and military conflicts between centralists and federalists and between liberals and conservatives characterized much of the 19th century in Zacatecas. When the liberals finally defeated conservatives and Benito Juárez (1806–1872) became president for a second time in 1867, Zacatecas experienced a period of social peace and economic progress. In 1880, Governor García de la Cadena ran against Porfirio Díaz (1830–1915) for the presidency of Mexico. He was defeated but revolted against Díaz who was just beginning what turned out to be the longest presidential tenure in the history of Mexico (1876–1910).

Different factions fought in Zacatecas during the Mexican Revolution, which started in 1910, but by 1917 the revolutionary victors were already in control of the region. Zacatecas joined the other states in sending delegates to write the new Mexican Constitution of 1917. During the rest of the 20th century, the Institutional Revolutionary Party (PRI), the dominant political party following the Mexican Revolution, tightly controlled politics in the heavily populated and agriculturally rich region.

9 ▊ State and Local Government

The highest authority in the state is the governor, elected democratically every six years for a nonrenewable term. The state legislature is a unicameral (single) chamber comprised of twenty-one members. Deputies are elected for nonrenewable three-year terms from both single member districts and by proportional representation. Until the opposition Party of the Democratic Revolution (PRD) won the gubernatorial election in 1998, the Institutional Revolutionary Party (PRI) governors exerted overwhelming influence over state powers.

The fifty-seven municipalities that comprise Zacatecas hold democratic elections for municipal presidents and council members every three years. Immediate re-election is not allowed. Although some decentralization initiatives are producing positive results, the state still has a long way to go to achieve successful decentralization.

10 ■ Political Parties

The three main political parties in all of Mexico are the Institutional Revolutionary Party (PRI), the National Action Party (PAN), and the Party of the Democratic Revolution (PRD). Although the PRI historically controlled politics in the state, the PRD won the 1998 gubernatorial elections. Ricardo Monreal became the first non-PRI governor of the state. Yet, the PRD is strongest in urban areas, with the PRI retaining a majority control of the rural vote. The PAN also has grown in urban areas and its support for Monreal was essential to defeating the PRI in one of its strongholds. A former PRI member, Monreal resigned from that party to join the PRD a few years earlier.

11 ■ Judicial System

The Superior Tribunal of Justice is the highest court in the state. The state governor appoints its seven members with approval from the legislature. Only qualified attorneys with a proven record can be appointed to the court. Justices can be reappointed at the end of their terms. Although the constitution guarantees the independence of the judiciary, the excessive influence exerted by PRI governors in the past prevented that autonomy from being freely exercised. In addition, an electoral tribunal and lower courts also comprise the state's judicial system.

12 ■ Economy

Agriculture and livestock account for about 25% of the economy. Service-based companies account for about 21% of the economy, followed by finance and insurance at 19%, trade activities at 14%, transportation and communications at 7%, construction at 5%, manufacturing at 5%, and mining at 4%.

13 ■ Industry

Most of the industries in the state are focused on food processing. There are some foreign companies with facilities in the state, including Oro Control and Packard Electric.

14 ■ Labor

The US Bureau of Labor Statistics reported that Mexican workers saw their wages increase 17%, from $2.09 per hour in 1999 to $2.46 per hour in 2000. (The average US worker earned $19.86 per hour in 2000.) After one year, workers are entitled by law to six days paid vacation.

15 ■ Agriculture

Agriculture is the main economic activity in the state. The most important crops include guavas, grapes, apples, peaches, and strawberries. Corn and potatoes are important staples. Cattle and sheep are the primary livestock animals.

16 ■ Natural Resources

Mexico produces approximately 17% of the world's total annual output of silver. Zacatecas produces about 40% of the country's total silver output. The largest mine is near Fresnillo.

© Robert Frerck/Woodfin Camp

This elaborate cathedral in the capital, Zacatecas, dates from the eighteenth century.

17 ■ Energy and Power

Almost all of the energy in Mexico is provided by the Federal Electricity Commission (CFE). In February 2002, the CFE introduced new electric rates. For households that use less than 140 kilowatt hours per month, there was no rate increase. (This is about 75% of all households in Mexico, according to CFE).

18 ■ Health

There are 14 general hospitals, 394 outpatient centers, and 34 surgical centers in the state of Zacatecas.

Most of the Mexican population is covered under a government health plan.

The IMSS (Instituto Mexicano de Seguro Social) covers the general population. The ISSSTE (Instituto de Seguridad y Servicios Sociales de Trabajadores del Estado) covers state workers.

19 ■ Housing

Only about one-half of the housing available in the state of Zacatecas is in good repair. More than 16% is in need of significant upgrading. Many homes do not have running water or access to electricity.

20 ■ Education

The system of public education was first started by President Benito Juárez in 1867.

Public education in Mexico is free for students from ages six to sixteen. According to the 2000 census, there were approximately 335,700 school-age students in the state. Many students elect to go to private schools. The thirty-one states of Mexico all have at least one state university. In Zacatecas, there is Universidad Autónoma de Zacatecas (Independent University of Zacatecas).

21 Arts

Most of the cities and towns of Zacatecas have local cultural centers. In all, the state has forty-nine local cultural centers and eight theaters. There is a large auditorium for performing arts groups in the city of Zacatecas.

22 Libraries and Museums

The state has 209 libraries and thirty-three museums. Major museums in the capital, Zacatecas, are a museum of abstract art, a science museum, a museum of pharmacy, a blacksmith museum, and a museum of local history. A mineralogy museum is located at the Universidad Autónoma de Zacatecas.

23 Media

The capital, Zacatecas, has two daily newspapers, *El Sol de Zacatecas* and *Imágen*.

24 Tourism, Travel, and Recreation

The capital, Zacatecas, is an old mining town founded in 1546. There are silver mines open to tourists. Zacatecas is known for its fine ironwork and for its buildings of pink sandstone. Tourists visit the cathedral (which dates from the 18th century) and Enrique Estrada Park, which has an aqueduct from the 18th century. Special events include the Zacatecas Fair (second week of September) and the De la Morisma Fair (celebrated the last three days in August).

25 Sports

There are two basketball teams in the state: Barreteros (in the capital, Zacatecas) and Gambusinos (in Fresnillo). The soccer team, Real Sociedad Zacatecas, plays in the 16,000-seat Francisco Villa stadium in the capital.

26 Famous People

Francisco "Pancho" Villa (born Doroteo Arango, 1878–1923) was born in Rio Grande but was known as a bandit revolutionary in Chihuahua and Durango. He has been called the Mexican Robin Hood. Composer Manuel María Ponce (1886–1948) may be best-known for his works for guitar. Refugio Reyes Rivas (1862–1945), a developer whose works transformed the city of Aguascalientes, was born in La Sauceda.

27 Bibliography

Books

DeAngelis, Gina. *Mexico.* Mankato, MN: Blue Earth Books, 2003.

Supples, Kevin. *Mexico.* Washington, DC: National Geographic Society, 2002.

Web Sites

Mexico for Kids. http://www.elbalero.gob.mx/index_kids.html (accessed on June 15, 2004).

Mexico

United Mexican States
Estados Unidos Mexicanos

Pronunciation: MEH-hee-koh.

Origin of state name: The country name comes from words in the language of the indigenous Náhuatl people: *metztli* (moon), *xictli* (center), and *co* (place).

Capital: Mexico City

Coat of Arms: The national coat of arms is an eagle with a snake in its beak, perched on a cactus.

Holidays: Año Nuevo (New Year's Day—January 1); Día de la Constitución (Constitution Day—February 5); Benito Juárez's birthday (March 21); Primero de Mayo (Labor Day—May 1); Revolution Day, 1910 (November 20); and Navidad (Christmas—December 25).

Flag: The national flag is a tricolor of green, white, and red vertical stripes; at the center of the white stripe is the national coat of arms.

Time: 6 AM = noon Greenwich Mean Time (GMT).

1 ■ Location and Size

Situated south of the United States on the North American continent, Mexico has an area of 1,972,550 square kilometers (761,606 square miles), including many uninhabited islands off the east and west coasts, which have a combined area of 5,073 square kilometers (1,959 square miles). Mexico is slightly less than three times the size of the US state of Texas, including the narrow peninsula of Baja. Mexico has a total boundary length of 13,683 kilometers (8,501 miles). The capital city, Mexico City, is located in the south-central part of the country.

Mexico's dominant geographic feature is the great highland central plateau, which occupies most of the width of the country, extending from the US border to the Isthmus of Tehuantepec (an isthmus is a narrow strip of land that connects two larger areas, in this case the Bay of Campeche on the north and the Gulf of Tehuantepec on the south). The plateau is enclosed by two high cordilleras (mountain chains), the Sierra Madre Oriental on the east and the Sierra Madre Occidental on the west, each separated from the coast by lowland plains. The ranges rise to over 3,000 meters (10,000 feet), and some volcanic peaks exceed 5,000 meters (16,400 feet). Pico de Orizaba, or

Citlaltépetl (5,700 meters/18,702 feet), is the highest point in the country. The Laguna Salada is the lowest point of the country (10 meters/33 feet below sea level).

The Río Bravo del Norte (known as the Río Grande in the United States) is a river that extends for about 2,100 kilometers (1,300 miles) of the boundary with the United States. The Papaloapan River is an important source of waterpower. The largest lake in Mexico is Lake Chapala (in the state of Jalisco), which covers about 1,686 square kilometers (651 square miles).

2 ■ Climate
The climate varies according to altitude and rainfall. The coastal plains, Yucatán Peninsula, and lower areas of southern Mexico have a mean temperature of 25°C to 27°C (77°F to 81°F). The temperate zone (tierra templada) has a mean temperature of 21°C (70°F). Mexico City and most other important population centers are in the cool zone (tierra fria), with a mean annual temperature of 17°C (63°F). The highest mountain peaks are always covered with snow.

Annual rainfall may exceed 500 centimeters (200 inches) in the Isthmus of Tehuantepec, while in parts of Baja California there is practically no rainfall. Precipitation is adequate in central Mexico, while in the northern states desert-like conditions prevail.

3 ■ Plants and Animals
Plant and animal life differs sharply with Mexico's varied climate and topography. The coastal plains are covered with a tropical rain forest, which merges into subtropical and temperate growth as the plateau rises. In the dry northern states, there are fewer trees and vegetation, with desert plants covering much of the area. Oaks and conifers are found in mixed forest regions along the mountain slopes. The Yucatán Peninsula has scrubby vegetation.

Among the wild animals are the armadillo, tapir, jaguar, bear, and several species of monkey, deer, and boar. Poisonous snakes and harmful insects also are found. In the coastal marshes malarial mosquitoes pose a problem. The only remaining elephant seals in the world are on Guadalupe Island west of Baja California.

4 ■ Environmental Protection
Mexico loses its forest at a rate of about 0.9% annually due to agricultural and industrial expansion. Mexico City has chronic smog, aggravated by the presence of thousands of factories, by more than two million motor vehicles, and by open burning of garbage by many citizens. Cities along the US-Mexican border also suffer from serious air pollution. Transportation vehicles are responsible for 76% of the air pollution. Water pollution results from the combined impact of industrial, agricultural, and public waste. In the north, fresh water resources are scarce and polluted. In the central-southeast region, water is frequently inaccessible and of poor quality.

Mexico has the fourth most extensive mangrove (a tropical evergreen) area in the world. In 2001, sixty-four of the nation's mammal species and thirty-six bird species were endangered, including the Mexican grizzly bear (possibly extinct), the southern bald eagle, the ridge-nosed rattlesnake, and two species of crocodile. At least thirty

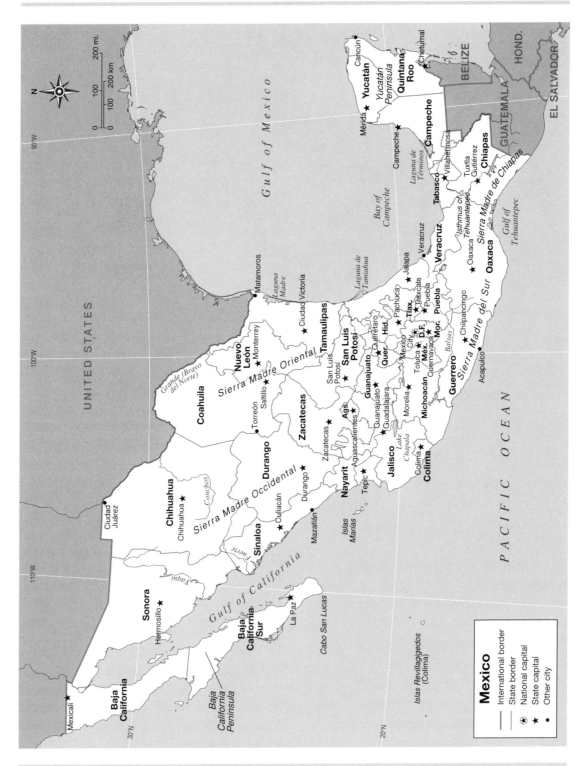

N

200 mi.

200 km

200 km

100

100

0

0

90°W

100°W

110°W

30°N

20°N

UNITED STATES

Gulf of Mexico

Grande (Bravo del Norte)

BELIZE

HOND.

GUATEMALA

EL SALVADOR

Cancún

Yucatán

Yucatán Peninsula

Quintana Roo

Chetumal

Mérida

Campeche

Campeche

Laguna de Términos

Bay of Campeche

Villahermosa

Tabasco

Tuxtla Gutiérrez

Chiapas

Sierra Madre de Chiapas

Veracruz

Veracruz

Jalapa

Isthmus of Tehuantepec

Oaxaca

Oaxaca

Sierra Madre del Sur

Gulf of Tehuantepec

Matamoros

Laguna Madre

Ciudad Victoria

Laguna de Tamiahua

Tamaulipas

Pachuca

Tlax.

Tlaxcala

Puebla

Puebla

Monterrey

Nuevo León

San Luis Potosí

San Luis Potosí

Querétaro

Quer.

Hid.

Mexico City

D.F.

Méx.

Mor.

Cuernavaca

Balsas

Chilpancingo

Guerrero

Acapulco

Coahuila

Saltillo

Sierra Madre Oriental

Zacatecas

Guanajuato

Guanajuato

Toluca

Michoacán

Morelia

Torreón

Zacatecas

Ags.

Aguascalientes

Guadalajara

Jalisco

Lake Chapala

Colima

Colima

Durango

Durango

Sierra Madre Occidental

Chihuahua

Chihuahua

Conchos

Ciudad Juárez

Culiacán

Sinaloa

Nayarit

Tepic

Fuerte

Mazatlán

Islas Marías

PACIFIC OCEAN

Sonora

Hermosillo

Yaqui

Gulf of California

Baja California

Baja California Sur

La Paz

Cabo San Lucas

Baja California Peninsula

Mexicali

Islas Revillagigedos (Colima)

Mexico

International border

State border

National capital

State capital

Other city

Cactii growing on San Pedro Martin Island.

species have become extinct, including the Mexican dace, Durango shiner, Tlaloc's leopard frog, and Caribbean monk seal.

5 ■ Population, Ethnic Groups, Languages

In 2003, the population of Mexico was estimated by the United Nations at 103.4 million. It is projected to total 119.6 million by 2015. In 2002, the population density averaged 52 persons per square kilometer (135 persons per square mile). In 2003, approximately 33% of the population was under fifteen years of age. About 74% of the population lived in urban areas in 2001.

In 1990, the US Census Bureau estimated that 13.5 million persons of Mexican ancestry were living in the United States. Likewise, the largest community of US citizens living outside the United States is found in Mexico.

The people of Mexico are mostly Mestizos, a mixture of native Amerindian and Spanish heritage. There are small numbers of persons of other European heritage. At last estimates, 60% of the population was Mestizo, 30% was pure Amerindian, 9% was white, and 1% was something other. Amerindian influence on Mexican cultural, economic, and political life is very strong.

Spanish is the official language and is spoken by nearly the entire population. This gives Mexico the world's largest Spanish-speaking community, since more Mexicans speak Spanish than do Spaniards. Only a small number of inhabitants, about 1% of the population according to the last estimate, speak only indigenous Amerindian languages or dialects. A larger percentage, some 7.5% at last estimate, speak an Amerindian language as well as Spanish. There are at least thirty-one different Amerindian language groups, the principal languages being Nahuatl, Maya, Zapotec, Otomi, and Mixtec.

6 Religions

According to the 2000 census, about 88% of the Mexican population is affiliated with the Roman Catholic Church and about 6% is Protestant. There are small Greek and Russian Orthodox communities. There are also small numbers of Seventh-Day Adventists, Jehovah's Witnesses, Mormons, Jews, Buddhists, and Muslims. While professing the Roman Catholic faith, a number of indigenous people include strong pre-Hispanic Mayan elements in their religion.

Veneration of the patron saints plays an important role in Mexican life, and the calendar is full of feast days (fiestas). These predominantly Roman Catholic celebrations include many ancient Amerindian rites and customs and, invariably, bands of mariachi musicians playing Mexican folk songs.

7 Transportation

In 2002, the country had about 323,977 kilometers (201,319 miles) of roads and 18,000 kilometers (11,185 miles) of railroads. In 2000, there were over 8.7 million registered vehicles, including 5.5 million passenger cars and 3.2 million commercial vehicles. Mexico has 2,900 kilometers (1,802 miles) of inland waterways and lakes, but these are not as important to transportation as are ocean and coastal shipping areas. There are 102 ocean ports, the most important being Tampico and Veracruz, on the Gulf of Mexico; Mazatlán and Manzanillo on the Pacific coast; and Guayamas on the Gulf of California.

In 2001, there were an estimated 1,852 airports and airfields. Principal airports include Juan N. Alvarez at Acapulco, Cancún International at Cancún, and Benito Juárez at Mexico City. Mexican commercial aircraft carried twenty million passengers on scheduled domestic and international flights in 2001. The main airline company is Aeroméxico.

8 History

The land now known as Mexico was inhabited by many of the most advanced Amerindian cultures of the ancient Americas. The Mayan civilization in the Yucatán Peninsula began about 2500 B.C., flourished about 300 to 900 A.D., and then declined until its conquest by the Spanish.

The Mayas were skillful in the construction of stone buildings and the carving of stone monuments. They built great cities at Chichen-Itzá and many other sites. In the early 10th century the Toltecs founded their capital of Tollan (now Tula), and made the Nahua culture, of which they were a part, predominant in the Valley of Mexico until the early 13th century. At that time, the Aztecs, another Nahua tribe, gained control.

The Kukulcán Pyramid at Chichén Itzá was planned so that the setting sun would cast a shadow of a serpent writhing down the steps of the pyramid during the vernal equinox (longest day of the year).

The Aztecs were skilled in architecture, engineering, mathematics, weaving, and metalworking. They had a powerful priesthood and a complex religion dominated by the sun god and war god Huitzilopochtli, to whom prisoners captured from other tribes were sacrificed.

The empire was at its height in 1519, when the Spanish, under Hernán Cortés (1485–1547), landed at present-day Veracruz. With superior weapons and the cooperation of local chieftains, the Spaniards conquered Mexico by 1521. First, Cortés imprisoned the Aztec emperor Montezuma II (1466–1520). Then Montezuma's nephew, Cuauhtémoc

(or Guatimotzin, c. 1495–1522), drove the Spanish from Tenochtitlán (ancient name of Mexico City) on June 30, 1520. This is now called "la noche triste" ("the sad night"), during which Montezuma died, probably at the hands of the Spaniards. Cortés later returned to Tenochtitlán and defeated Cuauhtémoc.

The Spaniards brought Roman Catholicism to Mexico, imposed their legal and economic system on the country, and enslaved many of the inhabitants. The combination of Spanish oppression and the diseases the conquistadors (Spanish conquerors) brought with them reduced the Amerindian population from an estimated 5 million in 1500 to 3.5 million a century later.

Spain ruled Mexico as the viceroyalty of New Spain for three centuries. Continued political abuses and Amerindian enslavement, combined with the political uncertainty that followed French emperor Napoleon's (1769–1821) invasion of Spain in 1807, produced a Mexican independence movement. Between 1810 and 1815, several unsuccessful revolts took place. In 1821, independence was finally proclaimed and secured. Agustín de Iturbide (1783–1824) proclaimed himself emperor of Mexico in 1822 but was deposed in 1823, when a republic was established.

Over the next twenty-five years, there were at least thirty changes of government. General Antonio López de Santa Anna (1794–1876) became the dominant figure in the 1830s and 1840s to attempt to centralize the new government. Texas gained its independence from Mexico in 1836 as a result of the defeat of Santa Anna at San Jacinto. It joined the United States in 1845 after a brief period as a republic. Mexico lost the subsequent war with the United States (1846–48), which began over a dispute about the border of Texas. Under the Treaty of Guadalupe Hidalgo, Mexico recognized the Rio Grande as the boundary of Texas and ceded half its territory (much of the present western United States) in return for $45 million.

A reform government was established in 1855 after a revolt against Santa Anna, and a new liberal constitution was adopted in 1857. In 1861, French troops under Emperor Napoleon III (1808–1873) intervened in Mexico, supposedly because Mexico had not paid its debts. They installed Archduke Maximilian of Austria (1832–1867) as emperor. The French withdrew in

1866. Maximilian was executed and the republic was restored in 1867.

Porfirio Díaz (1830–1915) seized power in 1867 and assumed the presidency. He held this position almost continuously until 1911. Under his dictatorship, Mexico modernized by opening its doors to foreign investors and managers. At the same time, all dissent was suppressed, and there was a complete lack of concern with improving the lives of Mexican peasants. An elite corps of mounted police, the Rurales, held the rural areas in check. Resentment among the middle classes and the peasantry continued to grow.

After Díaz was once again reelected to the presidency in 1910, the Mexican Revolution erupted. This revolution had claimed perhaps one million lives by 1917. It was, on the one hand, a protest by middle-class political liberals against the oppressive Díaz regime and, on the other hand, a massive popular rebellion of peasants who demanded the right to own land. The interests of these two groups sometimes coincided but more often clashed. Riots in Mexico City forced Díaz to resign and leave the country in 1911. Liberal politician Francisco Indalecio Madero (1873–1913) was elected president that year. Meanwhile, popular revolts led by Emiliano Zapata (1879–1919) and Francisco "Pancho" Villa (1878–1923), who refused to submit to Madero's authority, led the country into chaos. Madero was ousted and murdered in 1913 by General Victoriano Huerta (1854–1916).

When Huerta, a corrupt dictator, was driven from power in July 1914, a full-scale civil war broke out. This phase of the revolution ended in February 1917 when a new constitution was proclaimed. This document was considered by some to be the world's

A young girl celebrates during a festival honoring the Michoacan's ancient Purépecha empire and the indigenous Purépacha people.

first socialist constitution. It embodied the principle of the one-term presidency in order to prevent the recurrence of a Díaz-type dictatorship.

Venustiano Carranza (1859–1920) was elected president in 1917, but for the next decade Mexico was still beset by political instability and fighting between various revolutionary groups. Most of the revolutionary leaders met with violent deaths. Zapata, still regarded by many as a revolutionary hero, was assassinated in 1920.

Political stability at last came to Mexico with the formation in 1929 of an official government party that incorporated most of the social groups that had participated in the revolution. It has been known since 1945 as the Institutional Revolutionary Party (Partido Revolucionario Institucional—PRI). Although founded to support the interests of peasants, workers, and other disadvantaged groups, it has also been closely allied with business since the 1940s. Considered to be one of the most outstanding political leaders of the post-1929 era, Lázaro Cárdenas (1895–1970), who was president from 1934 to 1940, sought with some success to realize the social goals of the revolution. His reforms included massive land redistribution, establishment of strong labor unions, extension of education to remote areas of the country, and in 1938, the takeover of foreign petroleum holdings, mostly US-owned.

The years since World War II (1939–45) have been marked by political stability, economic expansion, and the rise of the middle class, but also by general neglect of the poorest segments of the population. An economic boom during the late 1970s, brought about by huge oil export earnings, benefited a small percentage of the people. Still, millions of peasants continued to be only slightly better off than in 1910. Declining world oil prices in 1981 led to a severe financial crisis in 1982. Mexico's new president, Miguel de la Madrid Hurtado, put economic austerity measures into place. He also promised a crackdown on corruption, which has long been a problem in Mexico. In October 1987, the PRI named Carlos Salinas de Gortari as its candidate to succeed President de la Madrid in December 1988. Salinas' legitimacy was questioned as there was a complete shutdown of the computer systems that were calculating the votes that brought him into office. Salinas promoted the privatization of state industries and free trade agreements. In September 1993, changes in federal electoral were designed to make elections free from corruption.

Mexico City was devastated by a major earthquake in September 1985. The official death toll was seven thousand, although unofficial estimates were as high as twenty thousand. In addition, 300,000 were left homeless. There was widespread protest over the fact that many of the buildings destroyed had been built in violation of construction regulations and claims that foreign emergency aid had been mishandled by the government.

In August 1992, formal negotiations regarding the North American Free Trade Agreement (NAFTA) were concluded, whereby Mexico would join the United States and Canada in the elimination of trade barriers, the promotion of fair competition, and increased investment opportunities. NAFTA went into effect on January 1, 1994.

In January 1994, a primarily Amerindian group calling itself the Zapatista Army of National Liberation resorted to an armed uprising against the government. The group initially took control of four municipalities in Chiapas to protest what it regarded as government failure to effectively deal with regional social and economic problems. Two months after the Zapatista uprising, the nation witnessed its first high-level political assassination in over sixty years when PRI presidential candidate Luis Donaldo Colosio was murdered in Tijuana, in Baja California. His replacement, Ernesto Zedillo, was elected at the end of the year in a closely monitored campaign.

In December 1994 the Mexican peso was devalued. The economy went into its worst recession in more than fifty years. Over a million Mexicans lost their jobs. The United States responded to its neighbor's distress with a multimillion-dollar bailout that kept the economy from getting worse.

The public discontent with the economic crisis, poverty, crime, corruption, and political instability, led in 1997 to a rejection of Mexico's nearly seventy-year-old system of one-party rule. In June of that year, the PRI lost its majority in the lower house of the National Congress to the combined power of the leftist Party of the Democratic Revolution (PRD) and the conservative National Action Party (PAN).

In December 2000, Vicente Fox Quesada of the conservative PAN Party became president, the first non-PRI ruler in more than seventy years. By mid-2003, Fox had lost popularity after his two most symbolic legislative initiatives failed to pass the divided congress. The president failed to solve the indigenous revolt in Chiapas. A tax reform aimed at increasing government revenues to beef up social spending was also significantly scaled back. President Fox's legislative and government agendas moved slowly and many Mexicans then looked to the PRI as a government alternative.

9 ■ Government

Mexico is a federal republic consisting of thirty-one states and the Federal District (Mexico City). The president is elected for a six-year term by universal adult vote (beginning at age eighteen) and is not eligible for reelection. The president appoints the attorney general and a cabinet, which may vary in number. There is no vice president. If the president dies or is removed from office, the congress elects a provisional president.

The two-chamber Mexican Congress, also elected by direct universal suffrage, is composed of a Senate (Cámara de Senadores) made up of 128 members (four from each state and four from the Federal District) and a Chamber of Deputies (Cámara de Diputados) made up of 500 members. Senators are elected for six-year terms with half the Senate being elected every three years. Deputies are elected for three-year terms. Both groups are ineligible for immediate reelection.

In an effort to unite various interest groups within the government party, a National Consultative Committee, composed of living ex-presidents of Mexico, was formed in 1961 by President Adolfo López Mateos (1958–64).

Mexico's 2,378 municipalities are the principal units of state government. Each state has a constitution, a governor elected for six years, and a one-chamber legislature, with representatives elected by district vote in proportion to population.

10 ■ Political Parties

From 1929 to 1997, the majority party and the only political group to gain national significance was the Institutional Revolutionary Party (Partido Revolucionario Institucional) or PRI. In the July 1997 elections, however, the PRI only retained 239 seats in the Chamber of Deputies, which was not enough to claim a majority. On July 2, 2000, Vicente Fox Quesada of the conservative National Action Party (PAN) was elected as president. That year, PAN also became the largest party in the Chamber of Deputies, with 223 seats. Also in 2000, the PRI won 60 out of 128 seats in the Senate. The Party of the Democratic Revolution (PRD) won 53 seats in the Chamber of Deputies and 17 in the Senate. Thus, no party had a majority within either chamber of the Mexican Congress.

The PRI includes only civilians and embraces all shades of political opinion. Three large pressure groups operate within the PRI: labor, the peasantry, and the "popular" sector (such as bureaucrats, teachers, and small business people). The PAN favors a reduced government role in the economy, backs close ties with the United States, and is closely linked to the Catholic Church. The PRD advocates active government intervention in economic matters and questions close relations with the United States.

11 ▪ Judicial System

Federal courts include the Supreme Court (with twenty-one magistrates), thirty-two circuit tribunals, and ninety-eight district courts, with one judge each.

The jury system is not commonly used in Mexico, but judicial protection is provided by the Writ of Amparo, which allows a person convicted in the court of a local judge to appeal to a federal judge. Low pay and high caseloads increase the possibility of corruption in the judicial system. Most lower court judges are selected by a competitive examination.

12 ▪ Economy

Although Mexico's economy once was mostly agricultural, commerce and industry have long been the nation's chief income earners. A great mining nation, Mexico is the world's leading producer of silver and has rich deposits of sulfur, copper, manganese, iron ore, lead, and zinc. Oil is also a leading product in Mexico. Oil accounted for 10% of the country's exports in 2002. Also in 2002, manufactured products accounted for 80% of exports.

Rapid population growth has been a burden on the economy. In 2001, an estimated 40% of the population was living below the poverty line. The economy showed improvement in the late 1990s; however, the recession and economic slowdown in the United States (beginning in 2001 and extending throughout the early part of the twenty-first century) affected Mexico's economy as well. In 2002, the economy only grew by 0.9%.

The North American Free Trade Agreement (NAFTA), in effect as of January 1, 1994, opened the domestic market to foreign trade by promising to eliminate trade barriers between Mexico, the United States, and Canada over the next twenty years. In 2001, free trade agreements were in place with the European Union (EU) and a number of Central American neighbors, as well, bringing over 90% of Mexico's trade under free trade agreements.

In 2001, Mexico's gross domestic product (GDP) was estimated at $920 billion, or about $9,000 per person. The average inflation rate in 2001 was 6.5%, and the growth rate in GDP was estimated at -0.3%.

13 ▪ Industry

Mexico is one of the leading manufacturing nations in Latin America. The principal manufacturing industries include food and beverages, tobacco, chemicals, iron and steel, petroleum, textiles, clothing, and motor vehicles. Other industries include footwear, metalworking, furniture, and other wood products. In 2001, Mexico produced 1.85 million motor vehicles. Leading manufacturers are Ford, Chrysler, General Motors, and Volkswagen.

Maquiladoras, which are facilities engaged in what is known as re-export processing, play an important role in Mexican manufacturing. Maquiladoras are usually located near the United States border and owned by foreign corporations. They assemble or process imported goods brought in from the United States and then re-export them duty-free. In 2002, there were some 3,200 maquiladora factories. However, due to recession and economic slowdowns, six hundred maquiladoras closed between 2001 and 2002, mostly in electronics and apparel. During that period, 250,000 jobs were lost, which amounted to 15% of the maquila workforce.

The fishing industry is largely handled by cooperative societies, which are

© Robert Frerck/Woodfin Camp

Silver shops on the Plaza Borda in Taxco.

problem, affecting primarily those in agriculture. According to official figures, unemployment was 3% in 2001, but that figure reflected only the largest metropolitan areas. Rural unemployment was believed to be much higher. About 25% of the labor force was unionized in 2002.

The workday is generally eight hours. Double or triple pay must be paid for overtime. The minimum age for child employment is fourteen, but there are laws restricting the number of hours and the conditions under which children can work. These child labor laws are fairly well-enforced among medium and large companies but not in smaller firms or in agriculture. There is no national minimum wage, but some municipalities have minimum wage laws.

15 ■ Agriculture

In 2001, agriculture contributed 4% to the gross domestic product and employed about 22% of the labor force. Only about 13% of Mexico's total land area is suitable for cultivation and only 6% is cultivated with permanent crops.

Mexico is self-sufficient in beans, rice, sugar, and most fruits and vegetables. In 1999, the principal crops included sugarcane (46 million tons), corn (18.3 million tons), sorghum (6.29 million tons), wheat (3 million tons), and barley (469,000 tons). Principal exports are coffee, cotton, fresh fruit, sugar, tobacco, and tomatoes. In 2001, the value of agricultural exports amounted to $7,631 million.

More than one-third of the total land area is suitable for pasture. In 2001, the livestock population was estimated at 30.6 million head of cattle, 16.5 million hogs, 9 million goats, 6.4 million sheep, 6.25 million horses (the third most in the world), 3.26

granted monopolies on the most valuable species of fish. Most fish processed in Mexico's canneries are consumed domestically. In 2000, Mexico's exports of fish products were valued at over $706.5 million.

14 ■ Labor

The labor force in Mexico numbered 39.8 million in 2000. Services accounted for 56% of those employed, with industry accounting for 24%, and agriculture accounting for the remaining 20%. Underemployment is Mexico's major labor million donkeys, 3.27 million mules, and 498 million chickens. Output of livestock products in 2001 included 9.47 million tons of cows' milk, 140,000 tons of goats' milk, 1.44 million tons of beef and veal, 1.97 million tons of poultry meat, 1 million tons of pork, and 1.89 million tons of eggs.

16 ■ Natural Resources

The waters of Mexico provide an abundant variety of fish. The main commercial catches are shrimp, sardines, bass, pike, abalone, Spanish mackerel, and red snapper. In 2000, the catch was 1,314,219 tons.

Mexico's forests are another important resource. About 55.2 million hectares (136.3 million acres) are classified as forestland. Mexico has seventy-two species of pine, more than any other country, and pine accounts for over 80% of annual forestry production. Besides wood, annual forestry production also includes an estimated 100,000 tons of resins, fibers, oils, waxes, and gums. The indigenous peoples living in Mexico's rain forests use up to 1,500 species of tropical plants to manufacture three thousand different products such as medicines, construction and domestic materials, dyes, and poisons.

Mexico is one of the leading producers of silver, arsenic, graphite, salt, mine copper, gold, and crude steel. Silver output in 2000 was 2.62 million kilograms (5.7 million pounds). Copper output was 364,566 tons. In 2000, Mexico also produced mercury, tin, nitrogen, talc, and wollastonite.

17 ■ Energy and Power

The total amount of electricity produced in 2000 was 193.9 billion kilowatt hours, of which 17% was hydroelectric and 4% was nuclear power. There are wide-ranging possibilities for geothermal electrical production, with more than one hundred thermal springs available for exploitation. Petroleum is used for more than half of Mexico's energy consumption.

Mexico's estimated oil reserves as of the beginning of 2002 were 26.9 billion barrels, second in the Western Hemisphere after Venezuela. The petroleum industry is operated by the government-owned company Mexican Petroleum (Petróleos Mexicanos—PEMEX). PEMEX is one of the world's largest oil companies, the largest civilian employer in Mexico, and the single most important business in the Mexican economy.

Crude oil production was about 3.6 million barrels per day during 2001. Mexico exports about half the oil it produces, mostly crude oil to the United States, Spain, and the Far East. Proven reserves of natural gas were estimated at 835 billion cubic meters (29.5 trillion cubic feet) in early 2002.

18 ■ Health

In 1997, the National Social Security System operated 14,978 outpatient clinics and 372 general hospitals. In 1999 the country had around 152,000 nurses. As of 1999, there were an estimated 1.7 physicians per 1,000 people. In 2000, average life expectancy was estimated at 73 years for both men and women.

Cholera, yellow fever, plague, and smallpox have been virtually eliminated and typhus has been controlled. Permanent campaigns are being waged against malaria, poliomyelitis, skin diseases, tuberculosis, and serious childhood diseases. Major causes of death include communicable diseases, injuries, and circulatory diseases. As of 2001, the number of people living with HIV/AIDS was estimated at 150,000. Deaths from AIDS that year were estimated at 4,200.

19 ■ Housing

Rapid population growth has led to housing shortages, particularly in rural areas and at the outskirts of major cities, such as Mexico City and Monterrey. The government has established several of its own housing programs and has received aid from international organizations such as the World Bank. In 2000, there were about 21,954,733 housing units; about 85% were detached homes. Most dwellings are privately owned; about 84% have running water and 78% have access to sewage services.

20 ■ Education

Primary schooling is compulsory and free. Except in the Federal District, where education is administered by the federal government, schools are controlled by the states.

Since the 1990s virtually 100% of primary-school-age children have been enrolled in school. In 1999, 57% of secondary-school-age children attended school. Mexican classes have 25 to 28 pupils per teacher.

Major universities include the National Autonomous University (founded in 1551), the National Polytechnic Institute, and Iberoamericana University, all in Mexico City, and Guadalajara University, the Autonomous University of Guadalajara, and the Autonomous University of Nuevo León. In each state there are other state and private institutions.

The government provides extracurricular education through special centers for workers' training, art education, social work, and primary education. As of 2003, the adult illiteracy rate was estimated at 8% (males, 6%; females, 9%).

21 ■ Arts

The National Foundation for the Arts and Culture of Mexico (Fondo Nacional para la Cultura y las Artes—FONCA) was established in 1989 to encourage and support both state and private arts institutions. The Fundación Cultural Omnilife was founded in 1996 to support and encourage Mexican artists and to promote the appreciation of Mexican art abroad. The National Advisory Committee for Culture and the Arts (Consejo Nacional para la Cultura y las Artes—CONACULTA) was established in 1988 as part of the Ministry of Education. Its mission is to work for the preservation of the Mexican cultural heritage and support art education in the country and abroad. There are several other arts associations throughout the country.

22 ■ Libraries and Museums

The Mexican public library system has over 4,800 branches with about twenty million volumes. The National Library, which is affiliated with the National University of Mexico, has about three million volumes. Other important collections include the Library of Mexico, the Library of the Secretary of the Treasury, and the Central Library of the National Autonomous University in Mexico City.

The National Museum of Anthropology in Mexico City, founded in 1825, has over 600,000 exhibits and a library of 300,000 volumes. Among its exhibits are the famous Aztec calendar stone and a 137-ton figure of

© Robert Frerck/Woodfin Camp

Seven wind turbines installed in Oaxaca in the narrow isthmus of Tehuantepec are the only wind-power generators in Mexico.

Tlaloc, the god of rain. The National Historical Museum has more than 150,000 objects ranging in date from the Spanish conquest to the constitution of 1917. The National Museum of Art exhibits Mexican art from 17th century to present. Several other art museums exhibit the works of leading European artists, including the Museum of Modern Art and the Museum of Popular Art. In Mexico City, the Frida Kahlo Museum is in the former home of Frida Kahlo (1907–1954) and Diego Rivera (1886–1957), both of whom were notable Mexican artists. Many public buildings in Guadalajara and elsewhere display murals by famous Mexican painters.

23 ■ Media

The number of mainline telephones in service in 2000 was 12.3 million. In 1998, there were also two million cellular phones in use. As of 2000, there were 851 AM and 598 FM radio stations and 236 television stations. Also in 2000, Mexico had 330 radios and 283 television sets for every 1,000 people. In 2001, about 3.42 million Internet subscribers were served by about fifty-one service providers.

Leading newspapers (with their estimated average daily circulations in 2002) include the following: *El Heraldo,* 373,600; *Esto,* 350,000; *El Nacional,* 210,000; *La Prensa,* 208,150; and *Excélsior,* 200,000.

Freedom of the press is guaranteed by law and is generally honored in practice.

24 ■ Tourism, Travel, and Recreation

Mexico is the second most popular tourist destination in the Americas (after the United States). About twenty million tourists enter Mexico each year, 95% of them from the United States. In 2000, there were 20,641,358 tourist arrivals, and receipts from tourism were $8.2 billion. That year there were 421,850 hotel rooms with a 55% occupancy rate.

Mexico's tourist attractions range from modern seaside resort areas, such as Tijuana, Acapulco and Cancún, to the Mayan ruins of Chiapas on the Isthmus of Tehuantepec and the Aztec monuments of the south-central regions. Mexico City, combining notable features from the Aztec, colonial, and modern periods, is itself an important tourist mecca.

25 ■ Sports

Mexico's most popular sports are baseball, soccer (called football), jai-alai (played on a court and similar to handball), swimming, and volleyball. Bullfights are a leading spectator sport; the Mexico City arena, which seats 50,000 persons, is one of the largest in the world, and there are about thirty-five other arenas throughout the country.

Mexico sponsored the Summer Olympics in 1968 and sponsored the World Cup Soccer Championship in 1970 and 1986.

26 ■ Famous People

The founder of Spanish Mexico was Hernán Cortés (1485–1547). One of the great heroes in Mexican history is Cuauhtémoc (or Guatimotzin, c. 1495–1522), the last emperor of the Aztecs, who fought the Spanish after the death of his uncle, Montezuma II (or Moctezuma, 1466–1520). The first years of independence were dominated by Antonio López de Santa Anna (1794–1876). Benito Juárez (1806–1872), the great leader of the liberal revolution, attempted to introduce a program of national reform. The dictator Porfirio Díaz (1830–1915) dominated Mexico from 1876 to 1911. He was overthrown largely through the efforts of Francisco Indalecio Madero (1873–1913), called the father of the Mexican Revolution.

Two revolutionary leaders—Doroteo Arango, known as Pancho Villa (1878–1923), and Emiliano Zapata (1879–1919)—achieved almost legendary status. The foremost political leader after the Mexican Revolution was Lázaro Cárdenas (1895–1970). Luis Echeverría Álvarez, who held the presidency from 1970 to 1976, made Mexico one of the leading countries of the developing world in international forums.

Painters Diego Rivera (1886–1957) and José Clemente Orozco (1883–1949) are renowned for their murals. Frida Kahlo (Magdalena Carmen Frida Kahlo y Calderon, 1907–1954), an artist who married Diego Rivera, became well-known in her own right for her symbolic self-portraits. Juana Inés de la Cruz (1651–95), a nun, was a poet and proponent of women's rights. Outstanding novelists include Martín Luis Guzmán (1887–1976), author of *El águila y la serpiente,* and Gregorio López y Fuentes (1897–1966), author of *El indio.* Well-known

© Peter Langer/EPD Photos

The Mexican Revolution Museum in the capital, Chihuahua, commemorates the history of the 20-year campaign for independence (1910–30).

contemporary authors include Octavio Paz (1914–1998) and Carlos Fuentes. An outstanding figure in recent Mexican literary life is the diplomat, dramatist, poet, essayist, and critic Alfonso Reyes (1889–1959).

Anthropologist Carlos Castaneda (1931–1998) was born in Brazil and was widely known for his studies of mysticism among the Yaqui Amerindians. Well-known Mexican composers include Manuel María Ponce (1886–1948) and Carlos Antonnio de Padua Chávez (1899–1978). Significant figures in the motion picture industry are the comedian Cantinflas (Mario Moreno, 1911–1993), Mexican-born actor Anthony Rudolph Oaxaca Quinn (1916–2001), and director Emilio Fernández (1904–1986).

Notable Mexican sports figures include Fernando Valenzuela, a pitcher for the Los Angeles Dodgers who won the Cy Young Award, for best pitcher in major league baseball, as a rookie. Hugo Sánchez Márquez is a well-known soccer player.

27 ■ Bibliography

Books

Chapman, Gillian. *The Aztecs.* New York: Beech Tree Books, 2000.

Gray, Shirley W. *Mexico.* Minneapolis: Compass Point Books, 2001.

Green, Jen. *Mexico.* Austin, TX: Raintree Steck-Vaughn, 2000.

Gritzner, Charles F. *Mexico.* Philadelphia: Chelsea House Publishers, 2003.

Marx, David F. *Mexico.* New York: Children's Press, 2000.

Meister, Cari. *Mexico.* Minneapolis, MN: Abdo and Daughters, 2000.

Meyer, Michael C., and William Beezley, eds. *The Oxford History of Mexico.* New York: Oxford University Press, 2000.

Park, Ted. *Mexico.* Austin, TX: Steadwell Books, 2000.

Reilly, Mary-Jo. *Mexico.* New York: Benchmark Books, 2002.

Web Sites

Mexico for Kids. http://www.elbalero.gob.mx/index_kids.html (accessed on June 15, 2004).

Visit Mexico. http://www.visitmexico.com/ (accessed June 17, 2004).

Index

Boldface numbers indicate the page range for the main entry of the state.

A

Acapulco Bay 112, 120
Aguanaval River 62, 91
Aguascalientes **1–8**
Aguascalientes Airport 2
Aguascalientes Museum 7
Aguilas, Nido 19
Agustín, Lara 90
Ajusco National Park 82
Alameda Central 89
Álvarez, Luis Echeverría 324
Ameca River 172
Anahuac Congress 115
Ángel, Sergio Guerrero 95
Apache Indians 250
Apizaco River 274
Arango, Doroteo 308, 324
Archduke Maximilian of Austria 315
Armería River 71
Arrieta, Domingo 95
Ash Wednesday 14
Assumption of the Hot Springs 1
"Athens of Mexico" 68
Atlantic Ocean 281
Atlético Celaya 110
Atoyac River 274
Autlan De Navarro 138
Autonomous University of Aguascalientes 7, 18
Autonomous University of Guadalajara 322
Autonomous University of Nuevo León 322

Autonomous University of Tlaxcala 279
Avenida Reforma 8
Avenue Hidalgo 304
Aznar, Tomás 35
Aztec Stadium 89, 146

B

Baja California **9–20**
Baja California Norte 15, 26
Baja California Sur **21–30**
Ballet Contemporánea 88
Ballet Folklórico Ehécatl 7
Ballet Folklórico of Guanajuato 108
Ballet Folklórico of Puebla 208
Ballet Neoclásico 88
Balsas River 111–112, 150, 274
Barrios, Fernando Gutiérrez 286, 289
Bartlett, Manuel 206
Basilica of the Virgin 88
Battle of Cross Mountain 139
Battle of Puebla 205
Bay of Campeche 34, 189, 255, 309
Beezley, William 326
Benito Juárez University of Oaxaca 199
Bernandino, Juan Diego 276
Biospheres 221
    Biosphere Reserve of the Wetlands 256
    Calakmul Biosphere Reserve 32, 38
    Celestun Biosphere Reserve 292
    El Cielo Biosphere Reserve 266
    El Pinacate Biosphere Reserve 248

El Triunfo Biosphere Reserve 42
La Encrucijada Biosphere Reserve 42
La Michilía Biosphere Reserve 94
Tehuacán-Cuicatlán Biosphere Reserve
202
Blanco River 282

C

Cabañas Institute 138
Cabo Catoche 221
Cabo San Lucas 12, 14, 22, 25–26, 28
Calakmul Biosphere Reserve 32, 38
Caldera Sierra 273
Calderón Bridge 154
Campeche **31–39**
Canastas River 62
CANMEX 238
Cape San Lucas *See* Cabo San Lucas
Cárdenas, Lázaro 35, 77, 155, 159, 175, 221,
231, 296, 316, 324
Cárdenas Solórzano, Cuauhtémoc 86
Carlos Pellicer Museum 262
Carlos V 41, 221
Carranza, Venustiano 65, 69, 175, 316
Carvajal, Rafael 35
Casamata Museum 271
Casas Grandes 249
Castaneda, Carlos 325
Catedral Metropolitana 89
Caxcán Indians 304
Cayo Arcas 31, 34
Cazones River 282
Celestun Biosphere Reserve 292
Central Breadbasket 161, 273
Central Plateau 209, 302, 309
Cervecería Cuauhtémoc-Moctezuma 185
Chamber of Deputies 5, 15, 65, 95, 259, 305,
318
Chankanaab Lagoon 225
Chapultepec Castle 89
Chapultepec Park 82, 89
Chapultepec Sierra 301

Chávez, Carlos 90
Chetumal International Airport 220
Chiapa Indians 42
Chiapas **41–49**
Chichén Itzá 295, 314
Chichimec Indians 230
Chichimec War 231
Chichinautzin Ecological Reserve 82
Chihuahua **51–60**
Chihuahua Cathedral 51, 58
Chinanteco Indians 193
Chirinos, Pedro Almendez 302
Cierro Prieto 59
Cisneros, Juárez 117
"City of Eternal Spring" 162
Ciudad Guzmán 138
Ciudad Juárez 52, 54, 58–60, 94
Ciudad Obregón 249, 253–254
Ciudad Victoria 263–264, 266, 271
Ciudad Xicotencatl 278
Clariond, Fernando Canales 185
Coahuila **61–69**
Colima **71–80**
Colima Volcano 71–72, 136
Colorado River 9, 13
Colosio, Luis Donaldo 250, 317
Columbus, Christopher 89, 221
Columns of Hercules 281
Conchos River 51–52
Contemporary Dance Company of Oaxaca
199
Copper Canyon 55, 57, 59–60
Coro Meced Chimalli 271
Cortés, Hernán 13, 25, 34, 85, 90, 105, 120,
124, 142, 153, 165, 174, 204, 221,
230, 258, 262, 266, 277, 281, 284,
295, 314, 324
Cortines, Adolfo Ruiz 286, 289
Costa Rica 74
Cota, Félix Agramont 26
Cozumel Airport 220
Crafts Institute of Jalisco 137

Cristero War 95, 106, 125, 133, 175, 213, 231
Cruz Azul 89
Cruz, Salina 196
Cry of Pain 110
Cuarto Poder 48
Cuernavaca Lookout 169
Cultural Center of Chiapas Jaime Sabines 48
Cuyutlán Lagoon 72, 75
Cy Young Award 254, 325

D
Dance of the Deer 245
Danza Contemporánea 234
Day of the Dead 108, 160
Desert of the Lions 84
Diablos Rojos 89
Diario Olmeca 262
Diary of Colima 79
Díaz, Joaquín Ernesto Hendricks 225
Díaz, José Antonio 75, 79
Díaz, Laura 90
Díaz, Porfírio 5, 26, 35, 65, 68, 76, 95, 105,
          116, 125, 133, 143, 154–155, 175,
          183, 195, 200, 205, 213, 231, 239,
          259, 267, 277, 305, 315, 324
Distrito Federal **81–90**
Domínguez, Antonio Echevarría 175, 177
Domínguez, Miguel 35
Durango **91–99**

E
Eduardo Ruiz National Park 150
El Boleo Centro Cultural 28
El Ceboruco 171
El Centenario Zoo 300
El Cerrito 216
El Chorro 216
El Cielo Biosphere Reserve 266
El Cimatario 210
El Cuchillo Dam 186
El Debate 242

El Diario 59, 89, 146, 158, 187, 216, 262, 271,
          288
El Dictamén 288
El Economista 89
El Eden Ecological Reserve 218
El Gordo Hill 129
El Heraldo 59, 89, 109, 323
El Imparcial 253
El Impartial 199
El Independiente 253
El Informador 137
El Jabalí 61
El Mañana 271
El Nacional 323
El Occidental 137
El Ocote 8
El Orbe 48
El Palomito 161
El Paso 52, 54
El Peñón Hill 273
El Periquillo Sarniento 90
El Pinacate Biosphere Reserve 248
El Pinal 2
El Porvenir 187
El Potosí National Park 228
El Sol 8, 19, 59, 68, 89, 99, 109, 120, 127, 146,
          158, 169, 208, 216, 234, 242, 271,
          280, 288, 308
El Sudcaliforniano 28
El Sur 39, 120, 288
El Tezoyo 161
El Triunfo Biosphere Reserve 42
El Tule 198
El Tunal 61
El Veladero National Park 112
Emperor Maximilian 35, 76, 89, 116, 133,
          195, 213, 239, 259, 286, 315
Emperor Montezuma II 85, 90, 314
Emperor Napoleon III 315
Emperor Zuuangua 153
Enrique Estrada Park 308
Espíritu Santo 21, 174

Estadio Hermanos Serdán 208
Estadio Monclova 68
Este Sur 48

F
Farías, Valentín Gómez 4, 8
"Father of the Revolution" 68, 324
Federal District *See* Distrito Federal
Florido River 91
Folk Art Museum 79
Fox, Vicente 106–107, 110, 318
Frida Kahlo Museum 88, 323
Fuentes, Carlos 90, 325

G
García, Patricio Martínez 57
Garrido Patrón, Francisco 214, 216
Garzas Plata 128
General Motors 66, 319
Gil, Emilio Portes 267, 271
González, Antonio 36
González, José Natividad 185
Grand Canyon 59
Grande Hill 301
Grijalva River 41, 46–47
Groupo Almalafa 19
Groupo Chuchumbe 288
Groupo Gente 169
Groupo Mal Paso 19
Groupo Mono Blanco 288
Grupo Mexico 58
Guadalajara Colony Reporter 137
Guadalajara Reporter 137–138
Guadalajara University 136, 138, 322
Guadalupe Victoria 285, 289
Guadiana Park 99
Guanajuato **101–110,** 149, 209
Guaymas-General Jose Maria Yanez
          International Airport 249
Guerrero **111–120**
Guerrero, Gonzalo 34, 221, 295

Guerrero Negro 27
Guerrero, Vicente 111, 115, 120
Gulf of California 313
Gulf of Tehuantepec 189, 255, 309
Guzmán, Diego 174, 249
Guzmán, Martín Luis 324

H
Hayek, Salma 90
Hidalgo **121–128**
Hidalgo, Dolores 105
Hidalgo, Miguel 5, 75, 94, 105, 115, 121, 124,
          128, 132–133, 165, 183, 212, 305
Hidalgo Park 300
Highlands of Chiapas 49
Hondo River 217, 221
Huamantla Sierra 273
Huasteco Indians 266
Huerta, Victoriano 175, 315
Hules River 121
Hurricane Pauline 112, 190

I
Iberoamericana University 322
Independent Confederation of Farm
          Workers 16
Independent University of Campeche 38
Independent University of Coahuila 68
Independent University of Guerrero 119
Independent University of Hidalgo 127
Independent University of Morelos 169
Independent University of Querétaro 216
Independent University of San Luis Potosí
          234
Independent University of the State 145
Independent University of Yucatán 299
Independent University of Zacatecas 308
Instituto Politécnico Nacional 88
Interactive Museum of Science 7
International University of La Paz 28
Iriarte, Rafael 4–5, 8

Isabel, Queen 273
Isla Contoy 292
Isla Isabela 172, 174
Isla Mujeres 225
Isla Tiburon 253
Islas Marías 172
Isle of Women 225
Isthmus of Tehuantepec 189–190, 255, 309–310, 323–324
Izta-Popo National Park 140, 146

J
Jacinto Canek 296
Jalisco **129–138**
Jalisco Stadium 138
Jiménez, Mariano 64

K
Kahlo, Frida 88, 90, 323–324
Kings
    Carlos V 41, 221
    Felipe II 182
    Ferdinand 273
    Karolus 273
Kino, Eusebio 20

L
La Afición 89
La Antigua 282
La Corona 161
La Cristiada 7
La Diana Cazadora 89
La Encrucijada Biosphere Reserve 42
La Extra 158
La Frontera 19
La Herradura 161
La Huasteca 126–127, 269
La Laguna 68, 96
La Michilía Biosphere Reserve 94
La Ola 146
La Opinión 68

La Parroquia 216
La Polvora Lagoon 262
La Prensa 89, 323
La Revista Peninsular 299
La Sauceda 308
La Silla Hill 179
La Venta 258, 262
Lady of the Assumption 1, 274
Laguna Azul 34
Laguna Madre 264
Laguna Salada 310
Laguna Tequesquitengo 162
Laguna Verde 287
Lake Chapala 130, 150, 310
Lakeside Little Theater 136
Las Bocas Sierra 301
Las Cañas 172
Las Cometas 216
Las Ilusiones 256
Las Lecheras 301
Las Marietas 172
Las Palmas 10
Las Pilas 169
Las Playas 271
Lavalle, Irineo 35
Lawrence of Arabia 60
Lerma River 101, 130, 150, 209
Liga Mexicana 39, 300
López Obrador, Andrés Manuel 87, 260
Los Alamos Sierra 301
Los Angeles Dodgers 254, 325
Los Arcos 28, 124
Los Cabos International Airport 25
Los Dorados 60
Los García Plateau 301
Los Guajalotes 129
Los Huacales 301
Los Huicholes 129
Los Lazos 302
Los Mochis 19, 236, 241–243
Los Novillos 61
Los Pericos 208

Los Remedios 91
Los Tigres 208
Los Valles 162

M

Madero, Francisco 65, 68, 95, 125, 175, 231, 315, 324
Madrazo, Roberto 260, 262
Malinche National Park 202, 276
Marabasco River 71
Márquez, Hugo Sánchez 325
Marshal Saint John Treaty 221
Matamoros International Airport 266
Matamoros, Mariano 194, 212
Mateos, Adolfo López 318
Maximilian, Archduke of Austria 35, 76, 89, 116, 133, 195, 213, 239, 259, 286, 315
Maya World Studies Center 299
Mayapan League 221
Mayo River 246
Medano Beach 28
Mendoza Aramburu, Ángel César 26, 29
Mérida Licenciado-Manuel Crescencio Rejon International Airport 294
Methodist Church 213
Mexica Indians 84, 193, 302
Mexican Riviera 120
Mexican–American War 14, 25, 65, 105, 124, 259, 267, 285
Mexico (country) **309–326**
México (state) **139–147**
Mexico City *See* Distrito Federal
Michoacán **149–160**
Miramar Beach 271
Mitote Jazz 169
Mixteco Indians 204
Mixtón War 132, 304
Moctezuma II 84, 85, 90, 153, 314, 324
Moctezuma Ilhuicamina 266
Moctezuma River 227
Molucas Islands 114

Monclova River 61
Monreal, Ricardo 306
Montaño, Leonel Cota 26
Monte Alto 139
Monterrey Institute of Technology 79
Morelos **161–170**
Morelos, José 115, 143, 149, 158-159, 161, 165-166, 194, 205
Moreno, Mario 90, 325
Murat, José 195
Murillo, Gerardo 138
Museo Ferrocarril 7
Museo Taurino 7
Museo Tonallán 137
Museum of Contemporary Art 7, 99, 187, 271, 299
Museum of the Mask 230, 234
Museum of Popular Art 137, 225, 323
Museum of Regional History 7, 79
Museum of Western Culture 79
Música Maestra 186

N

NAFTA *See* North American Free Trade Agreement
Nájera, Manuel Gutiérrez 90
Napoleon III 315
National Autonomous University 322
National Consultative Committee 318
National Folk Ballet of Mexico 88
National Historical Museum 323
National Library 7, 19, 28, 39, 48, 59, 68, 79, 88, 99, 109, 119, 137, 145, 169, 177, 187, 199, 271, 280, 288, 322
National Museum of Anthropology 277, 322
National Museum of Art 323
National Palace 110
National Parks
    Ajusco National Park 82
    Eduardo Ruiz National Park 150
    El Potosí National Park 228
    El Veladero National Park 112

Izta-Popo National Park 140, 146
Malinche National Park 202, 276
Parque Nacional Izta-Popo *See* Izta-Popo National Park
Pinacate National Park 251
Tulum National Park 218, 222
National Polytechnic Institute 88, 322
National Preparatory School 60
National Social Security System 321
National University of Mexico 88, 322
Nava, Salvador 231–232
Nayarit **171–178**
Necaxa River 202
Negrete, Pedro Celestino 94
Nicolas Alvarez Ortega Stadium 177
Noble Peace Prize 160
Nogales International Airport 249
North American Free Trade Agreement (NAFTA) 36, 44, 52, 55, 57, 66–67, 95–97, 107, 118, 215, 250, 267, 279, 317, 319
Novedades Acapulco 120
Nueva Galicia 132, 239
Nuevo Lardeo 271
Nuevo Laredo Fair 271
Nuevo Laredo-Qetzalcoatl International Airport 266
Nuevo León 94, **179–187**
Nuñez, Manuel Ángel 125, 128

O
Oaxaca **189–200**
Oaxaca Valley 189, 193
Obregón, Álvaro 5, 254
Ocampo, Melchor 61
Ojeda, Juan Antonio Flores 29
Orozco, José Clemente 138, 324
Our Lady of the Miracles 169

P
Palace of Fine Arts 88

Palacio, Gomez 96–97
Pan-American Road 94
Pánuco River 101, 121, 209, 227
Papaloapan River 190, 310
Páramo, Pedro 138
Parga, Pedro 4, 8
Parque La Junta 271
Parque Nacional Izta-Popo *See* Izta-Popo National Park
Partido Revolucionario Institucional 316, 318
Patrón, Patricio 297
Pátzcuaro Lake 157–158
Paz, Octavio 90, 325
Pecheco, Gaspar 296
PEMEX 37, 58, 135, 256, 321
Petróleos Mexicanos *See* PEMEX
Pinacate National Park 251
Plan of San Luis 231
Playa Bagdad 271
Playa Tortuguera Rancho Nuevo 266
Playas Tijuana 19
Plaza Art Center 60
Plaza Borda 118, 320
Plaza Calafia 19
Plaza Caletilla 120
Plaza Monumental 8, 60, 159
Plaza Revolución 110
Plaza Santa María 216
Ponce, Manuel María 308, 325
Por Esto 299
Puebla **201–208**
Puerto Peñasco 253
Puerto Vallarta Airport 130, 132
Purepecha Indians 304
Pyramid of Tepozteco 169

Q
Querétaro **209–216**
Que Payasos 88
Quijote, Don 109
Quinn, Anthony Rudolph Oaxaca 60, 325

Quintana Roo **217–225**
Quixote, Don 109–110

R
Ramírez, Sergio Estrada Cajigal 167
Rancho La Joya 99
Real San Luís 234
Real Sociedad Zacatecas 308
Reserve Estatal El Palmar 292
Revillagigedo Archipelago 72
Reyados Monterrey 187
Río Balsas 111–112, 150, 274
Río Blanco 287
Río Bravo 51, 179–180, 310
Río Grande 51–52, 64–65, 179–180, 267,
        308, 310, 315
Río Lerma 101, 150
Río Papaloapan 190
Río Salado 180
Río Santiago 101
Rivas, Refugio Reyes 308
Rivera, Diego 88–89, 109–110, 169, 323-324
Robles, Alfonso García 159
Roca Partida 72
Rodríguez, Juan 114
Rojano River 274
Rojas, Arturo Montiel 144
Roldán, Otto Granados 6
Rosarito Beach 19

S
Sabines, Jaime 48
Salado River 180
Salazar, Pablo 46
Saldaña, Vicente Guerrero 111, 120
San Andrés 302
San Benedicto 72
San Blas 176
San Carlos 264
San Cristóbal 41, 44, 46
San Diego Fort 120

San Dimas 97
San Felipe 13, 19, 182
San Francisco Fair 128
San Gervasio 225
San Gregorio 182
San Ignacio 22
San Isidro Mountains 129
San Jacinto 315
San José 14, 21, 24–25, 160, 264
San Juan 28, 42, 130, 171, 179, 186, 216
San Luis Potosí **227–234**
San Marcos National Fair 8
San Miguel Fort 39
San Pablo 200, 255
San Pedro Garza García 185
San Pedro Lagunillas 172
San Pedro Martin Island 312
San Rodrigo 62
San Ysidro 16
Sánchez, Alfonso Abraham 278, 280
Sandez, Braulio Maldonado 15, 20
Sandoval, Gonzalo 74, 165, 284
Santa Ana Chiauhtempan 278
Santa Anna 65, 116, 194, 285, 289, 315, 324
Santa Catalina 21
Santa Cruz 13, 21, 25
Santa Margarita 21
Santa Maria Bay 236
Santa Rosa 62
Santa Rosalía 27
Santana, Carlos 138
Santiago Baca Ortíz 95
Santiago Bay 72
Santiago River 101
Santos Laguna 68
Sea of Cortés 10, 19, 21, 245, 253
Sevilla, Juan 230
Shark Island 253
Sierra Alta 162
Sierra Atravesada 189
Sierra El Pino 61
Sierra Fria 2

Sierra Gorda 209–210, 263
Sierra Madre Occidental 2, 91, 94, 129, 235, 245, 301–302, 309
Sierra Madre Oriental 61, 101, 179, 186, 189, 209, 227, 263, 281–282, 301–302, 309
Sierra Mojada 61
Sierra Nevada 139–140
Sierra Norte 112, 192
Sierra Queretana 209
Sierra Tarahumara 59, 243
Sinaloa **235–243**
Sinaloa Science Center 242
Siqueiros, David Alfaro 60, 89, 169
Sombrerete Sierra 301
Sonora **245–254**
Sumidero Canyon 41, 46
Summer Olympics 324

T
Tabasco **255–262**
Tamaulipas **263–272**
Tamayo, Rufino 200
Tangolunda Bay 199
Tazmania Diablos 20
Teatro Carpa Carlos Ancira 208
Teatro Degollado 137
Teatro Hidalgo 79
Teatro Juárez 28
Teatro Morelos 7
Teatro Saltimbanque 186
Technical Institute of Aguascalientes 7, 18
Technological Institute of Colima 79
Tecolotes Dos Laredos 271
Tehuacán Airport 284
Tehuacán-Cuicatlán Biosphere Reserve 202
Tehuantepec Isthmus 189–190, 196, 255, 309–310, 323–324
Temple of Five Stories 39
Templo Mayor 85
Tepalcingo River 161
Tepaneca Indians 114

Terán, Hector 15
Términos Lagoon 32
Terra Nostra 90
Theater Calderón 304
Tlaxcala **273–280**
Tlaxcala Indians 182
Tlaxcaleca Indians 302
Tlaxcalteca Indians 277, 304
Tlaxco Sierra 273–274
Tlayotehuanitzin, Francisco Miguel 276
Toltec Indians 84
Toluca-Alfonso Lopez Airport 140
Tonalá Museum 137
Tonalá River 282
Transversal Volcanic Sierra 149
Treaty of Guadalupe Hidalgo 14, 25, 54, 315
Treaty of Hidalgo 14, 25, 54, 250, 315
Tulum National Park 218, 222
Turbio River 102
Tuxtla Gutiérrez 41–42, 48
TV Azteca 48

U
Universities
   Autonomous University of Aguascalientes 7, 18
   Autonomous University of Guadalajara 322
   Autonomous University of Nuevo León 322
   Autonomous University of Tlaxcala 279
   Benito Juárez University of Oaxaca 199
   Iberoamericana University 322
   Independent University of Campeche 38
   Independent University of Coahuila 68
   Independent University of Guerrero 119
   Independent University of Hidalgo 127
   Independent University of Morelos 169

Independent University of Querétaro 216

Independent University of San Luis Potosí 234

Independent University of the State 145

Independent University of Yucatán 299

Independent University of Zacatecas 308

Instituto Politécnico Nacional 88

International University of La Paz 28

National Autonomous University 322

Technical Institute of Aguascalientes 7, 18

Technological Institute of Colima 79

Universidad Michoacana 157

Universidad Veracruzana 288

University of the Americas 207

University of Colima 79

University of Guanajuato 108

University of Veracruz 288

V

Valdés, Miguel Alemán 286, 289

Valdez, Jorge Carlos Hurtado 36

Valenzuela, Fernando 254, 325

Valley of Mexico 81, 84–85, 122, 124, 259, 313

Vázquez Montes, Gustavo 76, 79

Velazco, Miguel Alemán 289

Veracruz **281–289**

Victoria Stadium 8, 288

Villa, Pancho 54, 60, 95, 99, 133, 166, 175, 239, 308, 315, 324

Villa Real 44

Vizcaíno, Sebastián 13, 25

W

Walther, Eugenio Elorduy 15–16

World Cup Soccer Championship 324

Writ of Amparo 319

X

Xalapeno Stadium 288

Xochitiotzin, Desiderio Hernandez 280

Y

Yáñez, Agustín 138

Yaquí Amerindians 325

Yaquí River 245, 249

Yarrington, Tomás 268, 271

Yucatán **291–300**

Yucatán Peninsula 31, 34, 217, 221, 310, 313

Yum Balam Protected Area 218

Z

Zacatecas **301–308**

Zahuapan River 274

Zapata, Emiliano 48, 161, 166, 170, 205, 315, 324

Zapatista Army of National Liberation 44, 46, 48, 317

Zapoteca Indians 193

Zaragoza Park 68

Zedillo, Ernesto 317

Zona Rosa 89

Zoológico Guadalajara 137

Zuldaca Sierra 301

Zuuangua, Emperor 153

Aguascalientes

Baja California

Baja California Sur

Coahuila

Colima

Distrito Federal

Hidalgo

Jalisco

México

Nuevo León

Oaxaca

Puebla

Sinaloa

Sonora

Tabasco

Yucatán

Zacatecas